Peterson's

Countdown

to the

LSAT®

Peterson's

COUNTDOWN

TO THE

LSAT®

3rd Edition

Mark Alan Stewart

PETERSON'S

A **nelnet** COMPANY

PETERSON'S

A ⓝelnet COMPANY

About Peterson's, a Nelnet company

Peterson's (www.petersons.com) is a leading provider of education information and advice, with books and online resources focusing on education search, test preparation, and financial aid. Its Web site offers searchable databases and interactive tools for contacting educational institutions, online practice tests and instruction, and planning tools for securing financial aid. Peterson's serves 110 million education consumers annually.

For more information, contact Peterson's, 2000 Lenox Drive, Lawrenceville, NJ 08648; 800-338-3282; or find us on the World Wide Web at: www.petersons.com/about.

Editor: Therese DeAngelis; Production Editor: Linda Seghers; Manufacturing Manager: Ivona Skibicki; Composition Manager: Gary Rozmierski

ISBN-13: 978-0-7689-2513-5
ISBN-10: 0-7689-2513-4

Printed in the United States of America

10 9 8 7 6 5 4 3 2 1   09 08 07

Third Edition

OTHER RECOMMENDED TITLES

Peterson's Master Series LSAT

Peterson's Logic & Reading Review for the GRE, GMAT, LSAT, MCAT

Contents

Contents

APPENDIX

Credits

"'I Am Christina Rossetti,'" by Antony H. Harrison, *Humanities,* vol. 14, no. 4 (July/ August 1993), pp. 33–37. Published by The National Endowment for the Humanities.

"Arnold's Double-Sided Culture," by John P. Farrell, *Humanities,* vol. 12, no. 3 (May/June1991), pp. 26–30. Published by The National Endowment for the Humanities.

"The Artful Encounter," by Richard Wendorf, *Humanities,* vol. 14, no. 4 (July/August 1993), pp. 9–12. Published by The National Endowment for the Humanities.

"The Debate Over Mozart's Music," by Neal Zaslaw, *Humanities,* vol. 14, no. 5 (September/October 1993), pp. 26–27. Published by The National Endowment for the Humanities.

Before You Begin

HOW THIS BOOK IS ORGANIZED

Taking the LSAT is a skill that requires discipline and practice to succeed. You can improve this skill through coaching, but ultimately, improvement also requires practice. This book gives you both.

Each of the main chapters in the book provides a bite-sized lesson plan that will help prepare you for taking the LSAT when you have a limited amount of study time before taking the test. As you count down to LSAT exam day, you'll review the following:

- **The Basics:** Here's where you can find essential information on the LSAT, including descriptions of exam sections, when and where to take the test, and how it's scored. You'll also learn how law schools evaluate your scores and how to register for the LSAT and Law School Data Assembly Service (LSDAS).

- **The Lessons:** The heart of the book consists of lessons on basic concepts and strategies for each LSAT question type, mini-tests and reviews, advice on sharpening your reasoning and essay-writing skills, and suggestions about how to spot wrong-answer ploys. Each lesson can be completed in a few hours.

- **The Practice Tests:** With the lessons under your belt, it's time to try some real test questions. We include two full-length LSAT exams—one divided into the sections you'll see on the actual LSAT, and the second a complete test in one chapter. Each includes reviews and complete answer explanations so you can track your progress. You'll also evaluate your own practice test performance using the included conversion table on page 6.

- **The Appendix**: We've provided a checklist of what you need to do in the weeks leading up to LSAT exam day, on exam day itself, and in the weeks following the exam.

As you'll learn in "Getting to Know the LSAT," the Logical Reasoning, Analytical Reasoning, Reading Comprehension, and Experimental sections of the actual LSAT can appear in any order before the Writing Sample (which is always last). We've arranged the lessons in this book accordingly to better prepare you for exam day. You'll also notice as you work through the lessons that each one builds upon what you've already learned. By the time you're ready for the two Practice Tests, you should be well prepared for anything the LSAT can dish out.

YOU'RE WELL ON YOUR WAY TO SUCCESS

You've made the decision to apply to law school. *Peterson's Countdown to the LSAT* will help prepare you for the steps you'll need to take to achieve your goal—from scoring high on the exam to being admitted to the law school program of your choice. Good luck!

GIVE US YOUR FEEDBACK

Peterson's publishes a full line of resources to help guide you through the graduate school admission process. Peterson's publications can be found at your local bookstore, library, and high school guidance office, and you can access us online at www.petersons.com.

We welcome any comments or suggestions you may have about this publication and invite you to complete our online survey at www.petersons.com/booksurvey. Or you can write to us at:

Publishing Department
Peterson's, a Nelnet company
2000 Lenox Drive
Lawrenceville, NJ 08648

Your feedback will help us make your educational dreams possible.

PART I

THE BASICS

Getting to Know the LSAT

In this first section, we'll focus on becoming familiar with the format of the LSAT and learning how the LSAT is scored. We'll also review a few basic success strategies.

THE LSAT AT A GLANCE

Total number of scored questions: 101–103

Total number of test sections: 6

Total testing time: 3 hours, 25 minutes

Section	Time	Number of Questions
Logical Reasoning	35 min.	25–26
Logical Reasoning	35 min.	25–26
Analytical Reasoning	35 min.	23–24
Reading Comprehension	35 min.	28
Experimental Section	35 min.	23–28
Writing Sample	35 min.	1 topic

The Writing Sample is always administered last (after other sections). Other sections may appear in any order before the Writing Sample.

Ground Rules

- Use of scratch paper is permitted only for the Writing Sample section (it is provided)

- You may use pencils or highlighters only (no pens), except when working on the Writing Sample section

- No penalty is assessed for incorrect responses

- Silent timing devices are permitted

- Working ahead or going back to other test sections is prohibited

LSAT Exam Sections

LOGICAL REASONING

Logical Reasoning questions are designed to evaluate your ability to understand, criticize, and draw reasonable conclusions from arguments. Each argument is presented in a brief one-paragraph passage. The LSAT includes two scored Logical Reasoning sections, so this type of question accounts for approximately 50 percent of all LSAT scored questions. The two scored Logical Reasoning sections are similar in format, style, and difficulty level.

ANALYTICAL REASONING

Analytical Reasoning questions measure your ability to understand a system of relationships and to draw appropriate deductive conclusions about those relationships. The questions are presented as a series of four distinct question sets, or "logic games." Each game is accompanied by five to eight questions. For each game, you need to draw diagrams in your test booklet to organize the information (premise and rules) and to analyze the questions. Each game will be presented on two facing pages of your test booklet. Thus, you respond to all questions for a game without turning pages.

READING COMPREHENSION

Reading Comprehension questions measure your ability to read carefully and accurately, to determine the relationships among the various parts of the passage, and to draw reasonable inferences from the material in the passage. The questions are presented as a series of four distinct question sets. Passages cover a variety of subjects, including the humanities, the social sciences, the physical sciences, ethics, philosophy, and law. Each question set will be presented on two facing pages of your test booklet.

THE EXPERIMENTAL SECTION

The 35-minute Experimental Section looks just like one of the scored sections (Logical Reasoning, Analytical Reasoning, and Reading Comprehension); however, this section itself is not scored. Instead, it's included to assess the integrity and difficulty level of new questions and, in turn, to determine whether to include them as scored questions on future exams. Experimental questions are not interspersed among scored questions within one exam section.

The Experimental Section may appear at any point during the exam, and you will not be able to tell which section it is while you're taking the exam. By the time you complete the exam, however, you will know which type of section was included as an Experimental Section. For example, if you have two Analytical Reasoning Sections on your exam, you can be certain that one of them was the Experimental Section.

THE WRITING SAMPLE

The 35-minute Writing Sample topic is designed to evaluate:

- Your ability to formulate persuasive and cogent arguments
- Your ability to write an organized, coherent essay in a short time period
- Your command of the language and the conventions of Standard Written English

The Writing Sample topic presents two alternatives and calls for you to argue in favor of one alternative over the other. This section always follows all other sections of the LSAT. You must respond in the writing space provided in the test booklet. Scratch paper is provided for taking notes and constructing outlines. The Writing Sample is not scored or evaluated by the testing service. Instead, the service provides a photocopy to the law schools to which you direct your LSAT scores.

Recent Changes and Possible Future Revisions

Two recent changes, both beginning with the June 2007 LSAT, are as follows:

- In the Reading Comprehension section, one of the four question sets is now based on two related passages, rather than one passage (as in previous versions). Most questions based on a passage pair involve both passages and how they relate to one another. The combined length of a passage pair is roughly the same as that of one longer passage, so the total amount of reading involved is about the same as before.

- For the Writing Sample, the writing prompt is now the same for every test-taker. You must decide between two given alternatives and defend your choice. Previously, some test-takers were prompted instead to analyze a given argument.

Neither of these two changes makes the LSAT easier or tougher than before—just a bit different.

Are any other changes in store for the LSAT? The most likely change in the near future will be procedural, not substantive. The Graduate Record Examinations® (GRE) and Graduate Management Admission Test® (GMAT) are now administered by computer, and the LSAT will no doubt follow suit before long.

HOW THE LSAT IS SCORED

First, the total number of correct responses (out of 101 scored questions) is determined. This is your raw score. Remember, there is no deduction from your raw score for incorrect responses.

Next, your raw score is converted to a scaled score ranging from 120–180. The purpose of converting raw scores to scaled scores is to account for slight variations in overall difficulty level and in total number of questions among the different exams administered over the years. For the two Practice Tests in this book, check the chart on page 6 to calculate an approximate score.

Evaluating Your LSAT Score

About five weeks after you take the LSAT, the testing service will send your results, including your raw score, your scaled score, and your percentile ranking (0 percent to 99 percent). The percentile ranking shows how you performed relative to all others taking the LSAT over a recent multi-year period. A percentile ranking of 60 percent, for example, indicates that you scored higher than 60 percent of all test-takers and lower than 39 percent of all test-takers. The percentile ranking is not reported to the law schools.

The following score worksheet and score conversion table, based on a 101-question LSAT, will help you evaluate your performance on practice tests. The figures in this table are average (mean) conversion figures for several previously administered exams. Keep in mind that scaled scores and percentile rankings vary slightly from exam to exam.

SCORING WORKSHEET

1. Enter the number of questions you answered correctly in each section.

    Section 1: _____

    Section 2: _____

    Section 3: _____

    Section 4: _____

2. Enter the sum here: _____ **This is your raw score.**

SCORE CONVERSION TABLE (FOR CONVERTING RAW SCORE TO THE 120–180 LSAT SCALED SCORE)

Raw Score Range	Scaled Score	Raw Score Range	Scaled Score
99–101	180	55–56	149
98	179	54	148
97	178	52–53	147
96	177	50–51	146
95	176	49	145
94	175	47–48	144
93	174	45–46	143
92	173	44	142
91	172	42–43	141
90	171	40–41	140
89	170	39	139
88	169	37–38	138
86–87	168	36	137
85	167	34–35	136
84	166	33	135
82–83	165	31–32	134
81	164	30	133
79–80	163	29	132
78	162	27–28	131
76–77	161	26	130
75	160	25	129
73–74	159	23–24	128
71–72	158	22	127
69–70	157	21	126
68	156	20	125
66–67	155	19	124
64–65	154	18	123
63	153	17	122
61–62	152	16	121
59–60	151	0–15	120
57–58	150		

Here are a few revealing observations about the figures in the score conversion table:

- You don't need to respond correctly to every question to attain a "perfect" score of 180.

- If you respond correctly to 3 out of 4 questions (on average), you will score higher than 90 percent of all test-takers.

- If you respond correctly to 2 out of 3 questions (on average), you will score higher than 75 percent of all test-takers.

- If you respond correctly to 1 out of 2 questions (on average), you will score higher than 40 percent of all test-takers.

- One additional correct response makes the biggest percentile difference near the middle of the performance curve. Here, one additional correct response can boost your percentile ranking by almost 5 percent.

How Law Schools Evaluate LSAT Scores

All of the nearly 200 American law schools accredited by the American Bar Association require that you take the LSAT to be considered for admission. Most nonaccredited and state-accredited schools, on the other hand, do not require LSAT scores.

Each law school develops and implements its own policies for evaluating LSAT scores. Some schools place equal weight on LSAT scores and grade point averages (GPAs), others weigh LSAT scores more heavily, and still others weigh GPAs more heavily. Your three most recent LSAT scores are reported by the Law School Data Assembly Service (LSDAS) to each law school receiving your scores and transcripts. Most law schools average reported scores, but a small number of schools consider only your highest reported score. A few schools have adopted a hybrid approach in which reported scores are averaged unless there is a sufficiently large discrepancy between scores, in which case the scores are not averaged.

WHEN SHOULD YOU TAKE THE LSAT?

The LSAT is offered four times each year, in February, June, October, and December. Most law schools admit new students for the fall term only. Although application deadlines vary among the schools, if you plan to take the LSAT no later than December prior to matriculation, you are certain to meet application deadlines at all but a few schools. Ideally, you should take the LSAT for the first time no later than October of the year before matriculation, so that you can take the exam a second time if necessary and still meet application deadlines.

You can take the LSAT at any time, even during your freshman or sophomore year of undergraduate school. However, because the intellectual abilities that the LSAT evaluates are developed to a large extent during your four years of college, postponing the test may allow for further intellectual development—and result in higher LSAT scores. Most college students take the LSAT for the first time either late in their junior year or early in their senior year.

Registering for the LSAT

To sit for the LSAT, you need to register using the form supplied by the Law School Admission Council (LSAC). You'll find this form and all the additional information you need to register at the LSAC Web site (www.lsac.org). Electronic registration is also available, or you can contact LSAC by telephone (215-968-1001) to request a printed copy of the current *LSAT/LSDAS Registration and Information Book* (also available online for downloading), which includes the LSAT registration form. Keep in mind, however, that the LSAC may phase out the use of preprinted forms and of its preprinted Registration Book. By the time you are ready to register, the LSAC Web site may be your only source for registration forms.

Registering for the LSDAS

The LSDAS is operated by the LSAC, the organization that designs and administers the LSAT. The function of the LSDAS is to collect your undergraduate transcripts and LSAT reports and assemble a report or summary to provide to the law schools that you specify. You will need to register for this service during the year you are applying for admission to law schools. Registration is for one year only, so if you register but postpone law school entrance for a year, you will need to re-register for the service later. Detailed information about the LSDAS and a registration form are available at the LSAC Web site (www.lsac.org).

TIPS FOR SCORING YOUR BEST

Find Your Optimal Pace and Stay There

Time is most definitely a factor on the LSAT. Almost every test-taker runs out of time before finishing at least one section of the exam. In fact, if you don't work constantly at a somewhat quicker pace than what is comfortable for you, you're not likely to finish any section.

Why does the testing service impose such great time pressure? Given enough time, most test-takers can respond correctly to perhaps 80 percent or more of the questions. Imposing a short time limit achieves a wide distribution of test scores.

To beat the odds, develop a sense of your optimal pace, one that results in the greatest number of correct responses. As you take the mini-tests and the full-length practice test in this book, learn to get comfortable with a quick pace by adhering strictly to the time limits imposed.

Don't Try to Be a Perfectionist

You can miss quite a few questions and still earn a very high score on the LSAT. Resist the temptation to stick with a "tough" question until you're sure your response is correct. Stubborn, perfectionist tendencies will only defeat you on the LSAT. All questions—difficult ones and easy ones alike—are worth one point each.

Don't Overanalyze

LSAT questions are not designed to trick you. The testing service takes every precaution to ensure that all questions are clear and unambiguous and that there is one best response to every question. As long as you believe your thinking is fairly clear as you read and consider a question, it's not useful to second-guess yourself about which response is correct. You'll only waste valuable time by overanalyzing a question.

Maintain a "Dialogue" with the Exam

While taking a timed exam such as the LSAT, it's remarkably easy to fall into a passive mode, in which you allow your eyes simply to scan the answer choices and hope that the correct response will jump out at you. This tendency is understandable, given the dry nature of the material on the LSAT. But you can fight it by "interacting" with the test as you read. As you work through the Reading Comprehension and Logical Reasoning sections, for example, keep asking yourself these questions:

- What's the point here?

- How is the test maker trying to trip me up?

- Why does the author make this point?

- Is there some portion of this paragraph that relates most directly to the specific question?

Use your pencil to help keep you in an active mode. Circle and underline key words and phrases; make brief notes in the margins; draw flow charts and other diagrams to help you understand what you are reading.

Don't Obsess About Your Practice Test Scores

When you take the mini-tests and practice tests in this book, you may not perform as well as you'd like to. You may have a particular law school in mind as your first choice, and you may think you need a particular LSAT score to gain admission to that school. It's understandable, therefore, to establish a particular LSAT score as your goal. Still, try not to concern yourself with your scores as much as with what constructive steps you can take between now and exam day to improve your performance.

Avoid "Cramming" and "Burnout"

Preparing for the LSAT is a bit like training for an athletic event. You need to familiarize yourself with the event, learn to be comfortable with each aspect of the event, and build up your endurance. At some point—hopefully, around exam day—your motivation, interest, and performance will peak. Because the LSAT does not measure substantive knowledge, "cramming" for the test makes no sense. Devoting a month or so of your attention, energy, and concern to the LSAT is plenty of time. Don't drag out the process by starting several months in advance or by postponing the exam to allow yourself more time than you really need for preparation.

HOW ELSE CAN YOU PREPARE?

The LSAT is not a test of substantive knowledge. Thus, no one specific academic course will provide you with a distinct advantage for the exam. Some academic fields, however, do have a more direct bearing than others on the LSAT in the kinds of intellectual abilities involved. The areas that correlate most closely with the LSAT in this respect include:

- philosophy and ethics

- English and literature

- political science

- history

Historically, test-takers with substantial philosophy course work perform better on the LSAT than those without such a background. That doesn't mean that you should rush over to the registrar's office and change your major just to score high on the LSAT. Remember that, to a large extent, the LSAT is designed to evaluate the kinds of intellectual abilities you develop over your lifetime, not specifically what you learn or study in college.

Likewise, be realistic about the benefits you should expect from this or any other LSAT preparation book. There is only so much you can do in a month, or even a year, to boost your LSAT score. Although theoretically, anybody is capable of attaining a perfect score on the LSAT, in reality each individual is constrained by his or her innate abilities and talents. With regular study and practice, you will perform as well as you can reasonably expect to perform.

Other Resources for LSAT Preparation

How much time and money should you invest in your LSAT preparation? The conventional wisdom is that since the LSAT is one of the most important tests you'll ever take, you should invest as much of both as possible. However, keep in mind that the law of diminishing returns applies to LSAT preparation as with other test-preparation strategies. This book, along with a few other thoughtfully selected books and online resources, can provide virtually all of the potential benefits of a full-blown LSAT prep course.

If you've already visited any major brick-and-mortar or online bookstore, you've probably been overwhelmed by the number of available books for LSAT prep. Here are some suggestions to help you cut through the glut:

- Peruse a book carefully before committing to it. Yes, this means visiting your local bookstore rather than simply ordering a book online.

- Look for a book that emphasizes skill development, not just practice questions.

- Rule out any book that does not include a complete analysis of all five answer choices for each Logical Reasoning and Reading Comprehension question. (You gain just as much from learning why wrong answer choices are wrong as you can in finding out why best answer choices are best.)

- Rule out any book that emphasizes so-called "secrets" and "shortcuts" or that makes the test out to be easier than it appears. Do you really think the LSAC would devise a test that can be "cracked" like a cheap safe? If so, think again.

- Limit the number of comprehensive LSAT books you use to two or three. Any more than that and you'll find yourself reading the same strategies and test-taking tips again and again.

- Identify your weakest skill area and supplement a comprehensive LSAT book with a workbook targeted for that particular area.

- If you must shop for LSAT books at an online bookstore, ignore customer comments and ratings, especially if there aren't very many.

The bottom line: You don't need to spend more than $40–$50 on three or four books at most to be fully prepared for the LSAT.

ONLINE LSAT RESOURCES

The Internet is littered with LSAT advice and practice questions, freely available for public consumption. To separate the wheat from the chaff, limit your LSAT Web-surfing to the official LSAC site (www.lsac.org) and the sites of test-prep publishers with a time-tested reputation for producing high-quality content, such as Peterson's (www.petersons.com). You'll also find links to these and other useful LSAT sites at the online supplement for this book (www.west.net/~stewart/lsat).

LSAT PREPARATION COURSES

Would it be worthwhile to enroll in an LSAT prep course? Here are some points to consider:

- The dynamics of a live classroom setting can help you learn difficult concepts by providing different perspectives. But why not start your own study group? You're just as likely to gain useful insights from your peers as from an LSAT instructor.

- Having made a substantial financial investment, you'll likely be motivated to get your money's worth out of the investment. But this can be an expensive head game—and if you can't afford the course to begin with, it won't matter anyway.

- You're less likely to procrastinate with a set class schedule. However, if you're disciplined enough, this is no advantage.

- All the materials are provided, so you don't need to decide which books and/or software to buy.

- You can commiserate and compare notes with your classmates. In fact, LSAT prep classes typically morph into de facto pre-law support groups. But again, there's no reason you can't start your own LSAT study/support group?

Here are some caveats to keep in mind if you're thinking about taking an LSAT prep course:

- They're expensive; you can easily spend $1,000 on one LSAT prep course. If you're near a university, you might find a course sponsored by the university for a fraction of the cost of a private course, or you could start your own study group.

- Despite their claims, private test-prep companies pass along no "secrets"—you'll learn nothing that you can't find for yourself in test-prep books.

- The popular test-prep services require each of their LSAT instructors to have taken the real LSAT and attained a high score (typically above the 90th percentile). Although this ensures that your instructor is intelligent and knowledgeable in the topics required to score high on the LSAT, it doesn't guarantee that he or she will be an effective teacher.

- During peak times of the year, you might have difficulty scheduling out-of-class time in a computer lab, at least during reasonable hours.

- If you're not located in a major urban area or near a large college or university, the class location might be too remote for you.

If you decide to enroll in an LSAT prep course, keep the following points of advice in mind:

- Ask about the policy for repeating the course. Insist on an option to repeat the course at least once without charge at any time (not just within the next year).

- Ask about merit-based or financial-based "scholarships" (fee reductions).

- If you repeat the course, be sure to arrange for a different instructor; just as with LSAT books, each LSAT instructor has his or her own pedagogical and communication style. You may find that a different teaching style better fits your needs.

- The most significant benefit of an LSAT course is the live classroom, so be sure to attend all classes, or at least as many as you can reasonably attend.

- Take full advantage of the opportunity to meet other students and set up out-of-class study sessions. As I've already noted, you can learn just as much from your peers as from an instructor.

PART II

THE LESSONS

Analytical Reasoning Basic Concepts and Strategies

In this lesson, you'll become familiar with the format of the Analytical Reasoning section and learn strategies for handling the questions.

ANALYTICAL REASONING AT A GLANCE

Total number of questions: 23–24

Total number of test sections: 1

Testing time allowed: 35 minutes

- Questions are divided into 4 sets.

- Each set involves a different logic game.

- Each logic game includes 4–8 questions.

Ground Rules

- No scratch paper is permitted (make notes in the test booklet).

- Only pencils and highlighters are allowed (no pens).

- No penalties are assessed for incorrect responses.

- Each question is considered independently of all others.

Here are the directions you'll see in the test booklet:

> Each group of questions in this section is based on a set of conditions. In answering some of the questions, it may be useful to draw a rough diagram. Choose the response that most accurately and completely answers each question and blacken the corresponding space on your answer sheet.

What Does the Analytical Reasoning Section Test?

The Analytical Reasoning Section tests your ability to:

- understand a system of relationships

- draw deductive conclusions about those relationships

- assimilate and organize information quickly and accurately

- visualize spatial relationships

ANATOMY OF A LOGIC GAME

On the LSAT, Analytical Reasoning questions appear in sets. Each set presents a distinct puzzle or logic game, which includes three elements:

1 **The premise:** A brief introductory paragraph establishing the setting for the game, identifying the subjects involved, and describing generally how the subjects are related to one another. The number of subjects in a game generally ranges from four to ten (five to eight is typical).

2 **A series of conditions or rules:** These conditions impose specific restrictions upon the relationships among the subjects. A logic game may include as few as two or as many as ten conditions, although the number of conditions typically ranges from four to six.

3 **The questions:** Questions involve the relationships defined by the rules. They require deductive analysis by which one and only one response can be proven beyond any doubt to be the correct one. The number of questions per game ranges from four to eight, although six or seven questions is most common.

Example: The "Roller Coaster" Game

An amusement park roller coaster includes five cars, numbered 1 through 5 from front to back. Each car accommodates up to two riders, seated side by side. Six people—Tom, Gwen, Laurie, Mark, Paul, and Jack—are riding the coaster at the same time.

Laurie is sharing a car.

Mark is not sharing a car and is seated immediately behind an empty car.

Tom is not sharing a car with either Gwen or Paul.

Gwen is riding in either the third or fourth car.

1. Which of the following groups of riders could occupy the second car?

    (A) Laurie only
    (B) Tom and Gwen
    (C) Laurie and Mark
    (D) Jack and Tom
    (E) Jack, Gwen, and Paul

2. If Gwen is riding immediately behind Laurie's car and immediately ahead of Tom's car, all of the following must be true EXCEPT:

    (A) Gwen is riding in the fourth car
    (B) Paul is riding in the third car
    (C) Tom is riding in the fifth car
    (D) Laurie is riding in the third car
    (E) The first car is empty

3. Which one of the following statements CANNOT be true?

    (A) Neither Tom nor Gwen is sharing a car with another rider.
    (B) Neither Mark nor Jack is sharing a car with another rider.
    (C) Tom is sharing a car, and Jack is sharing a car.
    (D) Gwen is sharing a car, and Paul is sharing a car.
    (E) Tom is sharing a car, and Gwen is sharing a car.

4. If Paul is riding in the second car, how many different combinations of riders are possible for the third car?

    (A) 1
    (B) 2
    (C) 3
    (D) 4
    (E) 5

5. Assume that Roger, a seventh rider, is riding with Jack in the first car, but that all other conditions remain unchanged. Which of the following is a complete and accurate list of the riders who might be riding in the fifth car?

    (A) Mark
    (B) Tom, Paul
    (C) Tom, Laurie, Paul
    (D) Tom, Laurie, Mark
    (E) Mark, Paul, Tom, Laurie

STRATEGIES FOR HANDLING A LOGIC GAME

In this section, you'll learn several strategies for handling any logic game—including the roller coaster game in the preceding section—as efficiently as possible. You'll find out how to:

- quickly size up a logic game

- organize a game's information using a master diagram

- respond appropriately to the questions

- Answers and explanations for questions 1–5 of the roller coaster game begin on page 23 ("Answers and Explanations").

Size Up the Game

- **Survey the game for key information.** Take a quick glance at the page to see what words and phrases appear frequently among the questions and answer choices. Then read the premise and conditions quickly. Try to determine:

    - what type of game you're dealing with

    - how many subjects are in the game

    - the game's difficulty level and whether you should skip it

    - how you might organize the information in a diagram

- **Don't let the "length" of the game fool you.** There is no automatic correlation between the length of a game (the number of questions or conditions) and the difficulty level of the game. Do not bypass a game merely because it either fills up more space on the page than the other games in the section or includes more (or fewer) questions than the other games.

- **Jot down a list, or "roster," of the subjects.** It's remarkably easy to forget how many subjects (people, events, etc.) a particular game involves unless you list them near your diagram. Use first letters as symbols, and use uppercase and lowercase letters (or any other binary distinction for which letter size is a clear indicator) to distinguish males and females. Put a box around the list to identify it clearly.

- **Don't let the wording of the rules trip you up.** Read the rules slowly and carefully. The single most common mistake test-takers make in logic games is to misread a rule or condition. These mistakes can be costly; they may taint your analysis of the entire game and cause you to respond incorrectly to several, if not all, of the questions.

- **Accept the rules at face value.** The rules are designed not to trick you but to be as clear as possible. Do not read into the rules what does not appear on their face. For example, in the roller coaster game we just reviewed, you may find yourself thinking, "Perhaps one person could ride in two cars at one time by straddling them in some fashion." Resist the search for subtle ambiguities or double meanings in the rules; you will only defeat your purpose.

Create a Master Diagram

- **Avoid listing all possible combinations.** When you attempted to solve the roller coaster game, did you try to jot down all the possible seat assignments for the riders, considering all rules simultaneously? If so, was the result a confusing mess? Probably.

Stop this "strategy" now before it becomes a bad habit. Instead, use one (or perhaps two) master diagrams that encompass all of the various possibilities. Depict the relationships spatially as pictures. Try to construct a picture that allows you to visualize the relationships among the subjects of the game at a glance. An effective picture or diagram can transform a seemingly impossible game into a piece of cake. For many games, a single basic diagram or picture can be used as a template for all questions.

- **Look for a key rule to begin diagramming.** Look for a rule that allows you to organize the game into two basic alternative scenarios. A rule that includes an "either/or" statement, for example, suggests two alternative situations and thus two alternative pictures. This technique will greatly simplify the game. Not every game includes a key rule, but you should always look for one.

Example: The "Roller Coaster" Game

All of the possibilities fall into one of two alternative scenarios based upon the last condition ("Gwen is riding in either the third or fourth car."). Accordingly, you can draw two distinct diagrams to represent these two scenarios:

SCENARIO #1	SCENARIO #2
1	1
2	2
3 G	3
4	4 G
5	5

- **Account for every rule, either in or around your diagram.** Use your pencil to display each and every rule in your workspace. Try to represent the rules as pictures that indicate visually how they fit into your diagram. If a rule cannot be expressed as a picture, restate the rule near your diagram, using symbols or shorthand. Otherwise, you may forget about it. Remember that every rule will come into play at some point in the game.

After creating two alternative diagrams based upon Gwen's position, consider the remaining rules. If we try to incorporate any of these rules directly into our diagram, we would have to add several scenarios to account for all of the additional possibilities. What if we overlook a possibility? Run out of space on our paper? Run out of time? Instead of complicating our diagram, let's simply indicate the remaining rules either as pictures or symbols near our master diagrams (the inequality symbol is used to signify that two riders are not sharing a car):

FINAL MASTER DIAGRAM

SCENARIO #1	SCENARIO #2
1	1
2	2
3 Ⓖ	3
4	4 Ⓖ
5	5

$$[L] \quad \boxed{\begin{array}{c}\boxtimes\\ \text{M}\end{array}} \quad T \neq \%_P$$

$$\boxed{\text{TGLMPJ}}$$

- **Based on the rules, draw useful conclusions.** Once you've displayed all of the rules in your workspace, ask yourself, "What conclusions can I draw from the rules?" This step is crucial. If additional information can be deduced, you will probably need to know this information to analyze most, if not all, of the questions. In looking for these hidden pieces to the puzzle, bear in mind the following:

- *Some conclusions are less helpful than others.* Conclusions about what cannot be true (in the roller coaster game, for example, which cars a particular rider cannot occupy) are generally not very useful. Focus instead on the affirmative.

- *Not all games contain clues to additional information.* With practice, you will develop an instinct for knowing when you can or cannot draw additional conclusions from the rules.

- *Limit your time looking for additional information.* In most cases, you will not be entirely certain that you have deduced all that you can from the rules. With enough practice, you will develop a sense for what type of additional information to look for, as well as a sense for when to move on to the questions.

What else can you deduce from the premise and conditions in the roller coaster game? Can you "fit" any other riders into the diagram? Not without adding restrictions. However, you can draw certain conclusions about the number of riders in each car. The game's premise states that each car can accommodate up to two riders, but one of the conditions states that Mark is seated alone behind an empty car. That leaves three other cars to accommodate the other five riders. Thus, accommodating all six riders requires this distribution:

- one and only one car (the car immediately ahead of Mark's car) is empty

- of the other four cars, two (including Mark's car) are occupied by one rider each

- two riders share each of the remaining two cars

This additional information is important in analyzing the questions. In fact, by drawing these conclusions before answering the questions, you've already done much of the work required to answer the questions.

- **Keep your diagrams neat.** Remember: Scratch paper is not permitted for this section of the exam. Use the margins and the bottom portion of each page (usually about one-fourth the area of the page) for diagrams and notes. Given this limited workspace, it is crucial that you keep your diagrams neat and compact.

Respond to the Questions

- **The first few questions will tell you whether you're on the right track.** They're usually somewhat simpler than the others and involve the more basic and obvious relationships established by the rules of the game. Some might require no analysis other than recognizing rule violations among the answer choices. Others might focus on just one or two of the rules without requiring more than one or two deductive steps. In fact, you might be able to respond to the first one or two questions without using a diagram. If you are stumped by the first few questions, then it's very likely you've misread or misinterpreted a rule, neglected to include a rule in or around your diagram, or overlooked a conclusion inferable from the rules. Before you invest more time in the remaining questions, go back and find out where you got off track.

Let's return to the roller coaster game. Question 1 is a typical first question. It does not require any analysis other than recognizing that particular answer choices violate particular rules. A diagram is not needed for this question.

- **Don't confuse the question with its "inverse."** It is easy to become confused as to what a question asks. To avoid this common error, follow these two steps:

  ① Review the question repeatedly as you analyze the answer choices.

  ② Underline the operative phrase in the question.

For example, Question 3 asks you to identify the one statement that "CANNOT be true." Be careful not to turn the question on its head by looking for a statement that must be true.

- **Predict the answer, if possible.** If the question stem provides additional information, begin to draw additional conclusions before reviewing the answer choices. Then scan the answer choices, looking for your predetermined answer.

In Question 2, you can determine the positions of Mark, Laurie, Gwen, and Tom from the information in the question stem. Accordingly, the correct response to the question ("All of the following must be true EXCEPT") will probably involve either Paul or Jack. The correct response, choice (B), jumps out at you as you quickly scan the choices.

- **Scan answer choices for clues.** Questions such as "Which of the following must be true?" can be time consuming, since you must analyze each answer choice in turn. If the correct answer turns out to be choice (E), you could spend an inordinate amount of time getting to it. The nature of the answer choices often provides a clue as to what rule or rules you should focus on. You may be able to identify the correct answer without analyzing the other choices.

For example, finding the correct answer to Question 3 is potentially time-consuming, since the question stem provides no clue as to what issues the question will focus on. However, by glancing quickly at the answer choices, you might intuit that the correct response will focus on single riders, and so you should first analyze answer choices (A) and (B).

- **Don't do more work than necessary to determine the answer.** You can answer most questions without considering every rule and without determining all that you can from the additional information supplied by the question stem. Avoid doing more work than necessary to determine the answer.

For example, Question 5 asks who might occupy the fifth car. In considering Scenario #1 in the diagram below (Gwen occupies the third car), you need only go as far as determining that Mark occupies the fifth car alone, even though the positions of all other riders can also be determined.

SCENARIO #1   SCENARIO #2
1   1
2   2
3 G   3
4   4 G
5   5

- **Beware of "sleeper" rules.** A game might include a rule that comes into play only in one or two of the later questions. Make sure to account for every rule as you diagram a game so that you don't forget about these rules.

   In the Roller Coaster game, for instance, the third rule—"Tom is not sharing a car with either Gwen or Paul"—is a sleeper. It does not come into play in drawing your initial conclusions; in fact, you do not need it at all until Question 5.

- **The last question may be easier than it looks.** While the final question is typically a bit more complex than the others, you'll probably be ready for it simply because you have become familiar and comfortable with the game. In fact, you may actually find it easier than some of the earlier questions.

- Question 5 on page 17 is a typical last question; every original rule comes into play, and the additional information does not permit you to eliminate either of the two basic scenarios. However, if you've successfully handled the other questions, you probably won't find this question all that difficult.

- **Use a highlighter or other method to preserve your master diagram.** Avoid the time and risk of error involved in redrawing your diagram for each question. Use your master diagram for as many questions as possible. Insert variable information, then erase that information before proceeding to the next question. In doing so, be careful not to erase part of your master diagram. No pens are permitted, so you may want to earmark "fixed" information with a highlighter or by circling those subjects in your master diagram that should remain fixed for all questions.

FINAL MASTER DIAGRAM
SCENARIO #1   SCENARIO #2
1   1
2   2
3 Ⓖ   3
4   4 Ⓖ
5   5

[L]   ⊠   T ≠ G/P
           M

TGLMPJ

In our final master diagram (above), notice that "G" (Gwen) is circled in both alternative diagrams. This technique ensures that those "Gs" won't be erased as you fill in the diagrams with variable information from question to question.

ANSWERS AND EXPLANATIONS

1. **The correct answer is (D).** Each of the other choices violates the premise or one of the conditions. Choice (A) violates the rule that Laurie is sharing a car; choice (B) violates the rule that Gwen is riding in either the third or fourth car; it also violates the rule that Tom is not sharing a car with Gwen (although either rule violation suffices to eliminate this answer choice). Choice (C) violates the rule that Mark is not sharing a car, and choice (E) violates the premise that states that each car can accommodate up to two riders.

2. FINAL MASTER DIAGRAM

   SCENARIO #1   SCENARIO #2

1	1
2	2
3 Ⓖ	3
4	4 Ⓖ
5	5

   [L_]   ⊠/M   T ≠ G/P

   TGLMPJ

   The correct answer is (B). Consider the information in the question stem in light of the two alternative scenarios in our final master diagram (above). Scenario #1 may be eliminated from consideration. Why? In Scenario #1, Laurie, Gwen, and Tom would occupy the second, third, and fourth cars, respectively. This arrangement, however, would not accommodate Mark seated alone immediately behind an empty car (as required by one of the game's conditions). Scenario #2 is the only one that applies to this question. Given the additional information in the question stem, Laurie must occupy the third car while Tom occupies the fifth car. Accordingly, Mark must occupy the second car, and the first car must be empty:

   SCENARIO #1   SCENARIO #2

1	1 ⊠
2 [L_]	2 M
3 Ⓖ	3 [L_]
4 T	4 Ⓖ
5	5 T

   However, Paul may occupy either the third or fourth car. Thus, choice (B) is not necessarily true.

3. **The correct answer is (A).** Mark and only one other rider are each seated alone; otherwise, the coaster could not accommodate all six riders. (Remember, each car can accommodate no more than two riders.) Thus, Tom and Gwen cannot both be seated alone.

4. **The correct answer is (C).** As with Question 2, this question provides additional information that allows you to eliminate one of the two alternative scenarios. In Question 4, however, Scenario #2 in our final master diagram (below) is the one that may be entirely eliminated.

FINAL MASTER DIAGRAM

SCENARIO #1	SCENARIO #2
1	1
2	2
3 (G)	3
4	4 (G)
5	5

[L_]　⊠/M　　T ≠ G/P

TGLMPJ

If Paul and Gwen occupy the second and fourth cars, respectively, Mark cannot sit alone immediately behind an empty car (as required by one of the game's conditions). Focusing, then, on Scenario #1 (Gwen occupies the third car), given that Paul occupies the second car, Mark must occupy the fifth car, and the fourth car must be empty:

SCENARIO #1	SCENARIO #2
1	1
2 P	2 P
3 (G)	3
4 ⊠	4 (G)
5 M	5

Considering the four remaining riders, the rules expressly prohibit Tom from riding with Gwen (in the third car). Accordingly, Gwen may occupy the third car, either alone or with Laurie or Jack. Thus, one of exactly three combinations of riders could be riding in the third car: Gwen only, Gwen and Laurie, or Gwen and Jack.

5. **The correct answer is (D).** Consider the two alternative scenarios in our final master diagram. In Scenario #1 (Gwen in the third car), given that Jack and Roger occupy the first car, Mark must occupy the fifth car alone. Next, consider Scenario #2 (Gwen in the fourth car). Given that Jack and Roger occupy the first car, Mark must occupy the third car (while the second car is empty). Since Tom cannot share a car with Gwen, Tom must occupy the fifth car. Since Tom cannot share a car with Paul, Paul must share the fourth car with Gwen. Accordingly, Laurie must share the fifth car with Tom.

SCENARIO #1	SCENARIO #2
1 J R	1 J R
2	2 ⊠
3 (G)	3 M
4 ⊠	4 (G) P
5 M	5 T L

Thus, either Mark alone (under Scenario #1) or both Tom and Laurie (under Scenario #2) must occupy the fifth car.

PACING AND TIME ALLOCATION: QUESTIONS AND ANSWERS

Q **How much time should I allot for any one logic game?**

A Some games are more complex than others and thus are inherently more time consuming. Most test takers require at least 7 or 8 minutes for even the simplest of games. Complex games may realistically take as much as 10 minutes to solve. Do not devote more than 10 minutes to any one logic game, unless you have decided to attempt fewer than all of the games in the section.

Q **Is there a pattern in difficulty level among games in an exam section? If so, should I skip the tough ones?**

A Logic games vary considerably in complexity and difficulty level. It is safe to say that the first game will not be the most difficult one. Beyond this, there really is no discernible pattern, so be ready for anything. Logic games are easier for some test takers than for others. You may find that you will achieve your best score by skipping one of the games in a section and devoting the entire time to the remaining three games. In any event, do not skip more than one game; allocating your entire time to only two of four games results in a pace that is far too slow and is not justifiable for even the most challenging games.

Q **How do I know when to give up on a game and move on?**

A Once you commit yourself to a game, it can be difficult to force yourself to throw in the towel and move on to the next game. Most test-takers tend to be stubborn and insist on figuring out every question before moving on. Do not succumb to this self-defeating mentality. Answer the easier questions; if you have time at the end (and you probably won't), return to the game and try again.

Q **What if I have only one or two minutes to attempt a game?**

A Perhaps your pace has been too slow and only a few minutes remain for your final game. You'll need to decide quickly which two or three questions of the final game to attempt. Bear in mind that some of the questions (most likely the earlier ones) might be answerable without reading the premise or all of the rules. A quick glance at the question stem, along with a quick reading of the rule(s) relating to the question, may give you an idea of which questions you can successfully attack.

FORMAL LOGIC: EVERYTHING YOU NEED TO KNOW FOR LOGIC GAMES

You do not need a formal college-level logic course to perform well on the Analytical Reasoning section of the LSAT. Much of what you would learn in such a course—particularly the terminology and symbols used in formal logic—is of little practical use in handling LSAT logic games. Nevertheless, one particular concept in formal deductive logic is so crucial for success in handling logic games that we must examine it.

Conditional Statements and the "Contrapositive" Rule

A conditional statement is one in which an event occurs or does not occur if some other event occurs or does not occur. Consider the following four statements:

1 If a shirt is red, then it must have long sleeves.

2 All red shirts have long sleeves.

3 Only long-sleeved shirts are red.

4 A shirt is red only if it has long sleeves.

All of the statements above are essentially the same in meaning—a shirt's being red is conditioned upon the shirt's having long sleeves. Given this premise, consider whether each of the following three statements may be logically deduced:

1 If a shirt does not have long sleeves, then it cannot be red.

2 If a shirt has long sleeves, then it is red.

3 If a shirt is not red, then it does not have long sleeves.

The first of the three statements immediately above is referred to in formal logic as the contrapositive of the conditional—it reverses the "if" clause and the "then" clause, and negates both. The conclusion of a conditional statement is such that the "then" clause is always inferable from the "if" clause. Neither Statement 2 nor 3, however, is inferable—long-sleeved shirts may also be any other color than red. To restate all of this more generally:

Premise:

If A, then B

(or) All A are B

(or) Only B are A

(or) A only if B

Conclusion:

1. If not B, then not A. (contrapositive—valid)

2. If B, then A. (not inferable)

3. If not A, then not B. (not inferable)

Conditional rules make a logic game more complex and more confusing. In these cases, you must do the following:

- Remember that the rule applies only under certain circumstances.

- Be alert to the contrapositive inference as you work through the questions.

- Be careful to avoid the two fallacious inferences (identified above).

Be ready for conditional statements! You can be sure that at least one game will include this feature.

Analytical Reasoning Linear Sequence Games

In this lesson, you will examine "linear sequence" games, the most common logic games on the LSAT.

WHAT ARE LINEAR SEQUENCE GAMES?

Linear sequence games are the most common of the LSAT logic games. Linear sequencing involves placing the game's subjects in order in a row, or sequence, from left to right (or perhaps from top to bottom). The nature of the order might be spatial, chronological, or quantifiable (e.g., size or weight). In any case, your task is the same: to line them up in proper order.

Several variations of sequencing appear on the LSAT. In this lesson, you will explore the six most common variations, looking at one example of each type. Note that each example in this lesson includes only one illustrative question. Keep in mind, however, that on the LSAT every logic game includes 4–8 questions. Also, each example involves exactly five positions or "slots" in a sequence, but remember that in the actual LSAT, the number of slots in a sequence game can vary.

The rules in sequencing games include certain terminology that you must be sure to interpret accurately. Consider a game in which several people, including A, B, and C, are seated in a row of chairs from left to right. In this scenario,

All of these rules carry the same meaning:

"A is seated next to B."

"A is seated adjacent to B."

"A is seated immediately next to B."

"A is seated directly next to B."

Both of these rules carry the same meaning:

"A is seated immediately to the left of B."

"A is seated directly to the left of B."

Both of these rules carry the same meaning:

"A is seated exactly two chairs from B."

"A is seated two chairs from B."

Both of these rules carry the same meaning:

"A is seated to the left of B."

"A is seated farther left than B."

All of these rules carry the same meaning:

"C is seated immediately between A and B."

"C is seated next to both A and B."

"Only C is seated between A and B."

Both of these rules carry the same meaning:

"Two chairs separate A from B."

"A is seated three chairs from B."

All of these rules carry the same meaning:

"A and B are seated two chairs apart."

"One chair separates A from B."

"A is seated two chairs from B."

THE SIMPLE SEQUENCE GAME

A simple sequence game involves nothing more than arranging the subjects linearly in a string of blank spaces, using a fill-in-the-blank approach. Make sure that you keep straight in your mind which end of the sequence is which, and you should not have much trouble with this type of game.

Example 1:

Five students—Joe, Kim, Linda, Mark, and Nicole—are enrolled in grades ranging from first to fifth. Each is in a different grade.

Mark is in a lower grade than Kim.

Nicole and Linda are in the first and fifth grades, although not necessarily in that order.

Which of the following statements provides sufficient information to determine that Kim is in the fourth grade?

(A) Linda is in a higher grade than Kim.
(B) Nicole is in a higher grade than Joe.
(C) Joe is in a lower grade than Mark.
(D) Linda is in a lower grade than Mark.
(E) Nicole is in a lower grade than Mark.

This is a straightforward linear sequence game in which two alternative diagrams based upon the last rule may be constructed:

The only major concern here is to keep straight in your mind that "lower" refers to the left of your diagram and that "higher" refers to the right.

The correct answer is (C). Before examining any of the answer choices, determine what must be true for Kim to be in the fourth grade. The diagrams above make clear that Joe must be to the left of (in a lower grade than) Kim to achieve this result. The correct answer is now easy to spot: If Joe is to the left of (in a lower grade than) Mark, then Joe is also to the left of (in a lower grade than) Kim.

THE DOUBLE-DECKER SEQUENCE GAME

Your task in a double-decker sequence game is to pair each subject with another subject and sequence the pairs. This type of game typically involves teams (of two subjects) competing in a race or other contest.

Example 2:

In a two-man bobsled race, ten athletes—A, B, C, D, E, F, G, H, I, and J—each finished in one of five places in the standings. There were no ties.

H and I were teamed together.

C and F were not teamed together.

E and G were teamed together and did not place last in the standings.

B placed immediately ahead of F in the standings.

If H and B placed second and third, respectively, which of the following must be true?

(A) C placed fourth.
(B) G placed first.
(C) F placed fifth.
(D) A placed fourth.
(E) D placed third.

Use a diagram such as the one below to assign each subject (athlete) to one of five positions:

```
1  ⎫           [H I]
2  ⎬ [E G]
3  ⎪           ⎡ B  ⎤
4  ⎭           ⎣ F∅ ⎦
5
```

10 ABCDEFGHIJ

Notice that the [EG] and [HI] teams are indicated to the right of the master diagram, ready to be pasted into the diagram as needed to respond to the question. The relationship between B and F is also indicated in picture form. Also notice the use of the elimination or "strikethrough" symbol (/) to indicate that a team including C and F is not permitted. In working with this diagram, keep in mind that left-right orientation between team members is irrelevant.

The correct answer is (B). Since B placed third, F must place fourth. According to one of the conditions, E and G did not place last; therefore, the only place in which E and G could finish is first.

```
1 [E G] ⎫
2 [H I] ⎬ [E G]
3  B    ⎪
4  F    ⎭
5
```

THE SEQUENCE/ATTRIBUTES GAME

In this type of game, your task is twofold: (1) line up (sequence) the subjects, and (2) assign one or two characteristics or attributes to each subject.

Example 3:

Five horses—A, B, C, D, and E—are kept in five adjacent stalls. Three of the horses are male, and two of the horses are female.

B is a male.

The females are not kept in adjacent stalls.

C is separated from E by one stall.

A is kept in one of the three middle stalls.

If all three males are kept in adjacent stalls, which of the following is a complete and accurate list of the horses whose gender (male or female) can be determined?

(A) A and B
(B) B and D
(C) A, B, and D
(D) A, B, C, and E
(E) B, C, D, and E

Your initial diagram for this game might include a sequence along with a shorthand restatement of the rules:

ABCDE

Now, considering the question, three males must be in stalls 2, 3, and 4 to satisfy the rule that the two females must be separated. Thus, although you have not constructed a sequence for the five horses, you do know the gender of the horse in each stall. B is a male and thus must be in one of the three middle stalls. A is in one of the three middle stalls and thus must be a male. That leaves D, C, and E. C and E cannot be in stalls 2 and 4 (in either order), because either A or B must occupy one of those stalls. (In the diagram below, A and B could be reversed.) C and E must therefore be either in stalls 1 and 3 (in either order) or in stalls 3 and 5 (in either order):

The correct answer is (C). In either event, you cannot determine the gender of either C or E (although they are not of the same gender). Finally, D must be in either stall 1 or 5, and thus must be female.

THE CLUSTER SEQUENCE GAME

In any type of sequence game, your task is to assign each subject to one position in a sequence. In a cluster sequence game, however, any number of subjects (perhaps none, perhaps all) might occupy a given position.

Example 4:

> Each of five detectives—Arkin, Billings, Cobart, Dansen, and Eckles—has been assigned to search one floor of the house of a murder victim for clues. The house includes five floors—the basement, the first floor, the second floor, the third floor, and the attic.
>
> Cobart has been assigned to a higher floor than any other detective.
>
> Billings has been assigned to a lower floor than Dansen.
>
> At least two detectives have been assigned to the second floor.
>
> Exactly one detective has been assigned to the first floor, and exactly one detective has been assigned to the third floor.

If exactly one floor separates the floor to which Eckles is assigned from the floor to which Arkin is assigned, which of the following must be false?

(A) Arkin is assigned to the basement.
(B) Billings is assigned to the first floor.
(C) Dansen is assigned to the second floor.
(D) Cobart is assigned to the third floor.
(E) Eckles is assigned to the third floor.

The key to working through this game quickly is to determine alternative scenarios based upon the number of detectives assigned to each floor. Given that exactly one detective is assigned to the first floor and one to the third floor, the three others must be allocated among the second floor, the basement, and the attic. Since at least two detectives are assigned to the second floor, three basic possibilities emerge. Because Cobart is assigned to a higher floor than any other detective, and because Dansen is assigned to a higher floor than Billings, the three alternative diagrams may be partially completed as follows ("X" indicates a floor to which no detective is assigned):

Floor			
A	X	C	X
3	C	–	C
2	– –	– –	ADE
1	–	–	B
B	–	X	X

(with C→D→B chain indicated beside the floor column)

Be careful in this game not to confuse the first floor with the bottom floor, which is the basement.

The correct answer is (E). The second alternative diagram above may be eliminated from consideration, since Eckles and Arkin would be assigned to the first and third floors (in either order), restricting both Dansen and Billings to the second floor, thereby violating the rule that Billings is assigned to a lower floor than Dansen. The third alternative diagram may also be eliminated, since it requires that Arkin and Eckles be assigned to the same floor. In the first diagram, Dansen and Billings must be assigned to the second and first floors, respectively, while Arkin and Eckles are assigned to the second floor and to the basement (in either order):

Floor	
A	X
3	C
2	DA
1	B
B	E

In neither scenario can Eckles be assigned to the third floor; thus, statement (E) must be false.

THE DUAL SEQUENCE GAME

Dual sequence games involve two separate and distinct sequences. Be careful in constructing your diagrams that you don't confuse the two sequences. Also, make sure you clearly identify which end is which in both sequences. In more complex dual sequence games (such as in Example 5 below), the two sequences might be related, requiring you to work back and forth between them.

Example 5:

Each of five museum tours—A, B, C, D, and E—is conducted once a day. All tours begin and end in the lobby of the museum. The five tours depart in 10-minute intervals and arrive in 10-minute intervals. Each tour is at least 10 minutes long.

Tour A departs before any other tour, and Tour A arrives before any other tour.

Tour B departs either 10 minutes before Tour C or 10 minutes after Tour C.

Tour C is the last tour to arrive, but Tour C is not the last tour to depart.

Tour D arrives after Tour B, and Tour D departs at least 10 minutes before at least two other tours, one of which is Tour E.

If the last of the five tours arrives exactly one hour after the first of the five tours departs, which of the following CANNOT be true?

(A) Tour A arrives before Tour C departs.
(B) Tour E arrives before Tour C departs.
(C) Tour B arrives before Tour E departs.
(D) Tour E arrives before Tour B departs.
(E) Tour A arrives before Tour B departs.

To handle this game, consider the possible departure sequences separately from the possible arrival sequences. You can deduce from the rules that Tour A and Tour D must depart first and second, respectively, while Tour E departs either immediately before or after both Tour B and Tour C. The result is exactly three possible departure sequences (Tour C cannot depart last). As for tour arrivals, Tour A and Tour C must arrive first and last, respectively, while Tour B must arrive before Tour D. The result is exactly three arrival sequences:

The correct answer is (B). Since the tours must depart and arrive in 10-minute intervals, the departure and arrival sequences overlap as follows:

Elapsed Time:	0	10	20	30	40	50	60
Departure:	A	D					
Arrival:	A	__	__	__	C		

If Tour C departs fourth, Tour A will arrive before Tour C departs; thus, (A) might be true. Tour E arrives no earlier than at the same time the fourth tour departs; since Tour C departs no later than fourth, Tour E cannot arrive before Tour C departs, and (B) must be false. Tour

E may be the last to depart, in which event Tour B may arrive before Tour E departs; thus, (C) might be true. Tour E could arrive second while Tour B departs last (10 minutes after Tour E arrives); thus, (D) might be true. Finally, since Tour A arrives at the same time that the third tour departs, Tour B might depart after Tour A arrives; thus, (E) might be true.

THE SEQUENCE FORMULA GAME

Sequence formula games, more than any other type of LSAT logic game, resemble the kind of games we've all played at the kitchen table with a special board, some dice, and different colored tokens. The "players" in a sequence formula game begin in a certain sequence and are then manipulated according to a designated set of simple rules.

Example 6:

A chess tournament among five boys involves one match at a time in which each player in turn elects to challenge the player either immediately above him or below him in the current rankings. At the outset of the tournament, Rodney, Kyle, Gary, Vladimir, and Peter are ranked first through fifth, in that order. The players must take turns making challenges in the order of their initial rankings.

If the challenger wins the match, his opponent is demoted to fifth in the rankings.

If the challenger loses the match, the challenger is demoted to fifth in the rankings.

If the match results in a stalemate, the challenger is demoted one position in the rankings.

Each time a player is demoted, the rankings of the other four players in relation to one another remain unchanged.

If the first two matches both result in stalemates, any of the following might represent the players' rankings, from first to fifth, after the first three matches EXCEPT:

(A) Rodney, Gary, Vladimir, Peter, Kyle
(B) Rodney, Kyle, Gary, Peter, Vladimir
(C) Rodney, Kyle, Vladimir, Peter, Gary
(D) Rodney, Gary, Kyle, Vladimir, Peter
(E) Rodney, Kyle, Vladimir, Gary, Peter

In sequence formula games such as this one, take the extra time to internalize the rules and visualize the game as it is played. The only written diagram you're likely to find useful for every question is a list of the subjects in their initial order or ranking.

The correct answer is (D). Since Rodney is initially ranked first, he makes the first challenge and must challenge Kyle (because a player may challenge another player only if they are positioned consecutively in the current rankings). Given that the first match results in a stalemate, Rodney is demoted one position, and the rankings after the first match are as follows:

R challenges K: K, R, G, V, P

The next match involves a challenge by Kyle since he was initially ranked second. Kyle must challenge Rodney, and a stalemate would return the players to their initial rankings:

K challenges R: R, K, G, V, P

The third match involves a challenge by Gary since he was initially ranked third. Gary may challenge either Kyle or Vladimir. In each case, one of three different rankings would result:

G challenges K:

      G wins R, G, V, P, K

      G loses R, K, V, P, G

      stalemate R, K, V, G, P

G challenges V:

      G wins R, K, G, P, V

      G loses R, K, V, P, G

      stalemate R, K, V, G, P

Only answer choice (D) is not among the possible rankings listed above.

Analytical Reasoning Mini-test and Review

In this lesson, you'll apply what you learned in Lessons 1 and 2 to three logic games. Take this mini-test under timed conditions; then review the explanations that follow. For each question, the game type and difficulty level are identified.

ANALYTICAL REASONING MINI-TEST

NUMBER OF QUESTIONS: 17 • SUGGESTED TIME: 26 MINUTES

Directions: Each group of questions in this section is based on a set of conditions. In answering some of the questions, you may find it useful to draw a rough diagram. Choose the response that most accurately and completely answers each question.

QUESTIONS 1–6:

A law firm occupies five of the six floors of a new office building. The remaining floor is still vacant. The law firm consists of four departments—civil litigation, tax, antitrust, and securities. Each of the four departments occupies a separate floor, and the antitrust department occupies two adjacent floors.

The securities department occupies the floor either immediately above or immediately below the tax department.

At least two floors separate the floor occupied by the tax department from each floor occupied by the antitrust department.

1. Which of the following lists, in order from the first floor to the sixth floor, is acceptable?

    (A) securities, tax, vacant floor, antitrust, antitrust, civil litigation
    (B) vacant floor, antitrust, civil litigation, antitrust, securities, tax
    (C) vacant floor, tax, civil litigation, securities, antitrust, antitrust
    (D) antitrust, antitrust, civil litigation, tax, securities, vacant floor
    (E) civil litigation, antitrust, antitrust, vacant floor, securities, tax

2. Which of the following is a complete and accurate list of the floors that may be vacant?

   (A) first, third, fifth
   (B) third, fourth, sixth
   (C) second, third, fourth, sixth
   (D) first, third, fourth, sixth
   (E) first, third, fifth, sixth

3. The antitrust department CANNOT occupy which two floors?

   (A) first and second
   (B) second and third
   (C) third and fourth
   (D) fourth and fifth
   (E) fifth and sixth

4. Which of the following is a complete and accurate list of the departments that may occupy the fifth floor?

   (A) antitrust, tax
   (B) securities, antitrust, civil litigation
   (C) civil litigation, securities, tax
   (D) antitrust, tax, securities
   (E) securities, antitrust

5. If the antitrust department occupies the third floor, how many different floor arrangements are possible?

   (A) 1
   (B) 2
   (C) 3
   (D) 4
   (E) 5

6. If the civil litigation department occupies the sixth floor, which of the following must be true?

   (A) The third floor is vacant.
   (B) The securities department occupies the second floor.
   (C) The tax department occupies the fifth floor.
   (D) The antitrust department occupies the first floor.
   (E) The securities department occupies the fourth floor.

QUESTIONS 7–11:

There are nine sponsors—A, B, C, D, E, F, G, H, and I—of a particular television program, each with its own commercial. The program is interrupted by five commercial breaks. Two commercials appear during each break, except for the fifth break, during which only one commercial appears. Each of the nine different commercials appears exactly once during the program.

E's commercial appears during an earlier break than C's commercial.

D's commercial appears during a later break than both F's commercial and B's commercial.

A's commercial appears during the same break as C's commercial.

B's commercial does not appear during the same break as E's commercial.

G's commercial appears during the same break as H's commercial.

7. Which of the following must be false?

   (A) C's commercial appears during the second break.
   (B) E's commercial appears during the fifth break.
   (C) D's commercial appears during the second break.
   (D) F's commercial appears during the third break.
   (E) G's commercial appears during the fourth break.

8. Each of the following pairs of commercials may appear during the same break together EXCEPT:

   (A) I's commercial and F's commercial
   (B) B's commercial and I's commercial
   (C) F's commercial and B's commercial
   (D) E's commercial and D's commercial
   (E) I's commercial and E's commercial

9. If two complete commercial breaks separate B's commercial from F's commercial, for how many commercials is it possible to determine the break during which the commercial appears?

   (A) 1
   (B) 2
   (C) 3
   (D) 4
   (E) 5

10. If C's commercial appears during the second break, how many different pairs of commercials could appear during the first break?

    (A) 1
    (B) 2
    (C) 3
    (D) 4
    (E) 5

11. If G's commercial appears during the third break, which of the following statements is sufficient to determine the break during which each and every commercial appears?

    (A) A's commercial appears during the fourth break.
    (B) B's commercial appears during the first break.
    (C) C's commercial appears during the second break.
    (D) E's commercial appears during the first break.
    (E) F's commercial appears during the fourth break.

QUESTIONS 12–17

The students in a music class must take turns changing a melody by making one and only one of the following alterations to the melody created by the previous student:

Each student may add one note at the end of the melody.

Each student may delete one note from the melody.

Each student may replace one note of the melody with a different note.

Each student may exchange one note with another in the melody, but the two exchanged notes must be different.

The initial melody consists of four notes. In order from first to last, the notes are: C, D, E, and F. In changing a melody, each student must also comply with the following restrictions:

Note D must neither immediately precede nor immediately follow note F.

Note E may be exchanged with note C only if neither note occurs as the first or last note of the melody.

Each of the four notes—C, D, E, and F—must occur in the melody at least once, and the melody must not include any notes of the musical scale other than these four.

12. The number of different five-note melodies that can be created by the first student is:

    (A) 0
    (B) 1
    (C) 2
    (D) 3
    (E) 4

13. Which of the following melodies can be created by the first student?

    (A) CFDE
    (B) EDCF
    (C) CFED
    (D) EDEFC
    (E) CDEFD

14. The fewest number of students that must take a turn to create a melody consisting of notes E, D, C, F, C, and D, in sequence, is:

    (A) 2
    (B) 3
    (C) 4
    (D) 5
    (E) 6

15. If a student wishes to exchange one note with another, which of the following melodies offers the greatest number of possible changes of this kind?

    (A) DCEF
    (B) CFED
    (C) EDCFC
    (D) CDDEF
    (E) EFFCD

16. Which of the following could not be the second and third notes, respectively, of the melody created by the first student?

    (A) D and E
    (B) F and E
    (C) D and C
    (D) E and E
    (E) E and D

17. Any of the following melodies might have been created by the second student EXCEPT:

    (A) DEFC
    (B) DCFE
    (C) EDCF
    (D) FCED
    (E) DECF

ANSWER KEY AND EXPLANATIONS

1.	E	5.	B	9.	E	12.	D	15.	A
2.	D	6.	A	10.	B	13.	C	16.	E
3.	C	7.	B	11.	E	14.	C	17.	C
4.	D	8.	A						

Questions 1–6: Simple Linear Sequence Game (Easy)

For this logic game, you could construct alternate diagrams—for example, representing all possible positions of the antitrust department (eliminating those that are inconsistent with the rules). A simpler and more elegant approach, however, is to draw one master diagram, depicting the rules near the diagram for reference:

$$\boxed{\text{T S A A C X}}$$

$$\overline{1}\ \overline{2}\ \overline{3}\ \overline{4}\ \overline{5}\ \overline{6}$$

$$[A\ A] \neq [\overset{\frown}{T\ S}]$$

* ≥ 2 Floors Between A & T

In the explanations below, letters are used to signify departments (e.g., "A" for antitrust department).

1. **The correct answer is (E).** Consider one rule at a time, eliminating answer choices that violate the rule. Choices (A) and (D) violate the rule that T must be separated from A by at least two floors. Choice (B) violates the rule that A must occupy adjacent floors. Choice (C) violates the rule that T and S are adjacent to each other.

2. **The correct answer is (D).** If either floor 2 or floor 5 were vacant, then A and T could not be separated by at least two floors. However, any one of the remaining floors might be vacant.

3. **The correct answer is (C).** A cannot occupy floors 3 and 4; otherwise, A and T would be separated by no more than one floor (floor 2 or floor 5), resulting in a rule violation.

4. **The correct answer is (D).** Try positioning each department on floor 5 to see whether a rule violation results. C cannot occupy floor 5 without violating the rule that A and T must be separated by at least two floors.

5. **The correct answer is (B).** If A occupies floor 3, then it must also occupy floor 2. Otherwise, A and T could not be separated by at least two floors. Accordingly, T must occupy floor 6, and S must occupy floor 5. C must occupy either floor 1 or floor 4; the remaining floor—either 1 or 4—is vacant. Thus, two possible sequences result:

    C [A A] X [S T]
    X [A A] C [S T]
    1 2 3 4 5 6

6. **The correct answer is (A).** If C occupies floor 6, only two arrangements will ensure that A and T are separated by at least two floors:

[A A]   [S T] C
[T S]   [A A] C
 1 2   3 4 5 6

In either case, the third floor must be vacant.

Questions 7–11: Double-Decker Sequence Game (Moderate)

As the diagram below suggests, each commercial break in the program includes two commercials. After displaying the information provided in the rules near your master diagram, you can deduce that either D or I must appear at the fifth break. Why? Only one commercial appears at the fifth break. C and A appear together, as do H and G. Thus, none of these four may appear at the fifth break. Also, since F and B both appear at an earlier break than D, neither F nor B may appear at the fifth break:

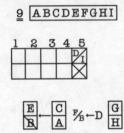

7. **The correct answer is (B).** Either D's commercial or I's commercial must appear during the fifth break (see general comments above); thus, choice (B) must be false.

8. **The correct answer is (A).** If I's commercial were paired with F's commercial, then B's commercial would have to be paired with E's commercial. This would result, however, in a rule violation. Thus, I's commercial cannot be paired with F's commercial.

9. **The correct answer is (E).** The condition in the question restricts the positions of B's commercial and F's commercial to the first and fourth breaks. Thus, the [GH] and [CA] pairs must appear during the second and third breaks, but in either order. Since E's commercial must precede C's commercial, E's commercial must appear during the first break. Since B's commercial and E's commercial cannot appear during the same break together, B's commercial must appear during the fourth break (and F's commercial must appear during the first break). Since D's commercial must appear during a later break than B's commercial, D's commercial must appear during the fifth break. Accordingly, I's commercial must appear with B's commercial during the fourth break.

```
 1 2 3 4 5
E G C B D
F H A I X
```

10. **The correct answer is (B).** If C's commercial (together with A's commercial) appears during the second break, then E's commercial must appear during the first break. B's commercial cannot appear with E's commercial, so B's commercial cannot appear during the first break. D's commercial must follow both B's and F's commercials, and so D's commercial cannot appear during the first break. Only F's commercial and I's commercial remain, either of which could appear during the first break with E's commercial.

11. **The correct answer is (E).** Given that G's commercial appears during the third break, H's commercial must also appear during that break. Now consider choice (E). If F's commercial appears during the fourth break, D's commercial must appear during the fifth break, since the rules stipulate that D's commercial appears during a later break than the break during which F's commercial appears. The [AC] pair must therefore precede the [GH] pair.

    Because E's commercial appears during an earlier break than C's commercial, E's commercial must appear during the first break, and the [AC] pair must appear during the second break. B's commercial cannot appear during the first break with E's commercial, and so B's commercial must appear during the fourth break with F's commercial, while I's commercial appears with E's commercial during the first break:

Questions 12–17: Sequence Formula Game (Challenging)

This sequence-formula game may appear intimidating at first because of its lengthy premise. Once you have internalized the rules of the game, though, analyzing the questions involves applying the same formula repeatedly to the initial sequence. No initial diagram other than the original sequence or "melody" (C D E F) is necessary.

Questions 14 and 17 are more difficult than the others in this group. Question 14 requires that you work backwards from a predetermined end result through unknown interim steps; to answer Question 17, you need a bit of intuition.

12. **The correct answer is (D).** To create a five-note melody, the first student must add one note to the end of the initial four-note melody. The last note of the initial melody is F. Thus, D cannot be added to this melody because F and D cannot occur in succession. However, any of the other three notes may be added. Thus, the first student may create any one of three different five-note melodies:

    C D E F C

    C D E F E

    C D E F F

13. **The correct answer is (C).** The first student can create the melody in choice (C) by exchanging D and F in the initial sequence. The melody in choice (A) violates the rule that F and D cannot occur in immediate succession; also, the first student cannot create the melody in choice (A) without also making another change. The melody in choice (B) can be created by the first student only by exchanging C and E in the initial melody; however, this exchange would violate the rule that C and E can be exchanged only if neither occurs as the first or last note of the melody. The melody in choice (D) can be created only by adding a note to the end of the initial melody and making some other change to the initial melody—but the first student is permitted to make one and only one change to the initial melody. The melody in choice (E) violates the rule that F and D cannot occur in immediate succession.

14. **The correct answer is (C).** Notes D and F remain in their initial positions. Notes C and D have been added to the end of the melody by different students, and notes C and E (the first and third notes in the initial melody) have been exchanged. However, one student could not have effected an exchange between C and E, since C initially occurred as the first note of the melody. Thus, a third student changed the C to an E and a fourth student changed the E to a C. For example:

original	C D E F
student 1	C D E F C
student 2	C D E F C D
student 3	E D E F C D
student 4	E D C F C D

Note that these four changes need not occur in the precise order indicated above.

15. **The correct answer is (A).** In the melody of choice (A), a student may make four different exchanges—D and C, C and E, E and F, or D and F. In the melody of choice (B), a student may make one of two different exchanges—C and F or F and D. In the melody of choice (C), a student may make one of three different exchanges—E and D, D and F, or F and the second C. In the melody of choice (D), a student may make one of two different exchanges—C and the first D or C and the second D. In the melody of choice (E), a student may make one of two different exchanges—E and the first F or E and the second F.

16. **The correct answer is (E).** The second and third notes—D and E—could remain unchanged by adding a note to the end of the melody; thus, choice (A) is a possibility. Choices (B), (C), and (D) each require that a note be replaced, but doing so would result in a four-note melody with only three different notes (a rule violation). Choice (E) requires that D and E be exchanged; the result, however, is that D would immediately precede F (a rule violation).

17. **The correct answer is (C).** Each answer choice includes four notes, suggesting one of two scenarios: (1) both students exchanged two notes (rather than adding, deleting, or altering notes), or (2) the first student added a note, then the second student deleted one of the two occurrences of that note (remember: the melody must include all four notes). Under the first scenario, the first student may exchange either D and F or C and D. The second student may then either reverse the exchange, restoring the initial melody, or create one of three new four-note melodies without violating a rule:

    F C E D

    D E C F

    D C F E

    Under the second scenario, the first student could add either a C, E, or F to the end of the original melody. The second student could then either restore the initial melody or create one new four-note melody without violating a rule:

    D E F C

    Answer choice (C) is not the original sequence and is not among the possible four-note melodies listed above.

Logical Reasoning Basic Concepts and Strategies

In this lesson, you'll familiarize yourself with the format of the LSAT's Logical Reasoning sections, learn strategies for handling the questions, and review the basic logical concepts presupposed on the LSAT.

LOGICAL REASONING AT A GLANCE

Basic format: a brief passage containing an argument, followed by a question and five answer choices.

Total number of questions: 25–26

Number of scored sections: 2

Testing time allowed: 35 minutes

Average time per question: 81–88 seconds

Ground Rules

- No scratch paper is permitted (make notes in the test booklet)
- Only pencils and highlighters are allowed (no pens)
- No penalties are assessed for incorrect responses
- Each question is considered independently of all others

Here are the directions you'll see in the test booklet:

> The questions in this section are based on the reasoning contained in brief statements or passages. For some questions, more than one of the choices could conceivably answer the question. However, you are to choose the best answer; that is, the response that most accurately and completely answers the question. You should not make assumptions that are by commonsense standards implausible, superfluous, or incompatible with the passage. After you have chosen the best answer, blacken the corresponding space on your answer sheet.

What Does the Logical Reasoning Section Test?

The Logical Reasoning Section tests your ability to:

- Identify the main point or conclusion of an argument
- Make inferences or draw conclusions from given premises
- Identify assumptions employed in specific arguments
- Assess the effect of additional information on an argument
- Identify principles that underlie or justify the reasoning employed in an argument
- Identify the method of reasoning employed in an argument
- detect reasoning errors
- Recognize arguments that have similar structure or employ a similar method

THE TERMINOLOGY OF LSAT LOGICAL REASONING PROBLEMS

For LSAT Logical Reasoning, you don't need to know the technical terminology of formal logic, except for a few basic terms. Here are the ones you should know before you proceed any further, along with their definitions:

Argument—The process of reasoning, from premises to conclusion.

Premise—A proposition helping to support the argument's conclusion; premises form the basis on which reasoning proceeds; they are often signaled with words and phrases such as "since," "because," and "given that."

Assumption—Something taken for granted to be true in the argument; strictly speaking, assumptions are actually unstated, assumed premises.

Conclusion—A proposition derived by inference from the premises of an argument. Conclusions are typically signaled by words and phrases such as "hence," "as a result," "consequently," "therefore," and "it follows that."

Inference—The process of deriving, from assumed premises, either the strict logical conclusion or a conclusion that is to some degree probable.

Don't get hung up on precise dictionary definitions. The LSAT won't ask you to define terms or try to trick you based on semantics; that's not what the exam is about. But the test makers will use these terms in phrasing Logical Reasoning questions, so you should have a basic understanding of what they mean.

Anatomy of a Logical Reasoning Problem

On the LSAT, Logical Reasoning problems have three elements:

❶ A brief passage that contains an argument or a set of facts. The writing style and format of the passages varies considerably from problem to problem. In addition, the content of the passages covers a broad spectrum of topics.

② A question dealing with the argument or the information stated in the passage. Although only eight basic question types are featured, they vary extensively in phrasing.

③ Five answer choices, from which you must choose the best.

Here are two typical examples.

Example 1:

Eighty percent of the homeless people interviewed in a recent survey said that they prefer to eat and sleep on the streets rather than go to shelters. Surprisingly, this survey proves that, contrary to popular opinion, homeless people prefer the discomfort and uncertainty of life on the streets to the comfort and security afforded by shelters.

Which of the following, if true, would cast most doubt on the conclusion of the above argument?

(A) Some of the persons interviewed in the survey possessed warm clothing and adequate sleeping bags.
(B) The survey was conducted in several small rural communities.
(C) The only question asked in the survey was: "Which do you prefer, eating and sleeping on the streets or eating and sleeping in shelters?"
(D) The survey was conducted by a person who was also homeless.
(E) The survey was conducted concurrently in several different metropolitan communities during the winter.

Example 2:

Politician: In opposition to the proposed reforms in welfare assistance, my esteemed colleague argues that children of welfare mothers ought to be sent to orphanages rather than remain a source of income for their work-dodging, lazy parents. My reply to him is that this is exactly the kind of argument we should expect from someone who abandoned his own children and left his wife penniless to fend for herself.

Which of the following argumentative techniques is employed by the politician in his reply to his esteemed colleague's argument?

(A) drawing attention away from the real issue of the argument and focusing attention on a side issue
(B) misrepresenting a person's argument for the purpose of making it easier to attack
(C) questioning the motives of the person advancing the argument
(D) attacking the character of the person advancing the argument rather than attacking the argument itself
(E) attacking an argument on the grounds that the person making it is guilty of the very thing he or she is arguing against

STRATEGIES FOR DEALING WITH LOGICAL REASONING PROBLEMS

As in any other aspect of life, it's important to have a plan in mind before you begin any complex task. This is especially true when dealing with the Logical Reasoning questions on the LSAT. Knowing in advance how you will approach each problem is just as important as having the requisite knowledge to solve the problem. The following four-step approach will help you work through the test methodically and answer the questions with the greatest possible speed and accuracy.

Step One: Read the Question Stem Carefully

Identify the problem type. When reading the question stem (i.e., the question itself, apart from the passage and answer choices), try to determine which logical reasoning skill is being tested in the problem and decide what task you need to perform to reach the answer.

If you cannot quickly decide which skill is being tested, don't bother reading the passage; just move on to the next problem. Since each problem is independent of every other, you need not proceed sequentially through the test. In fact, there are potential disadvantages to proceeding in this manner; the most significant of which is losing valuable time—and confidence in your abilities. The best way to gain confidence and use your time effectively is to skip the problems you find too difficult and focus initially on those you find solvable. Also, since some tasks require more time to perform than others, consider doing those that take less time first, even if you feel confident that you can handle the more time-consuming problems.

Follow directions carefully. Pay close attention to any special directions mentioned in the question. For example, if the question directs you to assume that the information stated in the passage is true, do so even if some or all of it appears false to you. Or, if the question directs you to assume that each of the answers is true, do so even if they state something that you believe is false.

Step Two: Read the Passage Carefully

Identify the premise(s) and the conclusion. With the task firmly in mind, read the passage very carefully. What you should look for when reading the passage depends entirely upon what task you must perform. In most cases, however, it is important to begin by determining which statements in the passage are premises of the argument and which is the conclusion. Once you've done this, it's a good idea to underline the key words in the premises and conclusion, leaving out as much of the unnecessary verbiage as possible.

Pay attention to key words. You must pay careful attention to detail when reading the passage, and you must confine your understanding of the topic under discussion to the information stated in the passage unless specifically directed otherwise. In other words, pay very close attention to facts, numbers, percentages, and the stated relationships among them, and do not make superfluous assumptions or draw unwarranted conclusions. Pay particular attention to words and phrases that have logical meanings. Words like "all," "some," "none," "most," and phrases like "only if" and "given that" signify logical relationships that are crucial to understanding the reasoning of an argument.

Put your knowledge of the topic aside. If you know about the topic of the passage, don't quarrel with the stated information. Treat the topic as though you know nothing whatsoever about it other than what is stated in the passage. It is extremely important that you focus on the logic of the argument rather than on the content. Never choose an answer simply because you happen to believe it is true or because you agree with it. Conversely, never reject an answer simply because you believe it is false or because you disagree with it. Keep this in mind: Logical Reasoning questions test your ability to recognize correct and incorrect reasoning; they *do not* test your knowledge of the topic under discussion. Remember this too: An argument can employ correct reasoning even if all of the statements in the argument are false; conversely, an argument can employ incorrect reasoning even if all of the statements in the argument are true.

Step Three: Read the Answers Carefully

When choosing your answer, keep in mind the directions stated at the beginning of the test. Remember, unless otherwise instructed, "you are to choose the best answer; that is, the response that most accurately and completely answers the question." If you don't know the answer or if none appear to be best, narrow down the alternatives by eliminating those that appear to be the worst answers and then make a guess. Never abandon a problem on which you have already spent time without selecting an answer. If you have time at the end of the test, you can always come back and change your answer if you find a better one.

Step Four: Go Back to Skipped Problems

Once you have worked your way through the entire section, return to the problems you skipped and spend the remaining test time on them. Check the time and divide it evenly among the skipped problems. Make sure that you answer every problem, even if you have to guess. Remember, there is no penalty for wrong answers. When making guesses, always eliminate the worst answers first, then choose from the ones remaining. Doing this will greatly enhance your odds of getting the right answer. It's a good idea to flag skipped problems so that you can return to them quickly. An easy way to do this is just to write a big "S" next to the problem number in the test booklet.

Managing Your Time

The advice in the strategies discussed above can be summed up in two simple maxims:

1 Know what you're looking for before you go looking.

2 If you're unsure of how to find what you're looking for, don't waste time looking.

This is important advice in light of the fact that you have an average of only 85 seconds to come up with the correct answer for each problem in this section. Of course, this does not mean that you can or should spend only 85 seconds on each problem, but it does highlight the importance of wise time management.

The first maxim points out the importance of being methodical in your approach to each problem. One obvious reason for doing this is that it saves time. The second maxim points out the importance of making the best use of your time in handling a problem—more specifically, the importance of not letting yourself get bogged down. The fact is that some questions are much more difficult than others. Moreover, there is no pattern in the difficulty level of the problems; the first problem on the test section might be difficult and the last one easy, or the other way around. This means that you may have to skip a few questions to finish in time. It also means that you are going to have to develop a strict schedule and keep close track of time. Basically, you should aim for completing 6–7 problems every 9 minutes to finish this section of the test. For this reason, it's a good idea to check the clock every 9 minutes or so to see how you are doing. If you're ahead of schedule, don't slack off; if you're behind schedule, don't panic. In other words, try to keep as even a pace as possible.

APPLYING THE STRATEGIES

Let's try applying the four strategies we reviewed above to Example 1 on page 51.

First, read the question again. Ask yourself, "Which logical reasoning skill is being tested in this problem?" Once you have determined that, ask yourself, "What is the task?"

> *Which of the following, if true, would cast most doubt on the conclusion of the above argument?*

This problem tests your ability to assess the effect of additional information on an argument. The task in this case is to find a statement that weakens the argument; that is, one that makes it less likely that the conclusion is true. Notice that the question directs you to assume that the statements in the answers are true.

Second, read the passage. To solve this particular problem, you are going to have to figure out which of the statements in the passage is the conclusion and which is the premise. This isn't hard to do in this case. List the premise first, followed by the conclusion.

> *Premise:* Eighty percent of the homeless people interviewed in a recent survey said that they prefer to eat and sleep on the streets rather than go to shelters.

> *Conclusion:* Homeless people prefer the discomfort and uncertainty of life on the streets to the comfort and security afforded by shelters.

Notice that the unnecessary verbiage in the passage has been eliminated in the above restatement of the argument.

In this argument, data gathered from a survey are offered in support of a general claim. Notice that the conclusion refers to all homeless people, not merely some. Notice also that only 80 percent of the homeless people interviewed agree with the conclusion. It's pretty clear from these two observations that the data gathered by the survey are going to have to be drawn from a sample that is sufficiently large and representative to support the inference in the argument. Any answer suggesting that the data are drawn from a sample that is not representative of the entire homeless community will cast doubt on the conclusion.

You may have noticed that this argument is flawed in that it draws a more general conclusion than is warranted by the premise. That is, to put it simply, the conclusion is too strong given the evidence. A more appropriate conclusion, given the evidence, would be that most homeless people would rather eat and sleep on the streets than to go to a shelter. The fact that this argument is flawed in this way, however, is irrelevant to the question being asked in this case.

The question does not ask you to criticize the argument; it asks you to assess the effect additional information would have on the argument.

Third, read the answers. Remember, you are looking for an answer that suggests that the data gathered in the survey are drawn from a sample that is not representative of the entire homeless community. Remember also that you are looking for the answer that does this best. Let's review them one by one.

Choice (A) does not suggest that the data are drawn from a sample that is not representative of the entire homeless community. In fact, choice (A) states something that we should expect to be the case if the sample is, in fact, representative of the entire homeless community. Had choice (A) stated that all or most or none of those interviewed possessed warm clothing and adequate sleeping bags, it would suggest that the sample was not representative, but this is not what choice (A) asserts. Eliminate choice (A).

Choice (B) suggests that the data are drawn from a sample that is not representative of the entire homeless community. After all, small rural communities are significantly different from large metropolitan communities, and these differences could bias the sample considerably. Keep choice (B) in reserve, but you should go on to see whether you can find a better answer.

Choice (C) does not suggest that the data are drawn from a sample that is not representative of the entire homeless community. It suggests that the survey may be unreliable because of the way the question was phrased, but it does not undermine the representativeness of the sample. Eliminate choice (C).

Choice (D) does not suggest that the data are drawn from a sample that is not representative of the entire homeless community. Clearly, the fact that the person conducting the survey was homeless does not, by itself, call the representativeness of the sample into question. Eliminate choice (D).

Choice (E) suggests that the data are drawn from a sample that is representative of the entire homeless community. Moreover, the fact that the survey was conducted during the winter gives even greater credence to the results. Rather than weaken the argument, choice (E) would strengthen it considerably. Eliminate choice (E).

You're left with choice (B) as the best response, so mark it as your answer.

Notice that some answer choices may be what we'll call "sucker bait." In this example, choices (A), (C), and (D) were sucker bait. Had you not first identified the task, then focused clearly on the task when reading the passage, chances are that you would have selected one of these as the correct answer. The way to avoid sucker bait answer choices is to know what you are looking for before you go looking.

REVIEW OF THE LOGICAL CONCEPTS PRESUPPOSED ON THE TEST

The LSAT Logical Reasoning questions do not presuppose knowledge of the terminology of formal logic. Specialized terms such as "syllogism," "valid," and "modus ponens" will not be used in asking questions. There are, however, some basic concepts that you will be expected to understand. The primary expectation is that you will be able to understand and critique the reasoning contained in arguments. To do this requires that you at least understand basic concepts such as argument, issue, premise, conclusion, main point, and assumption. Following is a brief discussion of each of these fundamental concepts.

The Concept of Argument

The word "argument" can be used in two quite different ways. When we say that two or more people are "having an argument" or "are arguing," we mean merely that there is a discussion going on in which the participants disagree about some topic. This is not the sense of "argument" intended in LSAT Logical Reasoning questions. In this context, to argue is to offer reasons in support of the truth of some claim or the correctness of some action. Since these reasons and the claim they are intended to support are expressed in statements, an argument can be characterized as a set of statements; the statements that express the reasons are called premises; those that express claims that are supported by reasons are called conclusions.

The topic or subject of an argument is simply what the argument is about (for example, censorship). The issue of an argument is the question that is being addressed on the topic (for example, "Does national security justify censorship?"). The main point of an argument is the particular claim or position on the issue that the author argues for (for example, "National security does not justify censorship."). The main point is typically expressed in the conclusion of the argument.

Unstated Premises

An argument may have any number of premises, but it must have at least one. Some of the premises of an argument might be unstated. Unstated premises in arguments are referred to as assumptions. Assumptions are statements that fill logical gaps in the stated argument. They are left unstated in most cases because the author believes that they are obvious or that they express claims that the audience already accepts as true or correct. Consider the following example:

Example 3:

Abortion is morally wrong for the simple reason that murder is morally wrong.

The argument in Example 3 can be rewritten as follows:

> *Premise:* Murder is morally wrong.

> *Conclusion:* Abortion is morally wrong.

The unstated premise that fills the logical gap in this argument is the statement: "Abortion is murder." This statement is an assumption in the argument.

Intermediate vs. Final Conclusions

An argument may have any number of conclusions, but it must have at least one. In complex arguments with more than one conclusion, some will be intermediate conclusions and one will be the final conclusion. Intermediate conclusions function as reasons supporting the final conclusion. That is, they are claims supported by reasons that, in turn, become reasons to support the final claim in the argument. Consider the following example:

Example 4:

Sexual harassment against women is often fostered by economic motives, since women generally have greater difficulty finding jobs, and hence can be intimidated more easily.

The argument in Example 4 has two conclusions. The claim "[Women] can be intimidated more easily," is an intermediate conclusion supported by the statement "Women generally have greater difficulty in finding jobs." In the argument above, this intermediate conclusion in turn becomes a reason for the final conclusion that is stated in the first part of the sentence.

Example 4 can be rewritten to explicitly reveal its structure as follows:

Premise: Women generally have greater difficulty finding jobs.

Intermediate Conclusion: Women can be intimidated more easily than men.

Final Conclusion: Sexual harassment against women is often fostered by economic motives.

Unstated Conclusions

The final conclusion or main point of an argument isn't always explicitly stated. Since it is a powerful rhetorical ploy to let readers reach the conclusion on their own, writers often leave it unstated. In these cases, however, the author usually presents the reasons in such a way that there is really only one obvious conclusion that can be drawn from them. This implicit conclusion, even though unstated in the argument, is the main point or final conclusion of the argument. Consider the following example:

Example 5:

Sexual orientation is not something over which persons have control. To hold a person accountable for something over which he or she has no control is irrational.

In Example 5, the implicit conclusion to be drawn is that it is irrational to hold a person accountable for his or her sexual orientation. This conclusion, while unstated, is clearly implied by the passage. Example 5 can be rewritten to explicitly reveal its structure as follows:

Premise: Sexual orientation is not something over which persons have control.

Premise: Holding a person accountable for something over which he or she has no control is irrational.

Unstated Conclusion: It is irrational to hold a person accountable for his or her sexual orientation.

Logical Reasoning
Basic Skills

In this lesson, you will learn four of the eight basic Logical Reasoning skills we reviewed in the previous lesson. Here's the list again, to refresh your memory:

- Identify the main point or conclusion of an argument

- Make inferences or draw conclusions from given premises

- Identify assumptions employed in specific arguments

- Assess the effect of additional information on an argument

- Identify principles that underlie or justify the reasoning employed in an argument

- Identify the method of reasoning employed in an argument

- Detect reasoning errors

- Recognize arguments that have similar structure or employ a similar method

IDENTIFYING THE MAIN POINT OR CONCLUSION OF AN ARGUMENT

The ability to identify premises and conclusions of arguments correctly is essential to answering almost all of the Logical Reasoning questions on the LSAT. Because of this, it is a skill that warrants close attention and complete mastery, even though only a small percentage (5 to 8 percent) of all Logical Reasoning questions test this skill directly.

Conclusion questions are typically worded as follows:

- Which of the following best expresses the main point of the passage?

- The conclusion of the argument is best expressed by which of the following?

The main point of an argument is typically expressed by the final conclusion of the argument. In arguments that contain more than one conclusion, the final conclusion is the statement that is supported by other statements but does not itself support any other statement; intermediate conclusions are statements that are supported by other statements and that, in turn, support further statements.

59

Look for Indicator Words and Phrases

In most cases, the conclusion of an argument can be quickly identified simply by paying close attention to key words and phrases in the passage. Here are some words and phrases commonly used to indicate that the sentence that follows is a conclusion:

therefore	entails that	allows us to infer that
shows that	as a result	hence
consequently	it follows that	proves that
implies that	so	it is likely that
thus	suggests that	demonstrates that

In cases where the above words and phrases are absent, it is possible to identify the conclusion by first identifying the premises and then looking for the sentence they are intended to support. Here are some words and phrases commonly used to indicate that the sentence that follows is a premise:

therefore	entails that	allows us to infer that
since	for	because
inasmuch as	follows from	given that
is suggested by	is proved by	for the reason that
is entailed by	assuming that	is substantiated by
is shown by	as a result	on the supposition that

Let's look at a few examples to see how these words and phrases can help you identify the conclusion of an argument.

Example 1:

Einstein is as great a cult figure as Madonna, so T-shirts with Einstein's picture on them will sell as well as shirts with Madonna's picture.

Example 2:

Since Einstein is as great a cult figure as Madonna, T-shirts with Einstein's picture on them will sell as well as shirts with Madonna's picture.

In Example 1, the word "so" indicates the conclusion; in Example 2 the word "since" indicates the premise. The argument in each of these examples is identical and can be rewritten as follows:

Premise: Einstein is as great a cult figure as Madonna.

Conclusion: T-shirts with Einstein's picture on them will sell as well as shirts with Madonna's picture.

Here's a more complicated example:

Example 3:

Inasmuch as Einstein is as great a cult figure as Madonna, it is likely that T-shirts with Einstein's picture on them will sell as well as shirts with Madonna's picture, so we should add them to our inventory.

Each of the three italicized expressions in Example 3 is an indicator. The first indicates a premise, the other two indicate conclusions. The final conclusion is indicated by the word "so." The intermediate conclusion is indicated by the phrase "it is likely that." This argument can be rewritten to reveal its structure as follows:

Premise: Einstein is as great a cult figure as Madonna.

Intermediate conclusion: T-shirts with Einstein's picture on them will sell as well as shirts with Madonna's picture.

Final conclusion: We should add T-shirts with Einstein's picture on them to our inventory.

Look for Rhetorical Questions

In addition to the indicator expressions listed above, another common way of signaling the conclusion of an argument is to express it as a rhetorical question or as an answer to a rhetorical question. The purpose of such questions is not to solicit information, but rather to emphatically express a particular point or to raise a particular issue. Rhetorical questions typically (but not always) appear at the very beginning of the passage. The remaining sentences in the passage are typically premises that support a position on the issue encompassed by the rhetorical question. Consider the following example:

Example 4:

Can anyone really deny that abortion is morally wrong? After all, killing humans is wrong, and abortion is just another way of killing a human.

The rhetorical question in Example 4 leaves little doubt about the author's position on this issue. The way in which the question is posed clearly indicates that, at least for the author, this is not an open question. Generally speaking, the more sarcastic the tone of the question the more obvious the author's position on the issue encompassed by the question. The converse of this is generally the case as well. The conclusion of the argument in Example 4 is simply a restatement of the rhetorical question expressed in the first sentence, specifically, abortion is morally wrong. The remaining sentences in Example 4 are premises that support this conclusion. The argument in Example 4 can be rewritten as follows:

Premise: Killing humans is wrong.

Premise: Abortion is just another way of killing a human.

Conclusion: Abortion is morally wrong.

Here's another example:

Example 5:

Is abortion morally wrong or not? I would answer "no!" because while killing humans is morally wrong, abortion kills a fetus, and a fetus is not a human being.

The first sentence in Example 5 is a rhetorical question that raises the issue the author wishes to address. Next, the author indicates which side of this issue will be argued for—specifically, that abortion is not morally wrong. This is the conclusion of the argument.

The remaining statements in Example 5 are intended as reasons in support of this claim. In this example, it is not obvious from the question itself which side of the issue the author will argue for. The way in which the question is posed indicates that this is an open question at least initially. In cases like this, you will have to read on to find out which side of the issue the author will argue for. The argument in Example 5 can be rewritten as follows:

Premise: Killing humans is morally wrong.

Premise: A fetus is not a human being.

Premise: Abortion kills a fetus.

Conclusion: Abortion is not morally wrong.

When Passages Contain No Indicator Expressions or Rhetorical Questions

In passages that contain no indicator expressions and no rhetorical questions, it is much more difficult to figure out which sentence is the conclusion. One way to proceed is to add indicator words to the passage and determine whether the result makes sense to you. Consider the following example:

Example 6:

There is a lot more to being an actress than having a pretty face. One has to learn how to move correctly. One has to learn how to project one's voice. One must learn how to speak clearly.

A plausible interpretation of the passage is that the author is giving reasons for the claim expressed in the first sentence. This interpretation is arrived at simply by adding the word "since" to the beginning of the second sentence. According to this interpretation, the argument goes as follows:

There is a lot more to being an actress than having a pretty face, since: (1) one has to learn how to move correctly, (2) one has to learn how to project one's voice, and (3) one must learn how to speak clearly.

When dealing with passages in which the conclusion is unstated, the best way to proceed is to ask yourself what the author is trying to establish in the passage. Consider the following example:

Example 7:

When we regard a person to be morally responsible for her actions, we regard her as being the object of praise or blame with respect to those actions. But it seems evident that a person cannot be the object of praise or blame for her actions unless she performed them of her own free will.

What is the author working toward or trying to establish? Asking this question while reading the passage will lead you to the conclusion of the passage. In this case, the unstated conclusion is that people are only morally responsible for actions that they perform of their own free will.

Checklist for Identifying a Main Point or Conclusion

Here's a brief summary of the three steps for identifying the main point or conclusion of an argument.

1. Scan the passage looking for conclusion and/or premise indicator words or phrases. These words and phrases provide important clues to the author's organizational scheme. Typically you are looking for the final conclusion of the argument, so in arguments with more than one conclusion, determine which sentences lead to or support other sentences in the passage. The final conclusion will be the one that is supported by others but does not itself support any others.

2. Alternatively, look for a rhetorical question in the passage—typically it will appear at the very beginning. The main point will be either a restatement of this question or a direct answer to this question. If the author's position on the issue addressed in the question is not obvious from the way in which the question is asked, a quick scan of the passage will usually tell you which side of the issue the author is supporting.

3. If there are no indicator expressions and no rhetorical questions in the passage, the best way to proceed is to ask yourself: "What is the author trying to establish in the passage?"

MAKING INFERENCES FROM GIVEN PREMISES

Inference questions test your ability to draw conclusions from the information stated in the passage; that is, your ability to determine what else must be true or is likely to be true, given that the statements in the passage are true. In problems of this type, the information in the passage functions as the premises of the argument, and the conclusions are found among the answer choices. In answering these questions keep in mind the admonition against making implausible, superfluous, or incompatible assumptions. You are, however, to assume that the information stated in the passage is true, even if you do not agree with it or believe that it is false.

Types of Inference Questions

Inference questions are typically worded as follows:

- If all of the statements in the passage are true, which one of the following must also be true?

- Which one of the following conclusions is most strongly supported by the statements in the passage?

- Which of the following statements can be properly inferred from the passage?

Notice that there are three basic types of questions:

1. Those that ask for the conclusion that must be true given the information in the passage

2. Those that ask for the conclusion that is most strongly supported given the information in the passage

3. Those that ask for the conclusion that can be properly drawn or inferred from the passage

The difference between the first two types of questions is significant. The conclusion that must be true given the information stated in the passage is the one that cannot conceivably be false, given this information. The conclusion that is most strongly supported by the information stated in the passage is the one that is most unlikely to be false (i.e., most likely to be true), given this information.

Questions that ask for what can be "properly inferred" or "properly drawn" from the passage are somewhat tricky. Strictly speaking, for an inference to be "proper" it must be made in accordance with acceptable inference rules or meet certain standards of acceptable inference. In the case of deductive reasoning, these rules and standards are designed to ensure that the truth of the premises guarantees the truth of the conclusion, whereas in the case of inductive reasoning they are designed to ensure that the truth of the premises makes it highly likely that the conclusion is true. Without getting bogged down with too many details here, the upshot is that questions that ask for what can "properly" be inferred or drawn from the statements in a passage can be understood in two ways. They can be understood as asking either for the conclusion that must be true, or for the conclusion that is most strongly supported.

Without training in formal logic you pretty much have to "fly by the seat of your pants" when dealing with these problems. Saying this, however, doesn't mean that you should just guess on these problems. There are some definite guidelines or procedures that you will want to follow.

"MUST BE TRUE" INFERENCE QUESTIONS

Here's the three-step procedure for dealing with questions that ask you to find the statement that must be true given the information stated in the passage.

1. Read the passage very carefully. If necessary, underline the premises (or list them on separate lines) leaving out any unnecessary verbiage.

2. Read each of the answers, and ask yourself whether it can conceivably be false given that the sentences in the passage are true.

3. The correct answer is the one that cannot conceivably be false given the information stated in the passage.

To illustrate this procedure, let's look at a simple example:

Example 8:

Cheating on your taxes is lying, and lying, as we all know, is morally wrong.

If the statements in the passage are true, which one of the following must also be true?

(A) Cheating on your taxes is illegal.
(B) Cheating is morally wrong.
(C) Cheating on your taxes is morally wrong.
(D) Lying is cheating.
(E) Cheating is immoral.

First, read the passage very carefully. Underline the premises leaving out the unnecessary verbiage as follows:

Cheating on your taxes is lying, and lying, as we all know, is morally wrong.

Second, read each answer in turn and determine whether it can conceivably be false, given the information stated in the premises. The correct answer is the one that cannot conceivably be false, given this information.

Could choice (A) conceivably be false given the stated information? The answer is "yes" because the given information does not explicitly mention anything about what is legal or illegal. Remember, don't make any assumptions beyond what is explicitly stated in the passage.

Could choice (B) conceivably be false given the stated information? Again, the answer is "yes" because the given information does not tell us that all kinds of cheating are lying. It tells us only that a particular kind of cheating is lying (i.e., cheating on your taxes).

Could choice (C) conceivably be false given the stated information? In this case the answer is "no" because if all tax cheating is lying and all lying is morally wrong, then all tax cheating must be morally wrong. **The correct answer is (C).**

Once you have found an answer that must be true given the information there is no need to look at the rest. Simply record it and go on to the next problem.

Here's a slightly more complicated example:

Example 9:

All professors are outgoing and all outgoing people are popular, but even so some introverts are professors.

If the above statements are true, which one of the following must also be true?

(A) All popular people are outgoing.
(B) All outgoing people are professors.
(C) Some introverts are popular.
(D) No introverts are professors.
(E) No introverts are popular.

First, read the passage very carefully. Underline the premises leaving out the unnecessary verbiage as follows:

> All professors are outgoing and all outgoing people are popular, but even so some introverts are professors.

Next, read each of the answers, and ask yourself whether it can conceivably be false, given that the underlined sentences are true.

Could choice (A) conceivably be false, given the information stated in the premises? The answer is "yes" because the passage states that all outgoing people are popular, and it is consistent with this that not all popular people are outgoing.

Could choice (B) conceivably be false, given the information stated in the premises? The answer is "yes" because the passage states that all professors are outgoing people, and it is consistent with this that not all outgoing people are professors.

Could choice (C) conceivably be false, given the information stated in the premises? The answer is "no" because if all professors are outgoing and all outgoing people are popular, then it must be true that all professors are popular. Moreover, if all professors are popular and some introverts are professors, then it must be true that some introverts are popular. **The correct answer is (C).**

A variation of this type of question asks not for the single statement that must be true, but rather for the answer that is the exception (i.e., the statement that need not be true given the stated information). In this case, the question is worded as follows:

> If the above statements are true, all of the following statements must also be true
> EXCEPT:

In this version of the question, four of the five answer choices must be true and only one need not be true. Your job is to find the one that need not be true given the information in the passage. The procedure for dealing with this type of question is the same as above. The only difference is the correct answer will be the one that could conceivably be false given the stated information.

"MOST STRONGLY SUPPORTED" INFERENCE QUESTIONS

Here's the three-step procedure for dealing with questions that ask you to find the statement that is most strongly supported given the information stated in the passage.

1. Read the passage very carefully. If necessary, underline the premises (or list them on separate lines) leaving out any unnecessary verbiage.

2. Read each of the answers, and determine how likely it is to be true given the information stated in the passage. Use a simple 4-point scale to score each of the answers:

   1 = very unlikely
   2 = not very likely
   3 = somewhat likely
   4 = very likely

3. The correct answer is the one that gets the highest score.

To illustrate this procedure, consider the following example:

Example 10:

> Dogs taken to humane shelters are routinely checked for rabies. The dog that bit the little boy was obtained from the humane shelter just a day before it bit the boy.
>
> If the statements in the passage are true, which of the following is most strongly supported?
>
> **(A)** The humane shelter technicians never make mistakes when testing dogs for rabies.
> **(B)** The dog contracted rabies after it was released from the shelter but before it bit the boy.
> **(C)** The dog does not have rabies.
> **(D)** The little boy has rabies.
> **(E)** The humane shelter technicians are incompetent.

With the information stated in the passage in mind, rank each answer using the 4-point scale.

The score for choice (A) is 2. This choice is not very likely because the information in the passage really doesn't address itself to the issue of whether or not the testing procedures are reliable.

The score for choice (B) is 2. While it is possible that the dog contracted rabies during this brief period, without additional information it is difficult to assess the likelihood that this is the case.

The score for choice (C) is 4. The fact that the dog was tested for rabies just a short time before the incident makes it very likely that the dog was not rabid at the time of the incident.

The score for choice (D) is 1. The likelihood that choice (D) is true is a function of the likelihood that choice (C) is true, so if it is very likely that the dog does not have rabies, then it is very unlikely that the little boy has rabies.

The score for choice (E) is 2. While it is possible that the technicians are incompetent, the stated information does not support that claim.

Looking back over the scores, choice (C) is most strongly supported. **The correct answer is (C).**

"PROPERLY INFERRED" INFERENCE QUESTIONS

The procedure above can also be used for dealing with questions that ask you to find the statement that is properly inferred from the information in the passage by simply expanding the 4-point scale to a 5-point scale, letting 5 equal "must be true."

IDENTIFYING ASSUMPTIONS INVOLVED IN AN ARGUMENT

An assumption of an argument is a statement that is not expressed in the argument but that must be true if the conclusion is true. Put simply, it's a missing piece of information that is required to support the conclusion.

In looking for the assumptions in an argument, you can use the author's stated information as a guide to the author's hidden assumptions. Typically, hidden assumptions in arguments connect key ideas in the author's reasoning. Authors don't state these ideas explicitly because they believe that their audience already accepts them or they are too obvious to state.

Problems of this type make up roughly 12 percent of the Logical Reasoning questions on the LSAT, so you can expect to see at least three assumption questions on each of the two Logical Reasoning sections in the exam.

Assumption questions are typically worded as follows:

- The conclusion of the argument is properly drawn if which of the following is assumed?

- For the argument to be logically correct, it must make which of the following assumptions?

- Which of the following is an assumption upon which the argument in the passage depends?

- Which of the following is a presupposition in the argument?

The exact conditions that must be satisfied for an argument to be "logically correct" or for the conclusion to be "properly drawn" will differ, depending upon the argument type. As a general rule, however, the more unlikely it is for the conclusion to be false given that the premises are true, the more "logically correct" the argument. Since this is the case, when looking for an assumption that will make the argument logically correct, you are looking for a statement that, when taken with the stated premises, will significantly increase the likelihood that the conclusion is true. Moreover, given a selection of possible assumptions, the one that increases this likelihood the most will be the best candidate.

Consider the following brief argument:

Example 11:

> All humans have inherent worth; this is why they have an inalienable right to privacy.

This argument can be rewritten as follows:

Premise: All people have inherent worth.

Conclusion: All people have an inalienable right to privacy.

As it stands, the above argument is not compelling; that is, the stated premise does not, by itself, ensure that the conclusion is true or even that it is highly likely to be true. The assumption required to make this argument logically correct must fill this logical gap. Moreover, to fill the logical gap, the assumption must connect the key ideas in the argument in such a way that it either impossible, or at least highly unlikely for the conclusion to be false given the stated premise. In Example 11, the logical gap in the argument can be filled with the following statement: Anything that has inherent worth has an inalienable right to privacy. Adding this statement to the argument ensures that the conclusion is true, given that the premises are true. This is clearly demonstrated in the following reconstruction of the argument.

> *Assumption:* Anything that has inherent worth has an inalienable right to privacy.

> *Premise:* All people have inherent worth.

> *Conclusion:* All people have an inalienable right to privacy.

Consider another brief argument:

Example 12:

> John stays at home whenever he is sick, so, he's probably at home.

This argument can be rewritten as follows:

> *Premise:* If John is sick, then he'll stay at home.

> *Conclusion:* John is probably at home.

To properly draw the conclusion in Example 12, you need additional information. The information required to increase the likelihood that the conclusion is true is that John is probably sick. As is evident in the following reconstruction of the argument, adding this statement to the argument increases the likelihood that the conclusion is true given that the premises are true:

> *Assumption:* John is probably sick.

> *Premise:* If John is sick, then he'll stay at home.

> *Conclusion:* John is probably at home.

Here's the procedure for finding assumptions:

- Identify the premises and the conclusion of the argument. To help keep things straight, underline the premises and the conclusion (marking premises with a "P," and the conclusion with a "C," for example) or list them on separate lines, placing the premises above the conclusion.

- Locate the logical gap in the argument. It will usually be obvious that something is missing because the argument just won't make sense. That is, it will seem to you that the stated reasons, by themselves, don't completely support the conclusion. Once you have located the logical gap between the premises and the conclusion, all you have to do is figure out what additional information would be required to fill it.

- Ask yourself the following question:

  > What additional information would be required to ensure the truth of the conclusion?

To illustrate this procedure, let's look at an example in the style of an LSAT problem.

Example 13:

> Captive animals exhibit a wider range of physical and behavioral traits than animals in the wild, and this is why researchers who study them are able to study a wider range of genetic possibilities than researchers who study wild animals.
>
> For this argument to be logically correct, it must make which one of the following assumptions?
>
> **(A)** Animals that are captive exhibit a wider range of physical and behavioral traits than animals that are wild.
> **(B)** Animals that permit researchers to study a wide range of genetic possibilities are better research subjects than animals that do not.
> **(C)** The wider the range of the physical and behavioral traits in a population of animals, the greater the range of their genetic possibilities.
> **(D)** Captive animals are studied more than wild animals.
> **(E)** Animals in the wild exhibit a narrow range of physical and behavioral traits.

The argument in the passage can be rewritten as follows:

Premise: Captive animals exhibit a wider range of physical and behavioral traits than animals in the wild.

Conclusion: Researchers who study captive animals are able to study a wider range of genetic possibilities than researchers who study wild animals.

This argument has an obvious logical gap between the premise and the conclusion. The assumption required to fill this gap can be determined simply by asking what information in addition to the stated premise would be required to ensure that the conclusion is true. In this instance, a little thought reveals that the required information must link the range of physical and behavioral traits with the range of genetic possibilities. Moreover, they must be linked such that the wider the range of physical and behavioral traits, the wider the range of genetic possibilities. Turning to the answer choices with this in mind, it is obvious that **the correct answer is (C).**

To sum up: To find an assumption that will make the argument logically correct, look for a statement that connects key ideas in the argument in such a way that when this statement is added to the stated premises of the argument, the conclusion of the argument either cannot be false or the likelihood of its being false is greatly diminished.

Assessing the Effect of Additional Information on an Argument

Questions of this type begin with a passage that contains an argument. Your job is to assess the effect additional information has on the argument. There are basically two types of these problems:

❶ Those that ask you to select the answer that will strengthen the argument

❷ Those that ask you to select the answer that will weaken the argument

Of the 25 problems in a typical Logical Reasoning section of the LSAT exam, roughly 20 percent will test your ability to assess the effect of additional information on an argument, so you can expect to see at least five of these problems on each of the two Logical Reasoning sections in the exam.

Additional information assessment (AIA) questions are worded in a wide variety of ways. To avoid confusion, remember that there are just two types of problems: those that ask you to strengthen an argument and those that ask you to weaken an argument. The following lists of questions illustrates the various ways these two types can be expressed.

Questions that ask you to select the choice that weakens the argument may be worded as follows:

- Which of the following, if true, would refute the argument in the passage?

- Which of the following, if true, casts the most doubt on the argument?

- Which of the following, if accepted by the author, would require him to reconsider his conclusion?

- Which of the following, if true, most seriously calls the conclusion above into question?

- The argument is most vulnerable to which of the following criticisms?

- Which of the following, if true, most seriously undermines the author's contention?

- Which of the following, if true, most substantially weakens the argument?

Questions that ask you to select the choice that strengthens the argument may be worded as follows:

- Which of the following, if true, most strengthens the argument?

- Which of the following would provide the most support for the conclusion above?

- Which of the following supports the conclusion in the above passage?

- The conclusion in the above argument would be more reasonable if which of the following were true?

- Which of the following, if true, would confirm the author's conclusion?

- Which of the following, if true, provides the most support for the argument?

WEAKENING AN ARGUMENT

There are essentially three ways to weaken an argument:

1. Undermine a major assumption of the argument.

2. Attack one of the premises of the argument.

3. Suggest an alternative conclusion that can be inferred from the given premises.

In problems that require you to choose a statement that will weaken an argument, the correct answer will do one of these three things. For this reason, it is important that at the outset you identify the premises, the conclusion, and the major assumption of the argument in the passage.

Here's the four-step procedure to find the statement that will weaken an argument.

① Identify the premises and the conclusion of the argument.

② Identify the major assumption of the argument.

③ Look for an answer choice that undermines the major assumption, attacks a stated premise, or suggests an alternative conclusion that could be inferred from the stated premises.

④ The correct answer is one that does any one of the above.

To illustrate this procedure, let's look at an example.

Example 14:

Mountain lion sightings in outlying areas of Los Angeles have increased dramatically over the past two years. Hence, the population of mountain lions must be increasing.

Which of the following, if true, most effectively weakens the above argument?

(A) People have become more active in outdoor activities during the past two years.
(B) Mountain lion habitat has dramatically diminished over the past two years.
(C) Human population in the outlying areas of Los Angeles has dramatically increased over the past two years.
(D) There has been a dramatic increase in the number of television programs about mountain lions during the past two years.
(E) Reports of people and animals being killed by mountain lions have increased dramatically over the past two years.

The premise and conclusion of Example 14 are easy to identify; the premise is the first statement and the conclusion is the statement that follows the word "hence." The major assumption in Example 14 is that the population of humans in the outlying areas of Los Angeles has remained relatively constant over the two-year period. Given this assumption, an increase in sightings would strongly indicate an increase in the population of mountain lions. Without this assumption, however, the argument is weakened considerably. The answer choice that most directly challenges this assumption is choice (C). **The correct answer is (C).**

STRENGTHENING AN ARGUMENT

There are two ways to strengthen an argument:

① Offer support for the major assumption of the argument.

② Provide additional evidence for the conclusion (i.e., beyond what is stated in the given premises).

In a problem that asks you to choose a statement that will strengthen an argument, the correct response will do one of these two things.

Here's the four-step procedure to find the statement that will strengthen an argument.

① Identify the premises and the conclusion of the argument.

② Identify the major assumption of the argument.

③ Look for an answer choice that offers support for the major assumption or provides additional evidence for the conclusion.

④ The correct answer is one that does either of the above.

Let's look at an example.

Example 15:

The portrayal of violence on television and in movies has increased dramatically over the past 10 years. It is primarily for this reason that we have seen a dramatic increase in the rate of violent crime during the last decade.

Which one of the following, if true, provides the most support for the argument?

(A) Liberal sentencing policies over the past 10 years have resulted in reduced sentences for perpetrators of violent acts.
(B) Persons who commit violent acts are less prone to being influenced by portrayals of violence.
(C) Recent studies have shown that repeated exposure to portrayals of violence significantly increases the tendency to commit violent acts.
(D) There has been a dramatic increase in the number of homeless people during the last decade.
(E) Due to severe overcrowding during the past decade, prisons have been forced to release violent criminals before their full sentences were served.

The premise and conclusion in Example 15 are relatively easy to identify. The phrase "It is primarily for this reason that" indicates that the first sentence in the passage is the premise; the conclusion follows this phrase. The major assumption of the argument is that exposure to portrayals of violence results in violent acts. Answer choices (A), (D), and (E) state plausible alternative reasons for the increase in violence and, as such, might be considered as providing additional support for the conclusion. However, none of these choices directly supports the argument's main contention that increased portrayal of violence is the "primary" reason for the increase in violent acts. Answer choice (B) weakens the argument, since it undermines the major assumption of the argument. You can eliminate this choice. Answer choice (C) supports the major assumption of the argument. **The correct answer is (C).**

Logical Reasoning
Mini-test and Review

lesson 6

In this lesson, you will apply what you've already learned about Logical Reasoning questions to a series of Logical Reasoning passages. Take the mini-test under timed conditions; then review the explanations that follow.

LOGICAL REASONING MINI-TEST

NUMBER OF QUESTIONS: 14 • SUGGESTED TIME: 18 MINUTES

Directions: The questions in this section are based on the reasoning contained in brief statements or passages. For some questions, more than one of the choices could conceivably answer the question. However, you are to choose the best answer; that is, the response that most accurately and completely answers the question. You should not make assumptions that are by commonsense standards implausible, superfluous, or incompatible with the passage.

1. Because animal liberationists place a higher value on protecting animals from harm than on protecting their autonomy, they cannot possibly be environmentalists. By insisting that we have a moral obligation to efficiently relieve animal suffering, animal liberationists are thereby committed to any plan that attains this goal. But this goal can be achieved most efficiently by converting our national parks and wilderness areas into humanely managed farms. The reasons for this are fairly obvious. The suffering of animals in the wild is unimaginable. Animal populations are violently managed by nature in a drama in which few individuals are spared injury or death. In comparison, animals live much longer and much less painful lives on the farm than in the wild. Any such plan, however, would be totally unacceptable to environmentalists since it would violate their guiding tenet that we have a moral obligation to preserve as much of the environment and its inhabitants in a natural state as is humanly possible.

75

The main point of the argument is best expressed by which of the following?

(A) The most efficient way to relieve the suffering of animals would be to convert our national parks and wilderness areas into humanely managed farms.

(B) Animal liberationists are committed to any plan that relieves animal suffering.

(C) Animal liberationism and environmentalism are incompatible.

(D) Animal liberationists place a higher value on protecting animals from harm than on protecting their autonomy.

(E) The plan of converting our national parks and wilderness areas into humanely managed farms would be totally unacceptable to environmentalists.

2. Is it wrong for doctors to lie about their patients' illnesses? Aren't doctors just like any other people we hire to do a job for us? Surely, we would not tolerate not being told the truth about the condition of our automobile from the mechanic we hired to fix it, or the condition of our roof from the carpenter we employed to repair it. Just as these workers would be guilty of violating their good faith contracts with us if they were to do this, doctors who lie to their patients about their illnesses violate these contracts as well, and this is clearly wrong.

The conclusion of the argument is best expressed by which of the following?

(A) Doctors who lie to their patients about their illnesses violate their good faith contracts with their patients.

(B) Doctors often lie to their patients about their illnesses.

(C) Doctors are just hired workers like mechanics and carpenters.

(D) It is wrong for doctors to lie about their patients' illnesses.

(E) Doctors, like mechanics and carpenters, enter into good faith contracts with us when we hire them.

3. Testifying before the Senate committee investigating charges that cigarette manufacturers had manipulated nicotine levels in cigarettes to addict consumers to their products, tobacco executives argued that cigarette smoking is not addictive. The primary reason they gave in support of this claim was that cigarette smoking was not regulated by the Food and Drug Administration.

For the tobacco executives' argument to be logically correct, which of the following must be assumed?

(A) Substances that are not addictive are not regulated by the Food and Drug Administration.

(B) Substances that are not regulated by the Food and Drug Administration are not addictive.

(C) Some addictive substances are not regulated by the Food and Drug Administration.

(D) There is no scientific proof that cigarette smoking is addictive.

(E) The tobacco executives lied when they claimed that cigarette smoking was not addictive.

4. *Sean:* I think the university orchestra's performance of Beethoven's symphony was terrible.

Kelly: Why do you say that?

Sean: Because the way they played it was not the way Beethoven intended it to be played.

What must be assumed for Sean's argument to be logically correct?

(A) Beethoven intended the symphony to be performed in a way different from the way the university orchestra performed it.

(B) Only the composer of a musical work knows how it should be performed.

(C) In general, university orchestras cannot perform Beethoven's symphony in the way it was intended to be performed.

(D) No performance of a composer's work that is not in keeping with the composer's original intention is a good performance.

(E) University orchestras lack the musical sophistication to do justice to Beethoven's symphony.

5. Nonhuman primates are excellent animal models for the study of human disease because of their close genetic relationship to humans. Indeed, comparisons of the chromosomes and DNA of nonhuman primates and humans reveal a startling similarity in their structure and primitive origin, and testify to the commonality of the genetic material between these phylogenetically related species.

Which one of the following is an assumption upon which the argument depends?

(A) Animals that are related to humans make good models for studying human disease.

(B) The more commonality of the genetic material between two species, the better one is as a model for studying the other.

(C) The more similar in structure and primitive origin of the chromosomes and DNA of species, the more commonalities in their genetic material.

(D) Phylogenetically related species make good models for studying one another.

(E) Nonhuman primates are closely related to humans.

mini-test

6. A study of native-born residents in Oonaland found that two thirds of the children developed considerable levels of nearsightedness after starting school, while their illiterate parents and grandparents, who had no opportunity for formal schooling, showed no signs of this disability.

If the above statements are true, which of the following conclusions is most strongly supported by them?

   (A) The nearsightedness in the children is caused by the visual stress required by reading and other class work.
   (B) People who are illiterate do not suffer from nearsightedness.
   (C) Only people who have the opportunity for formal schooling develop nearsightedness.
   (D) Only literate people are near-sighted.
   (E) One third of the children are illiterate.

7. Some of the most beautiful cars in the world are manufactured by Contempo Motors. Unfortunately, however, Contempo cars are notoriously unreliable, and as everyone knows, unreliable cars are exasperating.

If the statements above are true, each of the following must also be true EXCEPT:

   (A) Some of the world's most beautiful cars are exasperating.
   (B) Contempo cars are exasperating.
   (C) No Contempo cars are reliable.
   (D) No reliable cars are exasperating.
   (E) Some of the most beautiful cars in the world are unreliable.

8. The budget deficit will continue to grow unless taxes are raised soon. However, that's not going to happen in the foreseeable future. The upshot is that if the budget deficit continues to grow, the next generation of taxpayers will be burdened by an almost unbearable debt.

If the above statements are true, which of the following must be true?

   (A) Taxes will be raised soon.
   (B) The budget deficit will not continue to grow.
   (C) The political climate will not change in the foreseeable future.
   (D) The budget deficit will continue to grow but the next generation of taxpayers will not be burdened with an almost unbearable debt.
   (E) The next generation of taxpayers will be burdened with an almost unbearable debt.

9. Compare the human fetus at any stage of pregnancy with a newborn lamb. While it is evident that there are obvious differences between them because they belong to different animal species, they are similar in their capacities for pleasure and pain and in their levels of awareness and rationality. Yet the value placed on the newborn lamb's life is quite low; so low, in fact, that taking its life is a routine occurrence that happens every day without protest.

   Which one of the following is a conclusion that the statements above, if true, most strongly support?

   (A) It is wrong to take the lives of newborn lambs.
   (B) We should protest the practice of killing newborn lambs.
   (C) The differences between newborn lambs and human fetuses far outweigh the similarities between them.
   (D) We should not place a high value on the life of a human fetus.
   (E) Placing a higher value on the life of a human fetus than on the life of a newborn lamb is completely justified.

10. There is clear evidence that the mandated use of safety seats by children younger than age four has resulted in fewer child fatalities over the past five years. Compared to the five-year period before the passage of laws requiring the use of safety seats, fatalities of children younger than age 4 have decreased by 30 percent.

    Which one of the following, if true, most substantially strengthens the argument above?

    (A) The number of serious automobile accidents involving children younger than age 4 has remained steady over the past five years.
    (B) Automobile accidents involving children have decreased sharply over the past five years.
    (C) The use of air bags in automobiles has increased by 30 percent over the past five years.
    (D) Most fatal automobile accidents involving children younger than age 4 occur in the driveway of their home.
    (E) The number of teenage drivers has increased by 30 percent over the past five years.

11. Non-purebred horses are a better choice than purebred horses for potential horse owners who want to avoid costly medical bills. The main reason is that purebred horses are extremely susceptible to genetic abnormalities that can be corrected only by expensive surgery. Since non-purebred horses rarely suffer from these problems, they are obviously the better choice.

Which of the following, if true, most seriously undermines the author's contention?

(A) All horses are prone to the same environmentally determined diseases.

(B) Purebred horses are, for the most part, more attractive than non-purebred horses.

(C) Non-purebred horses have significantly longer life spans than purebred horses.

(D) Most genetically caused abnormalities in horses are cosmetic and do not impair the horse's general health.

(E) The initial cost of a purebred horse is much greater than that of a non-purebred horse.

12. Ten years ago, the death rate from Neural Synapse Deficiency (NSD)–related causes was 5 percent of all persons infected with the dreaded anti-synapse virus (ASV) that causes it. Today, the corresponding figure has risen to more than 15 percent. This is clear evidence that over the past ten years, the rate of propagation and the malignancy of the virus has increased substantially.

Which of the following, if true, most substantially strengthens the argument in the above passage?

(A) ASV screening and detection methods have been dramatically improved over the past decade.

(B) The number of ASV infected persons has increased tenfold over the past ten years.

(C) The number of persons who are willing to submit to ASV screening has increased significantly over the past ten years.

(D) The number of recognized NSD-related causes of death has remained relatively constant over the past ten years.

(E) New drugs have been developed over the past ten years that significantly lessen the debilitating effects of the NSD virus.

13. Lycopene, glutathione, and glutamine are powerful antioxidants that neutralize the free radicals produced in the body as a result of routine bodily processes. An excess of these free radicals in your system causes rapid aging because they accelerate the rate of cellular damage. Aging is simply the result of this damage. Thus, to slow down aging, it is necessary to supplement your diet daily with these antioxidants.

    Which of the following, if true, most seriously undermines the author's contention?

    (A) Most people aren't concerned with the effects of aging until it is too late to do anything about it.
    (B) Exercise associated with normal daily activities effectively neutralizes and dissipates the free radicals that are produced as a result of routine bodily processes.
    (C) The cost of antioxidants is exorbitantly high and well beyond the budget of most consumers.
    (D) Only overweight people who do not exercise daily are likely to have an excess of free radicals in their systems.
    (E) Smoking cigarettes is one of the main causes of cellular damage in humans.

14. Does having a large amount of money guarantee happiness? Results of a recent survey overwhelmingly confirm that having a sizable quantity of money is the key to happiness. In the survey, 78 percent of those who responded who claimed that they possessed a large amount of money said that they were happy.

    Which of the following, if true, most seriously calls the survey finding into doubt?

    (A) No clear quantitative definition of "large amount of money" was provided to the respondents.
    (B) No clear qualitative definition of "happiness" was provided to the respondents.
    (C) Most of the respondents who claimed to have a large amount of money in fact did not.
    (D) Many people are happy even though they do not possess a great deal of money.
    (E) Many people who have a great deal of money are not happy.

ANSWER KEY AND EXPLANATIONS

1. C	4. D	7. D	10. A	13. B
2. D	5. B	8. E	11. D	14. C
3. B	6. A	9. D	12. D	

1. **The correct answer is (C).** This is a challenging question that requires you to identify a conclusion. The main point of the argument is expressed in the first sentence, where it is concluded that animal liberationists "cannot possibly be environmentalists." This conclusion is based on the premise that "animal liberationists place a higher value on protecting animals from harm than on protecting their autonomy." The remainder of the passage is devoted to demonstrating that these two values are incompatible and that environmentalists are committed to the latter value. Choices (A), (B), (D), and (E) are all premises of the argument, so the correct answer must be choice (C).

2. **The correct answer is (D).** This is a moderately difficult question that requires you to identify a conclusion. The rhetorical question at the beginning of the passage introduces the issue to be discussed in the argument, which is whether it is wrong for doctors to lie about their patients' illness. In the final sentence, it is concluded that this practice is wrong because it would be a violation of the good faith contract we enter into when we hire the doctor. Choice (A) is a premise of the argument. Choice (B) is unsupported by the passage. The passage does not state that doctors often lie to their patients about their illnesses, nor is this the main focus of the passage. The main focus of the passage is to determine not whether they do, but whether they should engage in this practice. Choice (C) is a premise of the argument, and choice (E) is implied by the passage, so the correct answer must be choice (D).

3. **The correct answer is (B).** This is a moderately difficult question that requires you to find an assumption. The tobacco executives' argument can be represented as follows:

   Premise: Cigarette smoking is not regulated by the Food and Drug Administration.

   Conclusion: Cigarette smoking is not addictive.

The logical gap in the argument that needs to be filled is the link between substances that are regulated by the Food and Drug Administration and substances that are addictive. Moreover, to make the argument logically correct, the link between them must be such that the fact that something is not regulated entails that it is not addictive. Choice (B) is equivalent in meaning to the claim that all substances that are not regulated by the Food and Drug Administration are not addictive. This is exactly the assumption required to fill the gap in the tobacco executives' argument. Choice (A) does not fill the logical gap in the tobacco executives' argument and it is equivalent in meaning to the claim that all substances that are not addictive are not regulated by the Food and Drug Administration. The assumption required to fill the gap in the tobacco executives' argument is that all substances that are not regulated by the Food and Drug Administration are not addictive. Choice (C) does not fill the logical gap in the tobacco executives' argument. The fact that some of the substances regulated by the Food and

Drug Administration are not addictive is irrelevant to the tobacco executives' argument. Their conclusion is based on the premise that cigarette smoking is not regulated—not that it is regulated. Choice (D) brings in information not mentioned in the passage. The claim asserted in response (D), if true, could serve as an additional premise in support of the conclusion. Choice (E) also brings in information not mentioned in the passage. The issue of whether or not the tobacco executives lied when they claimed that cigarette smoking is not addictive is irrelevant to the logic of their argument.

4. **The correct answer is (D).** This is a moderately difficult question that requires you to find an assumption. Sean's argument can be restated as follows:

   Premise: The university orchestra's performance of Beethoven's symphony was not in accordance with the way Beethoven intended it to be performed.

   Conclusion: The university orchestra's performance of Beethoven's symphony was not a good performance.

The logical gap in Sean's argument that needs to be filled is the link between good performances and performances in accordance with the way the composer intended the music to be performed. Moreover, to make the argument logically correct, the link between them must be such that the fact that a performance is not in accordance with the composer's intentions regarding the way it should be played implies that it is not a good performance. Choice (D) is equivalent in meaning to the claim that any performance that is not in keeping with the composer's intentions regarding how it be played is not a good performance. This is exactly the assumption required to fill the gap in Sean's argument. Choice (A) is not an assumption of Sean's argument; rather, it is a restatement of the major premise of Sean's argument. Choice (B) does not fill the logical gap in Sean's argument; it is equivalent in meaning to the claim that all performances that are performed in the way in which the composer intended are good performances. This, in turn, is equivalent to the claim that all performances that are not good are not performed in a way in which the composer intended. This latter claim, however, does not entail that performances that are not in accordance with the way the composer intended are not good performances. Choices (C) and (D) provide plausible explanations of why the university orchestra's performance of Beethoven's symphony was not in accordance with the way Beethoven intended it to be performed; as such, (C) and (D) provide support for the major premise—they do not state assumptions of Sean's argument.

5. **The correct answer is (B).** This is a moderately difficult question that requires you to find an assumption. The argument in the passage can be restated as follows:

   Premise: Nonhuman primates are closely related genetically to humans.

   Conclusion: Nonhuman primates are excellent animal models for the study of human disease.

The logical gap in the argument that needs to be filled is the link between being closely related genetically to humans and being an excellent animal model for the study of human disease. Moreover, this link between them must be such that the fact that something is closely related genetically to humans implies that, or increases the likelihood that, it will be an excellent model for the study of human disease. Choice (B) states the general principle that the more closely related two species are genetically the better one is as a model for studying the other. The assumption required to fill the gap in the argument is an instance of this general principle. Choice (A) is too broad and does not specify the type of relationship required (namely, a close genetic relationship). Choice (C) is implied by the passage, which states that "comparisons of the chromosomes and DNA of nonhuman primates and humans reveals a startling similarity in their structure and primitive origin, and testifies to the commonality of the genetic material between these phylogenetically related species." From this information it can be reasonably inferred that the more similar in structure and primitive origin of the chromosomes and DNA of species, the more commonalities in their genetic material. Choice (D) is too broad. It is not the mere fact that the species are related phylogenetically to another that makes one a good model for studying the other; what is required is that they have a close genetic relationship to one another. Choice (E) is a paraphrase of the major premise of the argument.

6. **The correct answer is (A).** This is a relatively easy question in which you must make an inference. The task in this problem is to find the answer choice that is most strongly supported, that is, the one that is most likely to be true, given that the information stated in the passage is true. Choice (A) is the best response. The only difference cited in the passage between the children who developed nearsightedness and the parents and grandparents who did not have this disability is the fact that the children went to school, whereas the parents and grandparents did not. The inference to be drawn from this information is that school activities such as reading that require the use of vision are somehow causally related to the nearsightedness. Admittedly, the information stated in the passage would not, by itself, prove that these activities are the cause of the children's nearsightedness but it would provide strong support for this claim. Choice (B) is not strongly supported by the passage. From the information in the passage, it can be inferred that there are some people who are illiterate and who also do not suffer from nearsightedness (namely, the parents and grandparents of the children). However, it does not follow from this that all people who are illiterate do not suffer from nearsightedness, nor is this latter claim strongly supported by this inference. Choice (C) is unsupported by the passage; it is equivalent in meaning to the claim that all nearsighted people have had the opportunity for formal schooling. Admittedly, formal schooling is implicated with nearsightedness in the passage, but the implication is that formal schooling is, in some instances, a significant difference between persons who are nearsighted and persons who are not. Choice (D) is unsupported by the passage. It is equivalent in meaning to the claim that all nearsighted people are literate. While it is implied in the passage that some illiterate people are not nearsighted (namely, the parents and grandparents of the nearsighted children), it does not follow from this that all illiterate people are not nearsighted, nor is this claim strongly supported by this. Choice (E) is unsupported by the passage. The passage states only that "two thirds of the children developed considerable levels of nearsightedness after starting school." No inference regarding the remaining one third of the students is warranted.

7. **The correct answer is (D).** This is a moderately difficult question in which you must make an inference. The task in this problem is to find the answer choice that need not be true given that the information in the passage is true. The best way to proceed is to find all of those answers that must be true and by a process of elimination select the correct answer. The premises in the passage can be represented as follows:

> *Premise 1:* Some of the most beautiful cars in the world are manufactured by Contempo Motors.

> *Premise 2:* All cars manufactured by Contempo Motors are unreliable.

> *Premise 3:* All unreliable cars are exasperating.

Choice (D) is the best response. From premises 2 and 3 above, it follows necessarily that:

> *Conclusion 1:* All cars manufactured by Contempo Motors are exasperating.

Conclusion 1 eliminates choice (B). Premise 3 is equivalent in meaning to the claim that no cars that are manufactured by Contempo Motors are reliable. Since we are assuming that the statements in the passage are true it must also be true that:

> *Conclusion 2:* No Contempo cars are reliable.

Conclusion 2 eliminates choice (C).

From premise 1 and conclusion 1 it follows necessarily that:

> *Conclusion 3:* Some of the most beautiful cars in the world are exasperating.

Conclusion 3 eliminates choice (A).

From premise 1 and premise 2 it follows necessarily that:

> *Conclusion 4:* Some of the most beautiful cars in the world are unreliable.

Conclusion 4 eliminates choice (E).

Since answer choices (A), (B), (C), and (E) necessarily follow from the information stated in the passage, they each must be true given that this information is true, so the remaining answer choice, (D), is the correct answer. Choice (A) must be true if the statements in the passage are true. From premise 2 and premise 3 above it follows necessarily that:

> *Conclusion 1:* All cars manufactured by Contempo Motors are exasperating.

From premise 1 and conclusion 1 it follows necessarily that:

> *Conclusion 3:* Some of the most beautiful cars in the world are exasperating.

Choice (B) must be true if the statements in the passage are true. From premise 2 and premise 3 above, it follows necessarily that all cars manufactured by Contempo Motors are exasperating. Choice (C) must be true if the statements in the passage are true. Premise 3 is equivalent in meaning to the claim that no cars that are manufactured by Contempo Motors are reliable. Since we are assuming that the statements in the passage are true, it must also be true that no Contempo cars are reliable. Choice (E) must be true if the statements in the passage are true. From premise 1 and premise 2 above it follows necessarily that some of the most beautiful cars in the world are unreliable.

8. **The correct answer is (E).** This is a moderately difficult question in which you must make an inference. The task in this problem is to find the answer that must be true; that is, the one that cannot conceivably be false, given that the information stated in the passage is true. The premises in the passage can be represented as follows:

   Premise 1: Either the budget deficit will continue to grow or taxes will be raised soon.

   Premise 2: Taxes will not be raised soon.

   Premise 3: If the budget deficit continues to grow, then the next generation of taxpayers will be burdened with an almost unbearable debt.

   Choice (E) is the best answer. From premises 1 and 2 above, it necessarily follows that:

   Conclusion 1: The budget deficit will continue to grow.

   From conclusion 1 and premise 3 it necessarily follows that:

   Conclusion 2: The next generation of taxpayers will be burdened with an almost unbearable debt.

   Since conclusion 2 necessarily follows from the information stated in the passage, it cannot conceivably be false if this information is true.

   Choice (A) is contradicted by the passage, which states that "given the current political climate that's not going to happen in the foreseeable future." In this sentence, the pronoun "that" refers to the phrase "taxes are raised soon" in the previous sentence. Choice (B) is implicitly contradicted by the passage. From premises 1 and 2 above, it necessarily follows that the statement "The budget deficit will continue to grow" is true. Choice (C) is unsupported by the passage. No information in the passage supports a prediction about what the political climate will be in the foreseeable future. Choice (D) is contradicted by the passage. From premises 1 and 2 above, it necessarily follows that:

   Conclusion 1: The budget deficit will continue to grow.

   From conclusion 1 and premise 3, it necessarily follows that:

   Conclusion 2: The next generation of taxpayers will be burdened with an almost unbearable debt.

   Since answer choice (D) states a conjunction of two sentences, one of which must be false, then (D) must also be false.

9. **The correct answer is (D).** This is a moderately difficult question in which you must make an inference. The task in this problem is to find the answer choice that is most strongly supported; that is, the one that is most likely to be true, given that the

information stated in the passage is true. The major premises of the argument in the passage can be represented as follows:

Premise 1: The human fetus and the newborn lamb are similar in their capacities for pleasure and pain and in their levels of awareness and rationality.

Premise 2: The value placed on the newborn lamb's life is quite low.

Choice (D) is the best answer. The analogy between the human fetus and the newborn lamb points to significant and relevant similarities between them that suggest that the value placed on their lives should also be similar. Since the value placed on the lamb's life is quite low, it can be inferred that the value placed on the human fetus should be quite low as well. Another way to look at this is to consider how we could justify placing a higher value on the life of the unborn fetus than the life of the newborn lamb in light of the similarities stated in the passage. Choice (A) brings in information not mentioned in the passage. The rightness or wrongness of taking the lives of newborn lambs is not discussed. You can eliminate choice (A). Choice (B) is unsupported by the passage. While it is stated that "taking [the newborn lamb's] life is a routine occurrence that happens everyday without protest," it is not suggested that this practice should be protested. Choice (C) is unsupported by the passage. The relative number of differences and similarities cannot be ascertained only by the information in the passage. Choice (E) is unsupported by the passage. Given the information in the passage, it would be difficult to justify placing a higher value on the life of a human fetus than on the life of a newborn lamb. To do so would require pointing out some relevant difference between the two that would outweigh the similarities cited in the passage.

10. **The correct answer is (A).** This is a relatively easy question in which you must assess additional evidence. The task in this problem is to find an answer that strengthens the argument; that is, one that offers support for the major assumption of the argument or that provides additional evidence for the conclusion. The argument in the passage can be represented as follows:

Premise: Compared to the five-year period prior to the passage of laws requiring the use of safety seats by children, fatalities of children under age four have decreased by 30 percent.

Conclusion: The passage of laws requiring the use of safety seats by children under age four has resulted in fewer child fatalities over the past five years.

Choice (A) is the best answer. The major assumption of the argument is that there are no significant differences between the five-year period preceding the passage of the laws and the five-year period since their passage that could account for the decrease in fatalities. Choice (A) supports this assumption. Choice (B) weakens the argument by undermining the major assumption. Choices (C), (D), and (E) do not offer support for the major assumption of the argument, nor do they provide additional evidence for the conclusion of the argument.

11. **The correct answer is (D).** This is a moderately difficult question in which you must assess additional evidence. The task in this problem is to find an answer that weakens the argument; that is, one that undermines the major assumption of the argument, attacks a stated premise, or suggests an alternative conclusion that could be inferred from the premises. The argument in the passage can be represented as follows:

    Premise: Purebred horses are extremely susceptible to genetic abnormalities that can only be corrected by expensive surgery.

    Premise: Nonpurebred horses rarely suffer from genetic abnormalities that can only be corrected by expensive surgery.

    Conclusion: Nonpurebred horses are a better choice than purebred horses for potential horse owners who want to avoid costly medical bills.

    Choice (D) is the best answer. The major assumption of the argument is that it is necessary to correct the genetic abnormalities to protect the horse's health, and that consequently, costly medical bills will necessarily be incurred. Choice (D) undermines this assumption. Choice (A) brings in information not mentioned in the passage. The passage deals only with genetic abnormalities; environmentally determined diseases are not discussed in the passage. Choice (B) also brings in information not mentioned in the passage. The relative attractiveness of purebred and non-purebred horses is not discussed in the passage. Choice (C) strengthens the argument. It provides additional evidence for the conclusion by providing another reason for preferring non-purebred horses over purebred horses. Choice (E) brings in information not mentioned in the passage. The relative difference in initial costs of purebred and non-purebred horses is not discussed.

12. **The correct answer is (D).** This is a moderately difficult question in which you must assess additional evidence. The task in this problem is to find an answer that strengthens the argument; that is, one that offers support for the major assumption of the argument or that provides additional evidence for the conclusion. The argument in the passage can be represented as follows:

    Premise: Ten years ago, the death rate from Neural Synapse Deficiency (NSD) related causes was 5 percent of all persons infected with the anti-synapse virus (ASV) that causes it.

    Premise: Today, the death rate from Neural Synapse Deficiency (NSD) related causes is 15 percent of all persons infected with the anti-synapse virus (ASV) that causes it.

    Conclusion: The rate of propagation and the malignancy of the ASV has increased substantially over the past ten years.

    Choice (D) is the best answer. The major assumption of the argument is that no additional NSD-related causes of death have been discovered in the interim that could account for the increase in the death rate. In other words, the number of recognized NSD-related causes of death has remained relatively constant over the past ten years. Choice (B) is the second-best response. It provides additional evidence for the claim that the rate of propagation of the ASV has increased over the past ten years; however, it does not provide additional evidence for the claim that the malignancy of the virus has increased over this period. The conclusion of the argument states that both the rate of propagation and the malignancy of the virus have increased. Choices (A), (C), and (E) do not offer support for the major assumption of the argument, nor do they provide additional evidence for the conclusion of the argument.

13. **The correct answer is (B).** This is a moderately difficult question in which you must assess additional evidence. The task in this problem is to find an answer that weakens the argument; that is, one that undermines the major assumption of the argument, attacks a stated premise, or suggests an alternative conclusion that could be inferred from the premises. The argument in the passage can be represented as follows:

    Premise: Lycopene, glutathione, and glutamine are powerful antioxidants that neutralize the free radicals produced in the body as a result of routine bodily processes.

    Premise: An excess of the free radicals that are produced in the body as a result of routine bodily processes causes rapid aging.

    Conclusion: To slow aging, it is necessary to supplement your daily diet with these antioxidants.

    Choice (B) is the best answer. The major assumption in the argument is that daily ingestion of the antioxidants mentioned in the passage is the only way to rid your system of the free radicals produced as a result of routine bodily processes. Choice (B) undermines this assumption. Choice (A) brings in information not mentioned in the passage. Whether or not people are concerned with the problem of aging and the time at which that concern is realized are not discussed in the passage. Choice (C) also brings in information not mentioned in the passage. Admittedly, the high cost may prevent some people from using these antioxidants daily, but the fact that they are beyond the budget of most consumers does not attack a premise of the argument nor does it subvert the major assumption of the argument or suggest an alternative conclusion. Choice (D) does not undermine the major assumption of the argument, attack a stated premise, or suggest an alternative conclusion that could be inferred from the premises. Choice (E) brings in information not mentioned in the passage. Additional causes of cellular damage such as smoking are not discussed in the passage.

14. **The correct answer is (C).** This is a relatively easy question in which you must assess additional evidence. The task in this problem is to find an answer that weakens the argument; that is, one that undermines the major assumption of the argument, attacks a stated premise, or that suggests an alternative conclusion that could be inferred from the premises. The argument in the passage can be represented as follows:

    Premise: Seventy-eight percent of the respondents said that they were happy.

    Premise: The same 78 percent of the respondents claimed that they possessed a large amount of money.

    Conclusion: Having a sizable quantity of money is the key to happiness.

Choice (C) is the best answer. It directly attacks the second premise listed above, thereby seriously calling survey finding into doubt. If (C) is true, the second premise listed above is false. As a consequence, the argument falls apart because the connection between having money and being happy in the argument is completely severed. Choices (A) and (B) state possible problems that could have an adverse effect on the reliability of the survey, but neither of these responses directly attacks the truth of a stated premise, nor do they undermine the major assumption or suggest an alternative conclusion that could be inferred from the premises. Choice (D) is consistent with the conclusion of the argument. The conclusion does not state that everyone who is happy has a large amount of money; it states that people who have a large amount of money are happy. Choice (D) does not suggest an alternative conclusion that could be inferred from the premises, nor does it undermine the major assumption of the argument or attack a stated premise. Choice (E) contradicts the conclusion of the argument. The conclusion states that people who have a large amount of money are happy; choice (E) states the opposite of this claim. Choice (D) does not weaken the argument because it does not undermine the major assumption of the argument, attack a stated premise, or suggest an alternative conclusion that could be inferred from the premises.

Reading Comprehension Basic Concepts and Strategies

In this lesson, you will familiarize yourself with the format of the Reading Comprehension section and learn basic reading strategies.

READING COMPREHENSION AT A GLANCE

Basic format: The questions are divided into four sets. Each set involves a different reading passage (one of the sets involves two related passages). Each passage set consists of 5–8 questions.

Total number of questions: 28

Number of scored sections: 1

Testing time allowed: 35 minutes

Ground Rules

- No scratch paper is permitted (make notes in the test booklet)
- Only pencils and highlighters are allowed (no pens)
- No penalties are assessed for incorrect responses
- Each question is considered independently of all others

Here are the directions you'll see in the test booklet:

> Each passage (or passage pair) in this section is followed by a group of questions to be answered on the basis of what is *stated* or *implied* in the passage (or passage pair). For some of the questions, more than one of the choices could conceivably answer the question. You are to choose the best answer; that is, the response that most accurately and completely answers the question, and blacken the appropriate space on your answer sheet.

What Does the LSAT Reading Comprehension Section Test?

This section tests your ability to:

- Read carefully and accurately

- Determine the relationships among the various parts of the passage or between two passages

- Draw reasonable inferences from the material in the passage or passage pair

Questions and Answers About Reading Comprehension

Q Can I really improve my reading skills in a few weeks?

A Although a few weeks is probably not sufficient time to drastically alter your reading habits, it is enough time to train yourself to read more actively and efficiently and to learn how to better choose between best and second-best responses to LSAT Reading Comprehension questions.

Q Would it be worthwhile to increase my vocabulary by learning as many new words as possible before exam day?

A No. Reading Comprehension questions are not designed to test your vocabulary. Where a technical term is introduced in a passage but not defined, the passage will supply all you need to know about the term to respond to the questions.

Q From what sources are the Reading Comprehension passages taken?

A Passages are drawn from a variety of fields of knowledge, including the humanities, the social sciences, the physical sciences, ethics, philosophy, and law. Specific sources include professional journals and periodicals, dissertations, periodicals, and books that deal with sophisticated subjects of intellectual interest. Most passages are taken from sources written within the last 10 or 20 years and have been edited to increase their "density."

Q Am I at an advantage if a passage involves a topic that is familiar to me?

A Probably not. The testing service is careful to ensure that all questions are answerable based solely on the information provided in the passage. Also, the exam will include passages from a variety of disciplines, so it is unlikely that any particular test taker will be knowledgeable enough about two or more of the areas included on the test to hold a significant advantage over other test takers. You may nevertheless be at a slight advantage if you have some familiarity with the general area treated in a passage. You may find it easier to concentrate because the passage is more interesting and the terminology is familiar.

ANATOMY OF A READING COMPREHENSION SET

Each Reading Comprehension set consists of three elements:

1 A reading passage (or passage pair)

2 5–8 questions or other prompts

3 Five answer choices per question

Let's look closely at the anatomy of a set involving a single passage. (In Lesson 8, you'll examine a question set involving a passage pair.)

Single passages run 400–500 words each—about one full column on a two-column test page. These passages average 3–4 paragraphs each. Every fifth line is numbered (for questions that refer to particular parts of the passage). Passages vary in subject matter and complexity. The following passage is typical in length, but it's a bit tougher than average. Go ahead and read it now. You may find it useful to take brief notes as you read. Try to limit your time to 4 minutes.

Sample Passage:

Line   A "radiative forcing" is any change imposed on the Earth that affects the planetary energy balance. Radiative forcings include changes in greenhouse gases (such as carbon dioxide and ozone), aerosols in the atmosphere, solar irradiance, and surface reflectivity. A forcing may result from either a natural or an anthropogenic cause, or
5   from both, as in the case of atmospheric aerosol concentrations, which can be altered either by volcanic action or the burning of fossil fuels. Radiative forcings are typically specified for the purpose of theoretical global climate simulations. In contrast, radiative "feedbacks" are environmental changes resulting from climate changes and are calculated from scientific observation. Radiative feedbacks include changes in such
10   phenomena as clouds, atmospheric water vapor, sea-ice cover, and snow cover.

     The interplay between forcings and feedbacks can be quite complex. For example, an increase in the concentration of atmospheric water vapor increases solar irradiance, thereby warming the atmosphere and, in turn, increasing evaporation and the concentration of atmospheric water vapor. A related example of this complex interplay
15   also shows the uncertainty of future climatic changes associated with forcings and feedbacks. Scientists are unsure how the depletion of ozone will ultimately affect clouds and, in turn, the Earth's temperature. Clouds trap outgoing, cooling radiation, thereby providing a warming influence. However, they also reflect incoming solar radiation and thus provide a cooling influence. Current measurements indicate that
20   the net effect of clouds is to cool the Earth. However, scientists do not know how the balance might shift in the future as cloud formation and dissipation are affected by ozone depletion.

     Contributing to this uncertainty is the complexity of the mechanisms at work in the process of ozone depletion. The amount of radiation reaching the earth's surface and
25   the amount of reradiated radiation that is trapped by the greenhouse effect influence the Earth's temperature in opposite directions. Both mechanisms are affected by the vertical distribution of ozone. Also, the relative importance of these two competing mechanisms depends on the altitude at which ozone changes occur. In a recent NASA-sponsored aircraft study of the Antarctic ozone hole, chlorine monoxide was
30   measured at varying altitudes. The measurements suggest that chlorine plays a greater role, and oxides of nitrogen a lesser role, than previously thought in the destruction of ozone in the lower atmosphere. The study concluded that simultaneous

high-resolution measurements at many different altitudes (on the scale of 0.1 kilometer in vertical extent) are necessary to diagnose the operative mechanisms. These
35   findings have called into question conventional explanations for ozone depletion, which fail to adequately account for the new evidence.

Reading Comprehension questions are not designed simply to measure your ability to remember what you read. Rather, they are designed to gauge your ability to assimilate and understand the ideas presented. For example, consider the seven question "stems" below, all of which relate to the foregoing passage and all of which require you to go beyond merely memorizing or recalling what you have read:

1 Which of the following best expresses the author's primary purpose in the passage?

2 It can be inferred from the information in the passage that "burning of fossil fuels" (line 6) . . .

3 Based upon the information in the passage, it is reasonable to infer that decreased evaporation is most likely to result in which of the following?

4 According to the passage, radiative forcings can be distinguished from radiative feedbacks in which of the following ways?

5 The author discusses the effect of clouds on atmospheric temperature most likely in order to show that . . .

6 Based upon the information in the passage, the author would probably agree that scientists could more accurately predict the extent and direction of the greenhouse effect if they were to . . .

7 The information in the last paragraph does NOT: . . .

These seven question stems illustrate the following general observations about Reading Comprehension question sets:

- Some of the questions will be "memory" questions, requiring only that you recall specific information in the passage (for example, Question 4). However, most of the questions will require that you understand the ideas conveyed in the passage.

- One of the questions will ask about the passage as a whole, and that question will probably be either the first or last question in the set (for example, Question 1).

- With most questions, you will find all of the information needed to answer the question in one particular paragraph.

- Questions focusing on information in the first paragraph (for example, Question 2) typically appear early among the questions, while those focusing solely on information in the last paragraph (for example, Question 7) typically appear as the last question. Otherwise, there are no predictable patterns in question sequence.

- Questions vary somewhat in difficulty. Some require close judgment calls, while with others the "best" response is far better than any of the others. Questions requiring you to simply recall one or two specific bits of information are generally easier than those requiring you to assimilate and assess an entire paragraph or the entire passage.

The Answer Choices

Now, consider Question 1 along with five answer choices (we will examine answer choices for the other six questions in the next lesson):

1. Which of the following best expresses the author's primary purpose in the passage?
    (A) To examine the environmental effects of radiative forcings and feedbacks
    (B) To challenge conventional theories about the impact of radiative changes on ozone depletion and the greenhouse effect
    (C) To illustrate the complexity and uncertainty of some radiative changes
    (D) To evaluate current methods of determining radiative changes
    (E) To identify the factors that contribute to ozone changes and to the greenhouse effect

Your job in handling Reading Comprehension questions is to determine the best response among the five choices. In doing so, you must make qualitative distinctions among them. The two or three "worst" choices may jump out at you as obviously incorrect responses. However, the qualitative distinctions among the remaining choices can be subtle. Determining the best answer generally requires comparing the quality of the two (or three) best choices.

The correct answer is (C). In Question 1 above, choices (A) and (B) should have struck you as the worst choices. Choice (A) is far too broad a statement of the author's primary purpose. The author is primarily concerned with how radiative changes relate more specifically to ozone depletion and to the resulting greenhouse effect, not to the environment in general. Choice (B) is entirely off-focus and far too narrow to serve as a viable "best" response. The author makes no attempt in the passage to discuss the "conventional explanations" to which the last sentence of the passage refers. Moreover, the recent scientific study discussed in the final paragraph (which calls into question those "conventional explanations" about ozone depletion) illustrates the author's primary point that predicting radiative changes is difficult due to their complex and uncertain interaction.

Choices (D) and (E) have merit but are nevertheless incorrect. Either of these answer choices alone might be considered the best choice were it not for choice (C). With respect to choice (D), the author does point out the insufficiency of certain types of data in predicting climate changes (second paragraph), and the accuracy of previous explanations for Antarctic ozone depletion (final paragraph). These points are secondary, however, to the broader and primary point that predicting radiative changes is difficult due to their complexity and uncertainty. Thus, choice (D) is too narrow in its scope. Choice (E) is also too narrow in one sense, but is too broad in another sense. Although the author does indeed identify various factors contributing to ozone depletion, his or her concern is not merely with identifying these factors but also with pointing out problems in isolating and measuring these factors and the resulting problem of making accurate predictions about the greenhouse effect. In this sense, then, choice (E) is too narrow. In addition, there may be other factors that contribute to ozone depletion that are not discussed in the passage; the author does not necessarily intend to identify all such factors; in this sense, then, choice (E) is too broad.

Choice (C) is therefore the best response. While the first paragraph is introductory, the author stresses in the second paragraph that the effects of radiative changes can be complex and uncertain; in fact, the author devotes the second and third paragraphs (the bulk of the passage) to demonstrating this point.

TECHNIQUES TO HELP YOU READ MORE ACTIVELY

Most Reading Comprehension questions are designed to measure your ability to understand the ideas presented in the passage rather than simply to recall the information stated. To understand a passage, you must be able to: 1) identify the thesis (or main idea) and the author's primary purpose, and 2) follow the author's line of reasoning from paragraph to paragraph. Both of these tasks require an active frame of mind in which you are constantly interacting with the material as you read.

Poor scores on LSAT Reading Comprehension questions generally result from one of the following:

- poor concentration

- slow reading speed (inability to complete the section in time)

- the need to search the passage repeatedly for the information required to respond to each question

- difficulty narrowing down the answer choices to one clear best answer

All of these problems stem from the same bad habit: passive reading. You can add points to your LSAT score by becoming a more active reader. Begin right now by adopting this operating principle: Understand each paragraph well enough to be able to briefly explain the main point and line of reasoning to someone who has not read the passage.

Avoid the Passive Reading Mode

Most test takers take a rather passive approach to the Reading Comprehension passages. They give equal time and attention to every sentence in a passage, reading the passage from beginning to end without interruption and with very little thought as to what particular information is most important to respond to the specific questions.

This strategy is actually a non-strategy. What is the probable result of this approach? The reader may remember some scattered factual information and ideas, thereby enabling him or her to respond correctly to some easier questions. However, the reader is not likely to respond effectively to most questions, which require some insight into and assessment of the passage's information.

Pause After Reading Each Paragraph to Sum Up and Anticipate

After you read each paragraph, pause for a moment to evaluate the paragraph as a whole. Try to recapitulate or summarize the paragraph as two or three basic ideas. After each paragraph, answer the following questions for yourself:

- How would I sum up the discussion to this point?

- At what point is the discussion now?

- What basic points is the author trying to get across in this paragraph? Do these ideas continue a line of thought or do they begin a new one?

- Where is the discussion likely to go from here?

Example:

In the passage on pages 93 and 94, after reading the first paragraph, you might engage yourself in the following mental dialogue:

> "This paragraph doesn't express a thesis or main idea; it seems introductory in nature. The paragraph defines forcings and feedbacks, distinguishes them, and gives examples of each. I don't understand these concepts, but the general idea is that forcings and feedbacks are environmental changes that affect the Earth's climate. The passage might continue by focusing on one specific type of radiative change; or perhaps the passage will continue by discussing a theory or theories about radiative changes. I'm not sure."

Respond Tentatively to Certain Questions as You Read the Passage

After reading the first paragraph, scan the question stems for questions that you might respond to at this point, at least tentatively. The first paragraph will most certainly provide enough information for you to respond (tentatively) to any question that asks about the overall thesis, topic, or author's purpose. Additionally, the first paragraph might contain more detailed information being tested in one of the questions.

Example:

The first paragraph of the passage on page 93 probably provides sufficient information to respond to Questions 2 and 4. In addition, you might be able to respond tentatively to Question 1. Choice (E) appears to be too broad in scope, based upon the subject matter of the first paragraph. It's too early to tell about the other responses, though. They each look viable without knowing how the passage will continue. Tentatively eliminate choice (E) and keep the other responses in mind as you read on.

Return to the passage and read the next paragraph. Scan the question stems for any additional questions that you can respond to at present. Then take a few seconds to reconsider any thesis or primary purpose questions that you responded to after reading the first paragraph. Have you changed your mind about your tentative response after reading the second paragraph? Or has the second paragraph confirmed that your initial response was correct?

Example:

After reading the second paragraph, briefly reconsider Question 1. Choice (A) looks a bit broad now, and choice (B) appears to be narrow, considering you have read most of the passage and have yet to encounter any theories about ozone depletion. Eliminate choices (A) and (E). Keep in mind choices (C) and (D) as you read the rest of the passage.

Summarize the Passage After Reading It in Its Entirety

After reading the entire passage, take a few seconds to recap the passage. What was the author's main point and what were the major supporting points? Remind yourself at this point about the flow of the discussion only; don't be concerned with remembering all of the detailed factual information.

Example:

After reading the entire passage on pages 93 and 94, you might recap the discussion and formulate a thesis as follows:

> "To recap, the first paragraph defines forcings and feedbacks. The second paragraph gives an example (water vapor) of their complex interaction, then an example (clouds and ozone/greenhouse) of how this complex interaction makes it difficult to predict some forcings and feedbacks. The third paragraph goes into more detail about the second example (ozone/greenhouse), citing a recent ozone study showing that the relative importance of forcings having opposite effects varies with altitude."

> "What was this passage about as a whole? It is difficult to predict certain forcings and feedbacks because their interaction is complex and uncertain. Case in point: ozone depletion and the greenhouse effect."

Should You Preview Before Reading the Passage?

Test preparation publications typically recommend that, before reading a passage straight through (from beginning to end), you should perform one or both of the following "pre-reading" steps:

- Read all of the question "stems" (the questions but not the answer choices) for hints about the subject of the passage and possible thesis.

- Preview the passage by reading the first (and perhaps last) sentence of each paragraph.

- The first technique supposedly helps you anticipate the particular information in the passage that is tested. The second technique supposedly provides clues about the scope of the passage, the author's thesis or major conclusions, and the structure and flow of the discussion. Although these techniques make sense in theory, there are four main reasons why, in practice, they are rarely helpful on the LSAT:

1 Once immersed in the passage itself, you will quickly forget most if not all of what you learned from previewing.

2 These techniques call for you to read the same material twice. Does that sound efficient to you?

3 Previewing takes time (perhaps 30 seconds to a minute) that you probably cannot afford under testing conditions.

4 Although reading the beginning and end of each paragraph may be helpful for some passages, for others this technique will be of little or no help. (The passage on pages 93 and 94 is a good example of the latter type.)

There is one exceptional situation where previewing is appropriate—if you are running out of time (more on that later).

TECHNIQUES TO HELP YOU FOLLOW THE AUTHOR'S TRAIN OF THOUGHT

Look for Common Organization Patterns

How a passage is organized reveals the flow of the author's argument. Focusing on structure will help you to:

- understand the author's main idea and primary purpose
- identify supporting evidence
- understand the author's purpose in mentioning various details
- distinguish between main points and minor details

You can probably respond correctly to all of the more "general" questions (for example, "main idea" and "primary purpose" questions) just by determining the basic structure of the passage and organization of the materials.

Single passages tend to fall loosely into certain structural categories. Here are the four patterns that are most common (passage pairs follow their own distinct pattern, which you'll explore in Lesson 8):

1. Point and example
2. Theory and critique
3. Cause and consequence
4. Classification

Familiarizing yourself with these patterns will help you to anticipate the flow of the discussion in a passage. As you examine these patterns, bear in mind that not all passages fall neatly into one of these common patterns. A particular passage might, for example, do all of the following: reflect two patterns, present a variation of one of the three common patterns, or reflect a less common pattern not discussed below. (While the passage on pages 93 and 94 involves classifying various radiative changes as forcings or feedbacks, it really isn't a classification passage per se. Instead, it exemplifies a less common and simpler organizational pattern—point and example—in which a main point is asserted and examples are discussed to illustrate/explain that point.)

THEORY AND CRITIQUE

Introductory Sentences/First Paragraph. The author identifies the conventional (older, established, traditional) view, theory, or explanation of a phenomenon. The introduction also either implies or states that the conventional view is flawed. (If the conventional view could not be criticized, the author probably would not be interested in writing about the topic in the first place.)

Body. Look for one of the following patterns:

- The author focuses on one (or perhaps two) newer, more enlightened views. The author may attribute the new view either to a particular individual (for example, a scientist, author, sociologist) or to a school of thought in general (for example, the leaders of the feminist movement of the 1970s).

- The author points to specific examples, observations, data, or other evidence that support a different theory. The author may also point out that the evidence is conflicting (and so no firm conclusions can be reached).

Final Sentences. Look for one of the following typical patterns:

- The author admits that both views have their merits and shortcomings.

- The author suggests that all views are incomplete in their understanding and insight and that we need to study the subject further.

- The author introduces (but does not describe in detail) a new piece of evidence that suggests yet another view, an explanation for conflicting views, or a synthesis of numerous views.

In any case, the author will almost always have an opinion on the subject.

CAUSE AND CONSEQUENCE

Introductory Sentences/First Paragraph. The author describes the state of affairs either currently or at a relatively recent time in history; the author asserts that this state of affairs can be attributed to (i.e.—has directly or indirectly resulted from) certain previous historical phenomena.

Body. Look for one of the following typical patterns:

- The author discusses alternative theories regarding historical cause and effect (e.g., some historians believe X was the primary contributing cause of Y, while other historians disagree and believe instead that Z . . .). However, if this discussion turns out to be the author's primary concern, you are really dealing with a "theory and explanation" pattern rather than a "historical influence" pattern.

- The author traces in chronological order the events leading up to and contributing to a phenomenon.

Final Sentences. Look for one of the following typical patterns:

- The author recaps by concluding that the current phenomenon is rooted in one or more particular ideology, movement, school of thought, event, etc.

- The author concludes that no single influence adequately explains the course of events and that we should instead recognize all contributing factors.

CLASSIFICATION

Introductory Sentences/First Paragraph. The author identifies two or three basic types, categories, or classes of a phenomenon.

Body. Look for the author to accomplish all of the following:

- describe each class in some detail

- compare and contrast characteristics of members of the different classes

- further divide one or more classes into subclasses

Final Sentences. Look for one of the following patterns (the first pattern is by far the most common):

- The discussion concludes simply by finishing the description of the classes and subclasses (in other words, the author comes to no conclusions and asserts no arguments).

- The author points out new evidence that suggests an additional class or subclass.

- The author explains briefly how the classification system is used by practitioners to observe and test theories.

- The author points out a problem with the current classification system and suggests that some modification may be appropriate.

Look for Structural Clues or "Triggers"

"Triggers" are key words and phrases that provide clues about the structure and organization of the passage and the direction in which the discussion is flowing. The lists below contain many common trigger words and phrases. Underline or circle trigger words as you read the passage. By reviewing your annotations, you can effectively recap structure and organization of the passage.

These words precede an item in a list (e.g., of examples, classes, reasons, or characteristics):

first, second, third, etc.	also
in addition	another

These words signal that the author is contrasting two phenomena:

alternatively	on the other hand	while
by contrast	rather than	yet
however		

These words signal a logical conclusion based upon preceding material:

consequently	thus	as a result
in conclusion	therefore	accordingly
then		

These words signal that the author is comparing (identifying similarities between) two phenomena:

similarly	parallel	to
in the same way	likewise	also
analogous	just as	as

These words signal evidence (factual information) used to support the author's argument:

because	in light of
since	

These words signal that the author is providing an example of a phenomenon:

for instance	such as
e.g.	. . . is an illustration of

Don't Be Overly Concerned with the Details as You Read

LSAT Reading Comprehension passages are packed with details. If you try to absorb all of the details as you read, you will not only lose sight of the main points but you will also lose reading speed. Don't get bogged down in the details; gloss over them. In one of the margins, note where particular examples, lists, and other details are located. Then, if a particular question involving those details is included, you can quickly and easily locate them and read them in more detail.

Example: In the passage on pages 93 and 94, three examples are provided in the second paragraph to make the author's point that the effect of radiative changes on climate are complex and uncertain: 1) water vapor, 2) clouds, and 3) ozone depletion and the greenhouse effect. As you read the passage, as long as you briefly noted what each example dealt with and understood the author's broader purpose in discussing them, you would be able to handle the questions quite easily. However, if you were overly concerned with understanding the complex interactions described in any of these technical examples, you probably lost sight of the author's purpose and forgot what one or more of the examples was concerned with.

Annotate the Passage

Selective annotating (circling and/or underlining key words and phrases) serves three important purposes:

1. It helps you to maintain an active frame of mind, since you are shopping for ideas and information that are sufficiently important to earmark.

2. It provides an outline of sorts. After you read (and annotate) the entire passage, reviewing the annotated words and phrases can be an effective way to recap the passage for yourself.

3. It helps you to locate the relevant discussion quickly should you need to refer to the passage as you answer the questions.

What sort of information should you annotate? If you under-annotate, you will not be able to effectively recap the passage by reviewing your annotations. On the other hand, if you over-annotate, your annotations lose their meaning, and you might as well not have annotated at all. Consider the following seven suggestions for annotating the passage:

1. Mark areas of discussion that you may need to locate again to answer one or more questions.

2. Let your annotations provide an outline, so that you can recap the passage by reviewing only the annotated words and phrases.

3. Refrain from underlining complete sentences. Instead, select key words or phrases that "trigger" for you the idea or point that is made in this sentence or this part of the paragraph.

4. Mark structural connectors—key words that connect the logical building blocks of the passage.

⑤ In chronological passages, annotate historical benchmarks and divisions—centuries, years, decades, or historical periods—that help form the structure of the author's discussion.

⑥ Draw arrows to physically connect particular words whose connection is actually a logical, chronological, or conceptual one. For example, arrows can be used:

- to clarify cause and effect in the natural sciences or in the context of historical events

- to indicate who was influenced by whom in literature, music, psychology, and other fields

- to connect names (philosophers, scientists, authors, and others) with dates, events, other names, theories, or schools of thought, works, and so on

- to indicate the chronological order in which historical events occurred

⑦ Create your own visual cues to earmark:

- possible thesis statements

- major supporting points

- points of author disagreement

Make Margin Notes and Outlines

Choose a margin of the page for annotations and make shorthand notes summarizing paragraphs, earmarking areas of discussion, and otherwise providing signals for yourself so that you can locate details more quickly and recap the passage more effectively. Keep your notes as brief as possible; two or three words should provide a sufficient cue.

There is no need and not enough time to construct an outline of the passage per se. Instead, rely on your margin notes and other annotations to indicate the flow of the discussion. For certain high-density passages, however, some organized notes—a "mini-outline," so to speak—may be necessary. Some shorthand notes at the bottom of the page may help to keep particular details straight in your mind. The following scenarios typically call for a mini-outline:

- If the passage categorizes or classifies various phenomena, notes may help clarify which phenomena belong in which categories.

- If the passage mentions numerous individual names (for example, those of authors, artists, or political figures), use notes to link them according to influence, agreement or disagreement, and so forth.

QUESTIONS AND ANSWERS ABOUT PACING AND TIME ALLOCATION

One of the most common complaints about the LSAT Reading Comprehension section is that there is not enough time to finish all the questions. Reading speed, however, is not the key to success here. You are being tested not on how fast you read, but on how effectively—or how "smartly"—you read. Your effectiveness on the Reading Comprehension section(s) depends in part on how you pace yourself and how you manage your time, as explored in the following questions and answers.

Q **Should I skip one entire question set so that I have more time for each question set that I attempt?**

A By slowing down your pace and examining fewer passages in the allotted time (and random guessing for the remainder), you might actually improve your overall score. Most test takers discover, however, that this approach actually results in lower scores and that their overall comprehension actually suffers. Why? Most likely this occurs because, if you reads too slowly and too carefully, you tend to focus on details and lose sight of the larger picture, such as the flow of the argument and the author's main points. Also, if you have extra time to think about the answer choices, you may begin to overanalyze them, read too much into them, and ignore your intuition. Nevertheless, it's a good idea to try this approach as you practice; some test takers find that when they slow down and examine fewer than all question sets, some of the anxiety they feel over the time pressure disappears and their overall performance improves as a result.

Q **Should I move on to the next question set after a certain number of minutes, even if I haven't finished a question set?**

A Not necessarily. You have invested a certain amount of time in reading and assimilating the materials in each passage. Having made this investment, you should by all means take the time to consider every question in the set. However, if you have already responded to (made at least an educated guess for) all of the questions, it is probably not the best use of your time to re-examine those questions that you are least certain about. Even if you are ahead of your predetermined pace, move to the next question set and keep your momentum; otherwise, you will either become obsessed with a particular question or find yourself hunting through the passage again just to eliminate one answer choice for one question. Both of these actions are highly unproductive uses of your time.

Q **Should I reserve some time at the end of the timed section to re-examine questions about which I was uncertain?**

A Not as a hard and fast rule. By all means, earmark those questions for which you think another 30 seconds of consideration would help. However, do not assume that you will have extra time, and by all means do not hurry through the test or skip questions or passages to ensure that you have extra time left over.

Q **Should I read the passages in the order in which they appear?**

A Not necessarily. Begin with a passage that looks comfortable to you. Take a few seconds to size up the first passage. Consider starting with another passage if: 1) the topic is intimidating or unfamiliar, 2) the passage appears to be extremely dense in details, or 3) the passage is longer than average.

Q **Do the passages appear in ascending order of difficulty? If not, is there any pattern at all?**

A The passages do not necessarily appear either in ascending or descending order of difficulty. However, the first passage in a section is rarely the most challenging one. Accordingly, you should probably not skip the first question set.

Q **Should I skip a passage if it is not accompanied by as many questions as the other passages?**

A No. This may seem like a good strategy, since the return on your investment of time would seem to be greater for passages that are accompanied by more questions. However, the number of questions from passage to passage is not likely to vary by more than one or two. Your comfort level with the subject of the passage should be the determining factor when deciding whether to skip a passage.

Q **Are some types of questions inherently more difficult than others? If so, should I skip them?**

A Well, yes and no. Questions that require that you merely recall or locate factual information ("explicit detail" questions) do not require any insight or understanding on your part, so these would seem inherently easier. However, if the passage is extremely dense in details, it may be so difficult to recall or locate the specific information that you need to respond to one of these "easy" questions that in actuality the question is rather difficult.

Also, certain question types may seem more difficult than others to you, depending upon your own strengths and weaknesses. For example, if you have a great memory for details but often have trouble understanding broader concepts, you will probably find that the detail-oriented questions are easier than the more general questions. Even so, this fact would probably not justify your skipping the more general questions, except perhaps if you are very short on time.

Q **What if I'm running out of time?**

A If you do find yourself in a time crunch, try the following three steps to maximize what time you have remaining:

1. Find a question that includes a specific line reference (for example, "in lines 20–22") and requires specific factual information explicitly provided in the passage. Then, with that question in mind, read those lines as well as one or two lines immediately preceding and following those lines.

2. Make an educated guess at the "main idea" and "primary purpose" questions. Quickly read the first paragraph and the last sentence of the passage for clues.

3. Scan the passage for specific names, dates, events, titles, and proper (capitalized) nouns. These items are likely to be the focus of specific questions. Then scan the question stems to see whether you can respond to any questions merely by reading one or two sentences around the particular noun in the passage.

Sometimes these techniques work, and sometimes they don't. A passage that is more technical in subject and/or that includes a great number of facts and raw data is an ideal candidate, since in this kind of passage most questions are likely to focus on detailed information rather than general concepts.

Reading Comprehension Question Types and Wrong-Answer Ploys

In this lesson, you will examine the various Reading Comprehension question types, focusing particularly on common wrong-answer "ploys" you will encounter in the LSAT.

The question set in the previous lesson (about radiative forcings and feedbacks) includes examples of each of the six types of questions you will encounter in LSAT Reading Comprehension sets, distinguished by the skill that is being tested:

1 Recognizing the main idea or primary purpose of the passage

2 Recalling explicit information

3 Inferring from or interpreting specific information

4 Recognizing the function of specific information

5 Extrapolating from or applying passage ideas (this type appears less frequently than the others)

6 Comparing one passage with another

The wrong-answer choices in the question set in Lesson 7 illustrate many of the LSAT's favorite wrong-answer types, which include answer choices that:

- distort, understate, or overstate the ideas presented in the passage

- are mentioned in the passage but do not respond to the question at hand

- call for speculation or unsupported inference

- are contrary to or contradicted by the passage or are stated "backwards" (for example, reversing cause and effect)

- confuse one opinion or position with another

- are too narrow or too specific

- are too broad, too general, or too vague

- introduce extrinsic information (information not included in the passage)

Let's take a closer look at each of the six question types, focusing on the proper approach and wrong-answer ploys commonly used with each type. The questions we will be examining are all based on the passage in Lesson 7 (pages 93–94).

QUESTION TYPE #1: RECOGNIZING THE MAIN IDEA OR PRIMARY PURPOSE

Some questions test whether you recognize the author's main point or overall concern/ purpose. These questions require you to distinguish between the forest and the trees—that is, to distinguish broader ideas and points from supporting evidence and details. At least one such question accompanies every passage. Here's how to approach these questions:

- After reading the entire passage, formulate your own thesis statement and statement of author's purpose—before considering the answer choices. If you know what sort of response to look for, you will be far less tempted by the other (wrong) responses. Ask yourself these two questions:

    1 Toward what point is the author's effort primarily directed?

    2 What does the author spend most of his or her time discussing? (This may sound simplistic, but it helps to keep your thinking straight for this type of question.)

- Every passage has a "main idea" (thesis) and a primary purpose. You may find a particular sentence or two, usually in the first paragraph or at the very end of the passage, that sums up the passage. Don't insist on finding it, however; not all passages include explicit thesis statements or statements of purpose.

- The main idea of the passage and the author's primary purpose should be consistent. If both question types appear in the question set, be sure your answers to these two questions are also consistent.

- As you read the passage, pay particular attention to all words and phrases that indicate or suggest the author's attitude (tone, opinion, perspective). It's a good idea to circle all such words and phrases as you read the passage. The best response must reflect or at least show consistency with the author's attitude.

Look for These Wrong-Answer Ploys

- The response that is too narrow in scope. The response focuses on one element of the passage, ignoring other important elements. If a particular topic is discussed in only one of three or four paragraphs, you can pretty safely conclude that the author's primary concern is not with that specific topic. Be particularly suspicious of a response that refers to a single specific person, event, idea, or work. Here are three examples:

    1 If the passage is concerned with comparing two phenomena, a response that ignores this concern and focuses on only one of the two phenomena is too narrow to be a viable best response.

2 If the author uses specific examples to support an argument, a response that ignores the author's larger point and focuses on one of the examples is too narrow to be a viable best response.

3 If the author describes two existing theories and then proposes and describes a new and better theory, the author's primary purpose is not to examine, describe, or criticize current theories. The best response would go further and include the author's concern with proposing a new theory.

- The response that is too broad in scope. The response encompasses the author's main concern or idea, but extends that concern or idea beyond the author's intended scope—for example, in terms of topic, geographic region, or time frame.

- The response that distorts the author's position. For example, if the author's ultimate concern is to argue for a particular position or to propose a new and better explanation for some phenomenon, any response that ignores the author's opinion and instead implies objectivity on the author's part is not a viable best response.

Example (from the Question Set in Lesson 7):

1. Which of the following best expresses the author's primary purpose in the passage?

    (A) To examine the environmental effects of radiative forcings and feedbacks
    (B) To challenge conventional theories about the impact of radiative changes on ozone depletion and the greenhouse effect
    (C) To illustrate the complexity and uncertainty of some radiative changes
    (D) To evaluate current methods of determining radiative changes
    (E) To identify the factors that contribute to ozone changes and to the greenhouse effect

(For a detailed analysis of this question, see Lesson 7, page 95.)

QUESTION TYPE #2: RECALLING EXPLICIT INFORMATION

Some questions are designed to measure your ability to assimilate detailed information accurately as well as your efficiency in "looking up" information. The question may either ask which choice (among the five) is mentioned or which choice (among the five) is not mentioned. Here's how to approach these questions:

- Effective margin notes and annotations will help you locate the relevant information quickly. Wherever some sort of list is included in the passage—a list of characteristics, a list of examples, or some other list—earmark it. You can be sure that there will be an "explicit information" question that focuses on that list.

- Do not insist on finding a best response that repeats word-for-word what is stated in the passage. The best answer is usually not expressed exactly as it is in the passage; instead, it paraphrases the language used in the passage.

- Do not rely on your memory to answer these questions. Always go to the relevant portion of the passage at the time you are considering the question and read around the particular excerpt (from the preceding sentence to the following sentence) referred to in the question stem.

- Most "explicit information" questions focus on information contained in one particular paragraph. Some questions may explicitly refer to a specific line or paragraph in the passage. Even without a line reference, you can often locate the relevant portion of the passage within five or ten seconds based solely on the information in the question stem (quite helpful if you are in a time crunch).

Look for These Wrong-Answer Ploys

- The response that confuses the information in the passage by referring to unrelated details.

- The response that is not mentioned in the passage. One or more answer choices might provide information completely unsupported by or not mentioned anywhere in the passage. These wrong answers can be quite tempting; your natural reaction is that the information appeared somewhere in the passage, but you missed it. Well, probably not! Don't fall for this ploy.

- The response that contradicts the information in the passage. The response may appear viable at first glance, but it actually contradicts what is stated in the passage. This ploy will trap you if you fail to read each answer choice carefully.

Example (from the Question Set in Lesson 7):

4. According to the passage, radiative forcings can be distinguished from radiative feedbacks in which of the following ways?

   (A) Whether the radiative change is global or more localized
   (B) The precision with which the amounts of radiative change can be determined
   (C) The altitude at which the radiative change occurs
   (D) Whether the amount of radiative change is specified or calculated
   (E) Whether the radiative change is directed toward or away from the earth

The correct answer is (D). According to the passage, radiative forcings are normally specified in global climate simulations, while feedbacks are calculated changes based on observation (lines 6–9). Choice (A) is wholly unsupported by the passage. The author never discusses the geographic extent of radiative changes in any context. Choice (B) is also unsupported by the passage. The fact that feedbacks are "calculated" while forcings are "specified" does not in itself suggest that one can be more precisely determined than the other. Choices (C) and (E) confuse the information in the passage in a similar way. The subject of altitude is discussed in the third paragraph as a factor influencing the relative effects upon ozone changes (a radiative forcing) of radiation directed toward the earth and radiation directed away from the earth. This discussion does not, however, serve to distinguish forcings and feedbacks.

QUESTION TYPE #3: INFERRING FROM OR INTERPRETING SPECIFIC INFORMATION

Some questions require you to draw simple inferences or to recognize somewhat broader points by interpreting specific passage information. Here's how to approach these questions:

- Don't overlook the obvious! This question type calls for you to make only very "tight" inferences—in other words, the inference will be so strongly suggested in the passage that there really is no other reasonable interpretation. Do not fight the passage by looking for a more subtle or a deeper interpretation.

- An author inference usually requires that you piece together (logically speaking) no more than two consecutive sentences. To analyze the question, locate the relevant line or lines in the passage, read around those lines—the sentence preceding and the sentence following—and the inference should be clear enough to you.

- The question stem might refer to specific lines or a specific paragraph in the passage. In any event, based upon the information in the question stem, you will probably be able to locate the relevant portion of the passage within five to ten seconds (very helpful if you are in a time crunch).

Look for These Wrong-Answer Ploys

- The unwarranted or unsupported inference/interpretation. This response will leap to a conclusion that is not supported by the area of the passage where the inference occurs. It might bring in material that is outside the scope of the passage or exaggerate or distort the author's relatively narrow inference.

- The response that is either backwards or runs contrary to the passage. You might be surprised how easy it is to turn around certain facts or to confuse author agreement with author disagreement. The testing service knows this and will typically include an answer choice that is contradicted by, runs contrary to, or states certain information in the passage "backwards" (for example, reversing cause and effect).

- The response that confuses one thing with another. The response may mention details that are mentioned somewhere else in the passage but don't respond to the question at hand.

- The response that distorts the meaning of the information in the passage. This response may either twist or exaggerate the author's intended meaning.

Examples (from the Question Set in Lesson 7):

2. It can be inferred from the information in the passage that "burning of fossil fuels" (line 6)

   (A) is an anthropogenic cause of radiative forcings
   (B) results in both radiative forcings and radiative feedbacks
   (C) does not affect atmospheric forcings or feedbacks
   (D) is a significant type of radiative forcing
   (E) is an anthropogenic cause of radiative feedback

The correct answer is (A). The author states in the first paragraph that forcings can arise from natural or anthropogenic causes. In the sentence that follows, the author describes two specific causes of forcings, presumably to illustrate the point of the previous sentence. It can be reasonably inferred by considering both sentences together that the first example (volcanic activity) is a natural cause, while the second (the burning of fossil fuels) is an anthropogenic cause. Choice (B) is only partly supported by the passage. Although it can be inferred that the burning of fossil fuels causes radiative forcings, the author neither states nor suggests that this activity also causes radiative feedback. Choice (C) contradicts the information presented in this part of the passage, which states explicitly that the concentration of sulfate aerosols is affected ("can be altered") by burning of fossil fuels. Thus, although burning of fossil fuels may not affect radiative feedback, it can be inferred that such activity does affect radiative forcings. Choice (D) gets the passage information backwards. The burning of fossil fuels is a cause, not a type, of radiative forcing. Choice (E) confuses forcings with feedbacks.

3. Based upon the information in the passage, it is reasonable to infer that decreased evaporation is most likely to result in which of the following?

   (A) An increase in water vapor concentration
   (B) A decrease in solar irradiance
   (C) A decrease in other radiative forcings
   (D) An increase in atmospheric temperatures
   (E) A decrease in surface reflectivity

The correct answer is (B). According to the passage, increased evaporation leads to increased water vapor concentration (lines 13–14), which leads to an increase solar irradiance (lines 12–13). Accordingly, it is likely that a decrease in evaporation would lead to a decrease in the other two amounts. Choice (A) runs contrary (although not explicitly) to the information in the passage, which states that increased (not decreased) evaporation leads to increased water vapor concentration (see lines 13–14). Choice (C) confuses the information in the passage. The pertinent part of the passage (lines 7–10) deals solely with feedbacks and not forcings. Choice (D) runs contrary (although not explicitly) to the information in the passage, which states that increased (not decreased) evaporation leads to a warming of the atmosphere. Choice (E) confuses the information in the passage. The pertinent part of the passage (lines 7–10) deals solely with feedbacks. However, surface reflectivity is a type of forcing (lines 3–4).

7. The information in the last paragraph does NOT:

   (A) provide evidence of the variability of ozone amounts at different altitudes
   (B) underscore the complexity in measuring radiative changes
   (C) call into question current methods of determining radiative changes
   (D) support the author's position that predicting future ozone changes is problematic
   (E) explain a discrepancy between an earlier theory and more recent scientific evidence

The correct answer is (C). Choice (C) actually runs contrary (although not explicitly) to the information in the final paragraph. The author seems to accept the findings of the recent aircraft studies and certainly does not call into question the methods used in those studies. Choice (A) is incorrect based upon the last sentence of the passage. Since high (vertical) resolution observations are required to detect concentrations of greenhouse gases, it can be inferred that changes in such concentrations vary quickly with altitude. Moreover, the author suggests in the previous paragraph that this is the case when he or she refers to the "vertical distribution of ozone" (line 27) and to the dependence of climate forcings upon the altitude of ozone changes (lines 27–28). Choice (B) is incorrect since the studies discussed in the last paragraph suggest that determining the amounts of forcings is more complex than previously thought; specifically, that relative amounts vary quickly and significantly with altitude. Choice (D) is incorrect for essentially the same reason as (B). The newfound variability of chemical concentration among different altitudes adds to the difficulty in assessing the relative importance of competing forcings discussed in the previous paragraph (lines 27–28). Choice (E) is inferable. In the last sentence of the passage, the author refers to "conventional explanations," which can be characterized as "earlier theories." Since the new evidence calls into question those earlier theories, it is reasonable to infer that a discrepancy existed between earlier explanations and recent scientific evidence. In fact, the third paragraph as a whole explains that discrepancy.

QUESTION TYPE #4: RECOGNIZING THE FUNCTION OF SPECIFIC INFORMATION

Some questions are designed to test whether, in immersing yourself in the details, you lose sight of the author's reason for including the details. To avoid falling into this trap, be sure to read actively at all times, asking yourself what role or function specific information plays in the context in which it is mentioned. Here's how to approach these questions:

- Maintain an active mind set as you read. When you come across detailed information in the passage, ask yourself what role these details play in the discussion. Is the author trying to support his or her point with specific examples? Is the author observing similarities and differences between two things? As you read, remember that it is more important for you to understand why the author mentions details than to remember the details themselves (you can always look them up).

- Some inference is required. You will not find an explicit answer to this question in the passage. In other words, the author is not going to come right out and state, "The reason I am mentioning this particular detail is to support my assertion thatà" Instead, you must infer the author's purpose in mentioning the detail.

- As with "inference" questions (Type #3), these questions call for you to make only very "tight" inferences; in other words, the author's purpose will be so strongly suggested in the passage that there really is no other reasonable interpretation.

Look for These Wrong-Answer Ploys

- The response that is unsupported. This response will infer a purpose that is not supported by the information in the passage, possibly by bringing in extrinsic material (information from outside the passage).

- The response that exaggerates or distorts the author's purpose. As noted earlier, you must make only narrow, or "tight," inferences when inferring the author's purpose in mentioning details. A wrong answer might distort or exaggerate the author's relatively narrow inference.

- The response that confuses the information in the passage or does not respond to the question. The response will restate a point made elsewhere in the passage. This response will be tempting if you recall reading the statement and are confident that the statement is true. Don't be fooled. By focusing your attention on only the relevant portion of the passage, you can be confident that this response, while it may be an accurate statement, is a wrong answer.

- The response that confuses the author's position with that of another, possibly contradicting the information in the passage. The author may mention certain details to support his or her argument against a position or theory. Be sure not to confuse the author's argument with opposing views.

Example (from the Question Set in Lesson 7):

5. The author discusses the effect of clouds on atmospheric temperature most likely to show that

   (A) radiative feedbacks can be more difficult to isolate and predict than radiative forcings
   (B) the distinction between radiative feedbacks and radiative forcings is some-what arbitrary
   (C) some radiative feedbacks cannot be determined solely by global climate model simulations
   (D) the climatic impact of some radiative feedbacks is uncertain
   (E) the NASA-sponsored study is inconclusive as to the effect of ozone on cloud formation and dissipation

The correct answer is (D). Choice (D) restates the author's point in the first sentence of the second paragraph. Immediately thereafter, the author discusses clouds as an example of this point: it is difficult to predict the impact of greenhouse gases on clouds and thus on temperature. Choice (A) is unsupported by the passage. In the second paragraph, the author discusses two particular examples of radiative changes—one involving radiative forcings (lines 17–18) and the other involving radiative feedbacks (lines 18–19). The author's purpose in discussing these two phenomena is to illustrate the author's previous point that "the interplay between forcings and feedbacks can be quite complex" (line 11). However, the author makes no attempt to compare the relative complexity or uncertainty of these two effects. Choice (B) is unsupported by the passage. In the first paragraph, the author attempts to distinguish between forcings and feedbacks but does not assert or infer that the distinction is somewhat arbitrary. Choice (C) confuses the information in the passage and is somewhat nonsensical. It is forcings (not feedbacks) that are specified in (not determined by) global climate model simulations (lines 6–7). Moreover, choice (C) is wholly unsupported by the information in the second paragraph; nowhere does the author discuss or mention global climate simulations in relation to the effects of clouds on atmospheric temperatures. Choice (E) confuses the information in the second paragraph with the discussion in the third paragraph about the NASA-sponsored study; it is also unsupported insofar as the author does not indicate whether the study is conclusive or inconclusive.

QUESTION TYPE #5: EXTRAPOLATING FROM OR APPLYING PASSAGE IDEAS

These questions are not as common as the other types, but nevertheless appear in question sets from time to time. These questions ask you either to apply passage information to new situations or to speculate as to how the passage would continue. The approach here is similar to that of handling "inference questions" (Type #3).

Look for These Wrong-Answer Ploys

- The response that is unsupported by the ideas referred to in the question. It may require an unwarranted inference, or it may depart from the topic or be irrelevant to the ideas presented in the passage.

- The response that runs contrary to the ideas referred to in the question. This answer choice can fool you, since all the right words and phrases might be there. However, the answer turns around the idea presented in the passage, possibly by including or excluding a key word.

- If the questions ask for a logical continuation of the passage, beware of the response that covers old ground. The author's discussion is unlikely to reverse its "flow" and rehash material already treated in the earlier parts of the passage. However, don't rule out this possibility. For example, the author might continue by examining in more detail one of two key points made in the passage. If this is the case, the final sentences will in all likelihood provide a clue that this is the next area of discussion.

Examples (from the Question Set in Lesson 7):

6. Based upon the information in the passage, the author would probably agree that scientists could more accurately predict the extent and direction of the greenhouse effect if they were to

   (A) monitor radiative feedbacks and forcings over a longer time period
   (B) change the direction of research away from determining amounts of radiative changes
   (C) account for the altitude at which cloud formations appear
   (D) isolate those ozone changes caused specifically by anthropogenic factors
   (E) isolate the cooling influence of ozone changes from their warming influence

The correct answer is (E). According to the passage, a given vertical distribution of ozone affects atmospheric temperature in both directions at once (lines 24–26). Accordingly, by isolating the cooling influence of a given distribution of ozone from its warming influence, scientists might better predict whether changes in the vertical distribution of ozone will have a net cooling or a net warming effect. Choice (A) is the second-best response. It seems reasonable from a common-sense viewpoint that our ability to forecast the precise extent of the greenhouse effect improves as more data is acquired over time. However, this assertion is neither stated nor implied by the passage itself; thus, it is not adequately supported. Choice (B) runs contrary to the information in the passage. Radiative changes include changes in ozone, which are the very cause of the greenhouse effect. Thus, scientists should continue attempts to determine the amounts of such changes. Choice (C) confuses the information in the passage. The discussion of altitude relates to forcings, while the discussion of clouds relates to feedbacks. Choice (D) is unsupported—off the topic. Although the author does indicate in the first paragraph that forcings arise from both anthropogenic and natural causes (lines 4–5), nowhere in the passage does the author attempt to isolate their effects from each other, nor does the author suggest that doing so would enable scientists to better predict the extent of the greenhouse effect.

QUESTION TYPE #6: COMPARING ONE PASSAGE WITH ANOTHER

One (and only one) of the LSAT's Reading Comprehension sets will test you on what the test takers call Comparative Reading Skills. This set will consist of 6–8 questions based on two brief passages instead of one longer one. The total amount of reading involved will be about the same as for a longer passage. Both passages will involve the same specific topic or issue, but each will present its own distinct theory, viewpoint, or perspective on that topic or issue—as if the two passages were written by different authors.

A few of the 6–8 questions might involve just one or the other passage; these questions will look a lot like the ones you examined earlier in this lesson. However, most of the questions will be about how the two passages relate to each other. Before you learn what Comparative Reading questions look like and how to handle them, read the following two related passages. As you read, assume they were written by two different authors with different points of view on the same topic. Apply the active reading techniques you learned in Lesson 7, asking yourself these three questions:

1. What is the key issue, problem, or controversy that the two passages seek to address?

2. What is the essence of each viewpoint?

3. How does each author support his or her viewpoint?

Also ask yourself how the two passages are related—specifically, ask these three questions:

1. What are the similarities (points of agreement) between the viewpoints?

2. What are the dissimilarities (points of disagreement) between the viewpoints?

3. Is either viewpoint vulnerable to some criticism that the author of the other passage might seek to point out to bolster his or her own viewpoint?

To help you focus mainly on question types, the following two passages are a bit simpler and briefer than what you're likely to encounter on the actual test. During the mini-test in Lesson 9, however, you'll try your hand at a lengthier and tougher pair of Comparative Reading passages.

passage A:

Line   An apparent bird-dinosaur evolutionary connection, proposed early in the second half
of the twentieth century, is based on numerous anatomical similarities, and is supported by the fossils of a small number of seeming transitional forms uncovered in
Europe and Asia. The discovery of these fossil reptiles, equipped with feathers, wings,
5   and beak-like snouts, may be significant, but more likely provides only limited support
for a dinosaur-into-birds hypothesis. Convergent evolution often provides animals very
distant in lineage with similar appendages. Witness, for example, the similarities in
the body shape and presence of fins in fish and cetaceans such as whales and dol-
phins. We would never put forth the idea that orcas evolved from sharks based on the
10   morphological similarities of these creatures; it would be immediately deemed absurd.
It is more likely the case that birds and dinosaurs share a very different common
ancestor, perhaps from among the thecodonts. These prototypical reptiles of the late
Permian Age survived the largest mass extinction recorded in the planet's history to
bring forth many more recent lines—crocodiles, dinosaurs, pterosaurs, and birds being
15   the most notable among these.

passage B:

Line Studies of numerous dinosaur fossils make obvious that the lifestyles of dinosaurs were amazingly varied. No longer is it acceptable to view dinosaurs only as lumbering, cold-blooded monsters; indeed, the most frightening dinosaurs did not lumber at all. They were agile, swift, and some even possessed limited flying capabilities. Lightweight mus-
5 cular body structure would be crucial to the success of this type of predator.

Based upon this observation, along with a number of obvious physical similarities and evidence from the fossil record, it is likely that birds evolved from small, carnivorous dinosaurs called theropods. A mere examination of the forelimb, hindlimb, and feet of a theropod fossil, and a comparison to one of the five available specimens of
10 Archaeopteryx—a feathered reptile of the late Jurassic Era thought by many to represent an intermediate form between dinosaurs and birds—will bear this out. In addition, more recent discoveries of fossil dinosaurs with birdlike traits and habits, particularly the finds uncovered in the Liaoning province of China, lend further credible support to the assertion that birds are for all intents and purposes actual
15 members of the lineage Dinosauria living and thriving in our midst.

Look for These Wrong-Answer Ploys

All but a few of the questions accompanying a passage pair like the one above will be about how the passages relate to each other. These comparative-reading questions will focus on features such as the following:

- Points of agreement (either explicit or implicit) between the authors of the two passages

- Points of disagreement (either explicit or implicit) between the authors of the two passages

- How the author of one passage might critique or refute a viewpoint expressed in the other passage

- The effect of certain additional information on one author's thesis compared with the other author's thesis

- Similarities (or differences) in the scope or main concern of the two passages

- Structural similarities (or differences) between the two passages

As you might guess, the test maker's favored wrong-answer ploy for these questions is to confuse the two passages in some way. Also fair game are the ploys you studied earlier in this lesson. Don't fall for these ploys. Take good notes as you read each passage, so you can keep the details and viewpoints expressed in the two passages straight in your mind.

Example 1

1. Which of the following assertions is consistent with the theory proposed in passage A as well as the theory proposed in passage B?

   (A) Convergent evolution produces similar forms in diverse lineages.
   (B) Dinosaurs and birds may have evolved from the same ancestor.
   (C) Birds and dinosaurs arose out of completely separate lineages.
   (D) Birds arose out of a lineage of dinosaurs.
   (E) Birds first appeared at about the same time in evolutionary history as dinosaurs.

The correct answer is (B). The author of passage B believes that birds arose out of a lineage of dinosaurs, while the author of passage A believes that they did not. Neither belief is inconsistent with the assertion expressed in choice (B). Choices (A) and (C) are consistent with passage A's hypothesis but inconsistent with passage B's hypothesis. Choice (D) provides the essence of passage B's hypothesis but is antithetical to passage A's hypothesis. (E) runs contrary to both theories, which observe that birds first appeared later than any dinosaur.

Example 2

2. If genetic evidence were established to date the lineage of birds 85 million years prior to the rise of Archaeopteryx, this finding would tend to

   (A) support the theory proposed in passage A but undermine the theory proposed in passage B

   (B) support the theory proposed in passage B but have no affect on the theory proposed in passage A (This response is contrary to the information in both passages.)

   (C) support the theory proposed in passage A as well as the theory proposed in passage B

   (D) refute the theory proposed in passage A as well as the theory proposed in passage B

   (E) have no effect on the theory proposed in passage A or on the theory proposed in passage B

The correct answer is (A). The additional evidence mentioned in the question stem would contradict the theory proposed in passage B because its author suggests that birds arose from dinosaurs. The author of passage A suggests that the two arose from an extremely distant ancestor, and the theory of convergent evolution is not inconsistent with birds appearing before dinosaurs; hence the additional evidence would tend to support the theory proposed in passage A.

Example 3

3. The author of passage A would be most likely to criticize the evolutionary hypothesis set forth in passage B on which of the following grounds?

   (A) It ignores the possibility of the existence of transitional forms.
   (B) It ignores the impact of a very large mass extinction.
   (C) It assumes that morphological similarities are a result of direct lineage.
   (D) It proposes that the lineage from which dinosaurs arose is quite distinct from the one from which birds arose.
   (E) It presupposes that modern-day birds evolved from small, carnivorous dinosaurs.

The correct answer is (C). The hypothesis in passage B relies on the crucial assumption that there's no possible explanation for the body similarities between dinosaurs and early birds other than that birds descended directly from dinosaurs. Choice (A) contradicts the position of passage B's author, whose argument not just acknowledges, but actually relies upon, the possibility existence of transitional forms. Choice (B) provides an accurate statement, but so what? The large mass extinction that passage A mentions is irrelevant to the argument in passage B. Choice (D) provides the essential hypothesis of passage A, not passage B. Choice (E) restates the author's hypothesis in passage B, which that author supports with various evidence rather than merely presupposing the hypothesis to be true.

THE LSAT'S FAVORITE WRONG-ANSWER PLOYS

Here's a handy checklist of the eight common LSAT wrong-answer ploys, in order of frequency of use on the test. Keep this list in mind. It can help you narrow down the answer choices and find the best response.

1. Distorts the information in the passage: understates, overstates, or twists the information in the passage or the author's point in presenting that information

2. Mentioned in the passage, but does not respond to the question: includes information found in the passage but does not respond appropriately to the question posed

3. Speculation or unsupported inference: calls for some measure of speculation in that the statement is not readily (reliably) inferable from the information in the passage

4. Contrary to the passage or stated backwards: contradicts passage information or gets information backwards

5. Confuses one opinion or position with another: incorrectly represents the position or opinion of one person or group as that of another

6. Too narrow (specific): focuses on particular information in the passage that is too specific or narrowly-focused in terms of the question posed

7. Too broad (general): embraces information or ideas that are too general or widely-focused in terms of the question posed

8. Not mentioned in the passage: brings in information not found anywhere in the passage

TIPS FOR RESPONDING TO LSAT READING QUESTIONS

- **Don't second-guess the test maker.** The directions for the LSAT Reading Comprehension section instruct you to choose the "best" response among the five choices. Isn't this awfully subjective? True, there is an element of subjective judgment involved in Reading Comprehension. However, these questions are reviewed, tested, and revised several times before they appear as scored questions on an actual LSAT. Do not second-guess the test maker's judgment or command of the conventions of Standard Written English! If you think there are two or more viable "best" responses, you (not the test maker) have either misread or misinterpreted the passage, the question, or the answer choices.

- **Read every answer choice in its entirety.** Remember, you are looking for the "best" response. Often, more than one answer choice will be viable. Don't hastily select or eliminate answer choices without reading them all. LSAT test takers miss more questions for this reason than for any other!

- **Don't overanalyze questions or second-guess yourself.** If you believe you understood the passage fairly well, but a particular answer choice seems confusing or a bit nonsensical, do not assume that it's your fault. Many wrong answer choices simply don't make much sense! If an answer choice strikes you this way, don't examine it further; eliminate it! Similarly, if you've read and considered all five choices, and one response strikes you as the best one, more often than not, your initial response will be the correct one!

- **Don't overlook the obvious.** Reading Comprehension questions vary greatly in difficulty level, which means that many of the questions are really pretty easy. If a particular response seems obviously correct or incorrect, don't assume that you are missing something.

- **Cross-reference the questions.** Although each question in a set is distinct, it is possible to "check" your responses to certain questions by examining how you responded to certain other questions. Check to see if you have contradicted yourself in your responses. If so, go back and change your answers. For example, your response to a thesis or "main idea" question should be consistent with your response to questions that asks about the author's primary purpose, attitude toward the subject, and position on the issue at hand.

- **Eliminate responses that run contrary to the thesis.** Regardless of the type of question you are dealing with, keep in mind the overall thesis, main idea, or point that the author is making in the passage as a whole. Any answer choice to any question that runs contrary to or is inconsistent with that thesis can be eliminated. It's surprising how many questions can be answered correctly using only this technique.

- **Keep in mind common wrong-answer ploys.** Be assured: The LSAT will keep trying to bait you with its arsenal of wrong-answer ploys. Learn to recognize these ploys, and keep them in mind as you take tomorrow's mini-test as well as the Reading Comprehension section of the Practice Test later in this book.

Reading
Comprehension
Mini-test and Review

In this lesson, you will apply what you learned in the previous two lessons to three Reading Comprehension passages. After taking this mini-test under timed conditions, review the explanations that follow. The question type and difficulty level are indicated before the explanation for each question.

READING COMPREHENSION MINI-TEST

NUMBER OF QUESTIONS: 21 • SUGGESTED TIME: 27 MINUTES

Directions: Each passage in this section is followed by a group of questions to be answered on the basis of what is stated or implied in the passage. For some of the questions, more than one of the choices could conceivably answer the question. However, you are to choose the best answer; that is, the response that most accurately and completely answers the question, and blacken the appropriate space on your answer sheet.

QUESTIONS 1–7 ARE BASED ON THE FOLLOWING PASSAGE:

Line Non-indigenous species of plants and animals arrive by way of two general types of pathways. First, species having
5 origins outside of the United States may enter the country and become established either as free-living populations or under human cultivation—for
10 example, in agriculture, horticulture, aquaculture, or as pets. Some cultivated species subsequently escape or are released and also become
15 established as free-living populations. Second, species of either U.S. or foreign origin and already within the United States may spread to new
20 locales. Pathways of both types include intentional as well as unintentional species transfers. Rates of species movement driven by human transforma-
25 tions of natural environments as well as by human mobility— through commerce, tourism, and travel—dwarf natural rates by comparison. While geo-
30 graphic distributions of species naturally expand or contract over historical time intervals (tens to hundreds of years), species' ranges rarely expand
35 thousands of miles or across physical barriers such as oceans or mountains.

Habitat modification can create conditions favorable to the establish-
40   ment of non-indigenous species. Soil disturbed in construction and agricul-ture is open for colonization by non-indigenous weeds, which in turn may provide habitats for the non-indigenous
45   insects that evolved with them. For example, the European viper's bugloss, a weed common along roads and railroad tracks, provides a habitat for the Eurasian lace bug. Human-
50   generated changes in fire frequency, grazing intensity, as well as soil stability and nutrient levels, similarly facilitate the spread and establishment of non-indigenous plants. When human
55   changes to natural environments span large geographical areas, they effec-tively create conduits for species movement between previously isolated locales. The rapid spread of the
60   Russian wheat aphid to fifteen states in just two years following its 1986 arrival has been attributed in part to the prevalence of alternative host plants that are available when wheat
65   is not. Many of these are non-indig-enous grasses recommended for planting on the forty-million or more acres enrolled in the U.S. Department of Agriculture's Conservation Reserve
70   Program.
    A number of factors confound quantitative evaluation of the relative importance of various entry pathways. Time lags often occur between estab-
75   lishment of non-indigenous species and their detection, and tracing the pathway for a long-established species is difficult. Experts estimate that non-indigenous weeds are usually
80   detected only after having been in the country for thirty years or having spread to at least ten thousand acres. In addition, federal port inspection, although a major source of information
85   on non-indigenous species pathways, especially for agricultural pests, provides data only when such species enter via scrutinized routes. Finally, some comparisons between pathways
90   defy quantitative analysis. For ex-

ample, which is more "important": the entry pathway of one very harmful species or one by which many but less harmful species enter the country?

1. According to the passage, which of the following is true about the European viper's bugloss?

    (A) It serves as a host plant for the Russian wheat aphid.
    (B) Its natural rate of movement is comparable to that of the Eurasian lace bug.
    (C) It finds certain human path-ways to be habitable.
    (D) Its movement across physical barriers such as oceans is unlikely.
    (E) Its entry into the United States went undetected for more than thirty years.

2. Which of the following statements about species movement is best supported by the information in the passage?

    (A) Species movement is affected more by habitat modifications than by human mobility.
    (B) Human-driven factors affect the rate at which species move more than they affect the long-term amount of such movements.
    (C) Natural expansions in the geographic distribution of species account for less species movement than do natural contractions.
    (D) Natural environments created by commerce, tourism, and travel contribute significantly to species movement.
    (E) Movement of a species within a continent depends largely upon the geographic extent of human mobility within the continent.

3. According to the passage, the U.S. Department of Agriculture

    (A) contributed to the spread of the Russian wheat aphid.
    (B) provides data about non-indigenous species entering the United States through scrutinized routes.
    (C) has assumed the responsibility for preventing entry of non-indigenous species onto federal lands.
    (D) has attempted unsuccessfully to isolate the Russian wheat aphid.
    (E) favors the planting of non-indigenous grasses for the purpose of protecting certain species of insects.

4. It can be inferred from the passage that the movement of non-indigenous species is influenced by all of the following EXCEPT:

    (A) soil nutrient levels.
    (B) import restrictions.
    (C) popularity of aquaculture.
    (D) geographic terrain.
    (E) fire frequency.

5. Which of the following best expresses the primary purpose of the last paragraph?

    (A) To explain why it is difficult to trace the entry pathways for long-established non- indigenous species
    (B) To describe the events usually leading to the detection of a non-indigenous species
    (C) To discuss the role that time lags and geographic expansion of non-indigenous species play in species detection
    (D) To point out the inadequacy of the federal port inspection system in detecting the entry of non-indigenous species
    (E) To identify the problems in assessing the relative significance of various entry pathways for non-indigenous species

6. Based upon the information in the passage, whether the entry pathway for a particular non-indigenous species can be determined is LEAST likely to depend upon which of the following?

    (A) Whether the species is considered to be a pest
    (B) Whether the species gains entry through a scrutinized route
    (C) The rate at which the species expands geographically
    (D) How long the species has been established
    (E) The size of the average member of the species

7. Which of the following is the most appropriate title for the passage?

    (A) Determining Entry Pathways for Non-Indigenous Species
    (B) The Impact of Human Activity on Species Movement
    (C) Non-Indigenous Species: Intentional vs. Unintentional Entry Pathways
    (D) Non-Indigenous Plants: Pathways for Entry
    (E) Problems in Halting the Spread of Harmful Non-Indigenous Species

QUESTIONS 8–13 ARE BASED ON THE FOLLOWING PASSAGE PAIR:

passage A

Line   Why have governments typically assumed an active role with respect to health care—as if their role were obligatory? One answer is that, while
5   disease is omnipresent and prior to social organization, communal life creates special hazards. Trade and urbanization, with their consequent problems of sanitation and pollution,
10   exacerbate the risks of epidemics and other communicable diseases. An economist might assert that efforts to combat these risks should be considered public goods—the benefits from
15   such goods indivisible among beneficiaries—and hence within the legitimate

domain of governmental intervention. A sole private purchaser of health care would give others in society a free ride with respect to the benefits obtained. For example, one's vaccination protects another from infection. Conversely, the costs of failing to pay for such goods may be borne by others.

Yet, ill health is not a mere byproduct of economic activity. It is inevitably attendant to human existence. As a result, wherever there is human society there is public health. Every society must face the risks of disease, and hence must search to make disease comprehensible within the context of the society's own particular culture. To this end, theology once played the dominant role but has been supplanted by science. Health care is intrinsically public, then, not only because its benefits are indivisible and threats to it arise from factors outside of the individual, but also because communal life gives individuals the cultural context in which to understand it.

passage B

Line Those who criticize the United States government today for not providing health care to all its citizens equate the provision of health care with insurance coverage for the costs of medical expenses. By this standard, during the seventeenth and eighteenth centuries the U.S. lacked any significant conception of public health law. However, despite the general paucity of bureaucratic organization in pre-industrial America, the vast extent of health regulation and provision stands out as remarkable.

Of course, the public role in the protection and regulation of health was carried out in ways quite different from those today. Organizations responsible for health regulation were less stable than modern bureaucracies, tending to appear during epidemics and other crises, and wither away in periods of calm. Additionally, and not surprisingly, religious influence was significant, especially in the seventeenth

century. Finally, in an era that lacked sharp demarcations between private and governmental bodies, many public responsibilities were carried out by what we would now consider private associations. Nevertheless, the extent of public health regulation long before the dawn of the welfare state is remarkable and suggests that the nation's founding generations assumed a certain nexus of government and health that is not widely understood by proponents of universal health care today.

8. With which of the following assertions would both the author of passage A and the author of passage B most likely agree?

   (A) Government is ultimately responsible for ensuring the health of its citizenry.
   (B) The benefits and burdens of health care are indivisible among its beneficiaries.
   (C) Governments have typically acted as if they have a duty with respect to public health.
   (D) Disease can be understood only within the context of one's particular culture.
   (E) The costs of one person's failing to pay for health care should not be borne by others.

9. In passage A, its author suggests that all of the following serve to bring about epidemics EXCEPT:

   (A) inadequate health care.
   (B) commerce.
   (C) demographic trends.
   (D) inadequate sanitation.
   (E) pollution.

10. The theory about public health articulated in passage A would probably be viewed by the author of passage B as

   (A) theoretically unsound.
   (B) well-supported empirically.
   (C) culturally biased.
   (D) cogent but inadequate.
   (E) largely irrelevant today.

11. With which the following statements about government's role in the provision of health care would the author of passage A and the author of passage B most clearly agree?

   (A) The U.S. government today addresses health concerns that formerly were not considered serious enough to warrant government involvement.
   (B) What were once public health-care functions are now served by the private sector.
   (C) Philosophical considerations play a less significant role today in the formulation of public health-care policies than they did in previous eras.
   (D) Public health policy today is guided largely by secular rather than religious values.
   (E) Public health-care agencies today are typically established not as temporary measures but rather as permanent entities.

12. Which of the following best expresses the point of contention that the author of passage B has with "those who criticize the United States government today for not providing health care to all its citizens" (lines 43–45)?

   (A) They underestimate the role that insurance plays in the provision of health care today.
   (B) They fail to recognize that government plays a more significant role today in health care than in previous eras.
   (C) They misunderstand the intent of the nation's founders with respect to the government's duty to ensure the health of its citizenry.
   (D) They lack any significant conception of public health law.
   (E) Their standard for measuring the government's provision of health care is too narrow.

13. One difference between passage A and passage B is that they

   (A) present different perspectives regarding the role of government in the provision of health care.
   (B) argue for different levels to which the U.S. government's role in the provision of health care should be expanded.
   (C) provide different interpretations of the historical role of the U.S. government in the provision of health care.
   (D) propose different policies for addressing the public-health dangers of epidemic diseases.
   (E) provide different reasons for the ways that governments have fulfilled their perceived obligations with respect to health care.

QUESTIONS 14–21 ARE BASED ON THE FOLLOWING PASSAGE:

Line The origin of the attempt to distinguish early from modern music and to establish the canons of performance practice for each lies in the eighteenth
5 century. In the first half of that century, when Telemann and Bach ran the collegium musicum in Leipzig, Germany, they performed their own and other modern music. In the
10 German universities of the early twentieth century, however, the reconstituted collegium musicum devoted itself to performing music from the centuries before the beginning of
15 the "standard repertory," by which was understood music from before the time of Bach and Handel.

Alongside this modern collegium musicum, German musicologists
20 developed the historical subdiscipline known as "performance practice," which included the deciphering of obsolete musical notation and its transcription into modern notation, the
25 study of obsolete instruments, and the re-establishment of lost oral traditions associated with those forgotten repertories. The cut-off date for this study was understood to be around 1750, the year
30 of Bach's death, since the music of Bach, Handel, Telemann, and their contemporaries did call for obsolete instruments and voices and unannotated performing traditions—for
35 instance, the spontaneous realization of vocal and instrumental melodic ornamentation. Furthermore, with a few exceptions, late baroque music had ceased to be performed for nearly a
40 century, and the orally transmitted performing traditions associated with it were forgotten as a result. In contrast, the notation in the music of Haydn and Mozart from the second half of the
45 eighteenth century was more complete than in the earlier styles, and the instruments seemed familiar, so no "special" knowledge appeared necessary. Also, the music of Haydn and
50 Mozart, having never ceased to be

performed, had maintained some kind of oral tradition of performance practice.

Beginning around 1960, however,
55 the early musicians—the performers of early music—began to encroach upon the music of Haydn, Mozart, and Beethoven. Why? Scholars studying performance practice had discovered
60 that the living oral traditions associated with the Viennese classics frequently could not be traced back to the eighteenth century and that there were nearly as many performance mysteries
65 to solve for music after 1750 as in earlier repertories. Furthermore, more and more young singers and instrumentalists became attracted to early music, and as many of them graduated
70 from student and amateur status to become fully professional, the technical level of early-music performances took a giant leap forward.

As professional early-music groups,
75 building on these developments, expanded their repertories to include later music, the angry cries from the mainstream could be heard on five continents. The differences between the
80 two camps extended beyond the already fascinating question of which instruments to use and how (or whether) to ornament to the more critical matter of style and delivery. At
85 the heart of their disagreement is whether historical knowledge about performing traditions is a prerequisite for proper interpretation of music or whether it merely creates an obstacle
90 to inspired musical tradition.

14. It can be inferred that the "standard repertory" mentioned in line 15 might have included music

   (A) composed before 1700.
   (B) of the early twentieth century.
   (C) written by the performance-practice composers.
   (D) written before the time of Handel.
   (E) that called for the use of obsolete instruments.

15. According to the passage, German musicologists of the early twentieth century limited performance practice to pre-1750 works because:

    (A) special knowledge was generally not required to decipher pre-1750 music.
    (B) unannotated performing traditions had been maintained for later works.
    (C) generally speaking, only music written before 1750 had ceased to be performed.
    (D) the annotation for earlier works was generally less complete than for the works of Bach and Handel.
    (E) music written prior to 1750 was considered obsolete.

16. The author mentions the improved technical level of early-music performances (lines 71–73) in order to

    (A) call into question the fairness of the mainstream's objections to the expansion of performance practice to include later works.
    (B) explain why an increasing number of young musicians were being attracted to early music.
    (C) refute the mainstream's claim that historical knowledge about performing traditions creates an obstacle to inspired musical tradition.
    (D) explain the expansion of performance practice to include later works of music.
    (E) support the argument that the Viennese classics were more difficult to perform than earlier works.

17. The author refers to modern performance practice as a "subdiscipline" (line 20) probably because it

    (A) was not sanctioned by the mainstream.
    (B) required more discipline than performing the standard repertory.
    (C) focused on particular aspects of the music being performed at the German universities.
    (D) involved deciphering obsolete musical notation.
    (E) involved performing the works that were being transcribed at the universities.

18. According to the passage, performance practice in the early twentieth century involved all of the following EXCEPT:

    (A) deciphering outdated music notation.
    (B) varying the delivery of music to suit the tastes of the particular audience.
    (C) determining which musical instrument to use.
    (D) reestablishing unannotated performing traditions.
    (E) transcribing older music into modern notation.

19. Which of the following statements, if true, would best support the author's explanation for the encroachment by the early musicians upon the music of Mozart, Haydn, and Beethoven?

   (A) The mainstream approved of the manner in which the early-musicians treated the music of Bach and Handel.

   (B) Unannotated performing traditions associated with these composers were distinct from those associated with pre-1750 works.

   (C) Most instrumentalists are attracted to early music because of the opportunities to play obsolete instruments.

   (D) The music of these composers is notated more completely than is the music of Bach and Handel.

   (E) The early musicians and the mainstream both prefer the same style and delivery of music.

20. Which of the following statements is best supported by the passage?

   (A) The scope of performance practice expanded significantly during the latter half of the twentieth century.

   (B) Twentieth-century musicologists interpret early music differently than did musicologists of the eighteenth century.

   (C) Attempts to distinguish between early and modern music date back to the early eighteenth century.

   (D) The works of Mozart are now considered by the mainstream to be "early music."

   (E) Although the definition of early music has changed over the last century, the canons of performance practice have remained relatively unchanged.

21. Which of the following is the most appropriate title for the passage?

   (A) Performance Practice: The Legacy of the German Collegium Musicum

   (B) How Far Should Early Music Extend?

   (C) Unannotated Performing Traditions of the Eighteenth and Twentieth Centuries

   (D) Performance Practice and New Interpretations of the Viennese Classics

   (E) Competing Views Regarding the Necessity of Historical Knowledge for Inspired Musical Tradition

ANSWER KEY AND EXPLANATIONS

1. C	6. E	10. B	14. E	18. B
2. E	7. A	11. D	15. B	19. B
3. A	8. C	12. E	16. D	20. A
4. B	9. A	13. A	17. C	21. B
5. E				

1. **The correct answer is (C).** This is a moderately difficult question in which you must recall explicit details. According to the passage, the bugloss is common "along roads and railroad tracks"—that is, along human pathways. Choice (A) confuses the information in the passage. The bugloss serves as a host plant for the Eurasian lace bug, not for the Russian wheat aphid. Choice (B) calls for an unwarranted inference. Although it might be inferred that human-driven movement—i.e., movement associated with road construction—of the bugloss and lace bug are comparable, no such inference can be made about their natural movement. Choice (D) is too broad—although the bugloss's natural movement across physical barriers such as oceans is probably unlikely (based upon the information in the first paragraph), human-driven movement might very well be likely. Choice (E) is the second-best response. It is possible that choice (E) is an accurate statement. The European viper's bugloss is a type of weed, and the passage does indeed indicate that non-indigenous weeds usually go undetected for at least thirty years. However, it is unfair to infer that the European viper's bugloss was in fact one such weed.

2. **The correct answer is (E).** This is a moderately difficult question in which you must interpret specific information. Choice (E) restates the author's point in the first paragraph that rates of species movement driven by human transformation of the natural environment and by human mobility dwarf natural rates by comparison (lines 23–29).

   Choice (A) is unsupported by the passage. Although the author compares natural species movement to human-driven movement, no such comparison is made as between human modification of habitats and human mobility. Choice (B) is unsupported by the passage. The author makes no attempt to compare rate (interpreted either as frequency or speed) of species movement to total amounts of movement (distance). Choice (C) is also unsupported by the passage. The author makes no attempt to compare natural expansions to natural contractions. Choice (D) is nonsensical. Human mobility (commerce, tourism, and travel) do not create "natural" environments. It is human mobility itself, not the "natural environment" created by it, that contributes significantly to species movement.

3. **The correct answer is (A).** This is a relatively easy question in which you must interpret specific information. According to the information in the second paragraph, the rapid spread of the Russian wheat aphid resulted partly from the availability of alternative host plants (non-indigenous grasses) which were recommended for planting on lands controlled by the U.S. Department of Agriculture. Thus, the Department was partly responsible for the rapid spread of the Russian wheat aphid. Choice (B) confuses the information in the passage. Federal port inspection (not the U.S. Department of

Agriculture) provides data about species entering through scrutinized routes. Choice (C) is unsupported by the passage. The author neither states nor implies that this is one of the Department's duties. Choice (D) is unsupported by the information in the passage. The author neither states nor implies that the Department made any attempts to isolate the Russian wheat aphid either before or since the rapid spread of the species. Choice (E) is the second-best response. It is only partly supported by the information in the passage. Although it appears that the Department intentionally planted various non-indigenous grasses, as choice (E) suggests, the author makes no mention of the reason for this.

4. **The correct answer is (B).** This is a moderately difficult question in which you must recall explicit details. The only discussion in the passage related to importing is the discussion in the final paragraph about the limitations of federal port inspection in detecting the entry of non-indigenous species. While common sense might suggest that import restrictions would probably affect the movement of non-indigenous plants and animals, the subject of import restrictions is not mentioned in the final paragraph or anywhere else in the passage. Choice (A) is supported explicitly by the passage. According to the passage, human-generated changes in soil nutrient levels "facilitate the spread and establishment of non-indigenous plants" (lines 53–54). Choice (C) is the second-best response. Although not supported implicitly by the passage, "aquaculture" is mentioned in line 11 as a form of human cultivation which helps to establish non-indigenous species. Thus, it can be reasonably inferred that the popularity of this activity would affect the movement of certain non-indigenous species. Choice (D) is supported explicitly by the passage. According to the passage, physical barriers such as mountains (i.e., natural terrain) limit species movement (lines 34–37). Choice (E) is supported explicitly by the passage. According to the passage, human-generated changes in fire frequency "facilitate the spread and establishment of non-indigenous plants" (lines 53–54).

5. **The correct answer is (E).** This is a moderately difficult question in which you must interpret specific information. In the first sentence of the final paragraph, the author claims that "[a] number of factors confound quantitative evaluation of the relative importance of various entry pathways." In the remainder of the paragraph, the author identifies three such problems: 1) the difficulty of early detection, 2) the inadequacy of port inspection, and 3) the inherent subjectivity in determining the "importance" of a pathway. Choice (A) is off-focus. Although the author asserts that it is difficult to trace an entry pathway once a species is well established, the author does not explain why this is so. Choice (B) is also off-focus and is too narrow. Although the author does mention that a species is usually not detected until it spreads to at least ten-thousand acres, the author mentions this single "event" leading to detection as part of the broader point that the unlikelihood of early detection contributes to the problem of quantifying the relative importance of entry pathways. Choice (C) is off-focus as well. Although the author mentions these factors, they are not "discussed" in any detail, as choice (C) suggests. Also, the primary concern of the last paragraph is not with identifying the factors affecting species detection but rather with identifying the problems in quantifying the relative importance of various entry pathways. Choice (D) is too narrow. The author is concerned with identifying other problems as well as in determining the relative importance of various entry pathways.

6. **The correct answer is (E).** This is a relatively easy question in which you must recall explicit details. Nowhere in the passage does the author either state or imply that the physical size of a species' members is a factor in whether the entry pathway for the species can be determined. Choice (A) is the second-best response. Unlike choices (B), (C), and (D), choice (A) is not supported explicitly by the passage. However, the author mentions in the final paragraph that federal port inspection is "a major source of information on non-indigenous species pathways, especially for agricultural pests." Accordingly, whether a species is an agricultural pest might have some bearing upon whether or not its entry is detected (by port inspectors). Choices (B), (C), and (D) are all mentioned explicitly in the final paragraph as factors affecting how precisely the entry pathway(s) of a species can be determined.

7. **The correct answer is (A).** This is a challenging question in which you must recognize the main idea or primary purpose of the passage. Although choice (A) may not provide an ideal title for the passage, it is the best among the five responses in expressing the ideas presented in the passage as a whole: the various types of entry pathways (first paragraph), the effects of habitat modification by humans on the establishment of non-indigenous species (second paragraph), and the problems in determining the relative significance of entry pathways (final paragraph). Choice (B) is too narrow. Although the title suggested in (B) fairly characterizes the author's concern in the second paragraph, it fails to encompass the author's chief concern with identifying the problems in determining the relative importance of various entry pathways. Choice (C) is off-focus. Although intentional and unintentional pathways are distinguished (in the first paragraph), the remainder of the passage deals solely with unintentional entry. Choice (D) is too broad in one sense and too narrow in another sense. The author's specific concern is with unintentional entry pathways (not with both intentional and unintentional pathways); in this sense, then, (D) is too broad. At the same time, the passage is concerned not just with plant species but also with animal species; thus, in this sense, choice (D) is too narrow. Choice (E) distorts the passage. Although the final paragraph does identify some of the problems in obtaining information needed to prevent the establishment of non-indigenous species, the author does not focus on (or even suggest) the need to halt the spread of harmful non-indigenous species.

8. **The correct answer is (C).** This is a moderately difficult comparative reading question in which you must determine the similarities (points of agreement) between the authors' viewpoints. In the first sentence of passage A, its author presumes choice (C) is true. Twice in passage B, its author makes the point that the extent of government health regulation throughout U.S. history has been "remarkable," implying that, at least in one country (the United States), government has always acted as though it has an obligation to protect public health.

Choice (A) is the second-best answer. Passages A and B lay quite a bit of theoretical and empirical groundwork, respectively, for the case that government has a moral duty with respect to the health of their citizens. However, neither passage goes so far as to assert that duty as a general principle. For this reason, choice (A) is not as clearly a point of agreement for both authors as choice (C). Choices (B), (D), and (E) restate three reasons given in passage A for the inherently public nature of health care, and so the author of passage A would undoubtedly agree with them all. Passage B is not concerned with the same argument and has nothing to say about the ideas expressed in choices (B), (C), or (E). Thus, whether the author of passage B would agree with any of these statements is entirely unclear.

9. **The correct answer is (A).** This is a relatively easy comparative reading question that requires you to identify explicit points of agreement or disagreement between authors. In passage A, its author never mentions inadequate health care in the context of epidemics (or in any other context). Choices (B), (C), (D), and (E) are incorrect because passage A explicitly cites trade (commerce), urbanization (a type of demographic trend), and "the problems of [inadequate] sanitation and pollution" as contributing causes of epidemics.

10. **The correct answer is (B).** This is a moderately difficult comparative reading question in which you must determine the essence of each author's viewpoint. Passage A presents the theoretical basis for the argument that government should assume responsibility for public health. Passage B provides historical (empirical) evidence that the U.S. government has always done just that, and the rhetorical tone of passage B is at least sympathetic to the chief claim in passage A that, in any society, health is inherently public.

Choice (A) is contrary to the passage information. As noted above, the information in passage B and the context in which the author presents it suggest that the author would be sympathetic to the claim in passage A that health is inherently a public concern. Choice (D) is only partly supported. Nothing in passage B suggests that its author would find passage A's theoretical argument less than cogent (valid or appealing to reason). By the same token, however, passage B provides nothing that might discredit that theoretical argument. Choice (C) is unsupported. Nothing in passage A suggests any cultural bias on its author's part. Choice (E) distorts and confuses the passage information. Based on the passages, either author might consider theology (religious ideas) "largely irrelevant" to public-health policy today. But this point has nothing to do with the question at hand, which asks about one author's evaluation of the other's claims.

11. **The correct answer is (D).** This is a relatively easy comparative reading question in which you must identify explicit points of agreement or disagreement between authors. The author of passage A would clearly agree with choice (D), since passage A indicates that "theology, which once played the dominant role, has been supplanted by science." passage B indicates that government's role in health care is carried out in different ways today than in prior centuries, and that "religious influence was significant, especially in the seventeenth century." It is reasonably inferable from these statements that the passage's author does not consider religion a significant factor in today's public-health policy decisions.

Choices (A), (B), and (E) all find explicit support in passage B, which suggests that government health-care agencies are more stable and permanent today than in prior eras, when government intervened mainly during public-health emergencies and when "many public responsibilities were carried out by what we would now consider private associations." Nothing in passage A, however, suggests the extent to which its author would agree with choices (A), (B), or (E). Choice (C) finds little support in either passage, and so the extent to which either author would agree with this answer choice is unclear. Neither author suggests that government's current policies on health care are guided by philosophical considerations to a lesser extent than during previous eras. The term "philosophical" should not be equated with the term "religious"; otherwise, choices (C) and (D) would be essentially the same response.

12. **The correct answer is (E).** This is a challenging comparative reading question in which you must detect similarities (or differences) in the scope or main concern of the two passages. According to passage B, the critics equate the degree (extent) of healthcare provision with insurance coverage. The author contends that by this standard of measurement, public healthcare during the eighteenth century was practically nonexistent. In fact, however, the government played a significant role in healthcare during that century in ways other than providing insurance to its citizens. Thus, the critics' standard for measuring the extent of the government's role in healthcare is far too narrow in that it ignores all of the other possible ways in which government can play a role in healthcare.

Choice (A) is unsupported. Nowhere in passage B does its author state or imply that insurance plays a larger role in health care than the critics contend; also, choice (A) makes no distinction between private and public insurance. Choice (B) is not well supported. Based upon the information in passage B, it appears that the U.S. government has played a significant role in health care throughout history; the author does not contend that the government's role in health care is greater today than in previous eras. (Implicitly, some of the evidence in the second paragraph supports this contention, while other evidence undermines it.) Even if (B) were strongly supported by the passage, the statement is nevertheless not the author's point of contention with the critics. Choice (C) is unsupported and does not respond to the question. The author makes no attempt to evaluate the critics' understanding of the founding generation's intent. Even if choice (C) were supported by the passage, the statement is nevertheless not the author's point of contention with the critics. Choice (D) confuses the details in the second paragraph. It was the U.S. that, by the critics' standards, "lacked any significant conception of public health law." Choice (D) asserts, however, that the critics were the ones that lacked such conception.

13. **The correct answer is (A).** This is a challenging comparative reading question in which you must determine the similarities (or differences) in the scope or main concern of the two passages. passage A is mainly concerned with discussing the theoretical underpinnings—both from an economic and sociological perspective—for government's role in health care. passage B is concerned with examining that role from a U.S. historical perspective (in order to make the further point that those who advocate universal health care don't appreciate that perspective).

Choice (B) is unsupported. Both authors seem sympathetic to the view that government should play a significant role in health care, yet neither author goes so far as to suggest that the U.S. government's role in health care today is too small. While the author of passage B does refute the critics' argument that government is not providing health care to all citizens, that author does not go so far as to assert that the government's present role should be expanded. Choice (C) is also unsupported. passage B clearly discusses and interprets the historical changes regarding the U.S. government's role in health care. However, passage A does not, and so there's no clear disagreement between the two authors here. Choice (D) is also unsupported and is off-focus. Neither author offers any prescription for dealing with the underlying causes of epidemics. Choice (E) is off-focus and unsupported. passage B does examine some of the ways in which the U.S. government has fulfilled its perceived role in health care, but passage A provides no such examination. Although both passages suggest certain reasons (religious and secular considerations) for government involvement in health care, depending on the era, the two authors seem in agreement on those reasons.

14. **The correct answer is (E).** This is a moderately difficult question in which you must infer from or interpret specific information. It is reasonably inferable from the first paragraph as a whole that the "standard repertory" mentioned in line 15 refers to the music of Bach and Telemann as well as to other ("modern") music from their time (first half of the eighteenth century). In the second paragraph, the author mentions that the music of Bach, Telemann, and their contemporaries called for obsolete instruments (line 19). Thus, the standard repertory might have included music that called for the use of obsolete instruments, as (E) indicates. Choice (A) runs contrary to the information in the passage. The "standard repertory" refers to the music of Bach, Telemann, and other composers of the first half of the eighteenth century. Thus, it probably did not include music written prior to 1700. Choice (B) confuses the information in the passage. As noted above, the "standard repertory" refers to the music of Bach, Telemann, and other composers of the first half of the eighteenth century. Thus, it could not have included music written during the twentieth century. Choice (C) is nonsensical. "Performance practice" refers not to a group of composers but rather to a subdiscipline formed by German musicologists who deciphered and interpreted early works. Choice (D) runs contrary to the information in the passage. The passage suggests that Handel was a contemporary of Bach. Thus, the standard repertory included works written during, not before, Handel's time.

15. **The correct answer is (B).** This is a moderately difficult question in which you must recall explicit information. According to the passage, the German musicologists did not study the music of Mozart and Haydn (post-1750 music) because, among other reasons, their music, "having never ceased to be performed, had maintained some kind of oral tradition of performance practice" (lines 50–53). (B) restates this point. Choice (A) runs contrary to the information in the passage. The author states that later works were not included in the musicologists' studies because, among other reasons, the notation was more complete and the instruments seemed familiar, "so no 'special' knowledge appeared necessary" (lines 47–49). This statement implies, of course, that special knowledge was required to decipher pre-1750 music. Choice (C) distorts the information in the passage. Although the unannotated oral traditions may have ceased, the author neither states nor implies that the basic works of pre-1750 composers were no longer being performed. Choice (D) confuses the information in the passage. The works of Bach and Handel were included in the musicologists' early-music studies. The cutoff date for the study was 1750, the year of Bach's death. Whether notation of works prior to those of Bach or Handel were less complete than notation of works by Bach or Handel is not the issue.

Choice (E) distorts the information in the passage. The author refers to older musical notation, not the music itself, as obsolete (line 23).

16. **The correct answer is (D).** This is a moderately difficult question in which you must recognize the function of specific information. At the beginning of the third paragraph, the author states that, beginning around 1960, early musicians began to encroach upon the works of Haydn, Mozart, and Beethoven. The remainder of the third paragraph is devoted to explaining the reasons for this encroachment. One of the contributing reasons given is that the technical level of early-music performances had improved. Choice (A) is wholly unsupported by the passage. In the final paragraph, the author does mention that the mainstream objected to the early musicians' encroachment upon later works. However, the author neither defends the early musicians nor in any other way suggests that these objections were unfair. Choice (B) confuses cause and effect. It was because more young musicians were being attracted to early music that the technical level of early-music performances began to improve, not the other way around. Choice (C) confuses the information in the passage; it refers to information included in the final sentence of the passage and is irrelevant to the question posed. Choice (E) is the second-best response. According to the author, improvements in the technical skills of early musicians somehow contributed to the encroachment by early musicians upon the music of Mozart, Haydn, and Beethoven. However, the author does not spell out the precise causal connection. Although it might be inferred that these works were more difficult to perform than earlier works, the author does not make this point explicitly; thus, choice (E) exaggerates the author's purpose in mentioning this detail. The author mentions the improved technical level of the performances not so much to make a narrow point about how difficult the music was to perform, but rather to explain the reasons for the encroachment upon this music by the early-musicians.

17. **The correct answer is (C).** This is a relatively easy question in which you must infer from or interpret specific information. Performance practice, according to the passage, was developed alongside the modern (early twentieth century) collegium musicum, which was part of the German university. While the modern collegium musicum performed music from before the time of Bach and Handel, the field of performance practice involved certain aspects (e.g., choice of instruments, deciphering notation) of music from the same time period. Choice (A) does not respond to the question. In itself, choice (A) finds some support in the passage. The mainstream's objections to the expansion of early music to include later works (see the last paragraph) might be interpreted as disapproval. Even so, this discussion in the final paragraph of the passage is irrelevant to why performance practice is referred to as a "subdiscipline." Choice (B) is nonsensical. In the context of the passage, the term "discipline" refers to an area or field of study, and so "subdiscipline" refers to a component or more specific area within a broader field of study. An entirely different meaning of the word "discipline" is suggested by choice (B). Choice (D) is the second-best response. The fact that performance practice involves the specific task of deciphering musical notation is indeed relevant to why it is called a "subdiscipline"—it involves a narrow area of concern within a broader field of study. However, performance practice includes other concerns as well (most notably, the re-establishment of unannotated performing traditions). Thus, it is termed a "subdiscipline" not just because it involves deciphering musical notation but, more generally, because all of its concerns are also encompassed by a more broadly-defined field of study or discipline. Thus, choice (D) is too narrow.

Choice (E) confuses the information in the passage. Musicologists involved in the narrow subdiscipline of performance practice transcribed the works performed by musicians at the universities, not the other way around.

18. **The correct answer is (B).** This is a relatively easy question in which you must recall explicit information. Although performance practice did indeed involve varying the performance of a work of music from one time to the next (by including spontaneous vocal and instrumental ornamentation), the passage neither states nor implies that how the delivery of music varied from time to time depended upon the particular tastes of the audience. Thus, choice (B) is unsupported by the passage. Choices (A) and (E) are explicitly supported in the second paragraph, where the author states that performance practice "included the deciphering of obsolete musical notation and its transcription into modern notation" (lines 22–23). Choice (C) is the second-best response; it is not supported by the information in the passage as explicitly as choices (A), (D), or (E). The author does not state explicitly that performance practice involved determining which musical instrument to use. However, the passage does indicate that early music often called for the use of obsolete instruments and that one of the issues separating the mainstream and the early-musicians was "the already fascinating question of which instruments to use" (line 80–82). Thus, it is reasonably inferable that performance practice involved determining whether modern instruments or earlier (obsolete) instruments were appropriate for a particular piece of music. Choice (D) is explicitly supported in the second paragraph. The author asserts that the most important concern of performance practice is the "re-establishment of lost oral traditions" (line 25). The author then describes these lost oral traditions as the use of obsolete instruments and voices and unannotated performing traditions.

19. **The correct answer is (B).** This is a challenging question in which you must extrapolate from or apply passage ideas According to the passage, one reason for the encroachment was that some of the oral traditions associated with the Viennese classics (the works of Mozart, Haydn, and Beethoven) could not be traced back to the eighteenth century. Choice (B) supports this point by providing specific evidence that this was indeed the case. Choice (A) is irrelevant. No information in the passage supports the notion that the mainstream's approval or disapproval of how early-musicians treated other works would have been relevant to the early-musicians' encroachment upon the music of Mozart, Haydn, and Beethoven. Choice (C) is not responsive to the question. If this statement were true, and if the music of Mozart, Haydn, and Beethoven did indeed call for the use of obsolete instruments, then this might help to explain why the early-musicians encroached upon the music of Mozart, Haydn, and Beethoven. However, choice (C) would not support the author's explanation but rather would provide an additional explanation; thus, in this respect, choice (C) is irrelevant. Choice (D) would actually undermine (weaken) the author's explanation. Early-musicians are interested in exploring unannotated performance traditions. Music that is fully annotated does not allow for such exploration. Thus, if choice (D) were true, the early-musicians would not be interested in the music of Mozart, Haydn, and Beethoven. Choice (E) is irrelevant. Even if true, this statement would not support the author's explanation but rather provide an additional explanation.

20. **The correct answer is (A).** This is a relatively easy question in which you must infer from or interpret specific information. Choice (A) is the best answer. According to the passage, beginning around 1960 (i.e., in the latter half of the century), early-musicians began to expand the scope of performance practice to include works by major composers of a later period. (A) paraphrases this rather explicit point. Choice (B) is wholly unsupported by the passage. Although the scope of the music explored by twentieth-century musicologists may be greater than that of earlier musicologists, the author neither states nor implies that modern musicologists interpret early music differently than did their predecessors. Choice (C) distorts and runs contrary to the information in the passage. The first sentence of the passage indicates that the origin of the attempt to distinguish early from modern music lies in the eighteenth century. However, this sentence does not indicate that the attempt itself began during this time period. In fact, the passage makes no mention of any such attempt prior to the early twentieth century. Choice (D) is unsupported and actually runs contrary to the passage. Nowhere does the author indicate that the mainstream's definition of early music might embrace the music of Mozart. To the contrary, the mainstream would probably oppose this notion, since the mainstream objected to the early-musicians' encroachment upon Mozart's music. Choice (E) is partially accurate, but it is self-contradictory. The definition of early music has indeed changed during the twentieth century to include later works. It is not clear from the information in the passage exactly what all of the canons (rules) of performance practice are. However, one of the canons relates to the scope of music included within this subdiscipline, and the passage makes clear that this scope has indeed changed during the twentieth century. In this sense, then, the second clause of the statement in choice (E) contradicts the first clause.

21. **The correct answer is (B).** This is a moderately difficult question in which you must recognize the main idea or primary purpose of the passage. The author's primary concern in the passage is to trace the scope of works included in performance practice from the early twentieth century to the latter half of the century. The author identifies and explains the reasons for the trend of including later works within the scope of so-called "early music" (second and third paragraphs), then refers (in the final paragraph) to a controversy surrounding this trend. Choice (B) reflects the author's primary concern as well as embracing the controversy. Choice (A) is too broad. While the author does establish that performance practice originated in the German collegium musicum, the author's primary concerns are more specific—to explain why the scope of works included in this discipline has expanded and to identify a controversy concerning this expansion. Choice (C) is off-focus. The author does describe (in the second paragraph) some of the unannotated performing traditions of concern to early-musicians but does not discuss such traditions in much detail. Choice (D) is also off-focus. While the third paragraph does point out that new discoveries led to new interpretations of the music of Mozart, Haydn, and Beethoven, this is not the author's primary concern. The author does not mention what these new discoveries were, nor does the author describe any new interpretations of these works. Choice (E) is off-focus as well. The author mentions the competing views to which choice (E) refers for the first time in the final sentence of the passage.

Analytical Reasoning Attribute and Grouping Games

In this lesson, you will examine various types of "attribute" games and "grouping" games that appear commonly in the Analytical Reasoning section of the LSAT.

THE DUAL ATTRIBUTE GAME

Attribute games involve assigning to each subject in the game one or more characteristics. The dual attribute game involves assigning two characteristics or attributes to each of the game's subjects. More complex games incorporate conditional rules.

Example 1:

A basketball team consists of seven members—J, K, L, M, N, P, and Q. Each team member plays one of three positions—guard, forward, or center. At least two of the players are guards, at least two are forwards, and at least one is a center. Each player is on either the injured list or the active list.

K, N, and P are guards, and J and L are not guards.

No forward is on the injured list.

At least two guards are on the active list.

Assume that the team can play only if at least two guards, two forwards, and one center are on the active list. Which of the following statements, if true, would permit the team to play?

(A) Only M and Q are on the injured list.
(B) Only J and L are on the injured list.
(C) Only K and N are on the injured list.
(D) Only L and M are on the injured list.
(E) Only J and Q are on the injured list.

The following diagramming approach works well for this game type. Notice that the rules are depicted affirmatively in the grid. For example, the rule that "J and L are not guards" has been inverted (each is either a forward or a center) so that the choice between forward and center can be made by circling the appropriate letter. Also notice how the rule that "no forward is on the injured list" is depicted visually. The picture indicates the rule affirmatively (a forward must be on the active list) with a directional arrow that leads from "F" to "A."

	J	K	L	M	N	P	Q
G,F,C	F/C	G	F/C		G	G	
A,I							

≥ 2 G   [G/A]   [G/A]   F↓A
≥ 2 F
≥ 1 C

The correct answer is (C). You can determine the correct response by inserting the information from each answer choice in turn into the diagram. The following diagram for response (C) easily allows for two active guards (P and either M or Q), two active forwards (among J, L, M, and Q), and one active center (among J, L, M, and Q).

	J	K	L	M	N	P	Q
G,F,C	F/C	G	F/C		G	G	
A,I	A	I	A	A	I	A	A

You can also derive the solution more intuitively. In each answer choice, only two of the players are on the injured list. At least one of those two players must be either K, N, or P (the three players that must be guards); otherwise, two of the four remaining players would be on the injured list. Since those four remaining players must include a center and two forwards, it would not be possible to assemble an active playing team that includes two forwards and one center. Thus, you can eliminate all answer choices that fail to include either K, N, or P.

THE RANDOM ATTRIBUTE GAME

For some attribute games, it may not be feasible to construct a single grid or template to accommodate all of the rules. An attribute game involving more than two attributes generally calls for a more flexible approach. These games may not appear especially difficult at first glance. Nevertheless, they can be very confusing!

Example 2:

Four children—W, X, Y, and Z—are the only patients in the children's ward of a particular hospital. Each child has either red or brown hair. Each child is assigned to either a private room of his or her own or a semi-private room which is shared with either one or two other children. No two children are the same age.

X, a girl, is assigned to a private room.

The youngest child is assigned to a semi-private room.

At least one child is a red-haired boy.

Z is not the oldest child and does not share a room with the oldest child.

W and X both have brown hair.

If each of two red-haired children is assigned to a semi-private room, then each of the following, considered individually, could be true EXCEPT:

(A) W is the youngest child.
(B) Y is the oldest child.
(C) W is the oldest child.
(D) Z is the youngest child.
(E) X is the oldest child.

This game involves no fewer than four attributes for each child: hair color (red or brown), gender (male or female), room assignment (private or semi-private), and roommate (if any). It also includes a sequencing feature—relative ages of the children. With this many variables, don't try to use a grid-type diagram. Instead, take organized notes, listing the four children and noting those attributes that can be determined for each child:

```
        W  Brown
        X  Brown/Girl/Private
           Y
Red Boy <
           Z  Doesn't share w/oldest

     *Youngest shares
```

What else can be deduced from the rules? Since W and X both have brown hair, either Y or Z must be a red-haired boy, as indicated in the diagram.

The correct answer is (B). W and X both have brown hair. Thus, Y and Z must be the two red-haired children who are assigned to semi-private rooms. Although Y or Z, or both, may share a room with W, Y and Z must share a room with each other; otherwise, one of them would have to share a room with X, which would violate the rule that X is assigned to a private room. Since Z cannot share a room with the oldest child, Y cannot be the oldest child.

THE MATRIX GAME

The matrix game requires you to make the same series of yes-or-no decisions for each of the game's subjects. The term "matrix" refers to the suggested diagram approach.

Example 3:

During the high-school summer session, six different subjects—art, biology, calculus, driver education, English, and French—are offered. An academic day includes five class periods, and each subject must be offered exactly three times during the day.

Only calculus and driver education will be offered during the first period.

French and three other classes will be offered during the second period.

Only biology will be offered during the third period.

More subjects will be offered during the fourth period than during the fifth period.

Two subjects that must be offered during the same three periods are

(A) art and biology
(B) art and French
(C) driver education and calculus
(D) driver education and French
(E) English and calculus

In this matrix game, you must decide which of six subjects will be offered during each of five periods. Thus, the game potentially involves thirty "yes-or-no" decisions, which can all be displayed in a checkerboard or matrix.

In any matrix game, focus on the totals for each column and for each row of your matrix; these totals will probably be crucial to handling the game. List information about these totals around the perimeter of the matrix. In Example 3, each of the six subjects is offered exactly three times; thus, three check marks must appear in each column—a total of 18 check marks in the entire matrix. Display the number of check marks in each row to the right of the matrix.

Here's the key to this game: Since rows 1, 2, and 3 must include a total of seven check marks, rows 4 and 5 must include a total of eleven check marks. (Remember: the matrix must include 18 check marks altogether.) The only way to include eleven check marks between rows 4 and 5 is to assign six to one and five to the other. Since the rules specify that more subjects are offered during fourth period than during fifth period, six check marks must appear in row 4, and five check marks must appear in row 5. Next, evaluating the number of check marks in each column, you can determine that art, English, and French must each be offered during second, fourth, and fifth periods; otherwise, each of these three subjects would not be offered exactly three times.

	A	B	C	D	E	F	
1	✗	✗	✓	✓	✗	✗	(2)
2	✓				✓	✓	(4)
3	✗	✓	✗	✗	✗	✗	(1)
4	✓	✓	✓	✓	✓	✓	(6)
5	✓				✓	✓	(5)
	(3)	(3)	(3)	(3)	(3)	(3)	

The correct answer is (B). The question calls for you to compare columns in order to identify an identical pair. Art and French must both be offered during second, fourth, and fifth periods.

THE SEND-AND-RECEIVE GAME

A send-and-receive game involves matching each of the game's subjects to any number of other subjects. Think about each subject as potentially sending a message to each other subject (and each other subject potentially receiving that message).

Example 4:

Six firms—Jarco, Kanco, Listco, Mapco, Newco, and Optico—can transmit documents via a computer network, but only according to the following restrictions:

Jarco can transmit documents to three of the other firms, one of which is Kanco.

Kanco cannot transmit documents to any other firm.

Listco cannot receive documents from any other firm, although Listco can transmit documents to three of the other firms.

Mapco can receive documents from three of the other firms.

Newco can transmit documents to two of the other firms, one of which is Kanco.

Optico can transmit documents to four of the other firms.

All transmitted documents are received.

No firm can transmit documents to itself.

> If Jarco and Listco can each transmit documents to Newco and Optico, all of the following statements must be true EXCEPT:
>
> **(A)** Mapco can receive documents from Listco.
> **(B)** Kanco can receive documents from Listco.
> **(C)** Mapco can receive documents from Optico.
> **(D)** Optico can transmit documents to Newco.
> **(E)** Newco can transmit documents to Mapco.

As you read the premise and conditions above, did you visualize a map or flow chart in which the game's subjects are connected to one another by arrows? While a flow chart may be appropriate for some logic games, this approach unduly complicates a send-and-receive game. Let's try a simpler and more efficient approach: For each firm, list those firms to which the firm can transmit documents. There is no need to list separately the firms to which, for example, Jarco can transmit and the firms from which Jarco can receive. A second (reciprocal) diagram is unnecessary and will lead to confusion. Next, indicate to the right of each firm how many and which firms the firm can transmit to.

After filling in the lists as completely as possible based upon the information explicit in the rules, ask yourself what else you can deduce from the rules. Here, given that Listco cannot receive documents from any other firm, since Optico can transmit documents to four other firms, those four others must be Jarco, Kanco, Mapco, and Newco. Since Mapco can receive documents from Optico and two other firms, display two *M*s next to the diagram to indicate that a complete diagram must include two additional *M*s. Since Listco cannot receive documents from any other firm, indicate next to the diagram that no *L*s can be inserted. The final diagram, then, looks like this:

J: K̲_ ⌋
K: Ø
L: _ _ ⌋
M:　　　　MM
N: K̲_|　　no "L"
O: J̲ K̲M̲N̲|

In this diagram, a vertical line (|) at the end of a row signifies that no additional firms may receive documents from that firm.

The correct answer is (B). Given the additional information in the question, since Mapco can receive documents from Optico and exactly two other firms, those two firms must be Listco and Newco. Our initial diagram can be partially completed as follows:

```
J: K̲N̲O̲|
K: Ø
L: N̲O̲M̲|      MM
M:            no "L"
N: K̲M̲|
O: J K̲M̲N̲|
```

The diagram makes clear that Statements (A), (C), (D), and (E) must all be true. In contrast, Statement (B) cannot be true—Kanco cannot receive documents from Listco because Listco's transmittal roster is already full.

THE SIMPLE GROUPING GAME

Grouping games involve dividing a game's subjects into at least three different groups. Simple (easier) grouping games limit the game's parameters and possibilities in one or more of the following ways:

- the number of subjects allocated to each group is fixed

- the groups are distinct and identifiable

- the subjects are distinct and identifiable

Example 5:

The town of Smallville includes ten residents—A, B, C, D, E, F, G, H, I, and J. Each resident lives on one of three streets—Maple Street, Pine Street, or Elm Street. Either three or four residents live on each of these three streets.

C, E, and J all live on different streets.

B and I both live on Pine Street.

D, F, and H all live on the same street.

If J lives on the same street as A, how many distinct combinations of residents could live on Maple Street?

(A) 1
(B) 2
(C) 3
(D) 4
(E) 5

If you try to employ one of the diagramming techniques for attribute games to Example 5, you will discover that an "attribute" approach simply will not accommodate the rules here. Instead, create three distinct spaces or groups, each representing a different street. You can deduce several important pieces of information from the rules. First, since the ten residents must be allocated into groups of either three or four, three residents must live on each of two streets, while four residents live on the remaining street. Second, since D, F, and H all live on the same street, either C, E, or J must also live on that street (because C, E, and J all live on different streets). Thus, that street includes four residents. Accordingly, B, I, and exactly one other resident live on Pine Street, while A, G, and exactly one other resident live on the remaining street.

Maple	Pine	Elm
	[BI_]	

3/3/4
C ≠ E ≠ J
[AG_]
[DFH_]

The correct answer is (C). If J and A live on the same street, that street (either Maple or Elm) must include exactly three residents—A, G, and J. Alternatively, Maple Street could include D, F, H, and either C or E. Thus, three distinct combinations of residents could live on Maple Street.

THE COMPLEX GROUPING GAME

Grouping games are not always as simple as the one in Example 5. Any of the following features would result in a more challenging grouping game:

- the number of subjects allocated to each group is variable
- the groups are indistinguishable
- the subjects are indistinguishable

More "unknowns" in a grouping game generally make for a more complex and time-consuming game.

Example 6:

Three jars contain a total of twelve jelly beans. Five jelly beans are pink, three are green, two are yellow, and two are black. Each jar contains at least two jelly beans of different colors.

No two jars contain the same number of jelly beans.

No jar contains both pink and green jelly beans.

No jar contains both yellow and black jelly beans.

One of the three jars could contain any of the following assortments of jelly beans EXCEPT:

(A) two black jelly beans and one pink jelly bean
(B) two yellow jelly beans and three green jelly beans
(C) one yellow jelly bean and two pink jelly beans
(D) one pink jelly bean and one black jelly bean
(E) one green jelly bean and two yellow jelly beans

Two important pieces of information can be determined from the rules. First, although the precise number of jelly beans in each jar cannot be determined, certain parameters can be established. Each jar must contain at least two jelly beans, and no two jars may contain the same number of jelly beans. Thus, only three possible assortments result (excluding the issue of color):

    2 - 3 - 7
    2 - 4 - 6
    3 - 4 - 5

Second, two and only two different colors may be represented in each jar; otherwise, either pink and green jelly beans or yellow and black jelly beans would be included in the same jar. (Either result would violate a rule.) Because visualization is important in a grouping game, your diagram here should include a roster of jelly beans to the side of three distinct spaces representing the three jars. Indicate grouping parameters below the jars. Keep in mind that the jars are indistinguishable, and so you may arbitrarily establish the left jar, for example, as that which will contain the fewest jelly beans:

Y ≠ B   2/3/7   YY
G ≠ P   2/4/6   BB
         3/4/5   GGG
                  PPPPP

As you place jelly beans in the jars, simultaneously cross them off the roster. For example, try placing two *B*s and one *P* in the first jar. Since each jar may include jelly beans of two and only two different colors, the remaining jelly beans fall logically into their respective groups as follows:

BB	GGG	PPPP
P	Y	Y

The correct answer is (E). Using the same approach for the five answer choices in Example 6, you can quickly deduce the correct answer. Whether one green jelly bean and two yellow jelly beans are placed in the first jar or in the middle jar, a rule violation results. Assuming they are placed in the first jar, the middle jar must contain four jelly beans and the remaining jar must contain five. Since pink and black jelly beans cannot be included in the same jar, the last jar must contain all five pink jelly beans, violating the rule that each jar must contain jelly beans of two different colors. Assuming they are placed in the middle jar, the first jar must contain two jelly beans, while the last jar must contain seven. Since pink and black jelly beans cannot be included in the same jar, the first jar must contain both black jelly beans, again violating the rule that each jar must contain jelly beans of two different colors.

Analytical Reasoning Mini-test and Review

In this lesson, you will apply what you learned in Lesson 11 to three logic games. After taking this mini-test under timed conditions, review the explanations that follow. Preceding the explanation for each game, the game type and difficulty level are identified.

ANALYTICAL REASONING MINI-TEST

NUMBER OF QUESTIONS: 16 • SUGGESTED TIME: 26 MINUTES

Directions: Each group of questions in this section is based on a set of conditions. In answering some of the questions, it may be useful to draw a rough diagram. Choose the response that most accurately and completely answers each question and blacken the corresponding space on your answer sheet.

QUESTIONS 1–6:

On a particular day at a warehouse, each of five workers—Jackson, Klein, Lawry, Manning, and North—performs two different tasks. Each worker performs one task in the morning and one task in the afternoon.

Three tasks—assembling, boxing, and gluing—are performed in the morning.

Three tasks—gluing, stacking, and loading—are performed in the afternoon.

North and two other workers glue.

Three of the workers stack.

Jackson does not perform either task that Klein performs.

Lawry does not perform either task that Manning performs.

The five workers listed above are the only workers at the warehouse on that particular day.

1. Which of the following must be false?

    (A) Jackson assembles.
    (B) Klein glues.
    (C) Lawry stacks.
    (D) Manning loads.
    (E) North boxes.

2. If Jackson loads, which of the following must be true?

    (A) Jackson glues.
    (B) Klein stacks.
    (C) Lawry boxes.
    (D) Manning glues.
    (E) North assembles.

3. If Lawry loads, which of the following must be true?

   (A) Either Klein or Manning boxes.
   (B) Either Jackson or Manning glues.
   (C) Either Klein or Lawry glues.
   (D) Either Lawry or Manning boxes.
   (E) Either Jackson or Klein assembles.

4. If Klein is the only worker who assembles, which of the following could be true?

   (A) Manning glues in the morning.
   (B) Jackson loads in the afternoon.
   (C) Lawry glues in the afternoon.
   (D) Klein loads in the afternoon.
   (E) Jackson glues in the morning.

5. If Klein and North perform the same two tasks, all of the following must be true EXCEPT:

   (A) Jackson does not glue
   (B) Klein does not assemble
   (C) Lawry does not load
   (D) Manning does not stack
   (E) North does not box

6. If Jackson and Manning perform the same two tasks, one of which is assembling, how many different combinations of task assignments for the five workers are possible on that day?

   (A) 1
   (B) 2
   (C) 3
   (D) 4
   (E) 5

QUESTIONS 7–11:

Five classic cars—three hardtop models and two convertible models—appear consecutively in a parade. Each car is either a Ford or a Chevy, and each car is either gray, red, or white. Each car is one color only, and each of the three colors is represented at least once among the five cars.

The first and fifth cars to appear are both hardtops.

No Ford is white.

Only one of the hardtops is a Chevy.

7. Which of the following could appear in the parade?

   (A) two white hardtops
   (B) three Ford convertibles
   (C) three gray Chevys
   (D) two Chevy hardtops
   (E) three white Chevys

8. If exactly three of the cars are Chevys, which of the following must be true?

   (A) A convertible immediately follows another convertible.
   (B) A hardtop immediately follows another hardtop.
   (C) A Ford immediately follows another Ford.
   (D) A Chevy immediately follows another Chevy.
   (E) A white car immediately follows another white car.

9. If both convertibles are gray, which of the following must be false?

   (A) All Fords are hardtops.
   (B) All Fords are gray.
   (C) All Chevys are white.
   (D) All gray cars are convertibles.
   (E) All red cars are hardtops.

10. If the first three cars are white, all of the following must be true EXCEPT:

   (A) The first car is a Chevy.
   (B) The fourth car is a Ford.
   (C) The second car is a convertible.
   (D) The fourth car is a hardtop.
   (E) The fourth car is gray.

11. If all Ford hardtops appear consecutively in the parade, which of the following must be true?

   (A) The first car is a Ford.
   (B) The second car is a hardtop.
   (C) The third car is a convertible.
   (D) The fourth car is a Chevy.
   (E) The fifth car is a Ford.

QUESTIONS 12–16:

Bob has assembled a basket of fruit as a holiday gift for each of his four friends—Susan, Todd, Ursula, and Vadim. A total of fifteen pieces of fruit—five guavas, five mangoes, and five kiwis—are distributed among the four baskets according to the following conditions:

Susan, Todd, and Ursula will each receive exactly two different types of fruit.

Vadim will receive only guavas.

Todd will receive more pieces of fruit than Susan.

Each basket includes at least three pieces of fruit.

12. Which of the following sequence of numbers, representing the number of fruit pieces that Susan, Todd, Ursula, and Vadim receive, respectively, is possible?

   (A) 3, 6, 3, 3
   (B) 3, 3, 5, 4
   (C) 4, 5, 4, 3
   (D) 3, 3, 3, 6
   (E) 3, 4, 3, 4

13. Which of the following statements could be true?

   (A) Todd will receive exactly three pieces of fruit.
   (B) Todd will receive exactly six pieces of fruit.
   (C) Susan will receive exactly five pieces of fruit.
   (D) Vadim will receive exactly six pieces of fruit.
   (E) Ursula will receive exactly six pieces of fruit.

14. If Ursula's basket contains more pieces of fruit than Todd's basket, all of the following must be false EXCEPT:

   (A) Only Vadim will receive guavas.
   (B) Vadim will receive exactly four guavas.
   (C) Todd will receive exactly four kiwis.
   (D) Susan will receive exactly three mangoes.
   (E) Ursula will receive exactly two guavas.

15. If Susan's basket contains two guavas and two kiwis, but no other pieces of fruit, which of the following is the number of possible fruit combinations in Todd's basket?

   (A) one
   (B) two
   (C) three
   (D) four
   (E) five

16. If Vadim's basket contains exactly three pieces of fruit, and if Susan's and Ursula's baskets contain identical fruit assortments, which of the following could be true?

   (A) Todd will receive exactly two guavas.
   (B) Susan will receive exactly one kiwi.
   (C) Todd will receive exactly four kiwis.
   (D) Ursula will receive exactly two mangoes.
   (E) Todd will receive exactly three mangoes.

ANSWER KEY AND EXPLANATIONS

1. E	5. D	8. D	11. C	14. E
2. B	6. B	9. B	12. A	15. B
3. E	7. E	10. E	13. B	16. D
4. A				

Questions 1–6: Dual Attribute Game (Challenging)

This game can be troublesome unless you recognize that additional key facts can be deduced from the rules. Because three workers stack in the afternoon, North must stack; otherwise, either Jackson and Klein would both stack or Lawry and Manning would both stack, resulting in a violation either of the rule that Jackson does not perform either of the two tasks that Klein performs or of the rule that Lawry does not perform either of the two tasks that Manning performs. Accordingly, either Jackson or Klein (but not both) must stack, and either Lawry or Manning (but not both) must stack. As a result, during the afternoon, only one worker may glue (otherwise, no workers would load, which would violate one of the rules), and, in the morning, two workers must glue. One of the two workers who glue in the morning must be North, since the rules specify that North glues, and since we have determined that North must stack in the afternoon. Based upon this additional information, we can construct the following diagram:

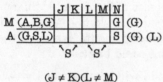

$$(J \neq K)(L \neq M)$$
*each worker does
2 <u>different</u> tasks

Given that each worker must perform two different tasks, that Jackson cannot perform either of the two tasks that Klein performs, and that Lawry cannot perform either of the two tasks that Manning performs, it is helpful to consider Jackson's and Klein's four tasks as a unit, bearing in mind that each task in that unit must be different (and the same for Lawry and Manning).

1. **The correct answer is (E).** As noted in the general comments above, N must glue in the morning and stack in the afternoon. Accordingly, N cannot box.

2. **The correct answer is (B).** As noted in the general comments above, either J or K must stack in the afternoon. Thus, if J loads (in the afternoon), K must stack (in the afternoon).

3. **The correct answer is (E).** Either L or M must stack; thus, if L loads, then M must stack. At least one of the workers must glue in the afternoon; thus, that worker must be either J or K (while the other stacks). Because J and K (in either order) glue and stack in the afternoon, J and K must (in either order) assemble and box in the morning; otherwise, either one would perform the same task in the morning and afternoon or both would perform the same task. As a result, either L or M must glue, while the other

either assembles or boxes. Thus, the only statement among the answer choices that must be true is choice (E).

4. **The correct answer is (A).** Among J, L, and M, two workers must box in the morning. Thus, either L or M must glue in the morning (otherwise, L and M would both box), and J must box in the morning. Since either L or M must glue in the morning, neither can glue in the afternoon, and so L and M (in either order) must stack and load in the afternoon. Finally, J and K (in either order) must glue and stack in the afternoon. Since M may either box or glue in the morning, choice (A) could be true.

5. **The correct answer is (D).** N must glue in the morning and stack in the afternoon. Thus, K must also glue in the morning and stack in the afternoon. Since J and K do not perform the same tasks, J must load in the afternoon and either assemble or box in the morning. As a result, L and M must (in either order) glue and stack in the afternoon and (in either order) assemble and box in the morning. Thus, of the five answer choices, only choice (D) could be false.

6. **The correct answer is (B).** Given that J and M perform the same afternoon task, that task must be stacking (see diagram and general comments above), while K and L perform the remaining two afternoon tasks—gluing and loading. Given that J and M both assemble (in the morning), K and L must perform the remaining two morning tasks—boxing and gluing. The same worker cannot glue both in the morning and afternoon, however. Thus, only two possibilities remain: K boxes and glues while L glues and loads, or vice versa.

Questions 7–11: Complex Attribute Game (Moderate)

In this game, each car includes three attributes: top, make, and color. Two conditional rules (the last two rules) and a sequencing feature add to the game's complexity. In order to work through this game efficiently, it is best to construct a diagram in which attributes are matched in roster form without regard to sequence:

```
            (1) (5)
            | H | H | H | C | C |
(Ch, F)     |Ch | F | F |   |   |  Ch
(w,g,r)     |   |g/r|g/r|   |   |  ↑
                                  w
```

The conditional rule that "Only one of the hard-tops is a Chevy" has been incorporated into the diagram. The conditional rule that "No Ford is white" has been restated as "All white cars must be Chevys" and expressed symbolically near the diagram.

7. **The correct answer is (E).** Two of the three hardtops must be Fords since only one of the hardtops is a Chevy. Fords cannot be white. Thus, no more than one hardtop (the Chevy) can be white, and choice (A) must be false. Choice (B) violates the statement in the premise that there are two convertibles (not three). Choice (C) is not possible. If three of the cars were gray Chevys, both remaining cars would be Fords; however, no Ford can be white, and so there could be no white car in the parade. This result would violate the statement in the premise that each color must be represented at least once. Choice (D) violates the rule that only one of the hardtops is a Chevy. Choice (E) is possible. One of the two Fords could be red, and the other could be gray.

8. **The correct answer is (D).** The two convertibles must both be Chevys. In order to disprove the statement in choice (D), the three Chevys would have to be first, third, and fifth. If so, hardtops could not appear both first and fifth. This result would violate one of the rules, and so choice (D) must be true.

9. **The correct answer is (B).** Either of the two convertibles could be a Chevy or a Ford. The Chevy hardtop must be white, since each color must be represented at least once. The roster in the diagram above can be filled in as follows:

H	H	H	C	C
Ch	F	F	?	?
w	g/r	g/r	g	g

Either convertible could be a Ford; thus, choice (A) could be true. At least one of the five cars must be red, and that car must be one of the two Fords; thus, choice (B) must be false. Both convertibles could be Fords; thus, choice (C) could be true. The second and third cars could both be red; thus, choice (D) could be true. Only cars 2 and 3 can be red, and these two cars are both hardtops; thus, choice (E) must be true.

10. **The correct answer is (E).** If a car is white, it must be a Chevy; thus, the first three cars are all white Chevys. The fourth and fifth cars must be the two Ford hardtops. The first car must be the Chevy hardtop, and the second and third cars must be Chevy convertibles:

(1) (5)   4   2   3

H	H	H	C	C
Ch	F	F	Ch	Ch
w	g/r	g/r	w	w

Statement (E) is not necessarily true; the fourth car could either be gray or red.

11. **The correct answer is (C).** The two Ford hardtops must appear either first and second or fourth and fifth; otherwise, the first and fifth cars could not both be hardtops. If the two Ford hardtops appear first and second, then the Chevy hardtop must appear fifth. On the other hand, if the two Ford hardtops appear fourth and fifth, then the Chevy hardtop must appear first. Two alternative sequences result:

```
1 2 3 4 5
H H C C H
F F ? ? Ch


H C C H H
Ch ? ? F F
```

In either sequence, the third car must be a convertible; thus, statement (C) must be true.

Questions 12–16: Complex Grouping Game (Moderate)

The key to working through this grouping game efficiently is to establish at the outset the minimum and maximum number of pieces of fruit that each person may receive. Susan, Ursula, and Vadim must each receive at least three pieces, but Todd must receive at least four pieces (because Todd must receive more pieces than Susan). The maximum number of pieces that any person may receive is six (6 + 3 + 3 + 3 = 15), and only Todd may receive six pieces.

(If any other person received six pieces, the total number of pieces would exceed fifteen because Todd must receive at least four pieces.) Ursula and Vadim may each receive as many as five pieces, while Susan may receive only four pieces at maximum. (If Susan received five pieces, Todd would have to receive six, and the total number would exceed fifteen.) We can construct the following initial diagram:

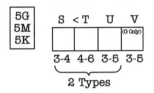

Having established these parameters, questions 12 and 13 are particularly straightforward. Question 16, on the other hand, is especially difficult, requiring a bit more insight than the others.

12. **The correct answer is (A).** Todd must receive more pieces that Susan, and the total number must be fifteen. Choice (A) conforms to these conditions. Choices (B) and (D) are not possible because Susan and Todd would receive the same number of pieces; choice (D) is not possible also because Vadim would receive six pieces, but there are only five guavas available, and the rules stipulate the Vadim receives only guavas. Choice (C) provides for a total of 16 pieces, while choice (E) provides for a total of only 14 pieces.

13. **The correct answer is (B).** As noted in the comments above, Todd can receive six pieces while the other three each receive three pieces. All four other statements, however, must be false, as the comments above make clear.

14. **The correct answer is (E).** Ursula may receive no more than five pieces, and Todd may receive no fewer than four pieces (see general comments above). As a result, if Ursula receives more pieces than Todd, then Ursula must receive five pieces, and Todd must receive four pieces.

   Accordingly, Susan and Vadim must each receive three pieces. The statements in choices (A) and (B) must be false—Vadim will receive three pieces (all guavas), two guavas remaining for the other three friends. Choices (C) and (D) must be false because each friend (including Todd) must receive at least two different types of fruit. Only choice (E) is possible.

15. **The correct answer is (B).** If Susan receives four pieces, then Todd must receive exactly five pieces while Vadim and Ursula both receive exactly three pieces (see general comments above). Given that Susan receives two guavas and two kiwis, three kiwis and five mangoes remain to be allocated between Todd and Ursula. A bit of experimenting reveals that only two allocation schemes are possible—either Todd receives one kiwi and four mangoes while Ursula receives two kiwis and one mango, or Todd receives two kiwis and three mangoes while Ursula receives one kiwi and two mangoes.

16. **The correct answer is (D).** Susan and Ursula must each receive exactly three pieces, and Todd must accordingly receive exactly six pieces (see general comments above). Vadim receives three of the five guavas. The remaining two guavas must be allocated

one each to Susan and Ursula. Why? The only other choice would be to allocate the two remaining guavas to Todd because Susan and Ursula must receive identical assortments. If this were the case, Todd would also have to receive four pieces of one other type of fruit, either four mangoes or four kiwis (each basket must contain exactly two different types of fruit). In this event, however, Susan and Ursula could not receive identical assortments (for example, if Todd were to receive four mangoes, either Susan or Ursula would receive the last mango). Thus, the two remaining guavas must be allocated one each to Susan and Ursula. Thus, Susan and Ursula must each receive (in addition to one guava) either two mangoes or two kiwis, while Todd receives either one mango and five kiwis or one kiwi and five mangoes.

Planning Your Writing Sample Essay

In this lesson, you will familiarize yourself with the LSAT Writing Sample. You will also learn how to take notes, organize the information presented, and formulate persuasive arguments for your essay response.

THE WRITING SAMPLE AT A GLANCE

Total number of questions: 1

Total number of test sections: 1 (not scored)

Testing time allowed: 35 minutes

The Writing Sample section appears last on the LSAT.

- Two criteria are presented
- Two alternatives are described
- Test-taker argues in favor of one alternative over the other

Ground Rules

- No scratch paper is permitted (you may make notes in the test booklet)
- Pens are provided
- There is no "correct" response

What Does the Writing Sample Test?

This Writing Sample section tests your ability to:

- argue persuasively and cogently
- present your thoughts in an organized, coherent fashion
- use the English language effectively and follow the conventions of Standard Written English

ANATOMY OF A WRITING SAMPLE TOPIC

In the Writing Sample section of the LSAT, you will be asked to decide between two alternatives and defend your choice based on two objectives or goals. Take a look at the sample topic on the next page. Notice that the topic includes three components:

1 A premise, which establishes a scenario

2 Two "bulleted" criteria or goals

3 Descriptions of two alternatives or choices

The sample topic below is typical; all LSAT Writing Sample topics include these three components. Also keep in mind the following about the Writing Sample format:

- There is no right or wrong choice. Each of the two stated choices will have its merits (strengths) and problems (weaknesses). It is not important to the exam reader which alternative you choose; what is important is how effectively you defend your choice.

- The two choices tend to polarize toward different goals. Invariably, one choice will be stronger in achieving one stated goal, while the other choice will be stronger in achieving the other goal. This feature is quite intentional and is really the heart of the Writing Sample. It's easy enough to argue for either choice based upon the more favorable of the two goals, but it's more challenging to defend your choice in light of the other, less favorable, goal.

- Exactly two alternatives and exactly two criteria are presented.

Writing Sample Topic:

"Cutters," a contemporary hair-care studio for men and women owned and operated by Jim and Joan Baxter, has been operating from the same downtown location for several years. However, the Baxters must move their studio when their lease terminates next month. They are considering two possible locations. Write an argument for one of the two following choices. Two considerations should influence your decision:

1 The Baxters wish to minimize the time and expense involved in starting up business in a new location.

2 The Baxters seek maximum potential for business growth and for return on their financial investment.

The Baxters are considering a location on Frye Street where a contemporary-style men's hair salon has recently failed. The Frye Street storefront is only a few blocks away from the Baxters' present location. Although the space would be just large enough to support the Baxters' current operation, they could expand to an adjacent retail space in the same building. While the Baxters' present location is on a busy thoroughfare, Frye Street is a quiet side-street lined with quaint older houses and a few neighborhood stores. Most Frye Street residents are either senior citizens or young couples in their twenties.

The Baxters are also considering a location in the new Fashion Place suburban mall, located about 3 miles from their present location. The space, which is positioned next to one of the mall's department stores, is large enough for the Baxters' current as well as potential future needs. The monthly rent is approximately twice that of the Frye Street location. Although parking at the mall is ample, no public transportation is available between the mall and the downtown area.

TESTING PROCEDURES AND MATERIALS

After all five multiple-choice sections of the LSAT have been administered, the exam proctor will collect test materials for those sections, then distribute the following materials for the Writing Sample section:

- A sealed two-page test booklet

- A sheet of light-colored scratch paper

- A black ball-point pen

The essay topic and space for your response are both included on two pages in the sealed test booklet. Attached to the back of the booklet is a yellow sheet on which a carbonless copy of your response is recorded. At the conclusion of the 35-minute Writing Sample section, the proctor will collect your original response but not the carbonless copy. You will tear off the carbonless copy to take home with you. The LSDAS will send photocopies of your response to each law school to which you direct your LSAT score.

The space available for your essay response will be about two pages long. Why isn't more space provided? Because among other abilities, you are being tested on your ability to consolidate information and to write in a concise, to-the-point manner. Besides, admission committee members at the law schools would rather read short essays than long ones. (This doesn't necessarily mean, however, that a shorter response is preferable to a longer one—more about that in the next lesson.)

The exam proctor will provide each test taker with a sheet of colored scratch paper. The use of distinctively colored paper guards a test taker trying to bring into the testing room a "cheat sheet" to use during the Writing Sample section. The proctor collects all scratch paper at the conclusion of the Writing Sample section.

No writing implements other than the black ballpoint pen provided by the proctor will be permitted during the Writing Sample section. Using a medium-tip black ballpoint pen helps to ensure legibility of photocopies and eliminates any possible advantage that might be gained through choice of writing implement. The use of liquid paper is permitted.

HOW THE WRITING SAMPLE IS EVALUATED

What Skills Are Being Tested?

The LSAT Writing Sample is designed to test your ability to support a position and express that position in writing. More specifically, the law schools are interested in:

- your ability to make persuasive and well-reasoned arguments in favor of one position and against another

- your ability to organize your thoughts under pressure of time and to express them in an organized manner

- your command of the language and of the conventions of Standard Written English (vocabulary, usage, grammar, syntax, and so forth)

You are not being tested on your knowledge of the law or of any other academic subject. Do NOT write on a topic other than the one specified.

The Evaluation Process

The testing service will not score your Writing Sample; instead, it will simply send a photocopy of your essay to the law schools to which you direct your LSAT score. Each law school determines its own evaluation guidelines and procedures, as discussed below.

Q **Is every applicant's LSAT essay read at the law school?**

A No. Law schools typically reject applicants out of hand who fail to meet some specified minimum GPA/LSAT composite score. In these cases, the law school does not read LSAT Writing Samples. In all other cases, each essay will be read by at least one person at the law school.

Q **Who reads LSAT essays and how carefully are LSAT essays scrutinized?**

A One or more members of the school's admission committee, consisting mainly of faculty members, may read your essay. If your acceptance at a particular school is highly probable based on your LSAT score and GPA, the essay will not affect your chances of admission unless you write something extremely inflammatory or careless in your essay. However, the closer you are to being a borderline candidate, the more closely your essay will be scrutinized. For such candidates, the essay may be read by more readers, and it may influence the ultimate admission decision.

Q **Are LSAT essays "scored" or "graded"?**

A The reader might make brief written comments about your essay and may annotate it by circling or underlining errors in spelling, usage, grammar, or mechanics. He or she will then score your essay according to the guidelines determined by the school. Some form of numerical scoring system is used by nearly all schools. By quantifying Writing Sample evaluations, the school can streamline the evaluation process. At some schools, essays are scored separately for content, organization, and mechanics; then a composite or total score is computed. Other schools employ a more holistic approach, assigning a single score to each essay from the outset.

A Model Scorecard for Self-Evaluation

The sample below provides a scoring system to illustrate how a law school might evaluate your essay on a scale of 1 to 5 (5 being best and 1 being worst). A score of 4 or 5 would help your chances of admission, a score of 3 would not work significantly for you or against you, and a score of 1 or 2 would probably hurt your chances of admission. Although each school has its own method of scoring essays, you can use this scorecard to evaluate the essays that you write in response to the topics in the Lesson 14 mini-test and in Practice Test 6. Keep in mind that this scorecard is *only* a model and that each law school develops its own method and criteria to evaluate essays.

5 (outstanding)

An outstanding essay includes well-reasoned and highly persuasive arguments and demonstrates a mastery of the English language and of the elements of effective writing. Specifically, an outstanding essay:

- expressly relates the two choices directly to the two stated criteria

- discusses the merits and weaknesses of both choices vis-à-vis both stated criteria

- incorporates into the analysis all key characteristics of each choice

- acknowledges and effectively rebuts possible opposing viewpoints

- confines the discussion to the stated criteria and choices

- is organized in a manner that clearly conveys the meaning and facilitates the persuasiveness of the arguments

- demonstrates superior facility with English grammar, syntax, and writing mechanics

- demonstrates superior control of the English language in spelling, usage, and diction

4 (strong)

A strong essay provides reasonably persuasive arguments in favor of one choice over the other in a well-organized essay that demonstrates a strong command of the language and the elements of writing. Specifically, a strong essay:

- expressly evaluates important features of both choices in terms of the two stated criteria

- acknowledges and rebuts possible opposing viewpoints

- confines the discussion to the stated criteria and choices

- is clearly organized

- demonstrates good facility with English grammar, syntax, and writing mechanics

- demonstrates good control of the English language in spelling, usage, and diction

- may omit to include key characteristics of one or both choices

- may fail to include a clear introductory or concluding statement

- may include occasional minor flaws in spelling, language use, or grammar

3 (adequate)

An adequate essay demonstrates basic competence in organizing and presenting relevant facts and in formulating reasonably effective arguments. Specifically, an adequate essay:

- weighs the relative merits of each choice by presenting relevant facts

- demonstrates some facility at formulating a cogent argument in favor of one choice over the other

- demonstrates an adequate ability to present an argument within a preconceived organizational format

- indicates adequate control of the language and the conventions of Standard Written English

- may ignore important features of one or both choices

- may fail to relate features of the two choices directly to the stated criteria

- may rely on reiteration of facts and circular arguments

- may include problems in spelling, usage, diction, or other mechanical aspects of writing, although such problems do not interfere significantly with the meaning

2 (limited)

A limited essay indicates a basic facility for organizing and presenting facts in support of a choice and demonstrates a basic facility in the use of the English language and the elements of effective writing. Specifically, a limited essay:

- presents relevant facts in support of at least one of the two choices

- demonstrates some ability to organize and present thoughts coherently and meaningfully

- demonstrates basic competence in the use of language and the conventions of Standard Written English

- may lack reasonably persuasive arguments in favor of one choice over another

- may fail to adequately address one of the two choices or one of the two criteria

- may fail to relate relevant facts to either criterion

- may depart from the stated criteria and discuss irrelevant issues or considerations

- may lack organizational coherence, suggesting inadequate forethought and planning

- may include mechanical errors and problems that interfere somewhat with the meaning

1 (seriously flawed)

A seriously flawed essay indicates significant deficiencies in formulating coherent arguments, organizing thoughts, or communicating using Standard Written English. It might also suggest an inability or unwillingness to follow directions. Specifically, a seriously flawed essay:

- fails to adequately communicate a coherent argument in support of either choice
- fails to demonstrate original thought, insight, or ability to argue persuasively
- may merely repeat or restate certain facts without any attempt to analyze or evaluate
- may deviate from the stated criteria and/or the stated choices
- may lack organizational structure
- may include significant spelling, grammatical, and syntactical problems that significantly distract the reader and obscure the test taker's intended meaning

TAKING NOTES AND ORGANIZING YOUR THOUGHTS

When you're working on the LSAT essay, resist the temptation to start writing your response immediately after you read the topic. Instead, take perhaps 6 to 8 minutes to formulate and organize your arguments using the strategies discussed below.

List the Key Features of Each Choice

Use the scratch paper provided to jot down the characteristics of each choice that relate to one or both goals. Try to cover all key features, but don't be too concerned if you omit a few details. A lot of facts are packed into the Writing Sample topic, and you are not expected to address every detail in your response.

Evaluate the Facts as You Take Notes

As you jot down a key characteristic, evaluate it in terms of one or both goals. Ask yourself:

- Is this characteristic a strength or a weakness in terms of the objectives? Why?
- Jot down a few words that express your idea. Then ask yourself:
- If I were to choose the other alternative, how would I respond to this strength (or weakness)?

	FRYE	MALL

Moving Time/Expense	+ hair studio set up already
	  − but renovate (men only)?
	+ rent $1/2$ mall rent
	  − expand next door adds $
	+ keep current customers
	  ? 3 blocks vs. 3 miles
		− install new fixtures
		+ will last long time
		+ Frye needs renovation
		− high rent (may not
		  survive short term)

Growth/Profit Potential	− failed business
	  ? low visibility
	  ? mismanaged
	+ expand next door
	  − may be occupied
	  − expensive
		+ dept. store (high traffic)
		  ? will mall succeed?
		  − high rent offsets
		− more competition
		  in suburbs
		+ larger customer base
		+ large space for growth

If an idea occurs to you, quickly jot down a few words that express that idea. By listing and evaluating key features, you are essentially formulating the points of your argument. To help you formulate effective arguments for your essay, a bit later we'll discuss various methods of argumentation.

Consolidate Related Facts

During the exam, you are severely limited in time and space (on paper) to express your arguments. Try to combine or consolidate features that make essentially the same point. Try to limit yourself to three or four points for each choice. This will allow you to achieve breadth of coverage within the time and space restrictions. In fact, the testing service is gauging your ability to achieve exactly that.

Consider Organizing Notes into "Quadrants"

If you think about it, there are really four distinct issues built into every Writing Sample topic:

1. The extent to which the first alternative achieves the first goal

2. The extent to which the first alternative achieves the second goal

3. The extent to which the second alternative achieves the first goal

4. The extent to which the second alternative achieves the second goal

Consider dividing your notes into four quadrants, one for each of these four issues. Admittedly, the quadrant approach is not perfect; it does not accommodate the fact that some characteristics will relate to both goals. Nevertheless, it can be a useful way to organize your thoughts. Try this method as you take the mini-test for the Writing Sample (see Lesson 14). The sample notes above use the quadrant approach for the topic provided at the beginning of this lesson. In the chart, a plus sign (+) indicates a strength and a minus sign (−) indicates a weakness.

FORMULATING PERSUASIVE ARGUMENTS

Law schools will evaluate your essay for 1) content, 2) organization, and 3) writing mechanics (spelling, grammar, and so forth). This lesson will focus solely on the first area; the other two areas are the subjects of Lesson 13.

Discuss Both Alternatives and Both Goals

A highly effective argument does not ignore an opposing position or an important objective. Even if cogent and well written, an LSAT essay that discusses only the "winner" or only one of the two goals will not work strongly for you in the admission process.

Acknowledge and Rebut Weaknesses of Your Choice and Strengths of the Other Choice

Your LSAT essay should do more than merely assert a position and reiterate some facts that tend to support that position. An effective participant in a debate will not ignore the weaknesses of his or her position or the merits of the opponent's position. Instead, the participant will acknowledge those weaknesses and merits, then rebut them in creative, well-reasoned, and convincing manner.

Applying this principle to the LSAT essay is easier said than done, of course. Persuasive argumentation, or rhetoric, is a bit of an art form. Some people have a natural talent in this area; others need to work at developing their rhetorical skills. If you fall into the latter category, the techniques discussed below will help you formulate effective arguments for your LSAT essay.

Engage in Reasonable Conjecture

As you evaluate the facts, you must venture beyond them to speculate about how those facts might or might not achieve the stated goals. You need to become comfortable with departing from the facts. Reasonable conjecture is essential to an effective argument. In the Writing Sample topic on page 156, for example, the following points would constitute reasonable speculation that would persuade the reader:

- The prior business at the Frye Street location may have failed due to factors other than lack of traffic.

- Current fixtures at the Frye Street location might not meet the Baxters' needs.

- The Baxters' current customers may be willing to drive to the mall.

- The mall location provides no assurance in itself of success.

Confine Your Arguments to the Stated Goals and Scenario at Hand

A brilliant idea should nevertheless be excluded from your essay if it departs somewhat from the topic or stated goals. Referring to the topic at the beginning of this lesson, the following ideas are probably too tangential and should be omitted:

- There is a trend toward urban redevelopment, which may help the Baxters' downtown salon in the future.

- There are other intangible benefits of a quaint, older urban location.

- It wouldn't be fair to the Baxters' longtime faithful clients to move out to the mall.

- The mall location would be more convenient for the Baxters' personal shopping needs.

- The Baxters should also consider the proximity of their salon to their suppliers.

Use Rhetorical Devices for Persuasive Arguments

With luck, ideas will occur to you naturally as you take notes for your essay response, without your consciously considering particular rhetorical techniques. If you do get stuck for ideas, however, draw upon the following five techniques to get your rhetorical juices flowing.

1 **Subordinate one goal to the other.** Argue that, while your choice is somewhat weak in terms of one of the two goals, that goal is not as important as the other goal.

Example:

The Baxters' primary concern should be with long-term investment return, as additional startup costs will prove insignificant over time.

2 **Explain it away.** Argue that an apparent weakness (strength) relies on contingencies that are unlikely or on factors that don't apply.

Example:

Although the prior salon failure on Frye Street might suggest poor growth potential, that failure may have been due to other factors, such as mismanagement or a narrow male-only client base.

3 **Turn it around.** Argue that an apparent weakness (strength) is actually just the opposite if one looks at it from a different perspective.

Example:

The mall space's high-traffic location might seem to provide more long-term profit potential. However, the Baxters may face greater competition in the suburbs from franchise salons.

4 **Trivialize it.** Argue that a particular weakness (strength), while real, is minor, trivial, or insignificant in comparison to another strength (weakness).

Example:

Although the Frye location's low rent would appear to help the Baxters to meet their objectives, any expansion at Frye would come at greater expense, thereby undermining long-term profit goals.

5 **Attack the opposing position.** Argue that the alternative choice is no stronger, or perhaps even weaker, in achieving a particular goal.

Example:

While the initial expense to equip the new space at the mall might be substantial, renovations at Frye Street needed to convert that space from a men-only salon may be just as costly and time-consuming.

Formatting and Writing Your Writing Sample Essay

In this lesson, you will learn how to structure your essay, how to find an effective style and "voice" for it, and how to avoid common mechanical errors.

PIECING TOGETHER YOUR ARGUMENT

How you organize (or fail to organize) your LSAT essay is just as critical as (and arguably more critical than) the essay's content. Your brilliant arguments may be rendered pointless and ineffective if your ideas wander aimlessly and the reader cannot follow your train of thought. A clear organizational structure suggests to the reader clear thinking, and therefore sound reasoning.

A well-organized essay can have one of two basic formats. Both formats include a brief introduction and conclusion (more on that later). In reviewing both formats, keep in mind that the primary goal is the goal toward which the "winner" polarizes, while the secondary goal is the goal toward which the "loser" polarizes.

Format A (Choice-Driven)

First paragraph:

- one-sentence introduction
- how the "winner" achieves the primary goal
- how the "winner" also achieves the secondary goal

Second paragraph:

- how the "loser" fails to achieve the secondary goal
- how the "loser" fails to achieve the primary goal

Third paragraph:

- one- or two-sentence conclusion

Format B (Goal-Driven)

First paragraph:

- one-sentence introduction
- how the "winner" achieves the primary goal
- how the "loser" fails to achieve the primary goal

Second paragraph:

- how the "winner" achieves the secondary goal
- how the "loser" fails to achieve the secondary goal

Third paragraph:

- (one- or two-sentence conclusion)

Make sure that your essay conforms to one of these two formats. Do not stray from your chosen format, and do not combine the two formats.

FINDING AN APPROPRIATE AND EFFECTIVE WRITING STYLE

The overall style of the LSAT essay should be relatively formal. Don't try to be conversational, informal, or "cutesy." The tone of your essay should be critical, but not inflammatory or emotional. Do not try to overstate your position by using extreme or harsh language. Do not attempt to elicit a visceral or emotional response from the reader. Appeal instead to the reader's intellect. Follow the guidelines below.

Avoid Gimmicky and Inappropriate Writing Techniques

Do not attempt to grab the reader's attention by using gimmicky devices. In general, it is best to avoid the following techniques:

- Dialogue
- Rhetorical questions
- Slang and colloquial expressions
- Quotations
- Puns or any other form of humor

Don't Try Too Hard to Impress with Your Vocabulary

While your writing style should be somewhat formal, do not try to impress the reader with an erudite vocabulary or with your knowledge of legal terminology. Using obscure, intimidating words or "legalese" may only serve to warn the reader that you are attempting to compensate for a lack of substance. There's nothing wrong with demonstrating in your LSAT essay a broad and educated vocabulary; just don't overdo it.

Develop an "Inventory" of Useful Phrases to Help Your Argument Flow

For many test takers, the most difficult aspect of the LSAT essay is not formulating persuasive ideas but rather finding the best words and phrases to express those ideas. Here is a list of transitional clauses, buzz-words, and rhetorical phrases that you will find useful in piecing together the components of your argument. They can add sophistication and style to your essay and help your ideas to flow.

Use these phrases to acknowledge your choice's weaknesses (or the other choice's merits):

Although it might appear that . . .   Admittedly, . . .

Although it would seem that . . .   The chief strength of _____ lies in

At first glance, it would seem/appear   its . . .
    that . . .

Use these phrases to respond to an apparent weakness (of your choice) or strengths (of the other choice):

However, . . .   In reality, . . .

Further examination reveals . . .   Actually . . .

Upon further inspection, . . .   When viewed more closely, . . .

Closer inspection/scrutiny reveals . . .   When viewed from another

Further consideration discloses . . .   perspective, . . .

A more thorough analysis . . .   Further observation shows . . .

Use these words to point out weaknesses of the other choice:

critical/significant/crucial problems   problematic

serious drawbacks   countervailing factors

Use these transition words to connect the components of your argument together:

furthermore   first, . . . second, . . .

additionally   moreover

in addition   most important/significantly

also   finally

Use these words to argue for your choice in terms of one of the goals:

promotes   accomplishes

facilitates   attains

provides a strong impetus   achieves

serves to   demonstrates

directly   suggests

furthers   indicates

Use these words to argue against the other choice in terms of one of the goals:

works against   runs contrary to

undermines   fails to achieve/promote/accomplish

thwarts   is inconsistent with

defeats   would impede

Use these words to subordinate one goal to the other:

ultimate goal/objective/purpose	subordinate
overriding	subsumed
primary concern	

Use these phrases for your concluding remarks:

In sum	. . . interests (objectives/purposes) would
In the final analysis	be better (more effectively) served (promoted)

Vary Sentence Length

You are no doubt aware that you can add interest and sophistication to your writing by varying sentence length and structure. Also consider, however, that short sentences are most effective to begin and end a train of thought (usually defined by paragraph breaks), especially if your goal is to persuade the reader. Try this technique in your LSAT essay to add some punch and sophistication.

Avoid Restating the Facts

Many test takers devote entire sentences and paragraphs to restating, paraphrasing, or reiterating facts. This is a waste of valuable time and space, and it suggests that the test taker has few ideas of his or her own to convey. Remember that the reader already knows the facts. While there's no way to avoid referring to the facts as you make your arguments, get right to the point—preferably in the same sentence.

Be Concise

Strive to write concisely and avoid superfluous words. Here are some commonly used LSAT essay phrases and their more concise counterparts (in parentheses):

In the event that . . . (If . . .)

Despite the fact that . . . (Although . . .)

. . . in achieving the goal of . . . (. . . to achieve . . .)

An additional consideration is that . . . (Also, . . .)

There are several factors that . . . (Several factors . . .)

Self-references are also superfluous. The reader knows that you are expressing your own opinions and thoughts in your essay. There's no need to remind the reader of this with phrases such as:

It is my opinion that . . .	If I were to choose between . . .
I believe that . . .	

Also, avoid meaningless rhetorical phrases. Although your objective is to persuade the reader, you are wasting valuable time and space with courtroom clichés such as:

Without a doubt, . . .	No reasonable person would disagree
It is clear that . . .	that . . .
	The evidence overwhelmingly . . .

Refer to the Two Choices as Briefly as Possible

It is perfectly acceptable to refer to the two choices throughout your essay in some shorthand fashion. In the Writing Sample topic in Lesson 12, for example, you might simply refer to the Frye Street location as "Frye," while referring to the Fashion Place Mall location as "the mall." There is no need to underline or set off the choices in quotes (unless your task is to choose between two books, plays, or movies).

INTRODUCTIONS

Effective introductory and concluding statements indicate strong organizational skills and help the reader to follow your train of thought. Forget what you've learned about writing introductions for theses, reports, and other papers for college. Those rules don't apply here. You're dealing here with a severely limited writing space and only 30 minutes. A simple, one-sentence introduction that indicates which is the better choice will suffice.

Example:

> The mall location would better meet the Baxters' objectives.

CONCLUDING REMARKS

Be sure to reserve enough time and space for a brief concluding remark that simply sums up or recapitulates the thrust of your argument. Keep it brief: just one or two sentences. Reiterate the main reasons why your choice is the better one.

Example:

> In sum, Frye is the better location; it would allow for a fast and inexpensive start-up and an uninterrupted flow of business, in turn ensuring both short-term survival and long-term success.

TIPS ABOUT PHYSICAL PRESENTATION

Your Handwriting Style

Put yourself in the position of the reader, who may be reading one hundred LSAT essays over one weekend during admission season. Yours may be the last essay he or she reads. Do the reader a favor and make sure that every word you write is legible. He or she will not take the time to try to interpret chicken scratches. Your handwriting doesn't have to be pretty, just legible. Hand-printing (instead of writing) is acceptable. Avoid using inordinately small or cramped writing just to pack more words into the space provided. Also avoid inordinately large handwriting; otherwise, you may run out of space before you run out of time and ideas.

Scratching Out Words and Phrases ("Strike-throughs")

If you want to delete or alter a few words here and there, cross them out. The reader will not look unfavorably upon the occasional strike-through. However, avoid frequent strike-throughs, especially if they involve long phrases or entire sentences. Otherwise, you will quickly run out of writing space and you will leave the reader with the impression that you have trouble organizing your thoughts before writing. If you need to delete lengthy phrases, consider using correction fluid (see below).

Using Correction Fluid

The use of correction fluid is permitted, but should you use it? For striking the occasional word or short phrase, using correction fluid is probably not worth your time. However, to strike entire sentences or multiple sentences, consider using it, especially if you need the writing space. Remember that the law schools receive a photocopy of your essay, so they can't scratch away your correction fluid to read what you deleted. The reader might detect the use of correction fluid in spots where you've whited out the horizontal guide lines or where your handwriting is a bit rough. However, as long as your writing remains clear and legible, the use of correction fluid will not negatively affect the reader's evaluation.

Writing in the Margins

Photocopies sent to the law schools will include only the writing space itself, not the margins around the perimeter of the writing space. Accordingly, don't use the margins to insert material into your essay; the reader will not even see that material.

Paragraph Breaks and Skipping Lines

By all means, use paragraph breaks to indicate organization and structure. If you use too many, however, you might sacrifice valuable writing space. Consider using two paragraph breaks: one between the two main paragraphs, and one before your conclusion. There is no need to set off your one-sentence introduction as a separate paragraph. Don't skip lines between paragraphs; while doing so might provide the reader with a visual break, it wastes valuable writing space.

MODEL RESPONSES TO THE LESSON 12 WRITING SAMPLE TOPIC

Here are two model responses, one arguing for each of the two choices described in the Writing Sample in Lesson 12 (page 156). These responses illustrate the organizational and stylistic devices discussed throughout this lesson. As you read these responses, keep in mind the following:

- The samples are models intended to exemplify the various suggestions discussed earlier in this lesson and in the lesson in Lesson 12. Don't expect that you will be able to write essays quite this polished in 30 minutes.

- Although they are models, they aren't perfect. Regardless of how effective an LSAT essay is, there's always some room for improvement.

- The length of these responses would fit in the space provided on the LSAT response sheet, although most test-takers' responses are a bit shorter.

- They are not all-inclusive. Effective arguments may have occurred to you that are absent in these model responses.

Response #1

(in favor of the Frye Street location)

The Frye Street location is the better choice for the Baxters. The time and cost of renovating the Frye shop would be minimal, since the store is already set up to accommodate a hair studio. Its close proximity would minimize the time and expense of moving as well as providing for uninterrupted business from current clients. A continued stream of business and a low initial rent would ensure short-term survival as well as making it financially feasible to expand to the adjacent space, thereby achieving long-term growth. Although the prior salon failure on Frye Street might suggest poor growth potential, that failure may have been due to other factors—such as mismanagement or a narrow male-only client base.

The mall space's high-traffic location might seem to provide more long-term profit potential. However, the Baxters may face greater competition in the suburbs from franchise salons. More importantly, the Baxters' primary concern should be with short-term survival, since otherwise they cannot achieve their longer-term profit goals. The additional expense of equipping a new retail space, along with a high initial rent, may jeopardize that survival, especially since it may take considerable time to develop a new clientele.

In sum, Frye is the better location; it would allow for a fast and inexpensive start-up and an uninterrupted flow of business, in turn ensuring both short-term survival and long-term success.

Response #2

(in favor of the Fashion Place Mall location)

The mall location would better meet the Baxters' objectives. The strategic high-traffic position next to a department store offers greater opportunity for long-term growth and profit. While the initial expense to equip the new space might be substantial, renovations at Frye Street to convert that space from a men-only salon may be just as costly and time-consuming. Even if not, the Baxters' primary concern should be with long-term investment return, as additional start-up costs will prove insignificant over time.

Admittedly, the relatively close and quiet Frye Street location might help the Baxters retain current customers, thereby offsetting moving expenses. However, failure of the previous hair studio suggests an insufficient demand among nearby elderly residents for a contemporary hair studio. This factor, along with the location's low visibility, is likely to prevent growth. Although low rent would appear to help the Baxters to meet their objectives, any expansion at Frye would come at greater expense, thereby undermining long-term profit goals; the mall location allows for expansion without additional rent.

In the final analysis, the mall is the better choice; while the relative start-up costs are uncertain, the mall location is more certain to achieve the Baxters' overriding objectives of long-term growth and profit.

Writing Sample
Mini-test and Review

In this lesson, you will apply what you learned in Lessons 12 and 13 to a new Writing Sample topic. Limit your time to 35 minutes for this mini-test. Then evaluate your essay, using the scorecard in Lesson 12 and comparing your response to the two model responses provided.

WRITING SAMPLE TOPIC

1 TOPIC • SUGGESTED TIME: 35 MINUTES

The Riverview city planners are considering various public improvement projects, particularly for the city's largely undeveloped and scenic riverfront. Write an argument in favor of one the following two projects, keeping in mind that the cost of the two projects would be the same. Also keep in mind the following two factors influencing the city's decision:

- The city wants to avoid projects that might undermine its residents' general opinion of the city as a great place to raise children.

- The city wants to stimulate its economy by reviving its waning tourist industry.

One project under consideration, the Riverview Plaza project, would involve converting a large 5-acre vacant parcel of land on the riverfront into an outdoor cultural center. The park-like setting would include a children's petting zoo, picnic facilities, a small botanical garden, and a miniature train ride which would encircle the Plaza. The focal point, however, would be a 1,000-seat amphitheater for showcasing popular performers from the musical and theatrical worlds as well as local talent. The amphitheater could also be used for other community events. The Plaza would also include an old-fashioned ice-cream parlor, a coffee house, and a gift shop. The amphitheater, train ride, and petting zoo would close during the cold-weather winter months, although the remaining facilities would be available year-round.

The other project under consideration is the Riverview Recreation Loop, a four-mile bicycle path around the city. All-weather fitness stations, paddle-ball and basketball courts, and new playgrounds would be installed at various other points around the Loop. The Loop would pass directly by the local high school and a local elementary school. Special overpasses would be constructed at the more heavily traveled roadways, although bicyclists would be required to cross traffic at numerous other streets. The Loop would extend along the riverfront, where a new indoor-outdoor skating rink, bearing the name of local resident and former Olympic figure-skating champion, would be constructed. The rink would provide ice skates—as well as bicycles, rollerblades, and pedal-power buggies for the bike path—year-round on an hourly rental basis.

Use the space below to respond to the Writing Sample topic. Do not write in the margins.

_____

_____

_____

_____

_____

_____

_____

_____

_____

_____

_____

_____

_____

_____

_____

_____

_____

_____

_____

_____

mini-test

EVALUATE YOUR WRITING SAMPLE

When you have completed your writing sample, evaluate it using the following techniques:

- Score your essay, referring to the scorecard in Lesson 12. Try to be as objective as possible. If you have trouble being objective, ask a friend or teacher to evaluate your essay for you.

- With a yellow highlighter, mark every sentence in which you accomplished nothing more than restating or paraphrasing the premise, criteria, or characteristics of the choices—that is, in which you merely rearranged and parroted back the facts to the reader. How great a portion of your essay did you highlight? Every sentence in yellow represents wasted space and wasted time that you want to use instead to formulate and present original ideas in the form of persuasive arguments.

- With a red pencil, circle or underline every grammatical error, awkward sentence, or other mechanical problem. If you're not sure what to circle, ask an English professor to do so. Does your essay look like a sea of red? If so, spend more time working on the mechanics of writing and on your writing style.

TWO MODEL ESSAY RESPONSES

Here are two model responses to the essay topic in this lesson. As you read these responses, keep in mind the following four points:

1. These responses are models intended to exemplify the various suggestions discussed in the lessons in Lessons 12 and 13. Don't expect that you will be able to write essays quite this polished in 35 minutes.

2. Although they are models, they aren't perfect. Regardless of how effective an LSAT essay is, there's always some room for improvement. And remember, there really is no such thing as a perfect LSAT essay.

3. These responses would fit in the space provided on the LSAT response sheet, although most test-takers' responses are a bit shorter.

4. The topic is loaded with facts that allow for a great variety of effective arguments. These model responses include only some possible arguments, so don't be concerned if your essay includes arguments that differ somewhat from those presented in these models. Instead, focus on how you performed according to the scorecard in Lesson 12.

Model Response #1

(in favor of the Riverview Plaza)

The Plaza project would be the better choice for the city. The amphitheater, gardens, zoo, and train are all likely to draw tourists while also providing educational opportunities and entertainment to residents and their children. The Plaza's appeal as a tourist attraction might seem to detract from the quality of life for local families. However, due to its location at the riverfront, local residents could easily avoid the area during the height of the tourist season.

The Loop is unlikely to attract a significant number of tourists, who are typically in search of entertainment and relaxation, not vigorous exercise. The Loop offers no activities for tourists that they could not engage in where they live. Admittedly, the various features of the Loop would be attractive to children, thus enhancing the city's reputation as a great place to raise children. However, the bike path itself may actually prove to be a source of worry for parents and danger for children, since it passes through the crowded and "touristy" riverfront and across a number of streets.

In conclusion, the Plaza would be a positive and safer addition to the city for local families, while providing more attractions for tourists. It is, therefore, a better plan than the Loop.

Model Response #2

(in favor of the Recreation Loop)

The city will better meet both of its goals with the Recreation Loop. Its various features would considerably enhance the quality of life for local children. At the same time, the variety and accessibility of its Riverfront features, enhanced by the notoriety associated with the skating rink, is sure to attract tourists year round. Although the cross-traffic at various points around the Loop may seem unsafe for small children, this problem would be partially abated with the planned overpasses and could be further abated with appropriate traffic signals and bicycle-safety education.

Although the Plaza would also attract tourists, especially if well-known performers are featured at the theater, nothing else about the Plaza is particularly unique or more compelling than the Loop. More significantly, the Plaza offers little improvement in the day-to-day quality of life for residents. In fact, in serving mainly as a tourist attraction, it may actually detract from the quality of life for local families.

In sum, while either project is likely to increase tourism, the Loop is the better choice overall considering the welfare of the resident's children.

STILL ROOM FOR IMPROVEMENT?

By now, you should have a fairly clear idea how effectively you respond to the LSAT Writing Sample topic. If you are not satisfied with your performance, take the following four remedial steps:

1. Review Writing Sample Lessons 12 and 13.

2. Rewrite the essay you wrote for this lesson, limiting yourself to about 17 minutes. Unless your essay is either "limited" or "seriously flawed," don't start from scratch. Instead, try to refine and build upon your basic arguments and approach.

3. Based upon the topic in this lesson, write a new essay in which you argue for the choice that you argued against in your first essay. Evaluate that essay as you did the first one. You may be pleasantly surprised to see some marked improvement in your work.

4. Recall from Lesson 13 the two alternative essay formats: 1) choice-driven and 2) goal-driven. Which one did you use in this mini-test? Perhaps the other format would be more natural or comfortable for you. Try it for your rewrite.

Logical Reasoning— Recognizing Reasoning Errors

In this lesson, you will learn how to recognize the various reasoning errors or fallacies that commonly appear in LSAT Logical Reasoning problems.

TEST QUESTIONS INVOLVING REASONING ERRORS

In LSAT problems involving reasoning errors, the passage contains an argument that employs a questionable argumentative technique or fallacy and your task is to identify the flaw or error in the reasoning. You will not be required to identify the fallacy by its traditional name, instead you will simply be required to select the best description of the reasoning error from the answer choices.

Reasoning error problems make up roughly 8 percent of the LSAT Logical Reasoning questions, so expect to see at least two problems of this type on each of the two Logical Reasoning sections. Your ability to recognize reasoning errors will also be tested indirectly in some of the parallel reasoning problems on the test.

Reasoning error questions are typically worded in one of the following ways:

- Which of the following is the best statement of the flaw in the argument?

- Which one of the following indicates an error in the reasoning leading to the conclusion in the argument?

- Which one of the following questionable argumentative techniques is employed in the passage?

The best way to prepare for this type of question is simply to become familiar with the various types of reasoning errors cataloged below.

STATISTICAL FALLACIES

The two most common statistical reasoning fallacies are the fallacy of the biased sample and the fallacy of the small or insufficient sample. Both involve sampling errors.

The fallacy of the biased sample is committed whenever the data for a statistical inference are drawn from a sample that is not representative of the population under consideration. Professional statisticians avoid this error through random sampling and other sampling techniques that are designed to eliminate bias in the data used to support their inferences.

The fallacy of the small or insufficient sample is committed whenever too small a sample is used to warrant confidence in the conclusion or whenever greater reliability is attributed to the conclusion than is warranted by the sample size. Professional statisticians avoid this error by choosing samples of sufficient size to reduce the margin of error in the conclusion. The fallacy of the insufficient sample is also known as the fallacy of "hasty generalization."

Egregious instances of these two statistical fallacies abound in ordinary discourse. For example, when one condemns all football players on the basis of the inappropriate behavior of a few, or lauds all politicians on the basis of the honesty and integrity of their representative, or vilifies all members of a race on the basis of encounters with only a few individuals, these fallacies are committed. Moreover, in most of the above cases, both forms of the fallacy are committed at the same time.

Here's an example of an argument that commits the fallacy of the biased sample.

Example 1:

> In a recent survey conducted on the Internet, eighty percent of the respondents indicated their strong disapproval of government regulation of the content and access of web-based information. This survey clearly shows that legislation designed to restrict the access or control the content of Internet information will meet with strong opposition from the electorate.

The data for the inference in the above argument are drawn from a sample that is not representative of the entire electorate. Since the survey was conducted on the Internet, not all members of the electorate have an equal chance of being included in the sample. Moreover, persons who use the Internet are more likely to have an opinion on the topic than persons who do not. For these reasons the sample is obviously biased.

Here's an example of an argument that commits the fallacy of the insufficient sample.

Example 2:

> I met my new boss at work today and she was very unpleasant. Twice when I tried to talk with her, she said she was busy and told me not to interrupt her again. Later, when I needed her advice on a customer's problem, she ignored me and walked away. It's obvious that she has a bad attitude and is not going to be easy to work with.

The data for the inference in this argument are insufficient to support the conclusion. Three observations of a person's behavior are not sufficient to support a conclusion about that person's behavior in general. Obviously, the boss could just have been having a bad day or been engrossed in other things.

CAUSAL FALLACIES

The "After This, Therefore Because of This" Fallacy

By far the most common causal fallacy, and the one most likely to appear on the LSAT, is the "after this, therefore because of this" fallacy. This is the fallacy of concluding on insufficient grounds that because some event X comes after some other event Y, Y must have caused X. Many common bad luck superstitions are examples of this fallacy (e.g., the black cat crossing one's path, walking under ladders, etc.). The error in arguments that commit this fallacy is that their conclusions are causal claims that are not sufficiently substantiated by the evidence. In most instances of this fallacy, the only evidence that is offered to support the causal claim is a positive correlation between two conditions or events; the one that occurs first is identified as the cause, the one that follows is identified as the effect. Typically, the causal connection between the two events is implausible given our general understanding of the world.

Here are two typical examples of the "after this, therefore because of this" fallacy.

Example 3:

> Ten minutes after walking into the auditorium, I began to feel sick to my stomach. There must have been something in the air in that building that caused my nausea.

Example 4:

> The stock market declined shortly after the election of the president, thus indicating the lack of confidence the business community has in the new administration.

In Example 3, a causal connection is posited between two events simply on the basis of one occurring before the other. Without further evidence to support it, the causal claim based on the correlation is premature. Example 4 is typical of modern news reporting. The only evidence offered in this argument to support the implicit causal claim that the decline in the stock market was caused by the election of the president is the fact that election preceded the decline. While this may have been a causal factor in the decline of the stock market, to argue that it is the cause without additional information and auxiliary hypotheses that make the causal connection plausible is to commit the "after this, therefore because of this" fallacy.

The "Necessary vs. Sufficient" Fallacy

Another common causal fallacy occurs when one confuses a necessary condition for the occurrence of some event with a sufficient condition for the event's occurrence. One source of this fallacy is a misunderstanding of the meaning of conditional statements. This fallacy is best understood with the help of a few examples.

Example 5:

> The car will start only if the battery isn't dead, so the car will start if the battery isn't dead.

Example 6:

> If you read this book carefully, you'll get a good score on the LSAT. Therefore, you won't get a good score on the LSAT unless you read this book carefully.

In Example 5, the confusion of necessary condition with sufficient condition is apparent. While having a "live" battery is certainly necessary for starting the car's engine, it is not sufficient to do this. Many other conditions including a "live" battery must be satisfied to bring this event about. Take special note of the difference between "only if" and "if" in this example. "A only if B" is not equivalent in meaning to "A if B." The former means that B is a necessary condition for A; the latter means that B is a sufficient condition for A. The former is equivalent to "If A, then B"; the latter is equivalent to "If B, then A."

The premise in Example 5 states that reading this book carefully is a sufficient condition for getting a good score on the LSAT. The conclusion states that reading this book carefully is a necessary condition for getting a good score on the LSAT. The premise asserts that anyone who reads this book carefully will get a good score; the conclusion asserts that anyone who gets a good score has read this book carefully. Obviously, these are quite different assertions.

UNWARRANTED ASSUMPTION FALLACIES

Unwarranted assumptions are assumptions that have no merit or independent justification. The two most common unwarranted assumption fallacies are the fallacy of composition and the division fallacy.

The Fallacy of Composition

The fallacy of composition is committed when a characteristic of individual members of a group is assumed without warrant to apply to the members of the group collectively. This fallacy is commonly referred to as the "part-whole" fallacy. While it is true that in some cases a property of an individual is transferable to the group of which it is a member, this certainly isn't always the case. The part-whole fallacy mistakenly assumes that this transference always holds.

Here is an example of the fallacy of composition.

Example 7:

> All physical objects are made of atoms. Atoms have no color. This book is a physical object, so it has no color.

In this example, a property that the parts lack is mistakenly assumed to be a property that the whole lacks as well. A little reflection shows that this assumption is false in this case.

The Division Fallacy

The division fallacy is the converse of the composition fallacy. In this case the fallacy is committed when a property of a group is mistakenly assumed to hold true for the individuals that make up the group. This fallacy is commonly referred to as the "whole-part" fallacy. While it is true that in some cases a property of a group is transferable to the individuals in the group, this certainly isn't always the case. The whole-part fallacy mistakenly assumes that this transference always holds.

Here is an example of the division fallacy.

Example 8:

>   The LSAT is a challenging exam. Therefore, every problem on the LSAT is a challenging problem.

In this example, a property of the whole exam is assumed to apply to each part of the exam. Clearly, the exam could be challenging even if some of the problems were not challenging.

The False Dichotomy Fallacy

The false dichotomy fallacy is also a common unwarranted assumption fallacy. This error is committed when one assumes without warrant that there are only two alternatives and then reasons that since one of the alternatives is false or unacceptable the other must be true or accepted. Of course, in cases where there are in fact only two alternatives, and this fact is obvious or can be justified, this pattern of reasoning is highly effective and acceptable. Typically, in arguments in which this fallacy occurs no evidence is offered to support the claim that there are only two alternatives available and a little reflection reveals that this claim is not self evident. This fallacy is commonly referred to as the "black-and-white" fallacy.

Here is an example of the false dichotomy fallacy.

Example 9:

>   Either we put convicted child molesters in jail for life or we risk having our children become their next victims. We certainly can't risk this, so we had better lock them up for the rest of their lives.

The argument in Example 9 assumes that there are only two possible alternatives open to us. No evidence is offered to support this claim and a little reflection reveals that it is not obviously the case. While child molestation is a difficult problem to deal with, it is unlikely that the only solution to the problem is the one mentioned in the argument. It is also unlikely that this is the only way that we can protect our children from becoming the victims of convicted offenders.

The Slippery Slope Fallacy

The "slippery slope" fallacy is so named because, like a slippery slope on which you cannot gain a foothold, once you start to slide you continue to slide until you crash to the bottom. Similarly, in this fallacy, it is assumed without justification or proof that once one event occurs a series of events will occur that will end with some undesirable consequence. Since the undesirable consequence is to be avoided, it is reasoned that the initiating event is also to be avoided. Typically, in arguments of this type no evidence is provided that the causal sequence depicted in the argument is the only possible scenario of events. In most cases, a little reflection reveals that the scenario is not even very likely. Without the assumption that each step in the sequence of events is inevitable, the argument is not convincing. This fallacy is also known as the "domino fallacy."

Here's an example of the slippery slope fallacy.

Example 10:

If pornography is not outlawed once and for all, the spread of pornographic literature will lead to an increase in sex-related crimes such as rape and incest. This in turn will lead to a general moral decay in the society that will cause an increase in crimes of all sorts. Eventually a complete breakdown of law and order will occur, leading ultimately to the total collapse of civilization as we know it. We certainly don't want this to happen, so we had better outlaw pornography before it's too late to do anything about it.

The "All Things are Equal" Fallacy

The "all things are equal" fallacy is committed when it is assumed without justification that background conditions have remained the same at different times or at different locations. In most instances this is an unwarranted assumption for the simple reason that things rarely remain the same over extended periods of time, and things rarely remain the same from place to place.

Here's an example of the "all things are equal" fallacy.

Example 11:

> Two years ago, when it rained for three days in a row, the river exceeded its banks and flooded the town. The latest weather forecast predicts that it will rain for at least three days, so it looks as though the town will be flooded again this year too.

The assumption operative in this argument is that nothing has changed in the two years since the last flood. No evidence or justification is offered for this assumption. Moreover, it is just as likely an assumption that things have changed and that measures were put in place to avoid a reoccurrence of the flooding.

IRRELEVANT APPEALS FALLACIES

Irrelevant appeals attempt to persuade others to accept a conclusion by appealing to matters that are not relevant to the truth or correctness of the conclusion. They are considered reasoning errors because they violate the requirement that the reasons offered in support of a claim should provide evidence that the claim is true or correct. In other words, such appeals mistakenly view the goal of argumentation to be simply persuasion, rather than the attainment of the truth.

Appeal to Ignorance

The appeal to ignorance is one of the most commonly used ploys to gain acceptance of a claim. The basic form of this fallacy is to argue that a claim is true (or false) solely on the grounds that no one has demonstrated or can demonstrate that the claim is false (or true).

Here's an example of an argument that employs an appeal to ignorance.

Example 12:

> Scientists have not established any causal link between smoking and lung cancer, hence we must simply accept the fact that smoking does not cause lung cancer.

Inability to prove that something is true (or false) cannot, by itself, be taken as evidence that it is false (or true). If this were accepted as a principle of logic, it would follow, for example, that our inability to prove the existence of God would lead immediately to the conclusion that God does not exist and that our inability to prove that UFO's don't exist, would lead immediately to the conclusion that UFO's exist. Likewise, our inability to prove that someone is guilty of a crime, would have to be taken as evidence, on this account, that they were innocent of the crime. This latter example has a ring of truth to it only because our system of law employs the rule that a person is innocent until proven guilty. Inability to prove guilt is not taken as evidence of innocence; rather, it is taken as inability to hold legally blameworthy.

Appeal to Public Opinion

Appealing to public opinion or to what most persons believe is another commonly used ploy to gain acceptance of a claim. Rather than use evidence or reasons that would support the truth of the claim, the author of the argument resorts to consensus prejudices, beliefs, traditions, or customs to gain acceptance of the conclusion. Peer pressure and peer acceptance are relied upon to persuade the unwary, uncritical listener or reader. Typically, no evidence that is relevant to the truth of the claim is offered in the argument. This fallacy is a favorite of politicians and advertisers.

Here's an example of an argument that employs an appeal to public opinion.

Example 13:

> Rick O'Flanagan's newest novel, *Seldom More Often Than Frequently*, has been on the best-seller list for twenty-five weeks in a row. It must be a good book; after all, 30 million readers can't be wrong.

In this example, the only reason given for the claim that the novel is a good book is that it has been read by 30 million people. A little reflection tells us that this, by itself, is not a good reason for this claim. After all, it is also true that 30 million people read tabloids on a regular basis and this is surely not evidence that they are in any sense good.

Appeal to Authority

Another common appeal used to gain acceptance of a claim is the appeal to authority. In place of evidence that supports the claim, author's often resort to the testimony or expertise of others to support the claim. This practice is not always suspect. As a matter of fact, we often rely on other persons or sources when accepting claims. We do this, for example, whenever we appeal to scientists, textbooks, doctors, and other experts to support our beliefs. This practice becomes suspect when there is a question about the competence, reliability, qualifications, motives, prejudices, etc., of the persons or sources upon whom we are relying.

The mere fact that an "authority" claims that some claim is or is not true is not, by itself, evidence that it is or is not true. It is a well-known fact among lawyers that, on any topic whatsoever, for every expert there is another expert who can be called to refute any claim made by the other. Similarly, the mere fact that some claim appears in a publication is not, by itself, evidence that the claim is true. After all, some publications, like the wolf in sheep's clothing, try to gain reliability and authoritativeness by mimicking publications that are authoritative and reliable sources of information. Dressing themselves up in the garb of respectable newspapers, tabloids try to fool us into believing that they are also reliable sources of information. Typically, in arguments that employ the appeal to authority to support the conclusion, no evidence is offered to justify our reliance upon the source cited. Once again, this fallacy is a favorite of politicians and advertisers.

Here's an example of an argument that employs an appeal to authority.

Example 14:

> Geena Goodlooks is one of this country's most respected and honored actresses. You
> can be certain that when she says welfare reform is needed, it has to be true.

In this argument, one has to wonder about the relevance of Geena's testimony to the truth of the claim it supports. No evidence is offered that would justify our reliance upon her testimony on this topic. The fact that she is a "respected and honored" actress hardly qualifies her as an expert on the need for welfare reform.

FALLACIES OF REFUTATION

Fallacies of refutation are committed in criticizing the arguments of others. Refutation fallacies occur whenever the critic focuses on aspects of the argument that are irrelevant to the reasoning employed in the argument or the truth of the claims that make up the argument. The basic tactic in criticisms that commit fallacies of this type is to scrupulously avoid attacking the argument, and instead attack the author, a side issue, or a deliberately weakened version of the argument. Needless to say, these fallacies are another favorite of politicians.

Attacking the Author

Attacks on the author of the argument take three forms. The attack is focused either on the character, or the motives, or the behavior of the person presenting the argument. The aim of the attack in all three cases is to discredit the conclusion of the person's argument. Assaults of this type are rarely, if ever, relevant to the reasoning employed in the argument or the truth or correctness of the conclusion. They are irrelevant for the simple reason that an arguer's personal character, motives, or behavior are rarely relevant to the correctness of the arguer's reasoning or the truth of the statements employed in the reasoning. Criticisms that employ attacks of these types are commonly known as "ad hominem arguments," which means "arguments against the person." It is a safe bet that you will see at least one problem on the LSAT in which this fallacy occurs.

ATTACKING THE AUTHOR'S CHARACTER

Here's an example of a counter-argument that employs an attack on the character of the person advancing the argument.

Example 15:

> When you realize that the man who is trying to convince you that he would be the best president this country has ever seen is in fact a womanizer and an illegal drug user, it's not difficult to draw the conclusion that his arguments are completely unacceptable.

In this example, the presidential candidate's arguments are attacked by pointing out repugnant characteristics of the candidate. No attempt is made to consider or attack the candidate's arguments.

ATTACKING THE AUTHOR'S MOTIVES

Here's an example of a counter-argument that employs an attack on the motives of the persons advancing the argument.

Example 16:

> The radio and television industry has been lobbying against proposed changes in the laws governing the use of publicly owned transmission frequencies. But just keep this in mind; no matter how good their arguments might be, they stand to lose a great deal if the proposed changes become law.

In Example 16, the radio and television industry's arguments are dismissed out of hand on the grounds that they have a vested interest in the outcome. The tactic exhibited in Example 16 is commonly called "poisoning the well" because the source of the argument is condemned in order to discredit the argument.

ATTACKING THE AUTHOR'S BEHAVIOR

Here's an example of a counter-argument that employs an attack on the behavior of the person advancing the argument.

Example 17:

> *Politician:* My esteemed colleague accuses me of misappropriating taxpayer's funds for my own personal use. Well, it might interest you to know that he has the unenviable distinction of having spent more on so-called fact-finding trips to exotic locations all around the world than anyone else in Congress.

The fallacy exhibited in Example 17 is commonly called the "you too!" or "two wrongs don't make a right" fallacy. In this example, no attempt is made to attack the colleague's argument, rather the focus of the attack is to accuse the person of similar questionable behavior or wrongdoing.

Attacking a Side Issue

The "red herring" fallacy. Another fallacious refutation tactic commonly employed is to divert attention away from the argument under consideration and focus instead on a side issue. The popular name for this refutation tactic is "red herring" which comes from the fox hunting practice of dragging a cooked herring across the fox's trail to divert the hounds off the scent. The aim of this tactic is simply to obfuscate and avoid the argument rather than offer apt reasons why it should not be accepted.

Here's an example of a counter-argument that employs the red herring fallacy.

Example 18:

Mandatory life sentences for three-time felons is a bad idea. People who think it's a good idea argue that it will stop violent crime. But, if we really want to stop violent crime, instead of locking people up we should stop portraying violence in movies and on television.

In Example 18, the critic shifts attention away from the issue of whether mandatory life sentences should be used to combat violent crime to a related but different issue. Instead of attacking the arguments of the proponents of mandatory life sentences, an alternative solution to the problem is proposed. Obviously, however, merely proposing a different solution to a problem cannot, by itself, be taken as evidence that competing solutions and the arguments that support them are necessarily mistaken or incorrect.

Attacking a Weakened Version of an Argument

The "straw man" fallacy. The "straw man" fallacy is committed when a person deliberately misrepresents an opponent's argument in order to make it easier to criticize, or make it so obviously implausible that no criticism is required. Although the misrepresented version is usually only a caricature of the opponent's argument, it is treated by the critic as equivalent to the original. Because the new version is a significantly weakened version of the original argument, the critic seldom has difficulty in defeating it.

Here's an example of a counter-argument that employs the "straw man" fallacy.

Example 19:

The "right-to-die" bill currently being considered by Congress implies that it's acceptable to take the lives of weak and frail old people who cannot defend themselves. However, anyone who has an ounce of decency knows that this is just plain wrong, so we must make every effort to defeat this legislation.

In Example 19, the critic distorts the argument in favor of the legislation by drawing a highly questionable inference from it. The attack then focuses on the purported implication which is quite easily defeated.

CONDITIONAL REASONING FALLACIES

Reasoning that involves conditional sentences can be somewhat tricky. Conditionals are sentences of the form "If A, then B." There are four basic patterns of reasoning involving these statements; two of them are correct forms of reasoning and two of them are fallacious forms of reasoning. The correct forms are illustrated in the following two examples.

Correct Forms of Conditional Reasoning

Example 20:

> If Felix is a cat, then Felix is an animal. Felix is a cat, so Felix is an animal.

Example 21:

> If Felix is a cat, then Felix is an animal. Felix is not a animal, so Felix is not a cat.

A little reflection is all that is required to convince yourself that these two patterns of reasoning are correct.

The basic pattern of Example 20 is:

> *Premise:* If A, then B.
>
> *Premise:* A.
>
> *Conclusion:* B.

The basic pattern of Example 21 is:

> *Premise:* If A, then B.
>
> *Premise:* Not B.
>
> *Conclusion:* Not A.

Every instance of the above two patterns is an argument which is such that if the premises are true, the conclusion must be true. That is, the truth of the premises guarantees the truth of the conclusion.

Fallacious Forms of Conditional Reasoning

The fallacious forms of conditional reasoning are illustrated in the following two examples.

Example 22:

> If Felix is a cat, then Felix is an animal. Felix is an animal, so Felix is a cat.

Example 23:

> If Felix is a cat, then Felix is an animal. Felix is not a cat, so Felix is not an animal.

A little reflection is all that is required to convince yourself that these two patterns of reasoning are fallacious.

The basic pattern of Example 22 is:

> *Premise:* If A, then B.
>
> *Premise:* B.
>
> *Conclusion:* A.

The basic pattern of Example 23 is:

> *Premise:* If A, then B.
>
> *Premise:* Not A.
>
> *Conclusion:* Not B.

Every instance of the above two patterns is a fallacious argument.

As a general rule, it's a good idea to proceed with caution when dealing with arguments containing conditional statements. The main source of potential confusion is that conditional statements can be expressed in a variety of ways. Whenever possible, restate conditionals and put them into the "If _____, then _____." form before you attempt to evaluate the argument. To appreciate the importance of doing this, consider the following example.

Example 24:

> The treaty will be signed only if both parties agree to end the hostilities. Both parties have indicated agreement to end the hostilities, so the treaty will be signed.

The argument in Example 24 is fallacious. This can be seen clearly by restating the argument as follows:

> *Premise:* If the treaty is signed, then both parties agree to end the hostilities.
>
> *Premise:* Both parties agree to end the hostilities.
>
> *Conclusion:* The treaty will be signed.

Notice that this restatement reveals that the argument in Example 24 has the same basic pattern as the argument in Example 22. Notice also that the restatement of the first premise accords with the advice stated earlier in the discussion of Example 5.

REASONING ERRORS INVOLVING LANGUAGE USE

The Fallacy of Equivocation

The fallacy of equivocation occurs when a key word or phrase that has more than one meaning is employed in different meanings throughout the argument. Since the truth of the premises and the conclusion is in part a function of the meanings of the words in the sentences that express them, a shift in meaning of key terms in the argument will enable one to draw conclusions from premises that do not in fact support them.

Here's an example of an argument that commits the fallacy of equivocation.

Example 25:

Logic is the study of arguments, and since arguments are disagreements, it follows that logic is the study of disagreements.

In Example 25, the word "argument" is employed in two different meanings. In the first premise, "argument" is used to mean "a discourse in which reasons are offered in support of a claim"; in the second premise "argument" is defined as meaning "a disagreement." If we adopt the second meaning, the first premise is false. If we adopt the first meaning, the second premise is false. Either way, the premises simply fail to provide support for the conclusion.

The Fallacy of Circular Reasoning

There are two basic forms of the fallacy of circular reasoning or "arguing in a circle." The first type occurs when one employs a restatement of the premise as the conclusion of the argument; the second type occurs when the truth of the conclusion is presupposed by the premises. Sound reasoning requires that the premises provide independent support for the conclusion. Obviously, the mere restatement of the premises in the conclusion can hardly be regarded as independent evidence that the conclusion is true. Nor can the use of premises that presuppose the truth of the conclusion be regarded as independent evidence that the conclusion is true. In both of these cases, one has merely argued in a circle. The circular reasoning fallacy is commonly referred to as the fallacy of "begging the question."

Here's an example of an argument that commits the first form of the fallacy of circular reasoning.

Example 26:

Honesty is the best policy for the simple reason that it's best to adopt a practice that will insure that people are treated in a fair, truthful, and trustworthy manner.

In Example 26, the conclusion is just a restatement of the premise, since "honesty" means being fair, truthful, and trustworthy.

Here's an example of an argument that commits the second form of the fallacy of circular reasoning.

Example 27:

My boss told me that I was her favorite employee, so it must be true because there's no way she would lie to her favorite employee.

In Example 27, the arguer is trying to prove that he is the boss's favorite employee, but to support the premise that the boss would not lie to her favorite employee, he would have to accept the claim that he was the boss's favorite employee. To do this, however, is to assume the very thing he is trying to prove.

Logical Reasoning
Basic Skills

In this lesson, you will learn three more of the eight basic logical reasoning skills listed in Lesson 4.

IDENTIFYING PRINCIPLES

In Lesson 4, you learned how to identify the factual assumptions required to make an argument logically correct. In this lesson you will learn how to identify the value assumptions required to make an argument acceptable or convincing to an individual.

Principle questions are typically worded as follows:

- Which one of the following principles, if accepted, would provide the most justification for the conclusion?

- On the basis of their statements, X and Y are committed to disagreeing about the truth of which of the following principles?

Principle questions make up only 5–8 percent of the Logical Reasoning problems on the LSAT, so you can expect to see only one or two of these problems on each Logical Reasoning section. There are two basic formats for these problems. In one, an argument is stated in the passage and your task is to ascertain the underlying principle that justifies the author's conclusion. In the other, an argumentative dialogue between two people is presented and your task is to ascertain the underlying principle that they would be committed to agreeing or disagreeing about, given their remarks.

A principle is a general rule that justifies a particular action or decision. In most cases, the principle functions as a value assumption in argument. This is especially true of arguments that prescribe a particular course of action or resolution.

Factual Assumptions vs. Value Assumptions

First, let's consider the basic difference between factual assumptions and value assumptions. A factual assumption is one that is operative in an argument that concludes that something is or is not the case. A value assumption is one that is operative in an argument that concludes that some action ought or ought not be performed. Arguments of the latter type are commonly referred to as prescriptive arguments, because their conclusions prescribe that certain types of conduct or courses of action should or should not be engaged in.

To best identify value assumptions, it is necessary first to be familiar with some basic values.

Some Commonly Held Values

justice	freedom of speech	creativity
wisdom	individual responsibility	tradition
honesty	equality of opportunity	peace
security	financial independence	cooperation
loyalty	obedience to authority	productivity
courage	equality of condition	tolerance
excellence	freedom from want	harmony
flexibility	autonomy	competition
novelty	generosity	comfort
happiness	profitability	efficiency

Obviously, the list is by no means complete, but it gives you the basic idea. Chances are that you and your friends and family share all or most of the values on the list, and a few more. What you may not share, however, are your value preferences. When two values conflict, you must make a choice as to which is to be given preference. For example, honesty and loyalty conflict when we have to choose between telling a lie or saving a friend. If we lie, the friend is saved; if we tell the truth, the friend is jeopardized. In cases like this, value preferences are made. Moreover, these preferences will, in many cases, be subconsciously codified and will function as personal rules or principles that will guide our conduct and our decision making. If we choose to tell the truth, for instance, and we thereby jeopardize the friend, the principle that guides us in this decision is that one ought to always tell the truth. Those who might choose to lie to save the friend are guided in their decision by a different principle, one that reflects a different value preference.

PRESCRIPTIVE ARGUMENTS AND VALUE ASSUMPTIONS

Recall that prescriptive arguments are arguments in which the conclusion prescribes that certain types of conduct or courses of action should or should not be engaged in. Such arguments will be convincing to an individual only if the individual shares the values and, more importantly, the value preferences of the person presenting the argument. Normally, the values and value preferences of the author are not explicitly stated in the argument; they are simply assumed. For example, consider this argument:

Example 1:

> Every day, new evidence is found to support the claim that cigarette smoking is harmful to the health of both the smoker and those in close proximity to the smoker. On the basis of this mounting evidence, the government should prohibit the sale and manufacture of cigarettes.

On the surface, it appears that this premise provides support for the conclusion; that is, it appears to provide a reason why the conclusion ought to be accepted. But notice that it does so only on the assumption that you believe that it is the government's responsibility to take care of people's welfare. If you believe that it is the individual's responsibility to take care of his/her own welfare, you will not find this argument convincing; in fact, from your perspective the premise will not even support the conclusion.

The underlying principle that readers would have to share for the argument in Example 1 to be acceptable is that government ought to protect people from harming themselves and others. This principle expresses the author's preference of one value over another; in this case, collective responsibility over individual responsibility. Those who agree with this principle will find the argument convincing; those who disagree with this principle will likely find the argument unacceptable.

In general, the best way to identify the principle underlying argument is to examine the premises provided in support of the conclusion and then determine what value preferences would be required so that those reasons are regarded as more convincing or more desirable than other reasons that might have been offered in support. Alternatively, ask yourself what values are involved in the argument and what preference regarding these values is required to justify the course of action or the decision expressed in the conclusion. Once you have located the value preference, look for an answer choice that reflects this preference.

Identifying the Method of Arguments

In problems that ask you to identify the method of an argument, an argument is stated in the passage and your task is to identify the reasoning technique employed in the argument. You will not be required to identify the technique by name; all that's required is to select the best description of the general reasoning strategy of the argument from the answer choices. Problems of this sort make up about 3 percent of the LSAT logical reasoning questions, so expect to see one or two of these problems on each Logical Reasoning section.

The method of an argument is simply the way in which the author goes about establishing the conclusion, or in the case of a critical response to an argument, the way in which the author attempts to defeat the conclusion. There are a great number of argumentative techniques that may be used when attempting to establish or defeat conclusions—too many to list all of them here, but familiarity with some of the basic strategies and techniques will prove to be helpful in dealing with these problems.

It is important to note that not all of the methods of establishing or defeating conclusions presented below are necessarily effective or logically correct. The issue in problems of this type is merely to identify the method used by the author, not to determine whether or not it is an effective or logically correct method. Determining the latter is an entirely different matter.

Method questions are usually worded as follows:

- Which of the following most accurately characterizes the argumentative strategy in the passage?

- The argument proceeds by:

- Which one of the following argumentative techniques is used in the passage?

- The method of the argument is to:

- The argument employs which one of the following reasoning techniques?

Reasoning by Analogy

A common method employed in arguing for a conclusion is to use an analogy. Starting with a claim or situation that is familiar and unproblematic, the author argues that the issue in question is very much like the familiar case, and hence that what is true of it is probably true of the case in question. The following example demonstrates this method.

Example 2:

> The mushrooms we saw in the forest yesterday are the same color, size, and shape as those we saw in the grocery store today. Obviously, the mushrooms sold in the grocery store aren't poisonous; hence, it is likely that the ones we saw in the forest aren't poisonous either.

Citing an Authority

Another technique often employed when attempting to establish a claim is to cite an authority as the grounds or reason for accepting it. In these cases the authority's or expert's testimony functions as the premise of the argument, and the author's reasoning is that we ought to accept the conclusion simply because some expert or authority claims that it's true. Here's an example.

Example 3:

> Professor Lipscomb, my Physics professor, warned us about the dangers of water and air pollution; that's why I'm supporting the Clean Air and Water initiative.

Statistical Reasoning

Many arguments use statistics to establish claims. These arguments normally begin with the recitation of a statistical claim to the effect that some percentage of a certain group have a certain characteristic. It is then indicated that since a given individual is in the group, it follows that the individual is likely (or unlikely) to have the aforementioned characteristic. Here are some examples.

Example 4:

> Two percent of all vegetarians contract colon cancer. Since Sally is a vegetarian, it is unlikely she'll get colon cancer.

Example 5:

> Eighty percent of all logic students scored high on the LSAT. Henry is a logic major, so he probably scored high on the LSAT.

Reasoning from Experience

Past experience is often taken as a reason for believing that something is the case or will be the case. Authors who use this type of reasoning typically begin with a statement that delineates some experience they or someone else has had. This stated experience then functions as a premise from which it is argued that some, as yet inexperienced, event or situation will occur. Here's a well-worn example.

Example 6:

> We have observed the sun rising countless times in the past; hence, we can be assured that the sun will rise tomorrow.

A variation of the above method is to argue that some general claim is true on the basis of the observation of a number of instances of the claim. Arguments that employ this kind of reasoning typically begin with premises that document the observed instances; the conclusion typically asserts that what is true of the observed instances is true of all or most instances. Here is an example.

Example 7:

> "Don't worry! All of the lettuce we checked in the shipment was in excellent condition, so you can be assured that all of the lettuce is OK."

Causal Conclusions

Causal conclusions (i.e., conclusions that assert a causal relationship between two events) are typically established either by eliminative reasoning, or by noting a significant correlation between events (causal reasoning).

ELIMINATIVE REASONING

Arguments that employ eliminative reasoning usually proceed by isolating a common feature of the events under discussion by a process of elimination. The common feature is then deemed to be the cause. The premises of such arguments usually describe testing procedures aimed at determining which, if any, of a set of properties are causally related to the event in question. Through experiment or observation an attempt is made to eliminate each of these features as a causal candidate. The one that resists these attempts is concluded to be the cause of the event under consideration. Here is an example.

Example 8:

> Six customers of a fast-food restaurant developed food poisoning shortly after eating lunch there. An investigation revealed that they had all drunk different beverages and not all had eaten salads or soups or French fries. However, they had all eaten chicken sandwiches prepared with different breads. The health department concluded that the cause of the food poisoning was poorly cooked chicken.

CAUSAL REASONING

Causal reasoning is based on a significant correlation. Arguments that assert a causal relation on the basis of a significant correlation between two circumstances typically begin with premises which document the correlation. The correlation is deemed significant if it is such that the suspected cause is not only present whenever the event occurs, but also absent whenever the event fails to occur. Once this is established, it is concluded that the relation between the two events is causal. Here is an example.

Example 9:

> Every time my car hits a pothole in the road the engine misfires, but it never misfires when the road is smooth. Hence, hitting potholes is the cause of the misfiring.

Disjunctive Reasoning

Another common method used to establish a conclusion is to show that it is the only acceptable alternative by ruling out all of the other possibilities. Here is an example.

Example 10:

> If Sean went to the beach, he either drove his own car or went with a friend. But Sean's car is in the garage; so he must have gone with a friend because he was seen at the beach early this morning.

Conditional Reasoning

Conditional arguments usually proceed by first stating a conditional statement, and then by asserting or denying the antecedent (i.e., the "if" clause) or the consequent (i.e., the "then" clause) of the conditional statement. Here are some examples.

Example 11:

> Pigs can't fly. If they could, they would, but they don't, so they can't.

Example 12:

> If it looks like a duck, walks like a duck, and quacks like a duck, then it's a duck. It looks, walks, and quacks like a duck, so obviously it's a duck.

Example 13:

> Sam is a basketball player if he's over 6 feet tall. But Sam is only 5' 9", so he's not a basketball player.

COMMON REBUTTAL TECHNIQUES

Discredit the Arguer

Among the most common methods employed to defeat or rebut an argument is to challenge the motives or the integrity of the person who is presenting the argument. The basic ploy here is to attempt to discredit the argument by discrediting the arguer. Here are some examples.

Example 14:

> The medical industry has argued vigorously that health-care reform is unnecessary, but we have to keep in mind that the medical industry stands to lose the most if new health-care legislation is passed.

Example 15:

> Professor Martini has presented some strong arguments in favor of the theory of evolution, but none of them are acceptable because it is a well-known fact that Martini is an atheist.

Redirect the Argument

Another common method used to defeat an argument is to direct attention away from the main point of the argument to a different, though perhaps related, point, and then attack or defend it rather than the main issue. Here is an example.

Example 16:

> Mandatory life sentences for three-time felons is a bad idea. People who think it's a good idea argue that it will stop violent crime. But if we really want to stop violent crime, instead of locking people up we should stop portraying violent crimes on television and in movies, because that's where these criminals get their ideas in the first place.

Reduce a Premise to Absurdity

Author's often attempt to defeat an argument by showing that one of its major premises is false or absurd. A common way in which this is done is by first assuming that the premise is in fact true, and then by showing that this assumption leads to an obviously false or absurd claim. By showing that the premise leads to this result, it is thereby shown to be itself false or absurd and hence the argument that employs it as a major premise is defeated. Here's an example of this technique.

Example 17:

> The evidence that condom use is an effective means to stop the spread of AIDS is hardly conclusive. But assume for the sake of argument that it is. By promoting condom use we encourage young people to think that it's okay to be promiscuous, to have sex with prostitutes, to engage in homosexual activities—in short, to engage in the very activities that spread AIDS. So, rather than limiting the activities that spread this disease, we promote them by promoting condom use.

RECOGNIZING SIMILARITIES BETWEEN ARGUMENTS

Parallel reasoning problems all begin with the same basic set-up. An argument is presented in the passage and in each of the answer choices. The task, however, can differ from problem to problem. In some cases you will be asked to find the argument that parallels the structure or pattern of reasoning of the argument in the passage, in other cases you will be asked to find the argument that employs the same method of reasoning, and in others you will be asked to find the argument that contains the same reasoning error as the argument in the passage. Problems of this type make up about 12 percent of the LSAT logical reasoning questions, so expect to see as many as three of these problems in each Logical Reasoning section.

Questions that ask you to find the argument that has the same structure or pattern of reasoning as the argument in the passage are typically worded as follows:

- The argumentative structure of which one of the following most closely parallels that of the argument in the passage?

- The pattern of reasoning displayed in the argument in the passage is most closely paralleled in which of the following arguments?

- Which of the following arguments contains a flawed pattern of reasoning parallel to that contained in the argument above?

- Which of the following, in its logical features, most closely parallels the reasoning in the passage?

Questions that ask you to find the argument that employs the same method of reasoning as the argument in the passage are typically worded as follows:

- Which of the following most closely parallels the reasoning in the argument presented in the passage?

- In which of the following is the method of reasoning most parallel to that in the argument above?

- Questions that ask you to find the argument that contains the same reasoning error as the argument in the passage are typically worded as follows:

- Which one of the following arguments contains a flaw that is most similar to the one in the argument above?

- The faulty reasoning in which one of the following is most parallel to that in the argument above?

Each of these question types requires a slightly different approach, as discussed below.

How to Handle Parallel Structure Problems

To get a basic idea of what is meant by logical "structure" or "pattern of reasoning" consider the following pair of arguments.

Example 18:

All men are mortal. Socrates is a man. Hence, Socrates is mortal.

Example 19:

> Every dog has a master. Fido is a dog. Therefore, Fido has a master.

While it is evident that the arguments in these examples are about different topics, and hence are quite dissimilar in their content, they are alike in the way in which the information about the topics is presented. Each begins with a general statement claiming that all individuals in a certain class have a certain characteristic, followed by a particular statement that claims that a certain individual belongs to the class mentioned previously, and concluding that the individual has the characteristic mentioned previously. Because of these similarities, the "pattern" or "structure" of these two arguments is the same.

The basic structure or pattern of Example 18 and Example 19 can be represented as follows:

> *Premise:* All A are B.
>
> *Premise:* C is an A.
>
> *Conclusion:* C is a B.

It is important to note when trying to determine the structure of the argument that the content of the argument is irrelevant; it is not what is said in the argument that's important, but the way in which it is said. The order of the premises and conclusion is also irrelevant when trying to determine the similarity of the structure of arguments. For example, consider the following pair of arguments that have the same structure but whose premises and conclusions are presented in different orders.

Example 20:

> People who are happy are content; hence, since Mary is happy she must be content.

Example 21:

> John must be tall because he is a basketball player and all basketball players are tall.

The similarity in structure of these two arguments becomes readily apparent when we restate them and reorganize them as follows.

> Example 20
>
> > *Premise:* <All> people who are happy are content.
> >
> > *Premise:* Mary is happy.
> >
> > *Conclusion:* Mary is content.
>
> Example 21
>
> > *Premise:* All basketball players are tall.
> >
> > *Premise:* John is a basketball player.
> >
> > *Conclusion:* John is tall.

Determining the pattern or structure of an argument is relatively easy to do as long as you focus on the way the argument is expressed rather than on what is expressed in the argument. To put this another way, focus your attention on the syntax of the sentences that comprise the argument, rather than on what the sentences mean.

Here's an example of a pair of arguments that have the same flawed pattern of reasoning.

Example 22:

If the propeller of an airplane breaks while the airplane is in flight, then the airplane will surely crash. The flight recorder clearly indicates that the propeller of John's airplane did not break in flight. Hence, we can be assured that John's plane did not crash.

Example 23:

If legislation is passed that completely prohibits pornography, then freedom of artistic expression will be greatly restricted. The legislature has indicated that it will not pass legislation that completely prohibits pornography. Hence, freedom of artistic expression will not be severely restricted.

The flawed pattern that Example 22 and Example 23 share is:

Premise: If A, then B.

Premise: Not A.

Conclusion: Not B.

Here's an example of a parallel structure problem as it would appear on the LSAT.

Example 24:

Either the safe wasn't locked or it was opened by the burglar. But it wasn't opened by the burglar unless he knew the combination. So either it was unlocked or the burglar knew the combination.

The pattern of reasoning displayed in the argument in the passage is most closely paralleled in which of the following arguments?

(A) Either the Slugs will win the Fruit Bowl or the Snails will. The Snails won't win unless they beat the Slugs. Hence, if the Slugs win the Fruit Bowl, the Snails didn't beat them.

(B) God is either unwilling to prevent evil or unable to do so. But he is not unable unless he is not omnipotent. Hence, he is either unwilling or he is not omnipotent.

(C) Either gun control laws are passed or the number of crimes involving handguns will continue to rise. But gun control laws won't be passed unless the NRA supports them. Hence, if the NRA supports them, gun control laws will be passed.

(D) Professor Lascola is either a realist or an empiricist. But he is not an empiricist if he believes that some concepts are innate. So, if he believes that some ideas are innate, he is not a realist.

(E) Either smoking is harmful or the Surgeon General is incorrect in his warnings about smoking cigarettes. But studies have shown conclusively that smoking is harmful, hence the Surgeon General is correct in his warnings.

Here's how you can handle parallel reasoning problems that ask you to find an argument that has the same structure or pattern of reasoning as the argument in the passage.

First, get clear about the structure of the argument in the passage. To do this, underline words such as "all," "some," "no" (and their synonyms), and words and phrases such as "and," "or," "if, then," "if and only if" (and their synonyms). Applying this advice to the passage in Example 24, you'll have something like the following:

> Either the safe wasn't locked or it was opened by the burglar. But it wasn't opened by the burglar unless he knew the combination. So either it wasn't locked or the burglar knew the combination.

So far, the structure looks like this:

> *Premise:* Either _____ or _____.
>
> *Premise:* _____ unless _____.
>
> *Conclusion:* Either _____ or _____.

Second, think about the sentences that fill the blanks. Notice that the first blank of the first premise and the first blank of the conclusion get filled by the same sentence. Notice also that the second blank of the second premise and the second blank of the conclusion also get filled by the same sentence. Notice further that the second blank of the first premise and the first blank of the second premise are not exactly the same sentence. The first blank of the second premise gets filled by the negation of the sentence that fills the second blank of the first premise. Filling in the blanks, the structure looks like this:

> *Premise:* Either A or B.
>
> *Premise:* Not B unless C.
>
> *Conclusion:* Either A or C.

Third, with this structure in mind, look at each of the answer choices to find the one with exactly the same pattern.

Choice (A) doesn't have the same structure as the argument in the passage. The structure of choice (A) is:

> *Premise:* Either A or B.
>
> *Premise:* Not B unless C.
>
> *Conclusion:* If A, then not C.

Choice (B) has the same structure as the argument in the passage. You can convince yourself that this is the case simply by replacing the letters in the above schema by the independent clauses of choice (B).

Choice (C) does not have the same structure as the argument in the passage. The structure of choice (C) is:

> *Premise:* Either A or B.
>
> *Premise:* Not A unless C.
>
> *Conclusion:* If C, then not A.

Choice (D) does not have the same structure as the argument in the passage. The structure of choice (D) is:

> *Premise:* Either A or B.
>
> *Premise:* If C, then not B.
>
> *Conclusion:* If C, then not A.

Choice (E) does not have the same structure as the argument in the passage. The structure of choice (E) is:

> *Premise:* Either A or not B.
>
> *Premise:* A.
>
> *Conclusion:* B.

Therefore, **the correct answer is (B).**

How to Handle Parallel Method of Reasoning Problems

Questions that ask you to find the argument that employs the same method of reasoning as the argument in the passage should be approached in a different way than those that ask for the argument that has the same structure or pattern of reasoning.

Here's an example of this type of question as it would appear on the LSAT.

Example 25:

> The economy is like a garden in that it experiences periods of growth and periods of latency. In order to thrive, gardens require human intervention by way of cultivation and fertilization, hence for the economy to thrive, human intervention by way of government regulation and monetary stimulus is required.

> In which of the following is the method of reasoning most parallel to that in the argument above?

> **(A)** It's true that domestic dogs are similar in many ways to wild wolves, but if dogs were immediately related to wolves, they could not be domesticated, because, to date, no one has ever successfully domesticated a wild wolf.

> **(B)** Provided that the teeth of the dinosaur stegosaurus are like the teeth of the modern herbivores such as the horse and the cow, they are probably ancient ancestors of these animals. However, no evidence can be found that clearly supports this hypothesis. Hence, it is unlikely that modern herbivores descended from stegosaurs.

> **(C)** Measurements taken from fossil remains of *Tyrannosaurus rex* are indicative of the entire species only if we can be assured that they are representative. But since we cannot be certain of this, we cannot conclude that all of these animals stood over twenty feet tall.

> **(D)** Computers and machines are extremely complex artifacts just as plants and animals are extremely complex organisms. Machines and computers are made by intelligent beings, hence plants and animals probably have an intelligent maker as well.

> **(E)** It's a well-known law that any two objects that are similar to a third object are similar to one another. Hence, since George's and Cosmo's cars are similar to Elaine's, they must be similar to one another.

HOW TO HANDLE SAME METHOD PROBLEMS

Here's the procedure for dealing with parallel reasoning problems that ask you to find an argument that employs the same method of reasoning as the argument in the passage.

First, get clear about the method employed in the argument in the passage. In Example 25 the method employed is analogical reasoning. In this argument the economy is likened to a garden and it is argued that because gardens require human intervention in order to thrive, it follows that the economy also requires human intervention in order to thrive.

Second, look for an answer choice that employs analogical reasoning to reach the conclusion. In the above example, **the correct answer is (D).** In choice (D), complex artifacts are likened to complex organisms and it is argued that because complex artifacts have an intelligent maker, it follows that complex organisms also have an intelligent maker.

How to Handle Parallel Reasoning Error Problems

Questions that ask you to find the argument that contains the same reasoning error or flaw as the argument in the passage should be approached in the same way as those that ask for the argument that employs the same method of reasoning.

Here's an example of this type of question as it would appear on the LSAT.

Example 26:

> If abortion on demand were to become legal there would be a great increase in abortions. And once abortion became commonplace there would be a weakening of respect for human life in general. Once the respect for human life was weakened we would see an increase in euthanasia of all kinds: the elderly, the mentally handicapped, and the physically disabled. Before long we would get rid of anyone who is unpopular or unproductive. In short, it would threaten our civilization. Therefore, we should oppose any move to broaden the grounds of legal abortion.

> The faulty reasoning in which one of the following is most parallel to that in the argument above?

> **(A)** The portrayal of violence on television and in the movies is the main cause of violence in our nation. Hence, to get rid of violence in our nation we must censor television shows and movies.
> **(B)** Mandatory life sentences for three-time felons is a bad idea. People who think it's a good idea think that it will stop violent crime. But if we really want to stop violent crime, instead of locking people up we should eliminate the root cause of violent crime by ceasing to glamorize violence in movies and on television.
> **(C)** It has been well established that smoking marijuana leads to heroin use and that heroin use leads to drug addiction. Drug addiction, in turn, leads to crime to support the drug habit. The epidemic of drug-related crime is threatening the very core of our existence as a nation. Hence, to stop it, we must not legalize marijuana use.
> **(D)** Parents are wrong to criticize their children for coming home late, smoking, watching too much television, and getting poor grades. After all, they do all of these things and they're not all that smart themselves.
> **(E)** Failure to comply with the directions contained in this chain letter will result in bad consequences. Jane Dugal received this letter and passed it on in the required seventy-two-hour period. A week later she won six million dollars in the lottery. Sam Dorfman received it but did not comply with the directions. Within a week after receiving it he was trampled to death by a renegade elephant at the circus.

HOW TO HANDLE SAME REASONING ERROR PROBLEMS

Here's how to deal with parallel reasoning problems that ask you to find an argument that contains the same reasoning error.

First, identify the reasoning error in the argument in the passage. The argument in the passage in Example 26 commits the "slippery slope" fallacy. In this argument, various events are purported to occur as a result of legalizing abortion. The terminus of this sequence of events is a catastrophic event that must be avoided; thus, it is argued, the initiating event should also to be avoided.

Second, look for an answer choice that commits the "slippery slope" fallacy. In the above example, **the correct answer is (C).** In choice (C), marijuana use is linked to heroin use, heroin use is linked to drug addiction, drug addiction is linked to crime, and crime in turn is linked to the downfall of the nation. Since the downfall of the nation is to be avoided, it is argued that marijuana use should be legally curtailed.

Logical Reasoning
Mini-test and Review

In this lesson, you will apply what you learned in Lessons 15 and 16 to a series of Logical Reasoning passages. After taking this mini-test under timed conditions, review the explanations that follow.

LOGICAL REASONING MINI-TEST

NUMBER OF QUESTIONS: 13 • SUGGESTED TIME: 18 MINUTES

Directions: The questions in this section are based on the reasoning contained in brief statements or passages. For some questions, more than one of the choices could conceivably answer the question. However, you are to choose the best answer; that is, the response that most accurately and completely answers the question. You should not make assumptions that are by commonsense standards implausible, superfluous, or incompatible with the passage.

1. To allow the press to keep their sources confidential is very advantageous to our country, because it is highly conducive to the interests of our nation that private individuals should have the privilege of providing information to the press without being identified.

   The faulty reasoning in which one of the following is most parallel to that in the argument above?

   (A) Freedom of the press is a fundamental feature of all democratic societies. Therefore, if a society has a free press, it is democratic.

   (B) The primary reason for widespread unemployment in this nation is that large numbers of people across this great country of ours are out of work.

   (C) In democratic societies the press has an inviolable obligation to publish any news that is in the public interest to have published. Thus, in democratic societies the press has a duty to publish news on any topic that the public shows interest in.

   (D) Free tuition for out-of-state students would be advantageous to students who otherwise could not attend this university. That's why free tuition ought to be implemented for these students.

   (E) Free speech is very advantageous to this country because allowing people to speak their minds without restraint provides a nonviolent means to dissipate their pent-up anger and frustration that results from governmental policies and decisions with which they do not agree.

207

2. Last month video production giant MovieCo announced that it was declaring bankruptcy due to insolvency. Today, another major video production studio—Vidfilms—filed for bankruptcy citing rising production costs as the primary reason for its failure. These facts clearly show that the video production business is in serious trouble and would make a poor investment for the future.

The reasoning in the above argument is most vulnerable to criticism on which of the following grounds?

   (A) The argument employs circular reasoning in which the conclusion is merely a restatement of the information stated in the premises.
   (B) The argument reaches a general conclusion on the basis of a small number of specific instances.
   (C) The argument explains one event as being caused by another event simply because one preceded the other.
   (D) The argument depends upon the assumption that there are only two possible alternatives, and having eliminated one, concludes that the other must be the case.
   (E) The argument involves an equivocation, in that the word "bankruptcy" is allowed to shift its meaning in the course of the argument.

3. Tax laws are fair only if people don't earn different amounts of money or don't pay the same amount in taxes. The reasons for this are clear. If people earn different amounts of money but everyone pays the same amount in taxes, then those who earn more wind up keeping more, and those who earn less keep less. But if this is the case, tax laws are clearly unfair.

Which of the following, in its logical features, most closely parallels the reasoning used in the passage?

   (A) If a person has talent but doesn't develop it, it is a waste. On the other hand, if one has talent and does develop it, it is a wonderful gift. Hence, talent is a wonderful gift only if it is not a waste.
   (B) If Oona doesn't go to preschool, she will either stay at home or remain in day care. But, if she doesn't go to preschool, she will not learn to get along with other children. So, if she stays at home or remains in day care, she won't learn to get along with other children.
   (C) Combustion will not occur if oxygen is not present. But if it doesn't occur, oxygen might nevertheless be present. Hence, the presence of oxygen is necessary but not sufficient for the occurrence of combustion.
   (D) If a person is depressed, they often lose the will to live. But if one loses the will to live, then life isn't worth living. Hence, life is worth living only if one is not depressed.
   (E) If the energy industry is deregulated but energy-related businesses do not profit from it, regulations will be reinstated by Congress. But this will occur only if it can be demonstrated that energy-related businesses are likely to fail in the near future. Hence, either the energy industry is deregulated or it can be demonstrated that energy-related businesses are likely to fail in the near future.

4. *Anti-disarmament spokesperson:*

If you accept the views of those who support disarmament, then you believe that it's all right to expose our spouses and children to the threat of nuclear attack just to save a few dollars on national defense. Personally, I don't think that risking my family for a few measly dollars is worth it. That's why I cannot accept their views.

Which of the following questionable argumentative techniques does the spokesperson employ in the above argument?

(A) Misrepresenting an argument for the purpose of making it easier to attack

(B) Drawing attention away from the real issue of an argument and focusing attention on a side issue

(C) Attacking the character of the person advancing the argument rather than attacking the argument itself

(D) Criticizing an argument by pointing out an inconsistency between what a person says and what he does

(E) Attacking the motives of the person advancing the argument rather than attacking the argument itself

5. The divorce rate of couples who live together before they get married is twice as high as that of couples who do not live together before marriage. Thus, it is evident that living together before getting married damages a couple's chance for a successful marriage.

The argument proceeds by:

(A) reaching a causal conclusion on the basis of a correlation between two circumstances.

(B) generalizing about all couples on the basis of evidence about only those who later divorce.

(C) neglecting evidence about couples who are happily married.

(D) isolating a common feature through a process of elimination and concluding that this feature is causally related to the event under investigation.

(E) reaching a general conclusion on the basis of an unrepresentative sample.

6. *Emily:* The best reason I can think of for not using drugs is that drug use is illegal, and one ought to obey the law.

David: How can you, of all people, think that's a good reason when you rarely drive within the legal speed limit!

Which of the following questionable argumentative techniques does David employ in his response to Emily?

(A) rejecting the conclusion of an argument on the basis of a claim about the motives of the person advancing the argument

(B) attacking the person's character rather than her argument

(C) criticizing an argument by pointing out an inconsistency between what a person says and the way in which she behaves

(D) misrepresenting an argument for the purpose of making it easier to attack

(E) drawing attention away from the real issue of the argument to a side issue and attacking it

7. If abortion on demand were to become legal, there would be a great increase in abortions. And once abortion became commonplace there would be a weakening of respect for human life in general. Once the respect for human life was weakened we would see an increase in euthanasia of all kinds: the elderly, the mentally handicapped, and the physically disabled. Before long we would get rid of anyone who is unpopular or unproductive. In short, it would threaten our civilization. Therefore, we should oppose any move to broaden the grounds of legal abortion.

Which one of the following questionable argumentative techniques is employed in the argument above?

(A) offering a solution to a problem that is based upon an oversimplified analysis of the cause of the problem

(B) reasoning, without appropriate evidence, that a particular action or event will cause a series of events leading ultimately to an obviously undesirable consequence

(C) reasoning that just because one event precedes another it must be the cause of it

(D) diverting attention away from the argument under discussion to a different or related point and arguing against it

(E) misrepresenting an argument and stating it in a way which makes it easy to ridicule or refute

8. The FatGo diet plan is simple and easy: just drink a can of delicious fruit-flavored FatGo in place of your meals each day. Everyone who has tried it has lost weight, and losses of 10 pounds in the first week are not uncommon. Start drinking FatGo today, and next week you'll be the thin person you've always wanted to be.

The faulty reasoning in which one of the following is most parallel to that in the argument above?

(A) My car was working perfectly until I let you drive it on Saturday. Now it won't even start. You must have done something to it that caused this problem.

(B) Studies reveal that people who do not smoke cigars or cigarettes are involved in far fewer serious automobile accidents than those who do. Thus, if you're involved in a serious accident, it's probably because you smoke.

(C) My former husband was a drunk and a wife beater. From that experience I've learned that all men are no good.

(D) Unregulated commercial interactions will confer on this nation the advantages that result when there is an unrestricted flow of products between countries. That's why free trade will be good for this country.

(E) The main cause of illegal drug use in America is unemployment. Thus, to get rid of the drug problem, we have to develop public works programs so that we can provide jobs for everyone.

9. *Sarah:* Possessing marijuana is not a serious offense because unlike offenses such as armed robbery, rape, and murder, in which other people's basic rights are violated, marijuana possession hurts no one. That's why I think it's unjust to send people to prison just because they have it in their possession.

Todd: I agree that possessing marijuana does not pose a threat to others, but I still think that sending people to prison for possessing marijuana is a good idea because it sets an example and lets others know that illegal drug use simply won't be tolerated.

On the basis of their statements, Sarah and Todd are committed to disagreeing about the truth of which of the following principles?

(A) The punishment should always fit the crime.

(B) Victimless crimes should not punished to the same degree as crimes in which victims are involved.

(C) People should be imprisoned only for crimes in which others are harmed.

(D) People should never be imprisoned just in order to set an example to others.

(E) Marijuana should be legalized.

10. When patients undergoing surgery receive positive reinforcement from their doctors, they invariably have fewer complications, and, as a general rule, when patients have fewer complications their recovery time is greatly reduced. Thus, to reduce a patient's recovery time, it is necessary for doctors to provide positive reinforcement to their patients.

The reasoning in the above argument is most vulnerable to criticism on which of the following grounds?

(A) It assumes that receiving positive reinforcement from their doctors will necessarily result in fewer complications.

(B) It assumes that reducing a patient's recovery time is a desirable goal.

(C) It reaches a general conclusion on the basis of insufficient evidence.

(D) It concludes that positive reinforcement by doctors is required to reduce a patient's recovery time, whereas the premises support only the conclusion that it is sufficient.

(E) It fails to consider other means of reducing a patient's recovery time.

11. If legislation is passed completely prohibiting pornography, freedom of artistic expression will be greatly restricted. The legislature has indicated that it will not pass legislation completely prohibiting pornography. Hence, it is likely that freedom of artistic expression will not be severely restricted.

The reasoning in the argument is flawed because:

(A) It fails to recognize the possibility of other factors that might restrict freedom of artistic expression.

(B) The issue of whether pornography is a form of artistic expression has yet to be resolved.

(C) It bases the conclusion on legislation the legislature may pass, rather than on what they have passed.

(D) It assumes that freedom of artistic expression should not be restricted.

(E) It assumes that pornography is an expression of artistic freedom.

12. Scientists cannot afford to mistreat research animals. To be a good research subject, the animal must be adequately fed and housed and kept free of any disease other than the one that may be under investigation. Poor care and treatment will reduce the reliability of the results of the study, and this is something researchers must take every precaution to prevent.

Which one of the following principles, if accepted, would best explain the position taken in the above argument?

(A) Scientists should not mistreat research animals.

(B) Only disease-free animals should be employed as research animals.

(C) Scientists should not deliberately infect research animals with diseases.

(D) Researchers should do everything necessary to ensure the reliability of their results.

(E) Only researchers who love animals should be allowed to use them in scientific experiments.

13. Based on measurements taken from fossil remains of ancient tyrannosaurs, we can reasonably conclude that all of these Upper Cretaceous dinosaurs stood more than 20 feet tall.

The method of the above argument is to:

(A) reach a conclusion about a particular member of a class on the basis of evidence about all members of the class.

(B) regard a claim that is merely probable as though it were certain.

(C) reach a general conclusion on the basis of observed instances.

(D) assert a general claim on the basis of insufficient evidence.

(E) attempt to establish a general statement whose truth can never be verified.

ANSWER KEY AND EXPLANATIONS

1. B	4. A	7. B	10. D	12. D
2. B	5. A	8. A	11. A	13. C
3. D	6. C	9. C		

1. **The correct answer is (B).** This is a moderately difficult question involving parallel reasoning. The argument in the passage can be represented as follows:

    Premise: It is highly conducive to the interests of society that private individuals should have the privilege of providing information to the press without being identified.

    Conclusion: To allow the press to keep their sources confidential is very advantageous to the country.

    An examination of the reasoning in the argument above reveals that it is circular; that is, the conclusion is just a restatement of the premise. What this argument boils down to is simply that it is good for the country to allow the press to keep their sources confidential because doing this is good for the country. Choice (B) is the best response. The argument in choice (B) can be represented as follows:

    Premise: Large numbers of people across this great country of ours are out of work.

    Conclusion: There is widespread unemployment in America.

    The reasoning of the argument in choice (B) is circular. An examination of the conclusion reveals that it is just a restatement of the premise. (A) is an incorrect response. The argument in response (A) can be represented as follows:

    Premise: Freedom of the press is a fundamental feature of all democratic societies.

    Conclusion: If a society has a free press, it is democratic.

    The reasoning in this argument is not circular. The conclusion of this argument is not a restatement of the premise. The premise is equivalent in meaning to the claim that all democratic societies have a free press; i.e., if a society is democratic, then it has a free press. This is not what is stated by the conclusion.

    Choice (C) is an incorrect response. The argument in this answer choice can be represented as follows:

    Premise: In democratic societies the press has an inviolable obligation to publish any news that is in the public interest to have published.

    Conclusion: In democratic societies the press has a duty to publish news on any topic that the public shows interest in.

    The reasoning in this argument is not circular because the conclusion is not a restatement of the premise. While the premise and the conclusion may initially appear to have the same meaning, a closer examination reveals that in the premise the phrase "in the public interest" means "that which is relevant to the public's well being," whereas in the conclusion what the "public shows interest in" means "that which they find fascinating."

Choice (D) is incorrect. Its argument can be represented as follows:

> *Premise:* Free tuition for out-of-state students would be advantageous to students who otherwise could not attend this university.

> *Conclusion:* That's why free tuition ought to be implemented for these students.

This reasoning is not circular because the conclusion is not a restatement of the premise.

Choice (E) is incorrect. Its argument can be represented as follows:

> *Premise:* Allowing people to speak their minds without restraint provides a non-violent means to dissipate their pent up anger and frustration that results from governmental policies and decisions with which they do not agree.

> *Conclusion:* Free speech is very advantageous to this country.

The reasoning is not circular because the conclusion is not a restatement of the premise.

2. **The correct answer is (B).** This is a relatively easy question involving a reasoning error. The conclusion of the argument in the passage is based on two specific examples of failed video production businesses. Since no indication is given in the passage that these two cases are representative of the condition of other video production companies or of the industry at large, the conclusion based upon them that all such businesses are in trouble is highly suspect. Choice (A) describes the reasoning in the argument incorrectly. The conclusion of the argument is "the video production business is in serious trouble and would make a poor investment for the future." This sentence is not a restatement of the premises of the argument. Choice (C) incorrectly describes the reasoning in the argument. Admittedly, the facts stated in the premises "precede" the conclusion in the sense that they appear at the beginning of the argument and the conclusion appears after them, but this is irrelevant to the reasoning. Choice (D) incorrectly describes the reasoning in the argument as well. No alternatives are mentioned in the passage. In choice (E), although the word "bankruptcy" appears in both premises, its meaning in both occurrences is the same.

3. **The correct answer is (D).** This is a challenging question involving parallel reasoning. The argument in the passage can be represented as follows:

> *Premise:* If people earn different amounts of money but everyone pays the same amount in taxes, then those who earn more wind up keeping more and those who earn less keep less.

> *Premise:* If those who earn more wind up keeping more and those who earn less keep less, tax laws are clearly unjust.

> *Conclusion:* Tax laws are just only if people don't earn different amounts of money or don't pay the same amount in taxes.

The logical pattern of this argument can be diagrammed as follows:

Premise: If P, then Q.

Premise: If Q, then not R.

Conclusion: R, only if P.

Choice (D) is the best answer. Its argument can be represented as follows:

Premise: If a person is depressed, they often lose the will to live.

Premise: If one loses the will to live, then life isn't worth living.

Conclusion: Life is worth living only if one is not depressed.

A comparison of this argument with the argument above reveals that they share exactly the same logical pattern.

Choice (A) is incorrect. Its argument can be represented as follows:

Premise: If a person has talent but doesn't develop it, it is a waste.

Premise: If a person has talent and does develop it, it is a wonderful gift.

Conclusion: Talent is a wonderful gift only if it is not a waste.

Unlike the argument in the passage outlined above, the "if" clause of the second premise of this argument is not the same as the "then" clause of the first premise.

Choice (B) is also incorrect, and its argument can be represented as follows:

Premise: If Oona doesn't go to preschool, she will either stay at home or remain in day care.

Premise: If Oona doesn't go to preschool, she will not learn to get along with other children.

Conclusion: If Oona stays at home or remains in day care, she won't learn to get along with other children.

Unlike the argument in the passage outlined above, the "if" clause of the first premise of this argument is the same as the "if" clause of the second premise.

Choice (C) is an incorrect response; its argument can be represented as follows:

Premise: If oxygen is not present, combustion will not occur.

Premise: If combustion does not occur, oxygen might nevertheless be present.

Conclusion: The presence of oxygen is necessary but not sufficient for the occurrence of combustion.

The main difference between this argument and the argument in the passage outlined above is to be found in the conclusions of these arguments.

Choice (E) is incorrect. The argument in choice (E) can be represented as follows:

Premise: If the energy industry is deregulated but energy related businesses do not profit from it, regulations will be reinstated by Congress.

Premise: Regulations will be reinstated by Congress only if it can be demonstrated that energy-related businesses are likely to fail in the near future.

Conclusion: Either the energy industry is deregulated or it can be demonstrated that energy-related businesses are likely to fail in the near future.

The main difference between this argument and the argument in the passage outlined above is to be found in the conclusions of these arguments.

4. **The correct answer is (A).** This is a moderately difficult question requiring you to identify the method of the argument. The spokesperson presents a distorted account of the views of those who support disarmament and then easily refutes it. The spokesperson's characterization of the pro-disarmament argument leads one to believe that the only reason they offer in support of their view is a savings on national defense, and furthermore, that they think this is more important than the potential risk to the lives of their loved ones. This characterization of the pro-disarmament argument is easy to refute, but it is highly doubtful that this is an accurate portrayal of the argument. Choice (B) is incorrect. The issue in the argument in the passage is whether disarmament ought to be pursued as a national goal. The spokesperson's argument is focused directly on this issue, and not on a side issue. Choices (C) and (E) are incorrect. The spokesperson does not directly attack the character or motives of persons who advocate disarmament, but admittedly, their characters and motives are denigrated by the suggestion that they care more about saving a few dollars on national defense than they do about protecting their families. Choice (D) incorrectly describes the spokesperson's argument.

5. **The correct answer is (A).** This is a moderately difficult question requiring you to identify the method of the argument. The method employed in the argument in the passage is to reach a causal conclusion on the basis of a correlation between two events. In this case, living together before marriage is correlated with a higher divorce rate. The conclusion drawn from this correlation is that living together before marriage increases the likelihood that the marriage will be unsuccessful. Choice (A) is the best response. Choices (B) and (C) are off-focus. The task in this problem is to identify the method of the argument in the passage, not to find fault with the argument. Choice (D) incorrectly describes the passage. In the passage there is no comparison of features possessed by couples who live together before marriage with features possessed by couples who do not, nor is one identified as the common feature by a process of elimination. Choice (E) is off-focus. The task in this problem is to identify the method of the argument in the passage, not to find fault with the argument. In any case, the "representativeness" of the sample on which the conclusion is based cannot be ascertained given the information stated in the passage.

6. **The correct answer is (C).** This is a moderately difficult question requiring you to identify the method of the argument. Emily's argument against using drugs is based on the premise that one ought to obey the law. David rejects this premise, not by challenging its truth, but by claiming that Emily often behaves in ways that are inconsistent with it. Choices (A) and (B) incorrectly describe David's response. Neither Emily's motives for advancing the argument nor her character are brought into

question by David. Choice (D) incorrectly describes the passage. David does not restate or misrepresent Emily's argument in the passage. Choice (E) is incorrect. The point of David's remark is not to draw attention away from the issue of Emily's argument, but rather to draw attention to an apparent inconsistency between Emily's pronouncement regarding obeying the law and her actions.

7. **The correct answer is (B).** This is a moderately difficult question involving a reasoning error. The argument in the passage proceeds by citing a chain of events that are thought likely to occur if the abortion on demand were to become legal. The chain ends with an event that is clearly undesirable, leading to the conclusion that to avoid the undesirable outcome of the series we should not allow the initiating event to occur. Choice (A) is incorrect; no analysis of the problem under discussion, oversimplified or otherwise, is mentioned in the passage. Choices (C), (D), and (E) do not provide correct descriptions of the argument in the passage.

8. **The correct answer is (A).** This is a moderately difficult question involving parallel reasoning. The argument in the passage is an example of "after this, therefore because of this" reasoning; that is, regarding an event that preceded another as being the cause of it. Basically, the argument in the passage is that since the weight loss followed the ingestion of FatGo in place of meals, FatGo is the cause of the weight loss. The reasoning in this argument is faulty because it completely overlooks other possible causes for the weight loss. Choice (A) is the best response because its reasoning is that, since the problem with the car followed the person's use of the car, the person's use of the car is the cause of the problem. The reasoning in choice (A) is similar to that of the passage. Choice (B) is incorrect; its reasoning confuses a correlation between two events with a causal relation between those events. While the occurrence of a correlation between events indicates the possibility that they are causally related, it is also possible that the correlation is just a coincidence. In any case, the reasoning in choice (B) is not similar to the reasoning in the passage. Choice (C) is incorrect. This is an example of reasoning to a general conclusion on the basis of insufficient evidence. The fact that one man behaves in a certain way is not sufficient grounds for the conclusion that all men behave in that way. In any case, the reasoning in choice (C) is not similar to the reasoning in the passage. Choice (D) is incorrect because it exemplifies circular reasoning. The premise and the conclusion of the argument in choice (D) express the same thing; its reasoning is not similar to that of the passage. Choice (E) is incorrect because the premise of its argument states an oversimplified account of the cause of the problem. The conclusion states a solution to the problem that addresses the cause identified in the premise. The reasoning in choice (E) is not similar to the reasoning in the passage.

9. **The correct answer is (C).** This is a challenging question requiring you to identify a principle. Sarah's main reason for not wanting to imprison people in possession of marijuana is that possession of marijuana is not an act that harms others. This indicates that Sarah subscribes to the principle that only crimes in which others are harmed should be punished with imprisonment. Todd's response indicates that he agrees that possessing marijuana does not harm others, but he maintains that persons who possess it should be imprisoned anyway. This indicates that he does not subscribe to the principle that only crimes in which others are harmed should be punished with imprisonment.

In choice (A), there is no indication in the passage that Todd and Sarah would necessarily disagree about the truth of this principle. In fact, it is because Sarah believes that the punishment does not fit the crime in the case of marijuana possession that she is opposed to sending persons to prison for doing this. Given the information in the passage, Todd's stance on this principle cannot be ascertained. Choice (B) also does not indicate that Todd and Sarah would necessarily disagree about the truth of this principle. Choice (D) is incorrect; Todd obviously does not subscribe to this principle because he is quite willing to send people who possess marijuana to jail to set an example to others that illegal drug use will not be tolerated. Sarah's stance on this principle, however, cannot be determined given the information in the passage. Choice (E) does not indicate that Todd and Sarah would necessarily disagree about the truth of this principle. Todd's opposition to marijuana possession appears to be based solely on the fact that it is an illegal drug. It is consistent with this opposition that he subscribes to the view that marijuana should be legalized. Sarah's stance on this principle, however, cannot be determined given the information in the passage.

10. **The correct answer is (D).** This is a moderately difficult question involving a reasoning error. The conclusion that can be correctly inferred from the premises of the argument is that when patients undergoing surgery receive positive reinforcement from their doctors, their recovery time is greatly reduced. This means that to reduce a patient's recovery time it is sufficient for the doctor to give the patient positive reinforcement; it does not mean that it is necessary to do this. Choices (A) and (B) are off-focus. Pointing out that an argument involves an assumption does not, by itself, show a weakness in an argument. To function as a criticism of an argument, in addition to pointing out that it involves a particular assumption, it would have to be shown that the assumption was questionable or false. Choice (C) incorrectly describes the argument in the passage. No evidence, in the sense of sample cases, is offered in the argument. Choice (E) is, like choices (A) and (B), off-focus. It is consistent with the conclusion of the argument that other ways of reducing a patient's recovery time might yet exist. In other words, the conclusion does not state that positive reinforcement by doctors is the only way to reduce the patient's recovery time.

11. **The correct answer is (A).** This is a moderately difficult question involving a reasoning error. The argument in the passage considers only one factor that might lead to the restriction of freedom of artistic expression. Concluding that freedom of artistic expression will not be severely restricted because this factor can be eliminated is warranted only if it can be shown that there are no other factors that might have this effect. Choice (B) brings in information not mentioned in the passage. The conclusion in choice (C) is stated in such a way as to take into account the fact that the legislature has not yet passed the legislation. Choices (D) and (E) do not point out flaws in the reasoning of the argument. The fact that an argument makes an assumption, even a false one, is not a reasoning flaw.

12. **The correct answer is (D).** This is a moderately difficult question requiring you to identify a principle. The only reason offered in the passage for not mistreating research animals is that to do so will reduce the reliability of the results of the study. Furthermore, it is maintained in the passage that this is "something researchers must

take every precaution to prevent." The underlying assumption in this argument is that researchers must take every precaution to ensure the reliability of the results of their studies. Choice (A) would not help to explain the position taken in the passage. The only reason offered in the passage for not mistreating research animals is that to do so will reduce the reliability of the results of the study. Mistreatment that would not jeopardize the results of the study is not discussed in the passage, but, conceivably, if mistreatment would ensure the reliability of the results, it would be allowed. Choice (B) is inconsistent with the passage. The passage states that research animals should be "kept free of any disease other than the one that may be under investigation." This implies that the research animals need not be disease-free. Choice (C) would not help to explain the position taken in the passage. If the deliberate infection of research animals would ensure the reliability of the results of the study, it would not be prohibited. Similarly, choice (E) would not help to explain the position taken in the passage. Whether researchers love the animals involved in their research is irrelevant to the position taken in the passage.

13. **The correct answer is (C).** This is relatively easy question requiring you to identify the method of the argument. The method employed in the argument in the passage is to reach a general conclusion on the basis of observed instances. In this case, observation of fossil remains of an animal is the basis for a conclusion about all animals of the type observed. The method described in choice (A) is the opposite of the method employed in the passage. Choice (B) incorrectly describes the passage. The phrase "we can reasonably conclude" indicates that the claim expressed in the conclusion is regarded as being probable, not certain. Choice (D) is incorrect; there is no indication in the passage of the extent of the fossil evidence. Whether or not this evidence is insufficient cannot be determined given the information in the passage. Choice (E) is off-focus. The task in this problem is to identify the method of the argument in the passage, not to find fault with the argument.

Analytical Reasoning Selection, Spatial, and Tree Games

In this lesson, you will examine and learn to handle additional types of logic games that appear commonly on the Analytical Reasoning section.

THE SIMPLE SELECTION GAME

Selection games involve dividing subjects into exactly two groups. The term "selection" is used here because your task is to select particular subjects from a roster or pool, while the remaining subjects remain deselected. Two groups result: those subjects that are selected, and those subjects that are not selected. In other words, for each subject you must make a yes-or-no decision—for example, is the subject:

- included or excluded?
- going or staying?
- on or off?

A simple selection game is one that involves a fixed number of selected subjects.

Example 1:

A particular two-story apartment building includes ten units. Apartments A, B, C, D, and E are located on the second floor. Apartments F, G, H, I, and J are located on the first floor. Each apartment is either vacant or occupied.

Six of the apartments are occupied.

Apartments B and C are not both occupied.

Either Apartment D or I, or both, are vacant.

Apartments G and H are either both vacant or both occupied.

Either Apartment E or Apartment J, but not both, is vacant.

If there are more vacant apartments on the first floor than on the second floor, all of the following must be true EXCEPT:

(A) Apartment F is vacant.
(B) Apartment I is vacant.
(C) Apartment B is vacant.
(D) Apartment D is occupied.
(E) Apartment E is occupied.

As in any logic game, ask yourself what you can deduce from the rules. Since a total of six apartments must be occupied, four must be vacant. Either E or J is vacant, either D or I must be vacant, and either B or C must be vacant. Thus, G and H cannot both be vacant; otherwise, at least five apartments would be vacant. Accordingly, G and H must both be occupied. The best diagramming approach to a game such as this involves the use of a simple roster, along with a shorthand restatement of the rules. Circle both G and H in the diagram:

```
(6 OCCUPIED)
                        * D/I (OR BOTH) VACANT
A  B  C  D  E           * J ≠ E
F  Ⓖ  Ⓗ  I  J           * B/C (OR BOTH) VACANT
```

Then, as you respond to the questions, indicate that an apartment is occupied by circling it on your roster, and indicate that an apartment is vacant by crossing it out on your roster.

The correct answer is (C). A total of four apartments must be vacant (because six are occupied). Since G and H are both occupied, the other three apartments on the first floor must be vacant, while only one apartment on the second floor is vacant. Since B and C cannot be occupied, either B or C must be the one second-floor apartment that is vacant. Accordingly, A, D, and E must all be occupied:

```
Ⓐ  B  C  Ⓓ  Ⓔ   (4)
F̶  Ⓖ  Ⓗ  I̶  J̶   (2)
```

THE COMPLEX SELECTION GAME

A complex (relatively difficult) selection game involves an unfixed number of selected subjects. Selection games can be further complicated by the inclusion of conditional statements, which you can easily misinterpret if you're not careful.

Example 2:

Nine people—P, Q, R, S, T, U, V, W, and X—all wish to go on a particular fishing trip.

Either V or S must go, but V and S cannot both go.

Among P, T, and X, exactly two must go.

If either T or U goes, both T and U must go.

X will not go unless R goes.

If P or Q (but not both) goes, then V or W (but not both) must go.

If fewer people go on the trip than do not go, how many different distinct groups can be assembled to go on the trip?

(A) 1
(B) 2
(C) 3
(D) 4
(E) 5

As in Example 1, the best diagramming approach here is to use a simple roster, along with a shorthand restatement of the rules. Arrange the subjects in your roster to reflect particular rules. Rephrase conditional statements that are expressed in a confusing manner, being very careful to interpret the statements correctly. For example, the rule that X cannot go unless R goes can properly be restated as "If X goes, then R must go" and expressed in shorthand form:

```
(1) V  S        (T U)
(2) P  T  X     X→R
    Q  R  U  W  P/Q (BNB)→V̸W (BNB)
```

As you respond to the questions, select subjects by circling them on your roster, and eliminate subjects by crossing them out on your roster.

The correct answer is (B). To satisfy the condition in the question stem, no more than four people can go. According to the rules, among P, T, and X, exactly two must go. Assume first that P and T (but not X) go. Since T goes, U must go. According to the rules, either S or V must go. In this case, it must be V that goes, because P is going without Q. (One of the rules requires either V or W to go in this situation.)

So one possible combination of four is: P, T, U, V. Next, assume instead that P and X (but not T) go. Since X goes, R must go. Again, V (not S) must also go. So a second possible combination of four is: P, X, R, V. Finally, assume instead that T and X (but not P) go. Since X goes, R must go. Since T goes, U must go. However, the rules require either S or V to go as well, which renders this scenario impossible, given that only four people go. So we're left with two possible combinations (of four) altogether.

SPATIAL GAMES

The Line-and-Node Game

Line-and-node games involve spatial connections between the subjects of the game. Your task is to determine how to get from one subject (or node) to the other subjects following the connecting lines. Some lines may be two-way streets, while others may be one-way streets. Also, some subjects might be impossible to reach from certain other subjects. The rules tend to be permissive in nature rather than mandatory; that is, the rules speak in terms of where you can go from any given point of departure, rather than compelling you to go. Do not be intimidated by a line-and-node game just because the game looks lengthy. These games tend to be relatively easy.

Example 3:

A commuter-subway schedule for a particular city lists all of the routes among seven stations—A, B, C, D, E, F, and G. Subways must stop as they pass through every station. In examining the schedule, a commuter has made the following observations:

He may ride from A directly to B and D only.

He may ride from B directly to only one station.

He may ride from C directly to E and F only.

He may ride from D directly to C only.

He may ride from E directly to only one station.

He may ride from F directly to A, C, and G only; he may ride to F directly from C only.

He may ride from G directly to A only.

He may ride from C to D by stopping at one other station first.

He may ride from B to E by stopping at two other stations first.

> If the commuter departs from F and makes five stops, which of the following is a complete and accurate list of the stations which might be the fifth stop?
>
> **(A)** C, D, E, F, G
> **(B)** A, B, D, E, G
> **(C)** A, B, C, E, F, G
> **(D)** B, C, D, E, F, G
> **(E)** A, B, C, D, E, F, G

Example 3 may look very much like the send-and-receive games we explored in Lesson 10. However, the recommended approach to send-and-receive games is awkward to use here, where you must trace a route from subject to subject. Instead, construct a line-and-node chart (or flowchart). It is not important how the stations are arranged; the key is to connect them in a way that accurately reflects the rules of the game. All of the rules, with the exception of the last two rules (involving interim stops), can be charted as follows:

```
G
↑↘
F → A → (B) → (?) (NOT F)
↑↓       ↓
C ← D
↓
E → (?) (NOT F)
```

Next, consider the two rules involving interim stops in light of this flowchart. First, if a commuter can ride from B to E by stopping at two other stations during the interim, a route must run directly from B to D. The commuter cannot ride from B through G and D to E, because from G he may ride to A only. A commuter cannot ride from B through F and C to E, because the only direct route to F is from C. A commuter cannot ride from B through A and D to E, because he may ride from D to C only. Secondly, if a commuter can ride from C to D by stopping at one other station during the interim, a route must run directly from E to D because E is the only station to which the commuter can ride directly from C:

The correct response to the question is (E). From F, the commuter might end at any of the seven stations after five stops. The commuter may ride back and forth between F and C as often as necessary to end at the desired fifth stop:

$$F \rightarrow C \rightarrow F \rightarrow C \rightarrow F \rightarrow A$$
$$F \rightarrow C \rightarrow F \rightarrow G \rightarrow A \rightarrow B$$
$$F \rightarrow G \rightarrow A \rightarrow B \rightarrow D \rightarrow C$$
$$F \rightarrow C \rightarrow F \rightarrow G \rightarrow A \rightarrow D$$
$$F \rightarrow C \rightarrow E \rightarrow D \rightarrow C \rightarrow E$$
$$F \rightarrow G \rightarrow A \rightarrow D \rightarrow C \rightarrow F$$
$$F \rightarrow C \rightarrow F \rightarrow C \rightarrow F \rightarrow G$$

The Multiple Row Game

Multiple row games involve arranging the game's subjects spatially among two or more rows. A diagram is usually provided to identify rows and columns. Do not be intimidated by a multiple-row game just because the game looks lengthy or complex. In actuality, these games tend to be easier-than-average.

Example 4:

A high-school debating team is traveling by airplane to compete in the national debating championships. The team consists of six students—K, L, M, N, O, and P. The team is accompanied on the trip by two teachers—X and Y. Each student and each teacher has been assigned a seat in either row 1 or row 2 of the airplane. Three executives have also each been assigned a seat in row 1 or row 2. Each row includes six seats, three on each side of the aisle:

```
SEAT:   A B C  D E F
row 1   _ _ _||_ _ _
row 2   _ _ _||_ _ _
```

L and M must sit next to each other, and M must occupy a window seat.

N and O must sit next to each other, and N must occupy an aisle seat.

P and K must sit next to each other, and P must occupy a window seat.

Passengers seated across the aisle from each other are not considered to be seated "next to" each other.

A passenger is seated directly ahead or behind another passenger only if the two passengers share the same seat letter but in adjacent rows.

If X and Y both occupy window seats, and if N is seated directly in front of one of the three executives, any of the following could be true EXCEPT:

(A)　O is seated next to an executive
(B)　Y is seated next to an executive
(C)　L and P occupy seats on different sides of the aisle
(D)　O is seated directly in front of K
(E)　M and O occupy seats on the same side of the aisle

Before you respond to the question, it is helpful to realize that two pairs of students (a "pair" includes two students that must sit next to each other) must sit on one side of the aisle while the third pair sits on the other side. The diagrams below indicate two of several acceptable arrangements (notice in the diagrams that P and M are each occupying window seats, while N is occupying an aisle seat, all conforming to the rules of the game).

One possible arrangement:

```
[PK]_| |[NO]_
[ML]_| |  _ _ _
```

Another possible arrangement:

```
[ML]_ |  |_ _ _
  _[ON]| |_[KP]
```

The question is really rather easy to analyze in light of the foregoing scheme. The question stem stipulates that X and Y both occupy window seats. According to the original conditions, P and M also each occupy window seats. Two basic alternatives emerge: either X and Y sit on the same side of the aisle (with PK and ML all on the other side) or X and Y sit on different sides of the aisle (with PK and ML on different sides). Here's an example.

One possible arrangement:

```
[PK]_| |[NO]X
[ML]_| | E_ Y
```

Another possible arrangement:

```
[ML]_ | |[NO]Y
 X _ _| |E[KP]
```

When you consider these diagrams, bear in mind that these do not represent the only possible positions for X and Y. For instance, the positions of X and Y could be reversed. Similarly, PK and ML could be reversed. Finally, the horizontal "mirror image" of each diagram would also be valid. In any event, however, NO must sit in row 1, and O must sit next to either X or Y. Why? Because the question stem stipulates that N sits directly in front of one of the executives. Thus, N must sit in row 1 as indicated in the diagrams above.

The correct answer is (A). O must sit between N and one of the two teachers and therefore cannot sit next to an executive.

The Circle Game

Circle games almost invariably involve people seated around a round table; and the seats are always equally-spaced. Circle games can be quite confusing because there is no definite starting place (or ending place) for the sequence. For example, in a circle of eight seats, a person seated two seats away from another person would also be seated six seats away from that person. If you are not ready with a systematic approach, this type of game can be quite confounding. The key to cutting through the confusion is in the diagram approach.

Example 5:

> Four people—A, B, C, and D—are to be seated at a round table. There are six chairs equidistantly spaced around the table.
>
> A must sit two seats from B.
>
> C must sit next to either A or B, or both.
>
> > If D sits next to A, which of the following must be true?
>
> **(A)**   A sits directly across from an empty chair.
> **(B)**   D sits directly across from an empty chair.
> **(C)**   D sits two seats from an empty chair.
> **(D)**   A sits next to an empty chair.
> **(E)**   C sits next to an empty chair.

Based on the rules alone, you can eliminate C from the only position which is next to neither A nor B, and the resulting diagram may look something like this:

Notice that, in the diagram above, only one of the two possible positions of B (relative to A) is accounted for. A second (alternative) diagram is not necessary, since the rules are not concerned with direction (left or right). Alternative diagrams would simply be mirror images of each other, and either diagram would be sufficient to analyze the question. In answering the question, however, accounting for both possible positions of D (either to the left or to the right of A) does suggest two distinct variations (which are not mirror images) of the basic diagram. The position of one of the empty chairs can now be determined (an empty chair is represented by an "X"). Notice that a total of four possible arrangements result—only the positions of C and the second empty chair remain undetermined:

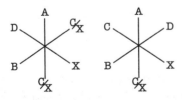

This diagram makes it clear that the correct response to the question is answer choice (C); in either diagram, D must sit two seats from an empty chair.

Keep in mind that Example 5 is a relatively simple game. A circle game may involve a greater number of seats and subjects. It may also incorporate some other issue; for example, whether each subject is male or female. Nevertheless, Example 5 illustrates a number of features that are unique to circle games. The following suggestions should help you avoid common mistakes and handle this game type efficiently.

DRAW SPOKES, NOT CIRCLES

The game may involve from 5 to 10 (and most likely either 6 or 8) different positions around the circle, usually described as seats around a table. Invariably, the seats are equidistant (spaced evenly) around the table. Represent the seats as ends of intersecting spokes rather than points around the perimeter of a circle. Spokes are easier to draw and they make clear whether two subjects are seated directly across from one another (a common issue in circle games).

CIRCLE SEQUENCES ARE "UNFIXED"

In all circle games appearing on past exams, the various positions around the circle have not been numbered or otherwise specifically identified. Unless the seats are distinguishable (and they probably won't be), you may arbitrarily choose any position (such as the top of the circle) as a starting point in building your diagram.

WATCH FOR MIRROR IMAGES

Often, the rules suggest two basic alternate diagrams, which are simply mirror images of each other. You can safely disregard one of the diagrams when answering the questions. Example 5 illustrates this point: the initial diagram omitted to account for the possibility that B sits two seats to the left of A. Accounting for this possibility results in two mirror image diagrams, either of which suffices to analyze the question.

LOOK FOR A KEY AXIS

A rule that stipulates that two particular subjects are positioned directly across from each other suggest an axis, and all of the remaining subjects must be grouped or separated on either side of that axis. Approach the game from this viewpoint.

DON'T BE CONCERNED WITH LEFT/RIGHT ORIENTATION

It is unlikely that any rule or question will involve direction (left or right), since direction is ambiguous without knowing whether a person is facing toward or away from the center of the circle.

THE LOGIC TREE GAME

The rules of a logic tree game can be characterized as the building blocks of logic trees. Your primary task is to construct the tree through repeated application of a formula or alternative formulas. Because these games deal with abstract relationships and conditional statements, they tend to be difficult.

Example 6:

Gremlins are always either white, orange, or brown in color.

Any mating involving an orange gremlin produces only brown gremlins.

Any mating involving a white gremlin produces only white gremlins.

No mating between two brown gremlins ever produces a brown gremlin.

Any of the following could be among the four grandparents of a brown gremlin EXCEPT:

(A) exactly four brown gremlins
(B) exactly three brown gremlins
(C) exactly two orange gremlins
(D) exactly one orange gremlin
(E) exactly three orange gremlins

Example 6 is typical of a logic tree game in that several alternative formulas result from the rules. For example, a brown gremlin can result only from the mating of either two orange gremlins or one orange and one brown gremlin. That is, there are two alternative formulas for producing a brown gremlin. An orange gremlin can result only from the mating of two brown gremlins (because an orange parent produces only brown offspring and a white parent always produces white offspring). That is, there is only one formula for producing an orange gremlin. As long as an orange gremlin does not participate in a mating, the mating might produce a white gremlin. Thus, there are three alternative formulas for producing a white gremlin. Listing each and every different formula may, however, result in confusion. Instead, indicate general formulas as follows:

$$O \rightarrow B$$
$$W \rightarrow W$$
$$(BB) \rightarrow \cancel{O}/W$$

The correct answer is (E). The arrows in this diagram suggest a rule of condition (an "if/then" statement), so the contrapositive rule of logic is likely to come into play (see "Formal Logic" in Lesson 1). Neither parent of a brown gremlin can be white (a white gremlin produces only white gremlins). Both parents of a brown gremlin cannot be brown. Thus, two possibilities exist with respect to the parents of a brown gremlin—one must be orange while the other is either brown or orange:

$$(O\,O) \rightarrow B$$
$$(O\,B) \rightarrow B$$

Orange offspring can be produced only by two brown parents. Thus, in the first scenario, all four grandparents must be brown. Brown offspring can be produced only from either two orange parents or one orange parent and one brown parent (the identical formula as that in the diagram immediately above). Adding this information to the diagram above:

(1) $\begin{matrix} (B\,B) \rightarrow \\ (B\,B) \rightarrow \end{matrix} \left.\begin{matrix} O \\ O \end{matrix}\right\} \rightarrow B$

(2) $\begin{matrix} (B\,B) \rightarrow \\ (O\,\cancel{B}) \rightarrow \end{matrix} \left.\begin{matrix} O \\ B \end{matrix}\right\} \rightarrow B$

At most, then, two of the grandparents can be orange. Thus, answer choice (E) is the correct response. Notice that analyzing the question required repeated application of one or more formulas. Remember that these formulas are the blocks with which you must construct a logic tree for a question.

THE FAMILY TREE GAME

Family tree games, as the term suggests, involve familial relationships among the subjects. The terms "paternal" and "maternal" are occasionally used in family-tree games. Remote relationships, such as second cousins and cousins once removed, are not included.

Family tree games always call for you to establish the relationships among various family members, but they may also require you to identify the gender (sex) of one or more family members. Example 7 involves both issues.

Example 7:

Six people—A, B, C, D, E, and F—are related to X—a woman—as X's husband, sister, son, daughter, mother, and aunt, although not necessarily in that order.

C and D are either both male or both female.

Either A or B, or both, are male.

Either E or F, or both, are female.

If B is F's daughter, which of the following statements could be true?

(A) A is X's sister.
(B) F is C's aunt.
(C) E is D's nephew.
(D) E is A's granddaughter.
(E) B is D's niece.

The correct answer is (E). A variety of alternative symbols and techniques can be used to construct a family-tree diagram. You may prefer to use your own symbols instead of those used below. You have several different options for distinguishing between male and female relatives in a family-tree diagram. One way is to indicate a male relative with a square and a female relative with a circle. Another helpful idea for indicating gender is to consistently place a husband to one side—for example, to the left—of his wife.

In the question at hand, two of X's six relatives are male and four are female. Since C is of the same sex as D, both must be female; otherwise, neither A nor B could be male. The gender combinations are displayed below. Roster #1 assumes that A and B are both male, while roster #2 assumes that either A or B, but not both, is male:

(1) $\boxed{A}$ $\boxed{B}$ $\bigcirc$ $\bigcirc$ $\bigcirc$ $\bigcirc$
   Ⓐ Ⓑ Ⓒ Ⓓ Ⓔ Ⓕ

(2) $A \neq B$ Ⓒ Ⓓ $E \neq F$

To visualize the various family relationships, you should also construct a family tree around X. Although X's aunt could be either X's father's sister or mother's sister, this distinction does not come into play in the game, so in the diagram below, X's aunt is indicated as X's mother's sister:

Given that B is F's daughter, B and F must either be X's daughter and husband, respectively, or X's sister and mother, respectively. Choice (E) could be true; F would be X's mother, D would be F's sister, and B would be X's sister. Choice (A) must be false—if A is X's sister, A and B would both be female, which is impossible. Choice (B) must also be false. None of the six relatives could be F's niece. Choice (C) must be false as well; E and D would have to be X's son and sister, respectively. Accordingly, F and B would have to be X's husband and daughter, respectively; however, E and F cannot both be male. Choice (D) must be false because E and A would have to be X's daughter and mother, respectively; if so, B could not be F's daughter.

Analytical Reasoning
Mini-test and Review

In this lesson, you will apply what you learned in Lesson 18 to three logic games. After taking this mini-test under timed conditions, review the explanations that follow. Preceding the explanation for each game, the game type and difficulty level are identified.

ANALYTICAL REASONING MINI-TEST

NUMBER OF QUESTIONS: 18 • SUGGESTED TIME: 26 MINUTES

Directions: Each group of questions in this section is based on a set of conditions. In answering some of the questions, it may be useful to draw a rough diagram. Choose the response that most accurately and completely answers each question and blacken the corresponding space on your answer sheet.

QUESTIONS 1–7:

From among eight volunteers—A, B, C, D, E, F, G, and H—a park ranger must select at least four for a search party. The park ranger's selections are bound by the following restrictions:

  If A is selected, B must be selected.

  If either C or D is selected, both C and D must be selected.

  If E is selected, D cannot be selected.

  Either E or G must be selected, but E and G cannot both be selected.

  H and B cannot both be selected if G is selected.

1. Which of the following could be a complete and accurate list of the search-party members?

   (A) H, G, A, F
   (B) H, D, C, F
   (C) B, D, G, F, H
   (D) E, A, B, F, H
   (E) G, C, D, B, H

2. If G is NOT selected, all of the following must be true EXCEPT:

   (A) B will be selected.
   (B) A will be selected.
   (C) E will be selected.
   (D) C will not be selected.
   (E) D will not be selected.

233

3. If the search party includes G and exactly four other volunteers, which of the following volunteers must be one of those four?

   (A) B
   (B) C
   (C) F
   (D) A
   (E) H

4. If the search party includes the maximum number of volunteers, which of the following is a complete and accurate list of the volunteers NOT included in the search party?

   (A) E
   (B) G
   (C) E, A
   (D) E, H
   (E) G, C, D

5. If A and H are both selected, with respect to how many volunteers can it be determined whether or not the volunteer is selected?

   (A) 4
   (B) 5
   (C) 6
   (D) 7
   (E) 8

6. If the search party includes A and exactly three other volunteers, how many distinct combinations of search-party members are possible?

   (A) 1
   (B) 2
   (C) 3
   (D) 4
   (E) 5

7. G must be selected for the search party if:

   (A) A is not selected
   (B) B is not selected
   (C) C is not selected
   (D) F is not selected
   (E) H is not selected

QUESTIONS 8–12:

Bob is planning a backpacking trip in Pine National Park. The park contains seven camps—A, B, C, D, E, F, and G. Bob must begin and end his trip as well as spend each interim night only among these seven camps. His trip is subject to the following restrictions:

> From Camp A, campers may hike directly to Camp B only.
>
> From Camp B, campers may hike directly to Camps A and D only.
>
> From Camp C, campers may hike directly to Camps B and F only.
>
> From Camp D, campers must not hike to any other camp.
>
> From Camp E, campers may hike directly to Camp C only.
>
> From Camp F, campers may hike directly to Camps A and C only.
>
> From Camp G, campers may hike directly to Camps E and F only.

Except where a round trip between two camps is possible, the elevation of each camp is higher than that of the next camp visited.

8. If Bob plans to visit all seven camps without visiting the same camp twice, which of the following routes can he follow, from first to last camp visited?

   (A) E, G, F, C, A, B, D
   (B) G, E, C, F, A, B, D
   (C) F, G, E, C, D, B, A
   (D) G, F, E, C, A, B, D
   (E) G, E, C, B, D, F, A

9. If Bob plans to begin and end his trip at the same camp, spending one interim night in the park, how many distinct routes may he follow?

   (A) 2
   (B) 3
   (C) 4
   (D) 5
   (E) 6

10. Any of the following could be true EXCEPT:

    (A) Camp C is higher in elevation than Camp A.
    (B) Camp E is lower is elevation than Camp D.
    (C) Camp C is higher in elevation than Camp F.
    (D) Camp E is neither higher nor lower in elevation than Camp A.
    (E) Camp F is neither higher nor lower in elevation than Camp D.

11. If Bob visits at least two camps in addition to the camp at which he begins his trip, with respect to how many different departure points is it certain that Bob will descend from each camp to the next?

    (A) 0
    (B) 1
    (C) 2
    (D) 3
    (E) 4

12. Assume that Bob visits a total of three different camps, including the camp at which he begins his trip. If he makes exactly two interim overnight stops between the beginning and the end of his trip, he could begin his trip at any of the following camps EXCEPT:

    (A) Camp A
    (B) Camp B
    (C) Camp C
    (D) Camp E
    (E) Camp G

QUESTIONS 13–18:

Around a circular table are seated four married couples—Bob and Connie, Dan and Ellen, Gary and Holly, and Jack and Karen. All eight people are equally spaced around the table.

No husband sits next to his wife.

Bob is seated next to Karen.

Dan and Ellen sit directly across from each other.

Connie is seated next to Holly.

13. With respect to which of the following pairs of people can the two people be seated next to each other?

    (A) Connie and Karen
    (B) Holly and Bob
    (C) Gary and Jack
    (D) Ellen and Holly
    (E) Karen and Jack

14. If Gary sits directly across from Jack, which of the following must be true?

    (A) Gary sits next to either Dan or Ellen.
    (B) One person separates Jack from Ellen.
    (C) Bob sits next to either Dan or Ellen.
    (D) Ellen sits next to either Holly or Connie.
    (E) Two people separate Connie from Gary.

15. If Holly is separated from Karen by only one other person, which of the following is a complete and accurate list of the people who may sit directly across from Karen?

    (A) Gary, Jack
    (B) Jack, Ellen
    (C) Connie, Gary
    (D) Bob, Connie
    (E) Jack, Connie

16. If Connie sits directly across from Bob and next to Ellen, which of the following people must sit next to Gary?

(A) Dan
(B) Karen
(C) Jack
(D) Bob
(E) Connie

17. If Jack sits next to Ellen, and if Gary sits next to Dan, then Bob may sit next to any of the following people EXCEPT:

(A) Ellen
(B) Gary
(C) Jack
(D) Karen
(E) Dan

18. If Jack sits directly across from Holly, how many different seating arrangements for the eight people are possible?

(A) 1
(B) 2
(C) 3
(D) 4
(E) 5

ANSWER KEY AND EXPLANATIONS

1.　D	5.　D	9.　C	12.　A	15.　A
2.　B	6.　C	10.　B	13.　D	16.　B
3.　B	7.　B	11.　A	14.　A	17.　E
4.　D	8.　B			18.　D

Questions 1–7: Complex Selection Game (Moderate)

Two alternative rosters can be used as a basic diagram. In the diagrams below, the one on the left assumes that E, but not G, is selected, while the right diagram assumes that G, but not E, is selected. According to the rules, if E is selected, D cannot be selected, and C and D must both be selected if either is selected. Thus, we can cross out (deselect) C and D in the left diagram.

$$\begin{array}{ll} \text{A B } \cancel{\text{C}} \; \cancel{\text{D}} & \text{A B C D} \\ \circledR \text{ F } \cancel{\text{G}} \text{ H} & \cancel{\text{E}} \text{ F } \circledG \text{ H} \end{array}$$

$$\text{A} \rightarrow \text{B}$$
$$[\text{C D}]$$
$$\text{G} \rightarrow \cancel{\circledH}\cancel{\circledB}$$

The rules are represented in symbolic form below the two alternative rosters. As you respond to the questions, circle volunteers on the roster as you determine that they must be selected, and cross out those volunteers that you determine cannot be selected. This approach is appropriate for all of the questions in this section except Question 1.

1. **The correct answer is (D).** The most efficient way to approach this question is to consider one rule at a time, scanning the answer choices to eliminate violators. For example, consider the rule that H and B cannot both be selected if G is selected. A quick glance at the answer choices reveals that choices (C) and (E) both violate this rule. Answer choice (A) violates the rule that if A is selected, B must also be selected. Answer choice (B) violates the rule that either G or E must be selected.

2. **The correct answer is (B).** If G is not selected, then E must be selected, Accordingly, we need to consider only the left diagram, in which G, C, and D are all de-selected. At least three volunteers among A, B, F, and H must be selected. One of those three must be B; otherwise, A, but not B, would be selected, which would violate the rule: "If A is selected, then B must be selected." Thus, all answer choices except choice (B) must be true.

3. **The correct answer is (B).** Only the right diagram, in which G is selected, applies here. According to the questions, exactly four other volunteers must be selected. If neither C nor D were selected, then A, B, F, and H would all be selected; this result, however, would violate the rule: "H and B cannot both be selected if G is selected." Thus, C and D must both be selected. (Remember that if either C or D is selected, both must be selected.)

4. **The correct answer is (D).** A bit of intuition helps you determine the maximum number of search-party members. Intuitively, it would seem that the largest possible search party would include C and D, since either both or neither must be selected.

Proceeding from this assumption, G, but not E, will be selected. Of the remaining four volunteers, the most that can be selected together is three—A, B and F may all be selected together. H cannot be selected under this scenario since B and G are both selected.

5. **The correct answer is (D).** Since A is selected, B must also be selected. Since G cannot be selected if B and H are both selected, G cannot be selected. Accordingly, E must be selected (only the left diagram applies), and neither C nor D may be selected. F is the only volunteer with respect to whom it is uncertain whether the volunteer is selected.

6. **The correct answer is (C).** Consider first the left diagram (E, but not G, is selected). Since A is selected, B must also be selected. Either of the two remaining volunteers—F and H—could be included in the four-member search party. Thus, two possible combinations result: A, B, E, and F or A, B, E, and H. Next, considering the right diagram. Again, since A is selected, B must also be selected. B and H cannot both be selected. The only remaining volunteer is F, resulting in only one possible combination: A, B, F, and G. The total number of possible combinations, considering both diagrams, is three.

7. **The correct answer is (B).** If B is not selected, A cannot be selected. Considering the left diagram, only three volunteers—E, F, and H—would be available. Thus, only the right diagram, in which G is selected, can be considered.

Questions 8–12: Line-and-Node Game (Easier)

The most difficult aspect of this game is understanding the premise and constructing a proper diagram. Once you do this, analyzing the questions is not a difficult task. The rules suggest a line-and-node or flowchart approach. As you construct a diagram, you must bear in mind that unless Bob can make a round trip between two camps, he will descend in elevation from one camp to the next.

For example, since Bob may hike directly from G to E but cannot hike directly from E to G, G must be higher in elevation than E. Continuing this analysis, E must be higher in elevation than C, since Bob can hike from E to C but not from C to E. Since Bob can hike from C to F as well as from F to C, it cannot be determined which camp (if either) is higher in elevation. Using this approach, a flow chart may be constructed as follows (a horizontal relationship indicates that relative elevation cannot be determined):

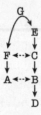

As you interpret this diagram, it is crucial to bear in mind that the elevations of F and A in comparison with E, C, B, and D cannot be determined. For example, it is possible that both F and A are actually lower in elevation than D.

8. **The correct answer is (B).** If Bob visits all seven camps, he must begin at Camp G and end at Camp D. To avoid visiting any camp more than once, only one route is available to Bob: G to E to C to F to A to B to D.

9. **The correct answer is (C).** For Bob to begin and end at the same camp, he must begin as well as end his trip at Camp A, B, C, or F. Four distinct routes are possible:

   A to B and back to A

   B to A and back to B

   C to F and back to C

   F to C and back to F

10. **The correct answer is (B).** Bob must descend in elevation from one camp to the next (except between camps where a round trip is possible); thus, Camp E must be higher in elevation than Camp D. Any of the other four statements could be true.

11. **The correct answer is (A).** Regardless of which camp Bob departs from, he might either move laterally or ascend in either direction across the dotted paths in the diagram. The only exception is Camp D; but the question stipulates that Bob must visit at least two camps, so he cannot depart from Camp D.

12. **The correct answer is (A).** To meet the conditions of the question, the route must include either F and C or A and B, and Bob must make a round trip between those two camps on either the first and second day of the trip or on the second and third day of the trip. Camp B is a possible departure point—B to A to B to D. Camp C is a possible departure point—for example, C to F to C to B. Camp E is a possible departure point—E to C to F to C. Camp F is a possible departure point—for example, F to A to B to A. However, if Camp A is Bob's departure point, he either makes two interim overnight stops but visits only two camps (A and B) or he visits three camps (A, B and D) but makes only one interim overnight stop (at Camp B).

Questions 13–18: Circle Game (Challenging)

In this circle game, alternative diagrams may be needed to help you work through some of the questions. The key to organizing this game is to recognize that Dan and Ellen create an axis (the vertical axis in the diagram below), that Connie and Holly must both sit on the same side of this axis, and that Bob and Karen must both sit on the side opposite Connie and Holly.

Both pairs cannot sit on the same side of the axis because only three positions are on each side. Accordingly, Gary and Jack must sit on different sides of the axis. The resulting core diagram might appear as follows (the positions in the diagram are numbered here solely for the purpose of facilitating the explanations that follow):

Since the game does not concern direction (left or right), it is not necessary to consider the mirror image of this diagram (however, see Question 6).

13. **The correct answer is (D).** Referring to the diagram above, Connie and Karen must sit on different sides of the axis. Holly and Bob must be similarly separated, as must Gary and Jack. Holly and Gary are married to each other and thus cannot sit next to each other. Therefore, all answer choices but choice (D) can be eliminated.

14. **The correct answer is (A).** Gary and Jack must sit either in positions 3 and 4 or in positions 1 and 6 to avoid separating Connie from Holly or Bob from Karen. In either case, Gary must sit next to either Dan or Ellen. Choice (B) must be false, since Jack cannot sit in positions 2 or 5. Choice (C) is not necessarily true because Bob may sit in position 5 as well as in positions 4 or 6. Choice (D) is not necessarily true because Holly and Connie may sit in positions 1 and 2 (in either order). Choice (E) is not necessarily true because Gary could sit in position 6 with Connie in position 3.

15. **The correct answer is (A).** Holly and Karen must sit either in positions 1 and 4, respectively, or in positions 3 and 6, respectively. In either event, Connie and Bob must sit in positions 2 and 5, respectively. Thus, either Gary or Jack may sit across from Karen.

16. **The correct answer is (B).** In the diagram above, Connie must sit in position 3, and Bob must accordingly sit in position 4. Since Connie must sit next to Holly and Bob must sit next to Karen, Holly and Karen must sit in positions 2 and 5, respectively. Jack cannot sit next to Karen (Jack's wife), and so Jack must sit in position 1, while Gary must sit in position 6. Thus, Gary sits next to Ellen and Karen.

17. **The correct answer is (E).** Construct two alternative diagrams to position Jack on either side of Ellen. Given that Gary sits next to Dan, Gary must sit directly across from Jack in order to avoid separating Connie from Holly and Karen from Bob:

In the first diagram, Bob may sit in position 5 or 6 next to either Gary and Karen or Ellen and Karen. In the second diagram, Bob must sit in position 5 and immediately between Jack and Karen (otherwise, Jack and Karen, who are spouses, would sit next to each other). In either case, Bob cannot sit in either of the two positions (1 or 4) next to Dan.

18. **The correct answer is (D).** In the initial diagram on page 184, Holly and Jack cannot sit in positions 2 and 5, respectively, since Bob and Karen would thereby be separated. Thus, Holly and Jack must sit either in positions 1 and 6, respectively, or 3 and 4,

respectively. In either event, only one arrangement is possible, since Holly cannot sit next to Gary and Jack cannot sit next to Karen:

[ch]
B ≠ c
G ≠ h

[Bk]
J ≠ k

[ch]
B ≠ c
G ≠ h

[Bk]
J ≠ k

The mirror images of each of the two diagrams must also be considered distinct arrangements. Thus, a total of four possible seating arrangements result.

PART III

THE PRACTICE TESTS

ANSWER SHEET PRACTICE MINI-TESTS 1–4

SECTION I: LOGICAL REASONING

1. Ⓐ Ⓑ Ⓒ Ⓓ Ⓔ	10. Ⓐ Ⓑ Ⓒ Ⓓ Ⓔ	18. Ⓐ Ⓑ Ⓒ Ⓓ Ⓔ
2. Ⓐ Ⓑ Ⓒ Ⓓ Ⓔ	11. Ⓐ Ⓑ Ⓒ Ⓓ Ⓔ	19. Ⓐ Ⓑ Ⓒ Ⓓ Ⓔ
3. Ⓐ Ⓑ Ⓒ Ⓓ Ⓔ	12. Ⓐ Ⓑ Ⓒ Ⓓ Ⓔ	20. Ⓐ Ⓑ Ⓒ Ⓓ Ⓔ
4. Ⓐ Ⓑ Ⓒ Ⓓ Ⓔ	13. Ⓐ Ⓑ Ⓒ Ⓓ Ⓔ	21. Ⓐ Ⓑ Ⓒ Ⓓ Ⓔ
5. Ⓐ Ⓑ Ⓒ Ⓓ Ⓔ	14. Ⓐ Ⓑ Ⓒ Ⓓ Ⓔ	22. Ⓐ Ⓑ Ⓒ Ⓓ Ⓔ
6. Ⓐ Ⓑ Ⓒ Ⓓ Ⓔ	15. Ⓐ Ⓑ Ⓒ Ⓓ Ⓔ	23. Ⓐ Ⓑ Ⓒ Ⓓ Ⓔ
7. Ⓐ Ⓑ Ⓒ Ⓓ Ⓔ	16. Ⓐ Ⓑ Ⓒ Ⓓ Ⓔ	24. Ⓐ Ⓑ Ⓒ Ⓓ Ⓔ
8. Ⓐ Ⓑ Ⓒ Ⓓ Ⓔ	17. Ⓐ Ⓑ Ⓒ Ⓓ Ⓔ	25. Ⓐ Ⓑ Ⓒ Ⓓ Ⓔ
9. Ⓐ Ⓑ Ⓒ Ⓓ Ⓔ		

SECTION II: READING COMPREHENSION

1. Ⓐ Ⓑ Ⓒ Ⓓ Ⓔ	11. Ⓐ Ⓑ Ⓒ Ⓓ Ⓔ	20. Ⓐ Ⓑ Ⓒ Ⓓ Ⓔ
2. Ⓐ Ⓑ Ⓒ Ⓓ Ⓔ	12. Ⓐ Ⓑ Ⓒ Ⓓ Ⓔ	21. Ⓐ Ⓑ Ⓒ Ⓓ Ⓔ
3. Ⓐ Ⓑ Ⓒ Ⓓ Ⓔ	13. Ⓐ Ⓑ Ⓒ Ⓓ Ⓔ	22. Ⓐ Ⓑ Ⓒ Ⓓ Ⓔ
4. Ⓐ Ⓑ Ⓒ Ⓓ Ⓔ	14. Ⓐ Ⓑ Ⓒ Ⓓ Ⓔ	23. Ⓐ Ⓑ Ⓒ Ⓓ Ⓔ
5. Ⓐ Ⓑ Ⓒ Ⓓ Ⓔ	15. Ⓐ Ⓑ Ⓒ Ⓓ Ⓔ	24. Ⓐ Ⓑ Ⓒ Ⓓ Ⓔ
6. Ⓐ Ⓑ Ⓒ Ⓓ Ⓔ	16. Ⓐ Ⓑ Ⓒ Ⓓ Ⓔ	25. Ⓐ Ⓑ Ⓒ Ⓓ Ⓔ
7. Ⓐ Ⓑ Ⓒ Ⓓ Ⓔ	17. Ⓐ Ⓑ Ⓒ Ⓓ Ⓔ	26. Ⓐ Ⓑ Ⓒ Ⓓ Ⓔ
8. Ⓐ Ⓑ Ⓒ Ⓓ Ⓔ	18. Ⓐ Ⓑ Ⓒ Ⓓ Ⓔ	27. Ⓐ Ⓑ Ⓒ Ⓓ Ⓔ
9. Ⓐ Ⓑ Ⓒ Ⓓ Ⓔ	19. Ⓐ Ⓑ Ⓒ Ⓓ Ⓔ	28. Ⓐ Ⓑ Ⓒ Ⓓ Ⓔ
10. Ⓐ Ⓑ Ⓒ Ⓓ Ⓔ		

SECTION III: ANALYTICAL REASONING

1. Ⓐ Ⓑ Ⓒ Ⓓ Ⓔ	9. Ⓐ Ⓑ Ⓒ Ⓓ Ⓔ	17. Ⓐ Ⓑ Ⓒ Ⓓ Ⓔ
2. Ⓐ Ⓑ Ⓒ Ⓓ Ⓔ	10. Ⓐ Ⓑ Ⓒ Ⓓ Ⓔ	18. Ⓐ Ⓑ Ⓒ Ⓓ Ⓔ
3. Ⓐ Ⓑ Ⓒ Ⓓ Ⓔ	11. Ⓐ Ⓑ Ⓒ Ⓓ Ⓔ	19. Ⓐ Ⓑ Ⓒ Ⓓ Ⓔ
4. Ⓐ Ⓑ Ⓒ Ⓓ Ⓔ	12. Ⓐ Ⓑ Ⓒ Ⓓ Ⓔ	20. Ⓐ Ⓑ Ⓒ Ⓓ Ⓔ
5. Ⓐ Ⓑ Ⓒ Ⓓ Ⓔ	13. Ⓐ Ⓑ Ⓒ Ⓓ Ⓔ	21. Ⓐ Ⓑ Ⓒ Ⓓ Ⓔ
6. Ⓐ Ⓑ Ⓒ Ⓓ Ⓔ	14. Ⓐ Ⓑ Ⓒ Ⓓ Ⓔ	22. Ⓐ Ⓑ Ⓒ Ⓓ Ⓔ
7. Ⓐ Ⓑ Ⓒ Ⓓ Ⓔ	15. Ⓐ Ⓑ Ⓒ Ⓓ Ⓔ	23. Ⓐ Ⓑ Ⓒ Ⓓ Ⓔ
8. Ⓐ Ⓑ Ⓒ Ⓓ Ⓔ	16. Ⓐ Ⓑ Ⓒ Ⓓ Ⓔ	24. Ⓐ Ⓑ Ⓒ Ⓓ Ⓔ

answer sheet

SECTION IV: LOGICAL REASONING

1. Ⓐ Ⓑ Ⓒ Ⓓ Ⓔ
2. Ⓐ Ⓑ Ⓒ Ⓓ Ⓔ
3. Ⓐ Ⓑ Ⓒ Ⓓ Ⓔ
4. Ⓐ Ⓑ Ⓒ Ⓓ Ⓔ
5. Ⓐ Ⓑ Ⓒ Ⓓ Ⓔ
6. Ⓐ Ⓑ Ⓒ Ⓓ Ⓔ
7. Ⓐ Ⓑ Ⓒ Ⓓ Ⓔ
8. Ⓐ Ⓑ Ⓒ Ⓓ Ⓔ
9. Ⓐ Ⓑ Ⓒ Ⓓ Ⓔ

10. Ⓐ Ⓑ Ⓒ Ⓓ Ⓔ
11. Ⓐ Ⓑ Ⓒ Ⓓ Ⓔ
12. Ⓐ Ⓑ Ⓒ Ⓓ Ⓔ
13. Ⓐ Ⓑ Ⓒ Ⓓ Ⓔ
14. Ⓐ Ⓑ Ⓒ Ⓓ Ⓔ
15. Ⓐ Ⓑ Ⓒ Ⓓ Ⓔ
16. Ⓐ Ⓑ Ⓒ Ⓓ Ⓔ
17. Ⓐ Ⓑ Ⓒ Ⓓ Ⓔ

18. Ⓐ Ⓑ Ⓒ Ⓓ Ⓔ
19. Ⓐ Ⓑ Ⓒ Ⓓ Ⓔ
20. Ⓐ Ⓑ Ⓒ Ⓓ Ⓔ
21. Ⓐ Ⓑ Ⓒ Ⓓ Ⓔ
22. Ⓐ Ⓑ Ⓒ Ⓓ Ⓔ
23. Ⓐ Ⓑ Ⓒ Ⓓ Ⓔ
24. Ⓐ Ⓑ Ⓒ Ⓓ Ⓔ
25. Ⓐ Ⓑ Ⓒ Ⓓ Ⓔ

Practice Mini-test 1

SECTION I: LOGICAL REASONING

NUMBER OF QUESTIONS: 25 • SUGGESTED TIME: 35 MINUTES

Directions: The questions in this section are based on the reasoning contained in brief statements or passages. For some questions, more than one of the choices could conceivably answer the question. However, you are to choose the best answer; that is, the response that most accurately and completely answers the question. You should not make assumptions that are by commonsense standards implausible, superfluous, or incompatible with the passage.

1. Softec, a small computer software company, has introduced more new software products than any of its competitors during the past year. This is undoubtedly the reason that it enjoyed greater financial success than its competitors during this period.

   Which of the following, if true, would provide the most support for the conclusion above?

   (A) The software products introduced by Softec were favorably reviewed by most major computer magazines.

   (B) None of Softec's competitors introduced new software products during this period.

   (C) Softec and its competitors are equally well-managed companies with insignificant differences in their marketing strategies.

   (D) Software innovations and applications are now the major driving force of the computer revolution.

   (E) Softec is one of the leading innovators in the fastest-growing segment of the computer software market.

247

2. A recipe for cooking potatoes states that potatoes should be cooked in boiling water for 20 minutes to be properly prepared. This holds only for potatoes that have been diced into one-inch cubes—smaller cubes would require proportionately less cooking time and larger ones proportionately more. It is important that potatoes not be overcooked, since this greatly diminishes their food value. Under-cooking also should be avoided because undercooked potatoes cannot be properly digested.

If the above statements are true, which of the following conclusions is most strongly supported?

(A) Whole potatoes, when properly cooked, cannot be properly digested.

(B) Potatoes that are diced into one-half-inch cubes and cooked in boiling water for 20 minutes will likely have little food value.

(C) Potatoes that are properly digestible must be cooked in boiling water for at least 20 minutes.

(D) Boiling in water is the only method of cooking potatoes that will ensure high food value and proper digestibility.

(E) To be prepared properly, potatoes must be boiled in water for at least 20 minutes.

3. Many rare or endangered plant species are sources of drugs and chemicals that have proven useful in medicine and in agriculture. It is likely, therefore, that many plants that are now extinct would have served as the source of useful drugs and chemicals as well. Thus, if we want to ensure that drugs and chemicals from plants are available in the future, we must make every effort to preserve these precious natural resources.

Which of the following is an assumption on which the above argument depends?

(A) Only rare or endangered plant species have proven to be useful as sources of drugs and chemicals.

(B) Extinct plant species would have provided useful drugs and chemicals.

(C) Efforts are not now being made to preserve plant species.

(D) Using plants as a source of drugs and chemicals will not threaten their survival.

(E) All plant species are sources of useful drugs and chemicals.

4. Lying is morally justified only if it is done to save a person's life. Yet, most people lie not because a life is in danger, but only to avoid the unpleasant consequences of telling the truth. Thus, most lies that are told are morally unjustified.

In which of the following is the pattern of reasoning most parallel to that in the argument above?

(A) Capital punishment is justified if it deters people from taking another's life. But it has been demonstrated conclusively that capital punishment is not an effective deterrent. Thus, capital punishment is not justified.

(B) Capital punishment is justified only if we are certain that the convicted offender is actually guilty of the crime. But there are many cases in which persons who are not guilty are convicted of capital offenses. Therefore, in many cases capital punishment is unjustified.

(C) Capital punishment is morally wrong only if it does not promote the greatest good for the greatest number of people. But sacred religious texts do not condemn capital punishment as being morally wrong. Thus, capital punishment promotes the greatest good for the greatest number of people.

(D) If the defendant in a murder trial is determined to be guilty beyond a reasonable doubt, the maximum penalty allowed under the law can be imposed. But most defendants in murder trials are not determined to be guilty beyond a reasonable doubt. Therefore, the maximum penalty is seldom imposed.

(E) Corporal punishment for persons who commit violent crimes is justified if and only if the punishment will alter the persons' behavior in the future. But most persons who commit violent crimes are corporally punished not in order to alter their future behavior, but only to exact revenge. Therefore, most instances of corporal punishment are unjustified.

5. Blood pressure varies over 24 hours, with a low point occurring when resting in a reclining position. Memory recall varies with blood pressure such that whenever blood pressure is lowered, recall time is lengthened. This correlation suggests that low blood pressure is the cause of slow recall and, consequently, that recall time should shorten when blood pressure is raised. However, tests show that recall time does not shorten when blood pressure is raised.

If the statements above are true, they provide the most support for which one of the following?

(A) People with neither high nor low blood pressure have normal memory recall time.

(B) Low blood pressure is not the cause of increase in memory recall time.

(C) There is no relation between blood pressure and memory recall time.

(D) Persons with high blood pressure will have fast memory recall.

(E) High blood pressure causes a decrease in memory recall time.

6. New genetic testing procedures have been developed that can detect the presence or absence of dirolin in foods. Dirolin is the toxin that causes food poisoning in humans. While rarely fatal if identified and treated in its early stages, food poisoning causes severe intestinal illness and vomiting. For this reason, the Department of Public Health and Safety should require that all processed foods be subjected to the new testing procedures.

Which one of the following, if true, would require the author to reconsider the conclusion?

(A) A recent Disease Control Agency report states that reported cases of food poisoning have declined steadily over the past decade.

(B) Death as a result of food poisoning is extremely rare in modern first-world countries.

(C) Current processing procedures employed in preparing foodstuffs are extremely effective in preventing and detecting dirolin contamination.

(D) The bacillus that produces dirolin can be easily treated with modern antibiotics.

(E) Improper preserving and processing procedures are responsible for the presence of dirolin in prepared foods.

7. In a recent medical experiment, 20 volunteers who were not immune to yellow fever lived for an extended period in a mosquito-proof environment with patients who had advanced cases of yellow fever. During this period, the volunteers were in constant contact with these patients, yet none of the volunteers developed the disease. When the experiment was repeated in a non-mosquito-proof environment, several of the volunteers were bitten by mosquitoes. In this instance, the ones bitten all developed yellow fever. That mosquito bites, and not contact with persons who have this disease, is the cause of yellow fever can be confidently concluded on the basis of these two experiments.

The argument above employs which one of the following methods of argumentation?

(A) Establishing a causal conclusion through a process of elimination of all but one of the candidate causes

(B) Establishing a causal conclusion on the basis of the identification of an event that precedes the effect

(C) Establishing a causal conclusion on the basis of an analogy between two different environments

(D) Establishing a causal conclusion on the basis of a significant correlation between two circumstances

(E) Employing the expert testimony of the experimenters as grounds for the conclusion

8. The overall demand for used computers has risen dramatically in the past few years. Most of this increase is a result of the explosion of entertainment software products aimed at young first-time computer users. As is to be expected, this demand has exerted an upward pressure on prices of used computers. As a result, we can expect that an increasing number of computer owners will be selling their old computers to buy the latest models.

Which of the following, if true, would most help to support the conclusion in the argument above?

(A) Computer technology is progressing so rapidly that computers purchased a year ago are now virtually obsolete.

(B) Exciting new software is being developed that can only run on the latest computer models.

(C) Most computer users do not know how to upgrade their old computers to accommodate the latest software products.

(D) It is less expensive to buy a new computer than to buy the components and build one yourself.

(E) The primary reason computer owners have not bought new computers or used computers that are newer models is that their old computers have little or no resale value.

9. Experiments with dogs to determine whether the Heimlich maneuver could be used effectively to resuscitate drowning victims are cruel and needless: cruel, because the dog's windpipe is often broken by the maneuver; needless, because a dog's respiratory system is not comparable to that of humans. For these reasons, these experiments are not condoned by state or federal medical review boards.

Which of the following is an assumption on which the argument depends?

(A) State and federal medical review boards do not condone experiments on dogs.

(B) State and federal medical review boards do not condone experiments on animals that are not comparable to humans or that suffer harm as a result of the experiment.

(C) State and federal medical review boards do not condone experiments involving drowning.

(D) State and federal medical review boards do not condone experiments that are cruel and needless.

(E) State and federal medical review boards do not condone experiments involving the Heimlich maneuver.

10. Unless a settlement can be reached, the truce will be violated by one of the parties to the dispute. But a settlement can be reached only if the border issues can be resolved, and the border issues can be resolved only if both parties are willing to give up the territory they captured during the hostilities.

If the statements above are true, but both parties are not willing to give up the territory they captured during the hostilities, then each of the following must also be true EXCEPT:

(A) A settlement can't be reached and the truce will be violated by one of the parties to the dispute.
(B) The border issues cannot be resolved.
(C) The truce will not be violated by either of the parties to the dispute.
(D) A settlement cannot be reached.
(E) The border issues cannot be resolved, nor can a settlement be reached.

11. Residential water use has been severely restricted in response to the current drought in our state. However, current reservoir levels are at the same height as during the drought that occurred here eight years ago. Because residential water use was not restricted then, it should not be restricted now.

Which of the following, if true, would most seriously undermine the author's contention?

(A) No new reservoirs have been constructed in the state since the last drought.
(B) The population of the state has grown at a steady rate of more than two million people a year since the last drought.
(C) Residential water use makes up more than 50 percent of the total water use.
(D) The restrictions on residential water use are projected to last for only two months during the summer.
(E) Since the last drought, water-conserving devices are required by law to be installed in all new residential construction.

12. Whenever inflation increases, the stock market declines; and whenever interest rates decrease, the stock market advances. However, since interest rates have not decreased nor has inflation increased, the stock market will neither decline nor advance.

Which one of the following arguments contains a flaw that is most similar to the one in the argument above?

(A) Whenever it rains, the streets get wet. But casual observation confirms that the streets aren't wet, so it can be confidently concluded that it hasn't rained.

(B) Whenever the president vetoes a bill, Congress attempts to override it; and whenever Congress attempt to override a veto, it runs into serious opposition from the president's supporters; so Congress rarely succeeds in overriding a presidential veto.

(C) When students receive individual tutoring, they invariably get good grades, and, as a general rule, when students get good grades, their self-esteem is greatly enhanced. Thus, to enhance a student's self-esteem, it is necessary to provide individual tutoring.

(D) When children study logic at an early age, they never have trouble learning mathematics, so if they have trouble learning mathematics, it's probably because they didn't study logic early on.

(E) Lawyers lose their cases whenever they go to trial without proper preparation. Good lawyers never go to trial without proper preparation, which is why they never lose their cases.

13. *Drug manufacturer:*

The drugs we now produce for the treatment of heart disease meet all current federal government standards but have significant detrimental side effects. Because recent medical research has discovered new drugs that are as effective as the ones we now produce but cause fewer side effects, we should begin phasing out our current products and take the necessary steps to begin manufacturing these new drugs.

Which one of the following principles, if true, would most help to justify the drug manufacturer's conclusion?

(A) Drug manufacturers should produce all new drugs that medical research discovers.

(B) Drug manufacturers should strive to produce drugs that treat illnesses with the fewest possible side effects.

(C) Drug manufacturers should make sure that their products are up to date with current medical research.

(D) Drug manufacturers should make sure that their products meet federal government standards.

(E) Drug manufacturers should be informed of current medical research.

14. Recent clinical tests clearly demonstrate that Psor-Be-Gone is an effective treatment in reducing the recurrence of psoriasis. Of 23 patients who previously had severe recurrent cases of psoriasis, only two had a recurrence after regular treatment with Psor-Be-Gone. This is a recurrence rate of less than 10 percent. In contrast, in a double-blind experiment 15 control subjects who were treated with a placebo in place of Psor-Be-Gone had a recurrence rate of 80 percent.

Which of the following, if true, would provide the most support for the conclusion in the above argument?

(A) Numerous independent studies have shown the active ingredient in Psor-Be-Gone to be an effective anti-bacterial agent for a wide spectrum of skin disorders.

(B) Most of the ingredients in Psor-Be-Gone are completely inert.

(C) None of the patients treated with Psor-Be-Gone had any adverse skin reactions.

(D) Psor-Be-Gone has been scientifically proven to be an effective treatment for numerous common skin diseases.

(E) The placebo used in the control group experiment did not contain the active ingredient found in Psor-Be-Gone.

15. It is the sacrosanct duty of the press to publish any news that is in the public interest to have published. There can be no doubt that the public has demonstrated considerable interest in the Adamson murder case, especially since the details of the private lives of the people involved have been displayed in the tabloid magazines and television talk shows every day. Thus, the press has an obligation to publish the details of the private lives of all of the people involved in this case.

A reasoning error in the argument is that:

(A) The reasons given in support of the conclusion presuppose the truth of that conclusion.

(B) The argument employs a key term or phrase in two different meanings.

(C) The argument assumes that just because the press has a duty to publish something, it should publish it.

(D) It bases the conclusion on the unwarranted assumption that whatever is in the public interest to have published ought to be published.

(E) It incorrectly assumes that just because the public is interested in some topic, they are also interested in the private lives of the people involved.

16. Excessive alcohol consumption has been conclusively demonstrated to be not only a serious health hazard to the individual who overindulges, but also a significant safety hazard to those in close proximity to that individual. Therefore, the government should ban all forms of public communication that promote or favorably depict excessive alcohol consumption.

Which one of the following principles, if established, would most strongly support the above argument?

(A) People should not be allowed to do things that harm themselves or pose safety risks to others.

(B) Beer, wine, and liquor advertisers should not be allowed to promote excessive consumption of their products.

(C) Depictions of drunkenness ought not to be tolerated in movies or on television.

(D) The various forms of public communication should be used only to promote and depict healthful and safe activities.

(E) Products that pose serious health and safety risks should be banned.

17. In the context of illegal drug trafficking, deterrence is a particularly unconvincing rationale for the death penalty. The main reason is that drug trafficking is extremely lucrative and may well be worth the gamble. This is true especially for the economically disenfranchised members of our society. Also, given the extremely high level of violence associated with illegal drug trafficking, the criminal justice system's penalties are unlikely to be a more effective deterrent than the violence to which one exposes himself or herself upon entering the trade.

The conclusion of the above argument is best expressed by which of the following?

(A) Drug trafficking is extremely lucrative and is worth the gamble, even if the price of being caught and convicted is the death penalty.

(B) The death penalty will not deter drug trafficking.

(C) The death penalty should be imposed on drug traffickers.

(D) The violence of the drug scene is not an effective deterrent to stop drug traffickers from entering the trade.

(E) Most drug traffickers are economically disenfranchised members of our society.

18. The use of computers has increased so much over the past ten years that now they are found in most homes and workplaces. Yet, relative to the number of computer users, the number of people who understand how computers work has dramatically decreased over this same period. This trend must be reversed in the future if computer users are to rely upon the accuracy of the information computers provide.

Which of the following, if true, would most seriously undermine the author's contention?

- **(A)** Computer technology is advancing faster than most people can keep up.
- **(B)** Knowledge of how a computer works is necessary for knowing whether the information provided by the computer is accurate.
- **(C)** The accuracy of the information computers provide can be independently verified without knowing how computers work.
- **(D)** Most computer scientists don't understand fully how computers work, so they couldn't teach others how they work.
- **(E)** It is not necessary to know how a computer works to know how to use one.

19. The medical licensing board of this state maintains that only medical schools that are accredited by the board should be permitted to train doctors. The primary reason given for this policy is that doctors who are trained at nonaccredited institutions may lack the training necessary to become competent practitioners. But since the licensing board is composed entirely of doctors and they obviously have a financial interest in limiting the supply of new doctors, their reasoning cannot be taken seriously.

Which one of the following argumentative techniques is used in the passage?

- **(A)** The licensing board's argument is undermined by pointing out that one of the statements used to support the conclusion is false.
- **(B)** The licensing board's argument is discredited by questioning the motives of the board in advancing it.
- **(C)** The licensing board's argument is discredited by showing that the board is not a reliable authority on the topic of the argument.
- **(D)** The licensing board's argument is discredited by pointing out that other institutions besides those accredited by the board can train competent doctors.
- **(E)** The licensing board's argument is challenged on the grounds that the major premise on which the board bases its conclusion is highly questionable.

20. Physicians should make every effort to identify the organism that is causing an infectious disease, for then they can use specific drugs instead of wide-spectrum antibiotics against that organism. This is desirable because specific drugs have fewer unwanted side effects and their use is less likely to produce multiple drug resistance.

What is the main point of the above argument?

(A) Physicians don't always know the specific cause of an infectious illness.

(B) Using wide-spectrum antibiotics is a good idea when the exact cause of an infectious disease is not known.

(C) Whenever possible, physicians should use drugs that have few unwanted side effects.

(D) Every effort should be made to identify the specific cause of an infectious disease before treating it.

(E) Multiple drug resistance should be avoided at all costs.

21. Every philosopher of science of the twentieth century who was either a realist or an empiricist was influenced by a group of philosophers known collectively as the logical positivists. The philosophical writings of this group deal primarily with the methodology of science and the question as to whether our belief that scientific theories are true can be justified. Their arguments on the latter topic are so compelling that no one who is influenced by them holds that scientific theories can be proven true.

If the statements above are true, which one of the following conclusions must be true on the basis of them?

(A) No twentieth-century philosophers of science who are realists maintain that scientific theories can be proven to be true.

(B) Every twentieth-century philosopher of science who believes that scientific theories cannot be proven to be true was influenced by the logical positivists.

(C) The logical positivists were the only twentieth-century philosophers to influence philosophers of science who believe that scientific theories cannot be proven to be true.

(D) Every philosopher of science in the twentieth century who was influenced by the logical positivists believes that scientific theories are false.

(E) Every twentieth-century philosopher of science who was not influenced by the logical positivists believes that scientific theories can be proven to be true.

22. Recent reports from waste management companies indicate that disposable plastic containers make up an increasingly large percentage of the waste they collect. As a result, landfills and incineration sites now deal almost exclusively with the disposal of plastics, whereas glass and metal containers previously made up the bulk of their refuse. It is evident from this radical change in disposal patterns that the use of plastic containers has virtually replaced the use of glass and metal containers.

Which of the following, if true, would most seriously call into question the conclusion above?

(A) Metal and glass containers are more expensive to manufacture than plastic containers.

(B) An increasing proportion of metal and glass containers are now being recycled.

(C) Plastic containers can be used over and over again before being discarded.

(D) Plastic containers decompose faster than metal and glass containers.

(E) Environmentalists have been unsuccessful in their attempts to decrease the production of plastic containers.

23. According to modern science, everything in the universe is composed of atoms that are exceedingly small; so small, in fact, that they cannot be seen even with the most powerful microscopes because they do not provide sufficient stimulus for the optic nerve, even when magnified. But if it is true that everything in the universe is composed of invisible atoms, surely it follows that everything in the universe is invisible. The patent absurdity of this, however, is clearly evidenced by the fact that tables, chairs, and everyday objects are visible. So it follows that modern science must be mistaken in claiming that everything is composed of atoms.

Which of the following best describes a flaw in the author's reasoning?

(A) The author's reasoning depends upon the mistaken belief that just because something occurred prior to something else it must be the cause of it.

(B) The author's reasoning depends upon the mistaken belief that what is true of the parts is necessarily true of the whole.

(C) The author uses the word "invisible" in two different senses.

(D) The author's reasoning depends upon the mistaken belief that the origin of a view is relevant to its truth or falsity.

(E) The author's reasoning depends upon the mistaken belief that whatever cannot be proven to be true must be false.

24. Contrary to popular belief, there are cases in which wearing a seat belt can actually endanger one's life rather than protect it. In one recent accident, for example, a car hit a tree and, except for a small space on the floor, was completely crushed. Luckily, the driver was not wearing a seat belt and was thrown to the floor on impact. Had he been wearing a seat belt, he would surely have been killed. Cases like this lead me to conclude that we should not be required by law to wear seat belts.

Which of the following is an assumption on which the above argument depends?

(A) Laws should not require an individual to engage in an act that may endanger his or her life.
(B) Most people believe that the mandatory seat belt law saves lives.
(C) Obeying the mandatory seat belt law will not necessarily protect the wearer in automobile accidents.
(D) The mandatory seat belt law should not be obeyed.
(E) Obeying the seat belt law isn't always a good idea.

25. Unequal pay for men and women is a completely indefensible practice and one that must be stopped immediately. After all, can anyone seriously doubt that women have as much right to self-esteem as men? Surely this fact alone is reason enough to justify their right to earn as much money as men.

Which of the following is an assumption on which the above argument depends?

(A) A person who has less money than another has less self-esteem.
(B) People who do not have jobs lack self-esteem.
(C) Women and men who perform similar jobs should earn similar salaries.
(D) Equal pay for equal work is a constitutionally guaranteed right of all workers.
(E) High self-esteem is as important to women as it is to men.

ANSWER KEY AND EXPLANATIONS

1. C	6. C	11. B	16. D	21. A
2. B	7. A	12. E	17. B	22. B
3. D	8. E	13. B	18. C	23. B
4. B	9. D	14. A	19. B	24. A
5. B	10. C	15. B	20. D	25. A

1. **The correct answer is (C).** This is a moderately difficult question that requires you to assess the effect of additional information. The task in this problem is to find an answer that strengthens the argument—one that offers support for the major assumption of the argument or that provides additional evidence for the conclusion. The major assumption of the argument is that there are no reasons other than the one stated (the introduction of more new software products than its competitors) that account for Softec's greater financial success than its competitors. Choice (C) supports this assumption by eliminating other relevant reasons that could account for Softec's greater success. The fact that Softec and its competitors do not differ in other respects that have direct bearing on their financial success provides support for the contention that the reason for Softec's superior financial success was its software products.

   Because it is consistent with choice (A) that Softec's competitors software products were also favorably reviewed, choice (A) does not provide additional support for the conclusion. Choice (B) is consistent with the stated premise of the argument. It does not provide additional evidence for the conclusion. Since Softec and its competitors are in the same industry, the fact stated in choice (D) would not account for Softec's greater financial success. The claim in choice (E) is consistent with the claim that some of Softec's competitors are also leading innovators. This claim does not provide additional evidence for the conclusion.

2. **The correct answer is (B).** This is a relatively easy question that requires you to make inferences from a given premise. From the information stated in the passage, it can be inferred that one-half-inch cubes would require proportionately less cooking time than the 20 minutes required for one-inch cubes. Cooking them for 20 minutes would consequently result in severe overcooking, and this in turn would result in a significant lessening of their food value. Choice (A) is unsupported by the passage and contradicts information stated in the passage, "undercooked potatoes cannot be properly digested." Choice (C) is unsupported by the passage, which clearly states that only potatoes that are diced into one-inch cubes will be properly prepared by being cooked in boiling water for 20 minutes; potatoes that are smaller than this would require proportionately less time to be properly prepared. Choice (D) is also unsupported by the passage because other cooking methods are not discussed. Choice (E) is unsupported by the passage and is too broad. This applies only to potatoes that are diced into one-inch cubes or larger. Smaller cubes would require less than 20 minutes to be properly prepared.

3. **The correct answer is (D).** This is a challenging question that involves detecting assumptions in an argument. The denial of the claim asserted in choice (D) is incompatible with the argument; that is, if using plants as a source of drugs and

chemicals threatened their survival, then efforts to preserve them would be thwarted. This indicates that the assumption operative in the argument is that using plants for these purposes will not threaten their survival. Choice (A) misstates information stated in a premise of the argument. Choice (B) is a paraphrase of a premise of the argument. Choice (C) brings in information not mentioned in the passage. Choice (E) overstates information mentioned in one of the premises.

4. **The correct answer is (B).** This is a challenging question that involves parallel structure problems. The argument in the passage can be restated as follows:

> *Premise:* Lies are morally justified only if they are told to save a person's life.

> *Premise:* Most lies are not told to save a person's life.

> *Conclusion:* Most lies are morally unjustified.

The argument in choice (B) can be restated as follows:

> *Premise:* Capital punishment is justified only if the convicted offender is guilty.

> *Premise:* Many convicted offenders are not guilty.

> *Conclusion:* Many instances of capital punishment are unjustified.

A comparison of this argument with the passage argument outlined above reveals a close similarity between the premises and conclusions of these arguments. In each, the first premise is constructed by connecting two independent clauses with the phrase "only if"; the second premise states the denial of the clause following "only if"; the conclusion states the denial of the clause preceding "only if." Choice (A) is incorrect; its argument can be restated as follows:

> *Premise:* Capital punishment is justified if it deters people from taking another's life.

> *Premise:* Capital punishment does not effectively deter people from taking another's life.

> *Conclusion:* Capital punishment is unjustified.

Contrary to initial appearances, the first premise of this argument is not comparable to the first premise of the passage argument outlined above. A simple example will demonstrate the difference. Compare the following two statements:

1. Combustion will occur only if oxygen is present.
2. Combustion will occur if oxygen is present.

These two statements have different meanings—the first states that the presence of oxygen is a necessary condition for combustion, the second states that it is a sufficient condition. The first is true; the second is false.

Choice (C) is incorrect; although its first premise is comparable to the first premise of the passage argument, the second premise and the conclusion of these arguments are not comparable. Choice (D) is incorrect. Its argument can be restated as follows:

Premise: If the defendant in a murder trial is determined to be guilty beyond a reasonable doubt, then the maximum penalty allowed under the law can be imposed.

Premise: Most defendants in murder trials are not determined to be guilty beyond a reasonable doubt.

Conclusion: The maximum penalty is seldom imposed.

This argument does not have the same structure as the argument in the passage.

Similarly, the argument in choice (E) can be restated as follows:

Premise: Corporal punishment for persons who commit violent crimes is justified if and only if the punishment will alter the persons' behavior in the future.

Premise: Most persons who commit violent crimes are corporally punished not in order to alter their future behavior but only to exact revenge.

Conclusion: Most instances of corporal punishment are unjustified.

This argument does not have the same structure as the argument in the passage. The first and second premises of this argument are not comparable to the first and second premises of the argument in the passage.

5. **The correct answer is (B).** This is a moderately difficult question involving making inferences from given premises. The information in the passage can be restated as follows:

Premise: If low blood pressure is the cause of slow recall, then recall time should shorten when blood pressure is raised.

Premise: Tests show that recall time does not shorten when blood pressure is raised.

The conclusion that can be inferred from these premises is that low blood pressure is not the cause of slow recall. Choice (B) is a paraphrase of this claim. Choice (A) is unsupported by the passage. The relationship between high and low blood pressure and "normal" recall time is not discussed in the passage. Choice (C) is inconsistent with information in the passage. The second sentence states that "memory recall varies with blood pressure such that whenever blood pressure is lowered, recall time is lengthened." It is this invariant relation between memory recall and blood pressure that suggests the hypothesis that the two are causally related. Choice (D) is unsupported by the passage. The relationship between high blood pressure and memory recall time is not discussed in the passage. Likewise, choice (E) is unsupported by the passage. The effect of high blood pressure on memory recall time is not discussed in the passage.

6. **The correct answer is (C).** This is a relatively easy question that involves assessing the effect of additional information. The task in this problem is to find an answer that weakens the argument; that is, one that undermines the major assumption of the argument, attacks a stated premise, or suggests an alternative conclusion that could be inferred from the premises. The major assumption in the argument is that current dirolin contamination detection methods are inadequate, ineffective, or completely

lacking. Choice (C) effectively undermines this assumption. Choices (A), (B), (D), and (E) bring in information that does not undermine the major assumption of the argument, attack a stated premise, or suggest an alternative conclusion that could be inferred from the premises.

7. **The correct answer is (A).** This is a moderately difficult question involving identifying the method of arguments. The only causes of yellow fever that are discussed in the passage are mosquito bites and contact with persons who have the disease. Experiments are devised to decide between them, and on the basis of the outcome of the experiments, contact with persons who have the disease is eliminated as the cause. Choice (B) is incorrect. No event that precedes the onset of yellow fever is identified in the passage. Choice (C) is incorrect because the two environments mentioned in the passage are not analogous. Choice (D) is incorrect because no correlation between two circumstances is mentioned in the passage. Choice (E) is incorrect because no expert testimony of the experimenters is cited in the passage.

8. **The correct answer is (E).** This is a moderately difficult question requiring you to assess the effect of additional information. The task in this problem is to find an answer that strengthens the argument; that is, one that offers support for the major assumption of the argument or that provides additional evidence for the conclusion. The primary reason given in the argument for expecting an increasing number of computer owners to sell their old computers is that increased demand for used computers has exerted an upward pressure on prices of used computers. This suggests that the reason computer owners had not sold their old computers previously is that their old computers did not have sufficient resale value to enable them to purchase newer models. Choice (E) explicitly states this reason and thus provides additional evidence for the conclusion.

Choices (A), (B), and (C) bring in information not mentioned in the passage. Admittedly, each of these responses provides a reason why computer owners might sell their old computers and buy newer models. However, none of these choices provide a reason for the expected increase in the number of computer owners who will do this. Consequently, none of them provide additional evidence for the conclusion. Likewise, choice (D) does not provide additional evidence for the conclusion, nor does it provide support for the major assumption of the argument.

9. **The correct answer is (D).** This is a relatively easy question requiring you to detect assumptions involved in the argument. In the passage, evidence is presented to support the premise that experiments with dogs to determine the effectiveness of the Heimlich maneuver in resuscitating drowning victims are cruel and needless. From this premise, it is concluded that the experiments are not condoned by state and federal medical review boards. The logical gap in the argument that must be filled is the connection between experiments that are cruel and needless and experiments that are not condoned by state and federal review boards. Choice (D) states the required connection.

Choice (A) does not fill a logical gap in the argument. The fact that the experiments are performed on dogs rather than some other animal is irrelevant to the logic of the argument. Choice (B) is too broad. The assumption required to fill the gap in the argument must link experiments that are cruel and needless to those that are not condoned. This answer choice links experiments that are cruel or needless to experiments that are not condoned. Choice (C) does not fill a logical gap in the argument. The fact that the experiments are concerned with drowning victims rather than some other topic is irrelevant to the logic of the argument. Choice (E) likewise does not fill a logical gap in the argument. The fact that the experiments involve the Heimlich maneuver is irrelevant to the logic of the argument.

10. **The correct answer is (C).** This is a moderately difficult question involving making inferences from given premises. The information in the passage and the question stem can be restated as follows:

> *Premise 1:* Either a settlement can be reached or the truce will be violated by one of the parties in the dispute.

> *Premise 2:* If a settlement is reached, the border issues can be resolved.

> *Premise 3:* If the border issues can be resolved, then both parties are willing to give up the territory they captured during the hostilities.

> *Premise 4:* Both parties are not willing to give up the territory they captured during the hostilities.

Choice (C) is the best response. From premises 4 and 3, it follows necessarily that the border issues cannot be resolved. From this claim and from premise 2, it follows necessarily that a settlement cannot be reached, and from this claim and premise 1, it follows necessarily that the truce will be violated by one of the parties to the dispute. This latter claim contradicts choice (C); consequently choice (C) cannot be true given the information in the passage.

Choice (A) states a conjunction of two claims that must be true given the information in the passage. From premise 4 and premise 3, it follows necessarily that the border issues cannot be resolved. From this claim and premise 2, it follows necessarily that a settlement cannot be reached, and from this claim and premise 1, it follows necessarily that the truce will be violated by one of the parties to the dispute. Since both of the underlined sentences follow necessarily from the premises, the conjunction of these claims must be true given that the premises are true. Choice (B) must be true given the information in the passage. From premise 4 and premise 3, it follows necessarily that the border issues cannot be resolved. Choice (D) must be true given the information in the passage. From premise 4 and premise 3, it follows necessarily that the border issues cannot be resolved. From this claim and premise 2, it follows necessarily that a settlement cannot be reached. Choice (E) states a conjunction of two claims that must be true given the information in the passage. From premise 4 and premise 3, it follows necessarily that the border issues cannot be resolved. From this claim and premise 2, it follows necessarily that a settlement cannot be reached. Since both of the underlined sentences follow necessarily from the premises, the conjunction of these claims must be true given that the premises are true.

11. **The correct answer is (B).** This is a relatively easy question that requires assessing the effect of additional information. The major assumption of the argument in the passage is that there are no relevant differences between the conditions present during the previous drought and the current drought that would necessitate the water use restrictions imposed in response to the current drought. Choice (B) undermines this assumption and, as a result, undermines the author's contention. The fact that there is a significant increase in the number of water users points to a relevant difference between the two situations that accounts for the difference in the restrictions.

    Choices (A), (C), (D), and (E) are incorrect responses. The task in this problem is to find an answer choice that weakens the argument; that is, one that undermines the major assumption of the argument, attacks a stated premise, or that suggests an alternative conclusion that could be inferred from the premises. The responses listed above do none of these.

12. **The correct answer is (E).** This is a challenging question involving involves parallel structure problems. The argument in the passage is composed of two sub-arguments, both containing the same flaw. The basic pattern of both of these sub-arguments is:

    Premise: Whenever A, B.

    Premise: Not A.

    Conclusion: Not B.

The flaw in this pattern of reasoning is apparent in the following example:

    Premise: Whenever it rains, the streets get wet.

    Premise: It's not raining.

    Conclusion: The streets aren't wet.

The conclusion does not follow from the premises for the simple reason that the streets might have gotten wet in some other way; for example, from a broken fire hydrant. The argument in the passage can be represented as follows:

1. *Premise:* Whenever inflation increases, the stock market declines.

    Premise: Inflation has not increased.

    Conclusion: The stock market will not decline.

2. *Premise:* Whenever interest rates decrease, the stock market advances.

    Premise: Interest rates have not decreased.

    Conclusion: The stock market will not advance.

Choice (E) is the best answer. Its argument can be restated as follows:

    Premise: Whenever lawyers go to trial without proper preparation, they lose their cases.

    Premise: Good lawyers do not go to trial without proper preparation.

    Conclusion: Good lawyers do not lose their cases.

A comparison of the pattern of this argument with the pattern above reveals the same flaw in reasoning.

Choice (A) does not contain a reasoning error or flaw that is similar to the one in the argument in the passage. The pattern of reasoning in response (A) can be represented as follows:

> *Premise:* Whenever it rains, the streets get wet.
>
> *Premise:* The streets are not wet.
>
> *Conclusion:* It has not rained.

This pattern is not similar to the argument in the passage.

Choice (B) does not contain a reasoning error or flaw that is similar to the one in the argument in the passage. The pattern of reasoning in response (B) can be represented as follows:

> *Premise:* Whenever the president vetoes a bill, Congress attempts to override it.
>
> *Premise:* Whenever Congress attempts to override it, they run into serious opposition from the president's supporters.
>
> *Conclusion:* Congress rarely succeeds in overriding a presidential veto.

This pattern is not similar to the argument in the passage.

Choice (C) does not contain a reasoning error or flaw that is similar to the one in the argument in the passage. The pattern of reasoning in choice (C) can be represented as follows:

> *Premise:* Whenever students receive individual tutoring, they invariably get good grades.
>
> *Premise:* Whenever students get good grades, their self-esteem is greatly enhanced.
>
> *Conclusion:* To enhance a student's self-esteem, it is necessary to provide individual tutoring.

This pattern is not similar to the argument in the passage.

Choice (D) does not contain a reasoning error or flaw that is similar to the one in the argument in the passage. The pattern of reasoning in this choice can be represented as follows:

> *Premise:* If children study logic at an early age, they never have trouble learning mathematics.
>
> *Conclusion:* If children have trouble learning mathematics, they probably did not study logic at an early age.

This pattern is not similar to the argument in the passage.

13. **The correct answer is (B).** This is a relatively easy question involving identifying the principle of an argument. The main reason given by the drug manufacturer for phasing out current drug products and manufacturing the new ones is that the new ones produce fewer side effects. The argument is basically as follows:

    Premise: The new drugs cause fewer side effects than our current drugs.

    Conclusion: We should produce these new drugs.

    The underlying assumption of this argument is that we should produce drugs that cause the fewest side effects. This assumption is an instance of the general principle stated in choice (B).

    Choices (A) and (C) are too broad. The drug manufacturer's rationale for producing the new drugs is not the fact that they are new or that they are up to date with current medical research but rather the fact that they cause fewer side effects. Choices (D) and (E) raise peripheral issues that are not germane to the argument. Being informed of current medical research or making sure that products meet federal standards would not help to justify the drug manufacturer's decision to produce the new drugs.

14. **The correct answer is (A).** This is a moderately difficult question requiring you to assess the effect of additional information. The task in this problem is to find an answer that strengthens the argument; that is, one that offers support for the major assumption of the argument or that provides additional evidence for the conclusion. Choice (A) provides additional evidence for the conclusion. The fact that the active ingredient in Psor-Be-Gone has been demonstrated to be an effective wide-spectrum antibacterial agent in independent tests adds credence to the claim that it is an effective treatment of the specific bacterium that causes psoriasis.

    Choice (B) is incorrect. Since "inert" means "having no active properties," the fact that most of the ingredients in Psor-Be-Gone are inert would not provide additional evidence for the claim that it is an effective treatment to reduce the recurrence of psoriasis. Choice (C) brings in information not mentioned in the passage. The nature of the reactions to treatment with Psor-Be-Gone are not discussed in the passage. Choice (D) is incorrect because, without knowing more about the causes of the skin diseases for which Psor-Be-Gone has been scientifically proven to be an effective treatment, this fact alone does not provide additional evidence for the claim that it is an effective treatment to reduce the recurrence of psoriasis. Choice (E) is incorrect because the medicine used in the control group experiment could not contain the active ingredient found in Psor-Be-Gone to qualify as a placebo. The fact that it did not is assumed in the argument.

15. **The correct answer is (B).** This is a challenging question requiring you to identify a reasoning error. The argument employs the key phrase "public interest" in two different ways. In the first sentence of the passage, the term is used to describe news that is "in the public interest"; that is, news that has some relevance to public well-being. In the second sentence the term is used to refer to news that the "public has . . . interest in";

that is, news that they find fascinating. The shift in the use of this phrase is apparent in the following simplified restatement of the argument:

Premise: The press has a duty to publish news that is in the public interest.

Premise: There is public interest in the private lives of persons involved in the Adamson murder case.

Conclusion: The press has a duty to publish news of the private lives of persons involved in the Adamson murder case.

Choice (A) is incorrect. The reasons given in support of the conclusion are the following:

Premise: The press has a duty to publish news that is in the public interest.

Premise: There is public interest in the private lives of persons involved in the Adamson murder case.

These reasons do not presuppose that the press has a duty to publish news of the private lives of persons involved in the Adamson murder case.

Choice (C) does not describe a reasoning error, nor does it state an assumption of the argument. Choice (D) is not an assumption of the argument; it is a restatement of the first sentence and functions as a premise in the argument. Choice (E) is incorrect because the argument does not depend on this assumption.

16. **The correct answer is (D).** This is a moderately difficult question requiring you to identify principles. The main reason given for advocating a ban of forms of public communication that promote or favorably depict alcohol consumption is that this activity is unhealthy and unsafe. The underlying assumption in this argument is that the promotion or favorable depiction of unsafe or unhealthy activities is not an appropriate function of these forms. Choice (A) provides support for this assumption by specifying that the forms of public communication should be used only to promote and depict healthy and safe activities.

The task in this problem is to find an answer that strengthens the argument; that is, one that offers support for the major assumption of the argument or that provides additional evidence for the conclusion. Choices (A), (B), (C), and (D) perform neither of these functions.

17. **The correct answer is (B).** This is a relatively easy question that requires you to identify the main point or conclusion of the argument. The conclusion of the argument is stated in the first sentence of the passage. The remainder of the passage consists of reasons that are offered in support of this sentence. The phrase "the main reason is that" signals that the second sentence states a premise. This premise is elucidated further in the third sentence. The word "also" at the beginning of the third sentence indicates an additional premise. Of all the answer choices, choice (B) comes closest to asserting what is asserted in the first sentence of the passage: that "deterrence is a particularly unconvincing rationale for the death penalty."

Choice (A) is a restatement of a premise of the argument. Choice (C) is off-focus. The issue in the argument is not whether the death penalty should be imposed on drug traffickers, but rather whether it would provide an effective deterrence to drug trafficking. Choice (D) is a plausible implication of the last sentence in the passage. This sentence expresses a premise of the argument, not the conclusion. Choice (E) misinterprets information in the passage. The passage states that economically disenfranchised members of our society may regard drug trafficking as worthy of the gamble. It is neither stated nor implied in the passage that most drug traffickers are economically disenfranchised members of our society.

18. **The correct answer is (C).** This is a moderately difficult question requiring you to assessing the effect of additional information. The task in this problem is to find an answer that weakens the argument; that is, one that undermines the major assumption of the argument, attacks a stated premise, or that suggests an alternative conclusion that could be inferred from the premises. The major assumption in the argument is that it is necessary to know how computers work in order to rely upon the accuracy of the information computers provide. Choice (C) directly contradicts this assumption, thereby seriously undermining the author's conclusion.

    Choice (A) supports the premise that "the number of people who understand how computers work has dramatically decreased." Choice (B) supports the major assumption of the argument, thereby strengthening rather than weakening the author's contention. Choice (D) brings in information not relevant to the argument. Choice (E) is off the topic. The relationship between knowing how a computer works and knowing how to use a computer is not discussed in the passage.

19. **The correct answer is (B).** This is a relatively easy question requiring you to identify the method of the argument. The medical licensing board's argument is criticized on the grounds that the board's membership is composed of doctors who have a vested interest in limiting the supply of new doctors, and that it is this self-serving motive that is the real reason for their position.

    Choice (A) is incorrect because the truth of the claim is not challenged in the passage. The primary reason offered in support of the medical licensing board's conclusion is "that doctors who are trained at non-accredited institutions may lack the training necessary to become competent practitioners." Choice (C) is off-focus. The medical licensing board's expertise on the topic is not questioned in the passage. Choice (D) is also off-focus. No reference to the capability of other institutions to train competent doctors appears in the passage. Choice (E) is incorrect because its premise is not attacked or criticized in the passage. The major premise on which the board bases its conclusion is "that doctors who are trained at nonaccredited institutions may lack the training necessary to become competent practitioners."

20. **The correct answer is (D).** This is a relatively easy question requiring you to identify the main point or conclusion of the argument. The final conclusion of the argument is stated in the first clause of the first sentence; the phrase "for then," that prefaces the second clause of this sentence, signals the major premise of the argument. The final

sentence states a reason in support of the major premise. Untangled, the argument looks like this:

Premise: Specific drugs have fewer unwanted side effects and their use is less likely to produce multiple drug resistance.

Intermediate Conclusion: It is desirable to use specific drugs against organisms that cause infectious diseases instead of wide-spectrum antibiotics.

Final Conclusion: Physicians should make every effort to identify the organism that is causing an infectious disease.

Choice (A) is unsupported by the passage. It is neither stated nor implied in the passage that physicians don't always know the specific cause of an infectious illness. Choice (B) is likewise unsupported by the passage. It is neither stated nor implied in the passage that the use of wide-spectrum antibiotics is a good idea when the exact cause of an infectious disease is not known. Choice (C) is supported by the passage, but it is an assumption of the argument, not the main point of the argument. Choice (E) is unsupported by the passage. It is neither stated nor implied in the passage that multiple drug resistance is to be avoided.

21. **The correct answer is (A).** This is a moderately difficult question that involves making inferences from given premises. The following information is stated in the passage:

1. Every philosopher of science of the twentieth century who was either a realist or an empiricist was influenced by the logical positivists.

2. No one who was influenced by the logical positivists maintains that scientific theories can be proven to be true.

From the information in the first statement above, it necessarily follows that every philosopher of science of the twentieth century who was a realist was influenced by the logical positivists. Moreover, given this and the information in the second statement above, it necessarily follows that no twentieth century philosophers of science who are realists maintain that scientific theories can be proven to be true.

Choice (B) does not necessarily follow from the information stated in the passage. The supposition that there is some twentieth-century philosopher of science who maintains that scientific theories cannot be proven to be true but was not influenced by the logical positivists is consistent with the information stated in the passage. Choice (C) is unsupported by the passage. The passage states that no one who was influenced by the logical positivists maintains that scientific theories can be proven to be true. From this it does not follow that the logical positivists were the only philosophers to have this influence. Also, choice (D) is unsupported by the passage, which states that no one who was influenced by the logical positivists maintains that scientific theories can be proven to be true. From this, it cannot be concluded that persons influenced by the logical positivists maintain that scientific theories are false; that is, the inability to prove that a theory is true does not logically imply that the theory is false. Choice (E) is likewise unsupported by the passage. The passage states that no one who was influenced by the logical positivists maintains that scientific theories can be proven true. This claim is equivalent to the claim that everyone who was influenced by the logical positivists maintains that scientific theories cannot be proven true; it is not equivalent to, nor does it logically imply, the claim that everyone who was not influenced by the logical positivists maintains that scientific theories can be proven true.

22. **The correct answer is (B).** This is a relatively easy question that requires you to assess the effect of additional information. The task in this problem is to find an answer that weakens the argument; that is, one that undermines the major assumption of the argument, attacks a stated premise, or suggests an alternative conclusion that could be inferred from the premises. The major assumption in the argument is that glass and metal containers are not being disposed of in some way other than the way mentioned in the passage. Choice (B) undermines this assumption, thereby calling into question the conclusion of the argument.

    Choice (A) brings in information not mentioned in the passage. The relative costs of manufacturing metal, glass, and plastic are not addressed in the passage, nor does this information undermine the major assumption of the argument, attack a stated premise, or suggest an alternative conclusion that could be inferred from the premises. Choice (C) also brings in information not mentioned in the passage. The fact that plastic containers are reusable is not an issue in the argument, nor does this information undermine the major assumption of the argument, attack a stated premise, or suggest an alternative conclusion that could be inferred from the premises. Choice (D) brings in information not mentioned in the passage. The fact that plastic containers decompose faster than metal and glass containers is not an issue in the argument, nor does this information undermine the major assumption of the argument, attack a stated premise, or suggest an alternative conclusion that could be inferred from the premises. Similarly, choice (E) brings in information not mentioned in the passage. The fact that environmentalists have not succeeded in their attempts to decrease the production of plastic containers is not an issue in the argument, nor does this information undermine the major assumption of the argument, attack a stated premise, or suggest an alternative conclusion that could be inferred from the premises.

23. **The correct answer is (B).** This is a moderately difficult question requiring you to identify a reasoning error. By arguing that "if it is true that everything in the universe is composed of invisible atoms, surely it follows that everything in the universe is invisible." The author relies upon the mistaken assumption that the whole must have the same properties as its parts, or more generally, that what is true of the parts is necessarily true of the whole.

    Choice (A) is incorrect because no antecedent event is cited as the cause of some other event in the passage. Choice (C) is also incorrect. Admittedly, the word "invisible" appears a number of times in the passage; however, its meaning remains the same in all occurrences: that which cannot be seen with the eye. Choice (D) is incorrect because, although modern science is cited in the passage as the origin of the view that everything in the universe is composed of atoms, this fact is not taken as a reason for rejecting the view. Choice (E) is incorrect because the argument does not rely upon this belief. No attempt is made in the passage to show that the claim that everything in the universe is composed of atoms cannot be proven to be true.

24. **The correct answer is (A).** This is a moderately difficult question requiring you to detect assumptions involved in an argument. The argument in the passage is essentially that we should not be required by law to wear seat belts because wearing them may endanger our lives. The argument can be represented as follows:

Premise: Wearing seat belts can endanger our lives.

Conclusion: We should not be required by law to wear seat belts.

The logical gap in this argument that must be filled is the link between acts that we are required by law to do and activities that may endanger us. Choice (A) expresses the necessary link.

Choice (B) is implied by the passage. The first sentence states that "contrary to popular belief, there are cases in which a seat belt can actually endanger one's life rather than protect it." This implies that most people believe that wearing a seat belt will save their life. Choice (C) is implied by the passage. The first statement, which states that "contrary to popular belief, there are cases in which a seat belt can actually endanger one's life rather than protect it," implies that wearing a seat belt will not necessarily protect the wearer in automobile accidents. Choice (D) is off-focus. The issue in the argument is not whether the seat belt law should be obeyed, but rather whether it should be a law in the first place. Choice (E) is a colloquial paraphrase of the first sentence of the passage.

25. **The correct answer is (A).** This is a moderately difficult question requiring you to detect assumptions involved in an argument. The argument in the passage is essentially that women have the right to earn as much money as men because they have as much right to self-esteem as men. The argument can be represented as follows:

Premise: Women have as much right to self-esteem as men.

Conclusion: Women have the right to earn as much money as men.

The logical gap in this argument that must be filled is the link between a person's self-esteem and the amount of money he or she earns. The suggestion is that a person's self-esteem is determined by the amount of money he or she has—the more money they have, the more self-esteem; the less money they have, the less self-esteem. Of the answer choices, choice (A) best expresses this assumption.

Choice (B) is off-focus. The argument is concerned only with unequal pay for men and women. This implies that they have jobs. Choice (C) is a paraphrase of the first sentence of the passage. The first sentence states that "unequal pay for men and women is a completely indefensible practice." Choice (D) brings in information not mentioned in the passage. The constitutionality of unequal pay for women and men is not discussed in the passage. Choice (E) is off-focus. The relative importance of self-esteem to men and women is not addressed in the argument. This answer choice expresses not an assumption of the argument, but another plausible reason why women and men should receive equal pay.

Practice Mini-test 2

In this mini-test, you will take a full-length Reading Comprehension section under actual test conditions. Allow yourself exactly 35 minutes to complete the 28 questions in this section.

SECTION II: READING COMPREHENSION

NUMBER OF QUESTIONS: 28 • SUGGESTED TIME: 35 MINUTES

Directions: Each passage in this section is followed by a group of questions to be answered on the basis of what is stated or implied in the passage. For some of the questions, more than one of the choices could conceivably answer the question. However, you are to choose the best answer; that is, the response that most accurately and completely answers the question.

QUESTIONS 1–6 ARE BASED ON THE FOLLOWING PASSAGE PAIR:

passage A

Line In a business organization, worker performance depends on both the provision of incentives and the credible threat of job
5 loss. For a government, the only viable approach to securing compliance with laws and maintaining social order is deterrence: the threat or use of
10 punishment. Simply put, human behavior flows chiefly from a desire to gain rewards or avoid punishments.
    The argument for legiti-
15 macy—that people will follow rules that coincide with their personal ethics and morality, even when there is little risk of being caught and punished—is
20 most often advanced during times when people demonstrate an unwillingness to defer to dubious government policies. But when the focus turns from
25 such issues as unjust wars and racial or gender injustice to those such as illegal drug use and intellectual property theft, the inefficacy of the argument
30 becomes all-too apparent. The high incidence of unchecked copying and downloading of illegal software, music, and movies today aptly illustrates
35 the point.
    Moreover, while its positive consequences are important, legitimacy often serves to justify policies of oppression.
40 Psychological research exploring legitimacy as a form of power that can shape people's

273

thoughts, feelings, and behavior
strongly suggests that when people
45 authorize another to make judgments
for them about what is appropriate
conduct, they no longer feel that their
own moral values are relevant to their
conduct. As a consequence, when
50 directed by that legitimate authority to
engage in immoral actions, people are
strikingly willing to do so.

passage B:

Line   Sanction-based governing and managerial strategies can carry deleterious
55   side effects. For the society it can mean
a swelling prison population and the
erosion of police-community relations.
For the corporation, it can spell disrup-
tive attrition and unfavorable labor
60   relations. Besides, ample research
about the influence of risk assessment
on rule-related behavior suggests that
the extent of such influence is often
insignificant. Studies of illegal drug
65   use, for example, show that only
around five percent of the variance in
illegal drug-use behavior can be explained by variations in risk estimates.
      Whether it is impossible or merely
70   impracticable to rule only by the sort of
control over resources that forms the
basis of power, it is widely agreed that
authorities find governance difficult
unless the feeling that they are
75   entitled to rule is widespread among
the governed, while the perceived
legitimacy of a corporation's policies
and practices is a key antecedent of its
employees' performance and loyalty.
80   And, this influence is distinct from the
risks of rule-breaking or nonperfor-
mance—for example, being fired or
passed over for a promotion or raise.
      In any case, people evaluate authori-
85   ties based upon their performance. The
police and courts gain legitimacy by
being effective in fighting crime, while
workers follow managers and companies that lead them to success. Legiti-
90   macy is linked neither to the fairness
of rules and policies nor to the fairness
of the procedures by which the rules
and policies are enforced, but rather to

the favorableness of decisions made or
95 policies pursued, as determined by the
dominant group.

1. The psychological research to which
   passage A refers (line 40) is cited by
   the passage's author in order to
   make the point that

   (A) people often betray their own
   moral convictions if they feel
   permitted to do so.
   (B) oppression is a nearly unavoid-
   able consequence of unchecked
   political authority.
   (C) people's thoughts, feelings, and
   behaviors are influenced
   primarily by their sense of
   morality.
   (D) the impulse to oppress other
   people is a natural aspect of
   human nature
   (E) people naturally engage in
   behaviors that carry no negative personal consequences.

2. Considered together, the references
   to "illegal drug use" in passage A
   (line 27) and in passage B (lines
   64–65) serve to show that

   (A) whether a law is legitimate
   depends on the cultural context
   in which the law is imposed.
   (B) different strategies for ensuring
   compliance with rules can often
   lead to markedly divergent
   results.
   (C) people will readily violate a law
   if they know that they are
   unlikely to be punished for
   doing so.
   (D) threat of punishment may in
   some cases not suffice as a
   deterrent to disobeying a law.
   (E) securing deference to authority
   by any means is problematic
   when it comes to certain kinds
   of prohibited activities.

3. Which of the following best characterizes the relationship between passage A and passage B?

   (A) Passage A raises theoretical and practical problems with a certain approach to gaining compliance with laws, and then passage B recommends circumventing those problems via an alternative approach.

   (B) Passage A examines the basis upon which people defer to political authority, while passage B conducts a similar examination but with respect to the authority of an employer.

   (C) Passage A provides the theoretical underpinnings of a strategy for ensuring deference to authority, and then passage B challenges the efficacy of that strategy.

   (D) Passage A examines the merits and drawbacks of two alternative approaches to maintaining social order, and then passage B argues for one approach over the other through the use of empirical evidence.

   (E) Passage A proposes one approach to deterring people from violating laws, while passage B argues for another approach because it is more broadly supported empirically.

4. The author of passage A might respond to the statement by the author of passage B that legitimacy is linked to "the favorableness of decisions made or polices pursued" (lines 94–95) by asserting that

   (A) what is deemed favorable by one group may be unfavorable to another group.

   (B) the link applies more to business organizations than to governmental authorities.

   (C) legitimacy should also be tied to the fairness of a decision or policy.

   (D) the basis for legitimacy is irrelevant to ensuring compliance with the law.

   (E) favorable polices are the ones that are most likely to be oppressive.

5. Which of the following would the author of passage A and the author of passage B both agree would best facilitate effective governance?

   (A) A bipartisan legislative committee's evaluation of the fairness of certain anti-discrimination labor laws

   (B) An employer's promise to pay bonuses to its sales force if their sales volume exceeds a certain level

   (C) The establishment of a volunteer task force to serve as mediators between community residents and the city's zoning commission

   (D) A whistle-blowing law that protects employees who report illegal activities on the part of their employer from retaliatory action by the employer

   (E) An employer's threat to fire any production supervisor whose subordinates fail to meet certain production quotas

6. Assume that a group of environmental activists knowingly risk fine and imprisonment by trespassing on private land in order to obstruct a legal timber-clearing operation which threatens the natural habitat of a certain endangered bird species. Which of the following expresses how the author of passage A and the author of passage B would most likely view the trespassers' activity?

(A) The author of passage A would characterize the activity as an illegitimate disruption of social order; the author of passage B would characterize the activity as a legitimate protest of a potentially unfavorable law.

(B) The author of passage A would view the activity as exceptional human behavior; the author of passage B would view the activity as typical of a non-dominant group.

(C) The author of passage A would view the activity as helping prove the case that deterrence is needed to maintain social order; the author of passage B would view the activity as an illustration of the point that the legitimacy of a law facilitates compliance with it.

(D) The author of passage A and the author of passage B would both agree that the activity is an understandable reaction to what a dominant group might consider an injustice.

(E) The author of passage A would characterize the activity as an unreasonable obstruction of justice; the author of passage B would characterize the activity as an unreasonable reaction to a legitimate policy of a ruling authority.

QUESTIONS 7–13 ARE BASED ON THE FOLLOWING PASSAGE:

Line Tuberculosis has two general stages relevant to its transmission and infectivity: tuberculosis infection (sometimes also called latent tuberculo-
5 sis) and active tuberculosis. Active tuberculosis manifests itself in a variety of ways, depending in part on the primary site of infection in the body. Pulmonary tuberculosis is the
10 most common form of the disease, leading to cavity formation and progressive destruction of lung tissue. Pathologic and inflammatory processes associated with pulmonary tuberculosis
15 produce weakness, fever, chest pain, cough, and when a small blood vessel is eroded, bloody sputum. Although only pulmonary and laryngeal tuberculosis are contagious through the
20 airborne route, another active form—extrapulmonary tuberculosis—can affect other sites in the body. Dissemination begins in the lungs, which are the initial site of the infection, and
25 travels through the body or through lymphatics to regional lymph nodes, resulting in the formation of small miliary (seed-like) lesions or life-threatening meningitis.
30 The cellular immune system is believed to play a central role in the development of tuberculosis. While some of the relevant immunologic processes have been identified, funda-
35 mental questions remain concerning the interplay and regulation of immunologic forces that both inhibit and actually contribute to the disease process itself. Airborne particles
40 containing tubercle bacilli that are inhaled and that reach the lower parts of the lung are initially engulfed by macrophages—a type of scavenger cell—in the alveoli (terminal air sacs in
45 the lung). If the bacilli are not destroyed by the alveolar macrophages, the bacilli multiply, killing the cell and attracting nonactivated macrophages from the bloodstream. In these new
50 macrophages, the bacilli multiply

logarithmically. Antigenic substances present within or secreted by tubercle bacilli stimulate T-lymphocytes (CD4 cells) to produce chemical substances
55 (lymphokynes), which activate these new macrophages, enabling them to destroy or inhibit the bacilli. This process of cell-mediated immunity (CMI) forms one part of the body's
60 immune response to tuberculosis.

A related immune process—delayed-type hypersensitivity (DTH)—is an inflammatory response that destroys bacilli-laden inactivated macrophages.
65 An overabundance of DTH is blamed for most of the tissue damage characteristic of pulmonary tuberculosis. Death of tissues leads to caseating granulomas and liquefaction of solid
70 caseous waste, producing cavities in the tissue. Within the liquefied caseum, tubercle bacilli multiply outside of the cells, reaching tremendous numbers. Host resistance may be
75 overwhelmed, and the bacilli may develop resistance to antimicrobial drugs. Liquefaction and cavity formation allow the disease to become contagious because the bacilli spread
80 via airways to other parts of the body and to the outside air.

7. In the passage, the author's primary concern is to

(A) examine the different stages in the development of tuberculosis in the body.

(B) describe the role of the body's immune system in the development of tuberculosis.

(C) distinguish between contagious and non-contagious forms of tuberculosis.

(D) describe the physiological effects of various forms of tuberculosis.

(E) discuss the interplay between two types of immune responses to tuberculosis.

8. Among the following, it is most reasonably inferable from the information in the passage that extrapulmonary tuberculosis

(A) is contagious through the airborne route.

(B) usually begins in the lymph nodes.

(C) is less common than pulmonary tuberculosis.

(D) is more likely than pulmonary tuberculosis to result in death.

(E) is disseminated by way of activated macrophages.

9. Among the following, which would the author probably agree contributes LEAST to the development or spread of tuberculosis?

(A) Liquefaction of caseous waste
(B) Tubercle bacilli
(C) T-lymphocytes
(D) Caseating granulomas
(E) Inactivated macrophages

10. According to the passage, lymphokynes

(A) are produced by tubercle bacilli.
(B) produce T-lymphocytes.
(C) attract macrophages from the bloodstream.
(D) aid in the destruction of bacilli.
(E) destroy inactivated macrophages.

practice mini-test

11. The passage provides information for answering all of the following questions EXCEPT:

(A) How do tubercle bacilli escape from the body to the outside air?

(B) In what ways does the body's immune system actually contribute to the development of tuberculosis?

(C) How do various forms of tuberculosis manifest themselves in the body?

(D) What is the mechanism by which the body produces macrophages?

(E) How does the body's immune system respond to the presence of tubercle bacilli?

12. Which of the following best expresses the main idea of the passage?

(A) The immune system both inhibits and contributes to the development of tuberculosis.

(B) Research suggests that airborne tubercle bacilli are primarily responsible for the development of contagious tuberculosis.

(C) The interplay and regulation of various immunological forces affecting tuberculosis remain largely uncertain.

(D) The immune system plays a more significant role in the development of contagious tuberculosis than in that of non-contagious tuberculosis.

(E) Immune-system responses play a more integral part in disease processes than previously believed.

13. Among the following, the passage would most likely continue by

(A) identifying treatments which may reverse the harmful effects of immune-system responses on the development of tuberculosis.

(B) defining latent tuberculosis and describing its manifestations.

(C) describing the process by which extra-pulmonary tuberculosis spreads through the body.

(D) raising questions about the interplay of immunological processes pertaining to the development of tuberculosis.

(E) examining the physiological factors that determine susceptibility to contagious tuberculosis.

QUESTIONS 14–20 ARE BASED ON THE FOLLOWING PASSAGE:

Line There are two cornerstones of economic reform in the formerly Communist states: liberalization of prices (including exchange rates) and privatization.
5 Radical economists call for immediate liberalization, with the only remaining wage regulation in the state sector, accompanied by a restrictive fiscal and monetary policy to harness inflation.
10 Conservative economists, however, favor gradual market deregulation in view of the dangers of inflation, unemployment, and economic instability. The "gradualists" would have the
15 government prepare enterprises for market shocks, for example, by breaking monopolies before prices and foreign trade are liberalized or by limiting production of heavy-industry
20 products such as coal and steel. If the gradualists have their way, however, economic reform could dissolve in the hands of bureaucrats incapable of facing the problems that a real transi-
25 tion to a market economy brings.

Privatization can also be approached either gradually or rapidly. Under the gradual approach, a state bureau would decide if and when an enterprise
30 is prepared for privatization and which form is most suitable for it. Slow

privatization, some experts claim, is
the only way to establish true private
ownership, because only those who
35 have to pay for property rights with
their own money will show an interest
in the enterprise and will be engaged
in its management. Although this
argument is not without merit, gradual
40 privatization would nevertheless only
prolong the core problems of inefficiency and misallocation of both labor
and capital. Under one approach to
rapid privatization, enterprise shares
45 would be distributed among employees
who would become the enterprise's
owners. This socialist-reform approach
discriminates in favor of workers
employed by modern, efficient enter-
50 prises; it also places workers' property
at great risk by requiring investment
in one specific enterprise rather than
diversifying investments.
      The better approach to rapid
55 privatization involves distribution of
enterprise shares, free of charge,
among all the people by means of
vouchers—a kind of investment money.
Some critics charge that voucher
60 holders would not be interested in how
their enterprises are managed, as may
be true of small corporate shareholders
in capitalist countries who pay little
attention to their investments until the
65 corporation's profits fail to meet
expectations, at which time these
shareholders rush to sell their securities. While the resulting fall in stock
prices can cause serious problems for a
70 corporation, it is this very pressure
that drives private firms toward
efficiency and profitability. Others who
oppose voucher privatization predict
that most people will sell their vouch-
75 ers to foreign capitalists. These
skeptics ignore the capacity of individuals to compare the future flow of
income secured by a voucher to the
benefits of immediate consumption.
80 Even if an individual should decide to
sell, the aim of voucher privatization is
not to secure equality of property but
rather equality of opportunity.

14. Which of the following does the
author associate with gradual market
deregulation?

(A) A restrictive monetary policy
(B) A policy requiring monopolistic
enterprises to split into two or
more enterprises
(C) Government subsidization of
steel producers
(D) State agencies' determining
when enterprises should be
privatized
(E) A fall in stock prices

15. With respect to which of the following pairs of terms does the author
implicitly equate the two terms with
each other?

(A) Voucher privatization and
gradual privatization
(B) Socialist-reform privatization
and investment-money privatization
(C) Price liberalization and market
deregulation
(D) Gradual privatization and
gradual liberalization
(E) Rapid privatization and voucher
privatization

16. Which of the following is LEAST
accurate in characterizing the
author's method of argumentation in
discussing the significance of falling
stock prices (lines 68–72)?

(A) Describing a paradox that
supports the author's position
(B) Asserting that one drawback of
an approach is outweighed by
countervailing considerations
(C) Rebutting an opposing position
by suggesting an alternative
explanation
(D) Discrediting an opposing
argument by questioning its
relevance
(E) Characterizing an argument
against a course of action
instead as an argument in its
favor

17. Which of the following is NOT mentioned in the passage as a possible adverse consequence of rapid privatization?

   (A) Instability in stock prices
   (B) Loss of ownership in domestic private enterprises to foreign concerns
   (C) Financial devastation for employees of private enterprises
   (D) Inequitable distribution of wealth among employees of various enterprises
   (E) Undue prolongation of inefficiency and misallocation

18. In responding to those "skeptics" who claim that people will sell their vouchers to foreign capitalists (lines 75–79), the author implies that

   (A) foreign capitalists will not be willing to pay a fair price for the vouchers.
   (B) the future flow of income is likely in many cases to exceed the present exchange value of a voucher.
   (C) foreign investment in a nation's enterprises may adversely affect currency exchange rates.
   (D) although the skeptics are correct, their point is irrelevant in evaluating the merits of voucher privatization.
   (E) foreign capitalists are less interested in the success of voucher privatization than in making a profit.

19. Which of the following would the author probably agree is the LEAST desirable outcome of economic reform in formerly Communist countries?

   (A) Effective allocation of labor
   (B) Equitable distribution of property among citizens
   (C) Financial security of citizens
   (D) Equal opportunity for financial success among citizens
   (E) Financial security of private enterprises

20. Which of the following best expresses the main idea of the passage?

   (A) The two most important principles of post-Communist economic reform are liberalization of prices and privatization.
   (B) Voucher privatization is the best approach to economic reform in the formerly Communist nations.
   (C) Economists disagree as to whether deregulation and privatization in formerly Communist nations should be accomplished rapidly or gradually.
   (D) A gradual approach to post-Communist economic reform is less likely to succeed than is a rapid approach.
   (E) Each proposed method of post-Communist economic reform has both its advantages and drawbacks.

QUESTIONS 21–28 ARE BASED ON THE FOLLOWING PASSAGE:

Line   Christina Rossetti's potent sensual imagery—the richest since Keats—compelled Edmond Gosse, perhaps the most influential literary critic in late
5   Victorian England, to observe that this Victorian poetess "does not shrink from strong delineation of the pleasures of life even when denouncing them." In the face of Rossetti's virtual canoniza-
10   tion by critics at the end of the nineteenth century, however, Virginia Woolf ignores her apparent conservatism, instead seeing in her curiosity value and a model of artistic purity and
15   integrity for women writers. In 1930, the centenary of Rossetti's birth, Woolf identified her as "one of Shakespeare's more recent sisters" whose life had been reclusively Victorian but whose
20   achievement as an artist was enduring.

   Woolf remembers Rossetti for her four volumes of explosively original poems loaded with vivid images and dense emotional energy. "A Birthday,"
25   for instance, is no typical Victorian

poem and is certainly unlike predictable works of the era's best known
women poets. Rossetti's most famous
poem, "Goblin Market," bridges the
30 space between simplistic fairy tale and
complex adult allegory—at once
Christian, psychological, and profemi-
nist. Like many of Rossetti's works, it
is extraordinarily original and unortho-
35 dox in form. Its subject matter is
radical and therefore risky for a
Victorian poetess because it implies
castigation of an economic (and even
marital) marketplace dominated by
40 men, whose motives are, at best,
suspect. Its Christian allusions are
obvious but grounded in opulent
images whose lushness borders on the
erotic. From Rossetti's work emerge
45 not only emotional force, artistic polish,
frequently ironic playfulness, and
intellectual vigor but also an intrigu-
ing, enigmatic quality. "Winter: My
Secret," for example, combines these
50 traits along with a very high (and
un-Victorian) level of poetic self-
consciousness.
    "How does one reconcile the aes-
thetic sensuality of Rossetti's poetry
55 with her repressed, ascetic lifestyle?"
Woolf wondered. That Rossetti did
indeed withhold a "secret" both from
those intimate with her and from
posterity is Lona Packer's thesis in her
60 1963 biography of Rossetti. Packer's
claim that Rossetti's was a secret of
the heart has since been disproved
through the discovery of hundreds of
letters by Rossetti, which reinforce the
65 conventional image of her as pious,
scrupulously abstinent, and semi-
reclusive. Yet the passions expressed in
her love poems do expose the "secret"
at the heart of both Rossetti's life and
70 art: a willingness to forego worldly
pleasures in favor of an aestheticized
Christian version of transcendent
fulfillment in heaven. Her sonnet "The
World," therefore, becomes pivotal in
75 understanding Rossetti's literary
project as a whole—her rhymes for
children, fairy tale narratives, love
poems, bleak verses of spiritual

desolation, and devotional commentar-
80 ies. The world, for Rossetti, is a fallen
place. Her work is pervasively designed
to force upon readers this inescapable
Christian truth. The beauty of her
poetry must be seen therefore as an
85 artistic strategy, a means toward a
moral end.

21. Based upon the information in the
    passage, Virginia Woolf would most
    likely agree that Rossetti's work

    (A) exposes a secret about Rossetti's
    life.
    (B) describes yet at the same time
    denounces life's pleasures.
    (C) has an enigmatic quality.
    (D) affirms that Rossetti was pious
    and reclusive.
    (E) serves as a model of artistic
    integrity.

22. All of the following are mentioned in
    the passage as qualities that emerge
    from Rossetti's work EXCEPT:

    (A) lush imagery.
    (B) ironic playfulness.
    (C) stark realism.
    (D) unorthodox form.
    (E) intellectual vigor.

23. The author implies that Rossetti's
    style was similar to that of

    (A) Keats.
    (B) Shakespeare.
    (C) Gosse.
    (D) Woolf.
    (E) Packer.

24. Which of the following statements is most reasonably inferable from the passage?

    (A) "Winter: My Secret" is Rossetti's best-known poem.
    (B) Rossetti was not among the best-known poets during her era.
    (C) The accounts of Rossetti's life contained in Packer's biography of Rossetti differ from those included in Woolf's biography of Rossetti.
    (D) Rossetti's display of poetic self-consciousness drew criticism from her contemporaries.
    (E) "Goblin Market" was published later than "A Birthday."

25. The passage mentions all of the following types of works by Rossetti EXCEPT:

    (A) the love poem.
    (B) the sonnet.
    (C) the one-stanza canzone.
    (D) the children's rhyme.
    (E) the devotional commentary.

26. The author discusses Packer's thesis and its flaws to

    (A) contrast the sensuality of Rossetti's poetry with the relative starkness of her devotional commentary.
    (B) reveal the secret to which Rossetti alludes in "Winter: My Secret."
    (C) call into question the authenticity of recently discovered letters written by Rossetti.
    (D) compare Woolf's understanding of Rossetti with a recent, more enlightened view.
    (E) provide a foundation for the author's own theory about Rossetti's life and work.

27. The author implies that Rossetti's "The World"

    (A) combines several genres of poetry in a single work.
    (B) was Rossetti's last major work.
    (C) is the most helpful expression of Rossetti's motives.
    (D) was Rossetti's longest work.
    (E) reflects Rossetti's shift away from her earlier feminist viewpoint.

28. Which of the following best expresses the main idea of the passage?

    (A) Newly discovered evidence suggests that Rossetti's works were misinterpreted by earlier critics and scholars.
    (B) Rossetti can be compared to Shakespeare both in her private life and in the enduring quality of her work.
    (C) Victorian poetry can be properly interpreted only by considering the personal life of the particular poet.
    (D) The apparent inconsistency between Rossetti's personal life and literary work are explained by Rossetti's poems themselves.
    (E) Rossetti's artistic integrity served as a model for later women poets.

ANSWER KEY AND EXPLANATIONS

1.	A	7.	B	13.	D	19.	E	24.	B
2.	E	8.	C	14.	B	20.	D	25.	C
3.	C	9.	C	15.	C	21.	E	26.	E
4.	D	10.	D	16.	C	22.	C	27.	C
5.	D	11.	D	17.	E	23.	A	28.	D
6.	B	12.	A	18.	B				

1. **The correct answer is (A).** This is a relatively easy comparative reading question requiring you to determine the main idea or primary purpose of the passage. The author of passage A explains that significance of the psychological research: it shows that people are "all too willing" to engage in immoral actions if directed to do so by whom they have authorized to make moral judgments on their behalf.

    Choice (B) distorts the author's viewpoint, which is that a deterrence strategy is the only viable means of preventing the kind of insidious oppression about which the results of the psychological research warns. Choice (C) expresses just the opposite of the author's point in referring to the psychological research: that under certain circumstance people will at behave contrary to their sense of morality. Choices (D) and (E) are irrelevant to the author's discussion in the third paragraph.

2. **The correct answer is (E).** This is a moderately difficult comparative reading question requiring you to infer from or interpret specific information. The author of passage A cites illegal drug use to elucidate the point that people find a legitimacy approach compelling only for certain types of laws (those involving social justice) and not for others (e.g., laws regulating private behavior such as drug use). The author of passage B cites statistics about illegal drug users to help show that a deterrence approach (the threat of punishment) is marginally effective at best. A reasonable inference from these two arguments, considered together, is that people will simply not defer to the law when it comes to certain activities (e.g., illegal drug use), regardless of the strategy (deterrence or legitimacy) to which the governing authority appeals.

    Choice (A) distorts the purpose of the reference in passage A. For the author of passage A, it is the effectiveness of a legitimacy approach to gaining deferring to a law, not the legitimacy of the law itself, that might depend on cultural context. Moreover, choice (A) finds no support whatsoever in passage B. Choice (B) runs contrary to the two passages, which together suggest that neither strategy is effective when it comes to the regulation of drug use. Choice (C) distorts the purpose of the reference in passage B. In mentioning illegal drug use, the author of passage B seeks to show that threat of punishment has little effect on human behavior, not to show that whether people break a law depends on their risk of being caught. Choice (D) does describe the point that the author of passage B is seeking to make; however, the author of passage A mentions drug use to argue against a legitimacy strategy and, by implication, for a deterrence strategy.

3. **The correct answer is (C).** This is a challenging comparative reading question requiring you to determine the main idea or primary purpose of each of the authors. Based on a theory about human motivation, passage A recommends a deterrence strategy for ensuring that people comply with laws. The first paragraph of passage B raises two practical problems with the strategy: it carries harmful consequences and is only marginally effective. The relationship between the two passages is a bit more complex than this. Nevertheless, choice (C) characterizes that relationship more accurately than any of the other choices.

Although B does recommend a different approach than A (legitimacy vs. deterrence), passage A is not concerned with raising problems with the deterrence approach that it recommends, so choice (A) is incorrect. Choice (B) accurately expresses the central point of passage A, but passage B presents a balanced examination involving both political authority and the authority of a business organization over its employees. Choice (D) is incorrect because passage A does not examine the merits of legitimacy (it only mentions in passing that there are such merits), nor does it discuss or even acknowledge any drawbacks of the deterrence approach that it favors. Choice (E) is incorrect because neither passage examines or compares different ways of deterring (preventing) people from violating laws.

4. **The correct answer is (D).** This is a moderately difficult comparative reading question requiring you to infer from or interpret specific information. The central idea of passage A is that deterrence, and not legitimacy, is the key to maintaining social order (including compliance with laws). Hence, the author of passage A would probably respond to the other author's entire discussion about the basis for legitimacy by arguing that the inquiry is beside the point.

Choice (A) is unsupported in passage A, which does not suggest any distinction between favorable and less favorable decisions or policies. Choice (B) is wrong for two reasons. First, in examining the proper basis for legitimacy, the author of passage B makes no claim that such basis depends on whether the environment is business or government. Secondly, the entire issue of the proper basis for legitimacy is not at issue as far as the author of passage A is concerned, at least not based on the passage information. Choice (C) is an idea that the author of passage B raises but explicitly rejects. Again, the entire issue of the proper basis for legitimacy is not at issue as far as the author of passage A is concerned, at least not based on the passage information. Choice (E) is the second-best response, since it is at least consistent with the point made by the author of passage A that legitimacy can breed oppression. However, passage A makes no distinction between favorable policies and other polices, and so choice (E) is not as well supported or on point as choice (D).

5. **The correct answer is (D).** This is a moderately difficult comparative reading question in which you must extrapolate from or apply passage ideas. The described whistle-blowing law would appeal to the deterrence approach (which passage A argues for), since the employer is put under a more credible threat of punishment for violating certain laws. The same whistle-blowing law would also appeals to the legitimacy approach (which passage B argues for), since the law would afford employees a certain

measure of power to check abuse of authority. Hence, both authors would agree that the whistle-blowing law facilitates effective governance.

Choice (A) describes efforts that the author of passage A would probably agree would facilitate effective governance, since antidiscrimination laws are just the type that this author carves out (in the second paragraph) as an exception to the general rule that a legitimacy approach doesn't work. However, the author of passage B would probably disagree; the explicit aim of the efforts described in choice (A) is to achieve fairness, but the author of passage B asserts that legitimacy is not linked not to fairness. Choice (B) describes an activity that the author of passage A, who asserts in the passage's first sentence that workers are motivated primarily by incentives, would no doubt agree would facilitate employee loyalty and hence effective governance on the part of the employer of its employees. On the other hand, the author of passage B maintains that threat of punishment and, by implication, promise of reward are less effective in this respect. Accordingly, the author of passage B would probably be inclined to disagree that the promises described in choice (B) would be effective in facilitating governance. Choice (C) describes an activity that the author of passage A would find of dubious efficacy in facilitating compliance with local zoning laws, since mediation aligns far more with a legitimacy strategy than a deterrence strategy. Hence, choice (C) cannot be the best answer. Choice (E) describes an activity that clearly appeals to the deterrence strategy, which only the author of passage A advocates.

6. **The correct answer is (B).** This is a challenging comparative reading question in which you must extrapolate from or apply passage ideas. The author of passage A claims that people obey laws chiefly out of fear of punishment. The activists know they will be punished for violating the law, yet they do so anyway. Hence the author of passage A would probably view their behavior as an exception to the norm. The author of passage B asserts (in the passage's final paragraph) that a rule's legitimacy is determined by the dominant group among the governed, according to whether the rule brings about desirable results. Since the tree-cutting operation is legal, the author of passage B would probably presume that the dominant group sees the economic favorableness of timber-clearing as more important than the undesirable ecological consequences of it. Hence the author would probably agree that the protest typifies the behavior of a nondominant group.

Choice (A) confuses the idea of legitimacy as the two authors examine it. Both authors are concerned with the legitimacy of authority and rules, not—as choice (A) wrongly suggests—with the circumstances under which disobeying rules might be legitimate. Choice (C) is incorrect in both respects. Regarding the first part of choice (C), far from illustrating this central idea of passage A, the activists' behavior tends to disprove it because the threat of punishment appears ineffective in this instance. The second part of choice (C) is unreasonable on its face: the activists' behavior seems to illustrate how laws governing the rights of land owners might facilitate disorder. Choice (D) finds insufficient support in either passage. Although both authors might consider the activists' behavior "understandable," passage A never broaches the concept of a "dominant group," and so choice (D) amounts to sheer speculation in this respect. Although the author of passage B does mention the concept of a "dominant group," nothing in passage B suggests that its author would agree that these activists are part of such a group. Choice (E) is partly nonsensical: the timber-clearing project described in the prompt has nothing to do with justice, as the first part of choice (E) suggests. The second part of choice (E) is unsupported: nothing in passage B suggests whether its author would view the activists' behavior as "unreasonable."

7. **The correct answer is (B).** This is a moderately difficult question requiring you to determine the main idea or primary purpose of the passage. While the first paragraph is introductory in nature (terms are defined and classified), the author's main concern in the remainder of the passage is to describe how different immune responses (two are described: CMI and DTH) both inhibit and contribute to the development of tuberculosis.

Choice (A) is off-focus. In the first sentence of the passage, the author identifies the two stages of tuberculosis—tuberculosis infection (latent tuberculosis) and active tuberculosis. However, there is no further discussion or mention of latent tuberculosis. The remainder of the passage deals with the various forms of active tuberculosis and with its development. Choice (C) is also off-focus. Although in the first paragraph the author does distinguish between contagious and non-contagious tuberculosis, the passage includes no further discussion of the differences between these two types. Choice (D) is off-focus as well. Although some of the physiological effects of pulmonary and extrapulmonary tuberculosis are listed in the first paragraph, there is no further discussion of symptoms or manifestations. Choice (E) is the second-best response. Admittedly, the author does indicate, in the first sentence of the final paragraph, that DTH and CMI are "related," suggesting that there is indeed some interplay between these two types of immune responses. However, the author's broader concern is to describe how each of these two responses both inhibits and contributes to the development of tuberculosis. The precise manner in which the two types of responses are related to each other is not discussed in any detail; thus, choice (E) is off-focus.

8. **The correct answer is (C).** This is a moderately difficult question requiring you to infer from or interpret specific information. Pulmonary tuberculosis is "the most common form of the disease" (lines 9–10). Since extrapulmonary tuberculosis is mentioned as "another form" of tuberculosis, it must be less common than pulmonary tuberculosis.

Choice (A) contradicts the passage. "Only pulmonary and laryngeal tuberculosis are contagious through the airborne route" (lines 17–20). Thus, extra-pulmonary tuberculosis (another form) cannot also be contagious in this manner. Choice (B) contradicts the passage; the lung is the initial site of the infection (line 24). Choice (D) is the second-best response. It is supported by the passage insofar as the author mentions that extrapulmonary tuberculosis can result in "life-threatening meningitis," while not mentioning any life-threatening results of pulmonary tuberculosis. However, just because no mention is made of the possible threat to life posed by pulmonary tuberculosis, it does not necessary follow that this form does not result in death. No information is provided to enable the reader to compare the rates of death resulting from the two forms. The author neither states nor implies that one form is more likely to result in death than the other. Thus, choice (D) requires an unwarranted inference.

Choice (E) confuses the information in the passage. Macrophages do not "disseminate" tuberculosis, as this choice suggests. Rather, they play a role in the body's immune response, engulfing tubercle bacilli that reach the lungs (lines 41–45).

9. **The correct answer is (C).** This is a relatively easy question requiring you to infer from or interpret specific information. T-lymphocytes, a type of cell, produce a chemical substance that activates macrophages, enabling the macrophages to destroy or inhibit bacilli. The spread and multiplication of bacilli seems to be the primary developmental process involved. Thus, it appears that T-lymphocytes inhibit rather than contribute to the development of the disease.

Choice (A) is explicitly contradicted by the passage. According to the passage, liquefaction of caseous waste is one of two factors that allow the disease to become contagious (lines 77–81). Thus, liquefaction clearly contributes to the spread of tuberculosis. Choice (B) is implicitly contradicted by the passage. The spread and multiplication of tubercle bacilli seem to be the primary developmental processes. Other aspects of the disease process mentioned in the passage are reactions to the invasion into the lungs and subsequent multiplication of bacilli. Choice (D) is implicitly contradicted by the passage. Caseating granulomas (along with liquefaction of solid caseous waste) contribute to the production of tissue cavities (lines 68–71), which in turn allows bacilli to spread via airways to other parts of the body and to the outside air (lines 77–81). Thus, caseating granulomas clearly contribute to the spread of tuberculosis. Choice (E) is implicitly contradicted. According to the passage, the body produces an inflammatory response (DTH) which destroys bacilli-laden inactivated macrophages. This response, however, results in tissue damage, leading to liquefaction and cavity formation which in turn allow the disease to become contagious. Thus, inactivated macrophages contribute indirectly to the spread of the disease.

10. **The correct answer is (D).** This is a relatively easy question requiring you to recall explicit information. According to the passage, lymphokynes activate macrophages, enabling them to destroy or inhibit bacilli. Choice (A) confuses the information. T-lymphocytes, not bacilli, produce lymphokynes. Choice (B) confuses the information in the passage. T-lymphocytes produce lymphokynes, not the other way around. Choice (C) confuses the information in the passage. According to the passage, it is the presence of tubercle bacilli (not lymphokynes) in the lung that attracts macrophages from the bloodstream. Choice (E) confuses the information in the passage. It is DTH, not lymphokynes, that destroys inactivated macrophages.

11. **The correct answer is (D).** This is a relatively easy question requiring you to recall explicit information. Although the passage indicates that macrophages are attracted from the bloodstream, no information is provided concerning how the body actually produces macrophages.

Choice (A) is answered explicitly by the last sentence of the passage. Choice (B) is answered implicitly in the passage. The body's immune system responds to the presence of bacilli in the lung by sending macrophages to the lung to engulf and destroy the invading bacilli. However, the passage notes that this response sometimes results in 1) the logarithmic multiplication of bacilli (second paragraph), or 2) a related immune-system response (DTH) which leads to tissue damage and the spread of bacilli to other parts of the body (third paragraph). Choice (C) is answered (partly) in the first paragraph, which mentions some symptoms of both pulmonary (lines 13–17) and extrapulmonary tuberculosis (lines 27–29). Choice (E) is answered explicitly and extensively in the passage. In fact, the second and third paragraphs are devoted entirely to answering this question.

12. **The correct answer is (A).** This is a moderately difficult question requiring you to recognize the passage's main idea or primary purpose. While the first paragraph is introductory in nature (terms are defined and classified), the author devotes the remainder of the passage to describing how different immune responses (two are described—CMI and DTH) both inhibit and contribute to the development of tuberculosis.

Choice (B) may be supported by the passage, but it is off-focus. The author implies that contagious tuberculosis is contracted by inhaling airborne bacilli (see, for example, the last sentence of the passage). However, this is not the passage's focus; nowhere in the passage does the author assert that research shows airborne bacilli, not some other phenomenon, to be primarily responsible for the contraction of tuberculosis. Choice (C) is supported by the passage, but it is off-focus. Admittedly, in the second paragraph the author states that "fundamental questions remain concerning the interplay and regulation of immunologic forces that both inhibit and actually contribute to the disease process." However, the author does not continue by raising any such questions. Instead, the discussion focuses more narrowly on the interplay of such forces. Thus, since choice (C) does not relate to the author's primary concern in the passage, it is not the main idea. Choice (D) is unsupported by the passage. The author neither states nor implies that the role of immune-system responses depends upon whether the tuberculosis is contagious or non-contagious. Choice (E) is too broad and is unsupported by the passage. The passage As concerned not about the disease process in general but rather about tuberculosis specifically; in this sense, choice (E) is too broad. Also, nowhere in the passage does the author discuss or mention any prior theories or explanations regarding the role of the immune system in the development of tuberculosis.

13. **The correct answer is (D).** This is a challenging question that requires you to extrapolate from or apply the ideas in the passage. The author mentions in lines 32–39 that while some immune responses relevant to tuberculosis have been identified, questions remain about immunological forces affecting tuberculosis. The author then devotes the remainder of the passage to discussing two immune-system processes that have been identified: CMI and DTH. However, the author never does identify or discuss the remaining "fundamental questions" mentioned earlier. Thus, it is reasonable that the author would continue by discussing these questions.

Choice (A) is wholly unsupported by the passage. Nowhere in the passage does the author either express or imply a concern with identifying any treatment for tuberculosis. Choice (B) is inconsistent with the focus of the passage. Latent tuberculosis refers to the infection stage (rather than the active stage) of the disease. The author mentions latent tuberculosis (lines 4–5) only to help define active tuberculosis, which is the author's more narrow concern. No information in the passage suggests that the author might return to discuss latent tuberculosis. Choice (C) runs contrary to the passage. Admittedly, in the first paragraph the author does distinguish extrapulmonary tuberculosis from other forms—i.e., the pulmonary and laryngeal forms. This distinction is based upon the primary site of the infection (lines 5–9). However, choice (C) suggests that the distinction lies in the immune-system response rather than the location of the infection. Moreover, nowhere in the second or third paragraphs (where the discussion of immune-system response occurs) does the author suggest that the responses discussed therein are different from those relating to extrapulmonary tuberculosis. Choice (E) is unsupported by the passage. The author neither expresses nor suggests a concern with how certain physiological traits affect susceptibility to tuberculosis.

14. **The correct answer is (B).** This is a relatively easy question that requires you to recall explicit information. One of the possible features of gradual deregulation mentioned in the first paragraph is the breaking of monopolies by the government. Choice (B) simply restates this possible feature.

   Choice (A) confuses two different areas of discussion in the passage. The passage associates a restrictive monetary policy with immediate rather than gradual deregulation. Choice (C) contradicts the passage. The author associates government limitation of steel production with gradual deregulation (lines 14–20). Government subsidization would, to the contrary, result in increased steel production. Choice (D) confuses two different areas of discussion in the passage. It is gradual privatization, not gradual deregulation, with which the author associates the feature mentioned in (D) (lines 27–31). Choice (E) confuses two different areas of discussion. The author associates falling stock prices (lines 68–69) with voucher privatization, not with gradual deregulation.

15. **The correct answer is (C).** This is a relatively easy question that requires you to infer from or interpret specific information. In the second sentence, the author indicates that one of the key features of immediate (price) liberalization is the elimination of wage regulation; thereby, the author equates, at least to an extent, price liberalization and wage regulation. Moreover, in the next sentence, the author contrasts "gradual market deregulation" with "immediate liberalization," further suggesting the interchangeability of the terms "market deregulation" and "price liberalization."

   Choice (A) is contradicted by the passage. Voucher privatization is one of two types of rapid, not gradual, privatization. Choice (B) is also contradicted by the passage. The third paragraph makes clear that voucher privatization and socialist-reform privatization are two separate and distinct approaches to rapid privatization. Since the passage indicates that a voucher is "a kind of investment money" (line 58), the two terms in (B) are not interchangeable. Choice (D) confuses two unrelated terms mentioned in the passage. Privatization and liberalization are two separate and distinct concepts. Liberalization is discussed in the first paragraph, while privatization is examined in the remaining paragraphs. Choice (E) is the second-best response. Although voucher privatization is discussed as an approach to rapid privatization, it is only one of two approaches; the other approach is socialist-reform privatization. Accordingly, it is unfair to equate the two terms listed in choice (E).

16. **The correct answer is (C).** This is a challenging question that requires you to infer from or interpret specific information. Although the author does respond to what might be one undesired result of voucher privatization—falling stock prices—as well as explain the cause of falling stock prices, the author does not offer an "alternative" explanation for this phenomenon, as suggested by choice (C). Moreover, the author's purpose in discussing falling stock prices is not to explain their cause but rather to acknowledge that what appears to be an undesirable consequence of voucher privatization may actually help to bring about a desirable result—see choices (B) and (E). Choice (A) is incorrect. The author acknowledges falling stock prices as one potential drawback of voucher privatization in that it might cause serious problems for an enterprise. However, the author asserts that it is the fear of this very consequence that will drive enterprises to efficiency and profitability. This phenomenon can be characterized, then, as a paradox, since what appears to be negative is actually positive when viewed differently. The author uses this paradox to undermine the critics' argument, thereby supporting the author's pro-voucher position.

Choice (B) is one way of characterizing the author's line of reasoning. The author does indeed acknowledge falling stock prices as one potential drawback of voucher privatization. Then, in the same sentence, the author goes on to assert that the fear of falling stock prices will drive enterprises to efficiency and profitability. This rebuttal, then, can be characterized as the author's attempt to introduce a countervailing (competing) consideration that is of overriding concern. Choice (D) is a good characterization of this discussion. The author does not disagree that voucher holders will have little interest in the management of their enterprises. The author does imply, however, that this fact is beside the point since it is the enterprises' fear of a sell-off that will drive the enterprise to efficiency and profitability, not the extent of voucher-holder involvement in management. Choice (E) is perhaps the best characterization among the responses of the author's line of reasoning. The author indeed acknowledges falling stock prices as one potential drawback of (argument against) voucher privatization in that it might cause serious problems for an enterprise. However, in the same sentence, the author suggests that, paradoxically, it is the fear of this very consequence that will drive enterprises to efficiency and profitability. This rebuttal, then, can be viewed as the author's attempt to recharacterize a negative feature as a positive one.

17. **The correct answer is (E).** This is a moderately difficult question that requires you to recall explicit information. The author foresees prolonged inefficiency and misallocation as a consequence of gradual, not rapid, privatization (lines 38–43).

Choices (A) and (B) are each explicitly mentioned in the last paragraph as possible consequences of voucher privatization (one of the two approaches to rapid privatization), at least according to critics of this approach. Choice (C) refers to the danger under the socialist-reform approach (one of two approaches respecting rapid privatization) that employees will expose themselves to undue risk if they are invested only in their employer-company (at least according to the author, who would agree with critics of rapid privatization on this point). Choice (D) refers to the discrimination in favor of those who happen to be employed by modern or efficient enterprises that may result under the socialist-reform approach (one of the two approaches to rapid privatization), at least according to the author, who would agree with critics of rapid privatization on this point. The shares of these employees, the criticism goes, will be more valuable than the shares of those who work for older or less-efficient firms.

18. **The correct answer is (B).** This is a moderately difficult question in which you must infer from or interpret specific information. The author responds to the skeptics' claim by pointing out that people are likely to weigh the future flow of income from a voucher against the benefits of selling their vouchers now and using the proceeds for consumption. Were people not likely (at least in many cases) to hold their vouchers after weighing these two alternatives, the author would not have made this argument. Thus, the author is implying that indeed in many cases the future flow of income from a voucher will exceed the present value of the voucher.

Choice (D) is the second-best response. Admittedly, the final sentence of the last paragraph does suggest that the author views the skeptics' argument as irrelevant; in this sense, (D) has some merit. However, in the preceding sentence, the author seems to disagree with the skeptics as to whether people will sell their vouchers to foreigners. Thus, the author does not acknowledge that the skeptics are correct. Choices (A), (C), and (E) are unsupported by the author's response to the skeptics' claim.

19. **The correct answer is (E).** This is a moderately difficult question in which you must extrapolate from or apply ideas in the passage. The author's willingness to place a private enterprise at risk for the broader purpose of achieving a free-market system is suggested by at least two areas of discussion in the passage. In the first paragraph, the author tacitly disagrees with the gradualists who favor bracing enterprises for the shock of deregulation to help them survive the transition. In the fourth paragraph, while advocating voucher privatization, the author admits that this approach may very well result in the instability of stock prices; yet the author seems to view the insecurity caused by market pressures as "good" for private enterprises in that it will drive them to efficiency—a sort of sink-or-swim approach.

Choice (A) is explicitly supported. The author identifies misallocation of labor as a core problem that must be addressed if economic reform is to succeed (lines 41–43). Choice (B) is supported implicitly by the passage. The author argues against the socialist-reform approach to privatization on the basis that distribution of enterprise shares under this approach would discriminate against employees of less profitable enterprises—i.e., that this distribution system would be inequitable (unfair). Note that the term "equitable" means "fair," not necessarily "equal." Choice (C) is the second-best response and is implicitly supported. One of the author's arguments against the socialist-reform approach is that employees of less profitable companies would be placed at undue financial risk. Accordingly, the author seems to value, at least to some extent, the financial security of employees (citizens). Although choice (C) is a less likely "objective" of economic reform than choices (A) or (D), the objective identified in choice (E) is clearly less "desirable" from the author's viewpoint than the objective referred to in choice (C).

Choice (D) is explicitly supported by the passage. The author states in lines 81–83 that the aim of voucher privatization (which the author advocates) is to secure equality of opportunity. The "opportunity" to which the author refers here is the freedom to determine what use of one's vouchers will be most advantageous financially.

20. **The correct answer is (D).** This is a moderately difficult question requiring you to recognize the main idea or primary purpose of the passage. Choice (D) encompasses the author's treatment of both liberalization and privatization by referring more generally to "economic reform," as well as referring to both the rapid and gradual approaches to each of these two aspects of economic reform. Just as crucial, choice (D) includes the author's position in the issue: The author favors rapid reform to gradual reform.

Choice (A) is too narrow in its scope. It restates the point in the first sentence of the passage which is intended to merely provide a framework for the discussion that follows. Choice (B) is too narrow in its scope. Voucher privatization may be the best approach to privatization, at least according to the author. However, choice (B) fails to encompass the second "cornerstone" of economic reform: liberalization (deregulation), which is the concern of the first two paragraphs. Choice (C) is the second-best response. It encompasses all approaches to economic reform discussed in the passage. However, it omits the author's position on the issue and therefore is not a viable best response. Choice (E) is too broad in that it incorporates ideas outside of the passage. The passage does not indicate "advantages" of either rapid or gradual deregulation and does not cite any "advantages" of the socialist-reform approach to privatization. It is also too narrow in the sense that it fails to reflect the author's position on the issues.

21. **The correct answer is (E).** This is a relatively easy question requiring you to recall explicit information. In lines 14–15, the author states that Woolf saw in Rossetti "a model of artistic purity and integrity for women writers."

Choices (A) and (C) confuse the opinions of Woolf with those of the author. The author does indeed discuss, in the third and fourth paragraphs, how some of Rossetti's works revealed a secret about her life and art. Also, in line 48 the author does claim that from Rossetti's work emerges (among other qualities) "an enigmatic quality." However, these are the author's opinions, not those of Woolf. Choice (B) confuses the opinion of Woolf with that of Edmond Gosse. It was Gosse, not Woolf, who commented that Rossetti "'does not shrink from a strong delineation of the pleasures in life even when denouncing them'" (lines 6–8). Choice (D) confuses the information in the passage. In the third paragraph, the author discusses how Rossetti's recently discovered letters confirm that she was pious, scrupulously abstinent, and semi-reclusive. These are not Woolf's impressions of Rossetti's work but rather the author's analysis of Rossetti's personal letters.

22. **The correct answer is (C).** This is a relatively easy question requiring you to recall explicit information. In describing Rossetti's work, the author never uses the words "stark" or "realism," nor does the author describe her work in any way that might be expressed by either of these terms.

Choices (A), (B), and (E) are all mentioned explicitly in the second paragraph (lines 45–48) as qualities that emerge from Rossetti's work. Choice (D) is the second-best response. The author refers to the form of Rossetti's works in reference specifically to "Goblin Market," claiming that in its unorthodox form "Goblin Market" is like many of

Rossetti's works. In this way, the author identifies "unorthodox form" as one quality that emerges from Rossetti's work.

23. **The correct answer is (A).** This is a relatively easy question requiring you to infer from or interpret specific information. The author claims that Rossetti's potent sensual imagery was "the richest since Keats" (line 2). Thus, it can be inferred that Rossetti's style was similar to that of Keats in that both writers used potent sensual imagery.

Choice (B) is the second-best response; it distorts the comparison in the passage between Rossetti and Shakespeare. It was Woolf who compared Rossetti to Shakespeare; also, the similarities Woolf noted between the two writers regarded their personal lives and the enduring quality of their works, not their writing styles. Choices (C), (D), and (E) are all discussed in the passage as critics of Rossetti. Their writing styles are wholly irrelevant to and are not discussed at all in the passage.

24. **The correct answer is (B).** This is a moderately difficult question requiring you to infer from or interpret specific information. In the first sentence of the second paragraph, the author states that "'A Birthday' is no typical Victorian poem and is certainly unlike predictable works of the era's best-known women poets." It is reasonably inferable that Rossetti was not among the era's best-known women poets, at least during her time.

Choice (A) is contradicted by the passage. The author states that "Goblin Market" is Rossetti's most famous poem (lines 28–29). Choice (B) confuses the information in the passage. Woolf reviewed but did not write a biography of Rossetti. Choice (D) distorts the information in the passage. The author does indicate that in "Winter: My Secret," Rossetti displayed a high level of poetic self-consciousness (lines 50–53). However, the author neither states nor implies that Rossetti drew criticism during her lifetime as a result. To the contrary, the fact that she was virtually canonized by critics at the end of the nineteenth century (lines 9–11) suggests her work was the object of very little negative criticism from her contemporaries. Choice (E) also distorts the information in the passage. Although the author discusses "Goblin Market" after "My Birthday," the author neither states nor implies which work was written earlier.

25. **The correct answer is (C).** This is a relatively easy question requiring you to recall explicit information. Choice (C) is the best response because the passage makes no mention of this literary form.

Choices (A), (B), (D), and (E) are all mentioned explicitly in the last paragraph as different types of works by Rossetti.

26. **The correct answer is (E).** This is a challenging question in which you are required to recognize the function of specific information or details. The author's threshold purpose in discussing Packer's biography is to affirm that Rossetti's style of writing was not a reflection of her personal lifestyle. Having dismissed the theory that Rossetti was keeping secrets about her life, the author goes on (in the final paragraph) to offer a better explanation for the apparent contradiction between Rossetti's lifestyle and the emotional, sensual style of her poetry.

Choice (A) distorts the information in the passage. First, the passage does not indicate that Rossetti's devotional commentary was in the form of prose rather than poetry. Second, nowhere in the passage does the author compare or contrast Rossetti's devotional commentary with her other works. Choice (B) distorts and actually runs contrary to the author's purpose. The author discusses Packer's biography to affirm that Rossetti's style of writing was not a reflection of her personal lifestyle—in other words, that she was not keeping secrets about her life. In this sense, choice (B) actually runs contrary to the author's purpose. Choice (C) distorts the information in the third paragraph. The author does not raise the issue of whether these letters were actually written by Rossetti. In fact, insofar as the author mentions these letters to disprove Packer's thesis, the author seems to affirm that the letters are indeed authentic. Choice (D) distorts and actually runs contrary to the information in the passage. The author compares Woolf's view only with that of Gosse, who actually preceded Woolf; in this sense, then, choice (D) distorts the information in the passage. Second, Packer's thesis does not reflect a more enlightened view; to the contrary, the author points out that Packer's thesis has been disproved.

27. **The correct answer is (C).** This is a moderately difficult question in which you must infer from or interpret specific information. In the final paragraph, the author states that "'The World'" is "pivotal in understanding Rossetti's literary project as a whole." Based upon the remainder of the final paragraph, the author seems to understand Rossetti's "literary project as a whole" as an attempt to convey an inescapable Christian truth to her readers (see lines 81–83). It is reasonably inferable, then, that "The World" provides significant insight into Rossetti's motives.

Choice (A) is contradicted by the passage. The author identifies "The World" as a sonnet (one type of poetry), never suggesting that it might incorporate other types of poetry as well. Choice (B) calls for speculation. Although "The World" is the last of Rossetti's works discussed in the passage, it does not necessarily follow that it was Rossetti's last major work. Choice (D) calls for speculation. The author neither states nor implies that "The World" is Rossetti's longest work; indeed, nowhere in the passage does the author mention the length of any of Rossetti's works. Choice (E) distorts the information in the passage. The author suggests that "The World" is pivotal in understanding Rossetti's general literary agenda—to convey an inescapable Christian truth to her readers. However, the author neither states nor implies that Rossetti's motives in writing "The World" or her viewpoint at the time she wrote it departed from earlier motives or viewpoints.

28. **The correct answer is (D).** This is a moderately difficult question in which you must recognize the main idea or primary purpose. The author's primary concern in the first two paragraphs is to point out that Rossetti's work conflicts with her apparently conservative personal life. The author's own impressions of Rossetti's work are corroborated by those of Woolf and Gosse. The third paragraph begins by asking how to reconcile this apparent conflict. (The newly discovered letters discussed in the third paragraph only reinforce the inconsistency between her personal life and literary work.) In the last paragraph, the author attempts to explain the inconsistency by examining Rossetti's love poems (particularly, her sonnet "The World").

Choice (A) is the second-best response. The newly discovered personal letters disprove Packer's thesis that Rossetti may have had personal affairs of the heart that she kept secret. Thus, Packer (and possibly Woolf) may have misinterpreted Rossetti's works by assuming that Rossetti wrote from personal experience. However, the author does not make this point explicit in the passage; moreover, this point is far too narrow. It ignores the author's own explanation (in the final paragraph) for the apparent inconsistency between Rossetti's personal life and her work. Choice (B) is off-focus. Admittedly, in the first paragraph the author does point out that Woolf compared Rossetti to Shakespeare in both of these respects. However, the author makes no further attempt to explain or describe these similarities. Moreover, the point made in choice (B) is Woolf's point, not the author's. Choice (C) distorts the author's argument and is too broad. First, in the last paragraph the author seems to claim that, through a proper reading of Rossetti's love poems, one can understand the ironic, enigmatic, contradictory nature of her work (in turn explaining the inconsistency between Rossetti's personal life and work). In this sense, choice (C) distorts and actually runs contrary to the author's argument. Second, the passage concerns only Rossetti, not Victorian poetry or poetry in general, as choice (C) suggests; in this sense, then, this answer choice is too broad. Choice (E) is off-focus. While the author does point out in the first paragraph that Woolf viewed Rossetti's work as a model for women writers, this is Woolf's point, not the author's. Moreover, the author does not elaborate on this point—there is no further discussion of particular women writers who might have seen Rossetti as a model for their own work.

Practice Mini-test 3

In this mini-test, you will take a full-length Analytical Reasoning section under actual test conditions. Allow yourself exactly 35 minutes to complete the 24 questions in this section.

SECTION III: ANALYTICAL REASONING

NUMBER OF QUESTIONS: 24 • SUGGESTED TIME: 35 MINUTES

Directions: Each group of questions in this section is based on a set of conditions. In answering some of the questions, it may be useful to draw a rough diagram. Choose the response that most accurately and completely answers each question.

QUESTIONS 1–7:

Of nine members on a baseball team, four bat right-handed, three bat left-handed, and two are switch-hitters. Each of the nine players bats once and only once in the batting order.

Exactly two left-handed batters bat consecutively.

The switch-hitters do not bat consecutively.

No two right-handed batters bat consecutively.

A right-handed batter bats fourth.

1. All of the following are possible batting assignments in order from first to third EXCEPT:

   (A) Right-handed batter, switch-hitter, left-handed batter
   (B) Right-handed batter, left-handed batter, switch-hitter
   (C) Switch-hitter, left-handed batter, right-handed batter
   (D) Switch-hitter, right-handed batter, left-handed batter
   (E) Left-handed batter, right-handed batter, switch-hitter

2. Which of the following is an acceptable batting order for the fifth, sixth, and seventh positions, in that order?

   (A) Right-handed batter, left-handed batter, left-handed batter
   (B) Left-handed batter, switch-hitter, switch-hitter
   (C) Switch-hitter, right-handed batter, left-handed batter
   (D) Left-handed batter, right-handed batter, right-handed batter
   (E) Switch-hitter, left-handed batter, left-handed batter

3. If a right-handed batter bats second, it must be true that

   (A) a right-handed batter bats ninth.
   (B) a left-handed batter bats fifth.
   (C) a switch-hitter bats seventh.
   (D) a right-handed batter bats sixth.
   (E) a left-handed batter bats eighth.

4. If left-handed batters bat second and eighth, all of the following must be true EXCEPT:

   (A) A right-handed batter bats first.
   (B) A switch-hitter bats fifth.
   (C) A right-handed batter bats sixth.
   (D) A switch-hitter bats seventh.
   (E) A right-handed batter bats ninth.

5. Assume that left-handed batters bat both fifth and sixth. Considering only whether a batter is right-handed, left-handed, or is a switch-hitter, what is the total number of possible batting orders?

   (A) 2
   (B) 3
   (C) 4
   (D) 5
   (E) 6

6. If all left-handed batters bat after all switch-hitters, all of the following must be false EXCEPT:

   (A) A left-handed batter bats seventh.
   (B) A switch-hitter bats second.
   (C) A left-handed batter bats ninth.
   (D) A right-handed batter bats eighth.
   (E) A switch-hitter bats fifth.

7. If both switch-hitters bat after all left-handed batters, which of the following must be true?

   (A) A switch-hitter bats seventh.
   (B) A left-handed batter bats fifth.
   (C) A left-handed batter bats first.
   (D) A switch-hitter bats sixth.
   (E) A right-handed batter bats eighth.

QUESTIONS 8–12:

Eight voters—Perez, Quinn, Raffi, Sperry, Trager, Utley, Villar, and Wieser—are voting in two elections. Each voter must vote for either Able or Berman, and each voter must vote for either Cargis or Dorsey. The election results are as follows:

Berman received exactly four votes.

Raffi, Sperry, and Trager voted for Able.

Villar did not vote for the identical two candidates as either Wieser or Utley.

Wieser did not vote for the identical two candidates as Utley.

8. The elections must have resulted in

   (A) a tie between Able and Berman.
   (B) a tie between Cargis and Dorsey.
   (C) Berman defeating Able.
   (D) Cargis defeating Dorsey.
   (E) Dorsey defeating Cargis.

9. With respect to which of the following pairs of voters is it NOT possible that the two voters voted for the same two candidates?

   (A) Raffi and Sperry
   (B) Trager and Perez
   (C) Villar and Trager
   (D) Utley and Quinn
   (E) Wieser and Perez

10. What is the greatest number of voters who could have voted for Cargis?

    (A) 4
    (B) 5
    (C) 6
    (D) 7
    (E) 8

11. If Perez and Quinn voted for different candidates in the election between Cargis and Dorsey, then it CANNOT be true that:

    (A) exactly two voters voted for both Berman and Cargis.
    (B) exactly three voters voted for both Berman and Dorsey.
    (C) exactly four voters voted for both Able and Dorsey.
    (D) exactly one voter voted for both Able and Cargis.
    (E) exactly three voters voted for both Able and Dorsey.

12. If Villar and six other voters voted for Dorsey, which of the following is a complete and accurate list of those voters whose choices with respect to both elections can be determined?

    (A) Villar, Perez, Quinn
    (B) Raffi, Sperry, Trager
    (C) Villar, Wieser, Utley
    (D) Raffi, Sperry, Trager, Utley, Villar
    (E) Raffi, Sperry, Trager, Perez, Quinn

QUESTIONS 13–18:

In a series of chemistry experiments, each experiment involves combining the contents of two different beakers. A beaker may contain one of three chemical compounds—X, Y, or Z—in either a gaseous or liquid medium. Two beakers containing the same chemical compound must never be combined, and gaseous Z must never be combined with liquid Y. The results of the series of experiments are as follows:

> Each experiment produces exactly one chemical compound—X, Y, or Z—in exactly one medium—gas or liquid.
>
> Combining X and Y produces Z.
>
> Combining X and Z produces X.
>
> Combining Y and Z produces Y.
>
> A gas may result only by combining a liquid and a gas.
>
> Combining a gas and a liquid produces a liquid if and only if X is used.

13. An experiment in which gaseous Y and liquid Z are combined produces:

    (A) liquid X.
    (B) liquid Y.
    (C) liquid Z.
    (D) gaseous X.
    (E) gaseous Y.

14. Liquid X will be produced by combining:

    (A) gaseous X and liquid Y.
    (B) liquid X and gaseous Z.
    (C) liquid Y and liquid Z.
    (D) gaseous Z and gaseous Y.
    (E) gaseous Y and liquid Z.

15. How many different results are possible from a single experiment?

    (A) 2
    (B) 3
    (C) 4
    (D) 5
    (E) 6

16. If each chemical compound is used exactly four times in six simultaneous experiments, which of the following statements must be true?

    (A) Exactly one of the experiments produced Z.
    (B) Exactly two of the experiments produced X.
    (C) Exactly three of the experiments produced Y.
    (D) Exactly two of the experiments produced a gas.
    (E) Exactly two of the experiments produced a liquid.

17. Two and only two possible different experiments will produce which of the following?

    (A) Liquid X
    (B) Liquid Y
    (C) Liquid Z
    (D) Gaseous X
    (E) Gaseous Y

18. If the results of two simultaneous experiments are combined in a third experiment to produce a gas, any of the following might have been used in at least one of the three experiments EXCEPT:

    (A) gaseous X.
    (B) gaseous Y.
    (C) gaseous Z.
    (D) liquid X.
    (E) liquid Y.

QUESTIONS 19–24:

Six commuters—C, D, E, F, G and H—participate in a van pool together. The seating capacity of the van is eight; two of the seats are empty. The seats are arranged in three rows as follows:

(front of van)

row 1:	1		2
row 2:	3	4	5
row 3:	6	7	8

Seat 1 is the driver's seat. Seats 4 and 7 are the only two seats that are considered "middle" seats. Two commuters can converse with each other only if they are sitting either immediately next to each other or diagonally from each other. However, the driver cannot converse with any other commuter. A commuter is seated "diagonally" from another commuter if the commuter is in an adjacent row and one seat to the left or right from the other commuter. The commuters' seating arrangement is subject to the following conditions:

Either E, F, or G always drives the van.

Neither C nor D will sit in a middle seat.

G will not sit in row 3.

H and D must sit next to each other.

19. Which of the following is an acceptable seating arrangement, in order, for seats 1, 2, 3, and 4?

    (A) G, D, empty seat, empty seat
    (B) F, C, E, H
    (C) G, empty seat, F, C
    (D) E, F, C, empty seat
    (E) C, G, F, E

20. Among the following pairs of commuters, with respect to which pair is it always true that the two commuters CANNOT converse with each other?

    (A) G and H
    (B) F and C
    (C) C and D
    (D) E and F
    (E) D and E

21. If seat 6 and seat 8 are empty, which of the following must be true?

    (A) H occupies seat 4.
    (B) G occupies seat 1.
    (C) F occupies seat 2.
    (D) E occupies seat 7.
    (E) D occupies seat 3.

22. The fewest number of commuters that can converse is

    (A) 0
    (B) 1
    (C) 2
    (D) 3
    (E) 4

23. If D converses with G during a commute, which of the following must be true?

    (A) E is driving the van.
    (B) Seat 3 is empty.
    (C) H occupies seat 7.
    (D) D occupies seat 5.
    (E) Seat 2 is empty.

24. If H can converse with exactly two other commuters, with respect to which of the following seats is it NOT possible to determine whether the seat is occupied?

    (A) Seat 1
    (B) Seat 2
    (C) Seat 4
    (D) Seat 6
    (E) Seat 7

ANSWER KEY AND EXPLANATIONS

1. C	6. A	11. B	16. B	20. C
2. C	7. B	12. E	17. B	21. A
3. A	8. A	13. E	18. C	22. D
4. D	9. B	14. B	19. D	23. C
5. D	10. D	15. C		24. D

Questions 1–7: Simple Linear Sequence Game (Easier):

One viable approach to this game is to jot down the possible sequences, considering together that a right-handed batter bats fourth and that no right-handed batters bat consecutively. First consider a right-handed batter batting first (sequences 1–3 below), then consider a right-handed batter batting second (sequences 4–6 below). Also consider that unless a sequence contains at least two adjacent empty slots, it can be eliminated, since two left-handed batters bat consecutively. (Eliminate sequence 4 below.) Finally, insert those two left-handed batters wherever you can. The result is five alternative scenarios:

```
1.  R L L R _ R _ R _
2.  R _ _ R _ R _ _ R
3.  R _ _ R _ _ R _ R
X4. _ R _ R _ R _ R _
5.  _ R _ R _ R L L R
6.  _ R _ R L L R _ R
```

Another (and probably more efficient) approach is to simply construct one initial diagram which indicates that a right-handed batter must bat fourth, while indicating the other rules near that diagram:

```
            ®
_ _ _ _ _ _ _ _ _
1 2 3 4 5 6 7 8 9
```

```
┌─────┐
│RRRR │   [L L] ≠ L
│ LLL │   S ≠ S
│  SS │   R ≠ R
└─────┘
```

1. **The correct answer is (C).** The quickest way to locate the correct answer here is to consider, one at a time, each restriction regarding the first three batters. Then scan the answer choices for violations. If you consider that a right-handed batter cannot bat third, a quick glance down the list of third batters reveals the correct answer immediately—only in answer choice (C) does a right-handed batter bat third.

2. **The correct answer is (C).** Narrow down the choices by considering the conditions one at a time and scanning the answer choices for violations. Considering that a right-handed batter bats fourth and that right-handed batters cannot bat consecutively, (A) can be eliminated. Considering that the two switch-hitters cannot bat consecutively, (B) can be eliminated. (D) and (E) each require that two or more right-handed batters bat consecutively. (C) is the only choice that does not violate any rule.

3. **The correct answer is (A).** Given that a right-handed batter bats second, then the remaining two right-handed batters must bat either sixth and ninth or seventh and ninth. (In either case, a right-handed batter must bat ninth.) Otherwise, either no two left-handed batters would bat consecutively or two right-handed batters would bat consecutively. Either result would violate a rule.

4. **The correct answer is (D).** Given that left-handed batters bat second and eighth, a bit of experimenting reveals that only two viable sequences result:

   ```
   R L L Ⓡ S R S L R
   R L S Ⓡ S R L L R
   1 2 3 4 5 6 7 8 9
   ```

   Thus, either a switch-hitter or a left-handed batter can bat seventh.

5. **The correct answer is (D).** Given that left-handed batters bat fifth and sixth, two initial possibilities result:

   ```
   R   Ⓡ L L R   L
   _R_ Ⓡ L L R _R_
   1 2 3 4 5 6 7 8 9
   ```

   The first diagram above presents two possible sequences—a switch-hitter batting eighth while a left-handed batter and the other switch-hitter bat second and third, in either order. The second diagram presents three possible sequences—a left-handed batter batting first, third, or eighth, with the two switch-hitters occupying the remaining two positions.

6. **The correct answer is (A).** A bit of intuition and experimenting reveals that the first left-handed batter in the order must bat fifth, and no later, resulting in two possible sequences:

   ```
   S R S Ⓡ L R L L R
   S R S Ⓡ L L R L R
   1 2 3 4 5 6 7 8 9
   ```

   The foregoing sequences make clear that answer choice (A) could be true, while each of the other four statements must be false.

7. **The correct answer is (B).** Given that both switch-hitters bat after all left-handed batters, a bit of experimenting reveals that a switch-hitter can bat sixth at the earliest. Two possible sequences result:

   ```
   R L L Ⓡ L S R S R
   R L L Ⓡ L R S R S
   1 2 3 4 5 6 7 8 9
   ```

   In either case, a left-handed batter must bat fifth.

Questions 8–12: Complex Grouping Game (Moderate):

In this game, your task is to allocate eight subjects (the voters) among four different groups (who they voted for):

- the group who voted for Able and Cargis

- the group who voted for Able and Dorsey

- the group who voted for Berman and Cargis

- the group who voted for Berman and Dorsey

According to the rules, Berman receives exactly four votes. As a result, Able must also receive exactly four votes (from Raffi, Sperry, Trager and one other voter). Considering together the last two conditions, Utley, Villar, and Wieser must all be included in different groups. Accordingly, one of those three voted for Able, while the other two, along with Perez and Quinn, voted for Berman. The rules can now be incorporated into a group-oriented diagram as follows:

$$(RST) \begin{cases} [A\ C] \\ [A\ D] \end{cases}$$
$$(PQ\_) \begin{cases} [B\ C] \\ [B\ D] \end{cases}$$
$$U \neq V \neq W$$

In the following explanations, voters and candidates are identified by the first letter of their last name, as in the diagram above.

8. **The correct answer is (A).** Because A received exactly four votes, B must also have received exactly four votes.

9. **The correct answer is (B).** R, S, T, and one other voter voted for A. That other voter must be either U, V, or W. Therefore, T and P could not both have voted for A.

10. **The correct answer is (D).** V, U, and W must all be included in different groups. Thus, at least one voter among these three must have voted for D rather than for C.

11. **The correct answer is (B).** P and Q both voted for B (see general comments above). If one voted for C while the other voted for D, then P and Q must each be joined by exactly one other voter (among V, U, and W) in their respective groups (see diagram above). Otherwise, among V, U, and W, two would be in the same group together, resulting in a rule violation.

12. **The correct answer is (E).** According to the question, seven of the eight voters voted for D. As a result, exactly one voter voted for C. Accordingly, either the AC group includes one voter while the BC group includes no voters, or vice-versa. However, if that one voter is assigned to the AC group rather than the BC group, V, W, and U cannot all be separated into different groups. Thus, one voter must be assigned to the BC group while none of the voters are assigned to the AC group. Accordingly, R, S, and T must all have voted for A and D, while P and Q must both have voted for Berman and D. (Group assignments for W, U, and V cannot be determined.)

Questions 13–18: Logic Tree Game (Challenging):

In approaching this game, begin by listing the formulas suggested by the rules. In doing so, several important additional facts may be deduced. Considering the last two rules together, if either two liquids or two gases are combined, the result must be a liquid, while if a liquid and a gas are combined, the result is a gas if Y and Z are used or a liquid if either X and Y or X and Z are used. Since a gas may be produced only if Y and Z are combined, any experiment combining X and Y or X and Z must produce a liquid. This additional information is necessary to analyze the questions.

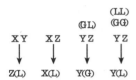

13. **The correct answer is (E).** Combining Y and Z produces Y. Combining a liquid and a gas produces a gas if X is not used. Thus, the experiment produces gaseous Y.

14. **The correct answer is (B).** According to the rules, combining X and Z in any form produces liquid X.

15. **The correct answer is (C).** Without restriction, a total of six different results would be possible—X, Y, or Z each in either liquid or gaseous form. However, any experiment using X must produce a liquid rather than a gas (see general comments above). Thus, an experiment combining X and Y or X and Z must produce liquid Z and liquid X, respectively. Gaseous Z and gaseous X are impossible results.

16. **The correct answer is (B).** A bit of intuition or experimenting reveals that three experiments—combining X with Y, X with Z, and Y with Z—must each be performed twice if each chemical compound is to be used four times in six experiments. Thus, Z, X, and Y must each be produced twice. Accordingly, answer choice (B) must be true, while choices (A) and (C) must be false. A liquid may result from a minimum of four to a maximum of six of the experiments (see general comments above). Accordingly, choice (D) is not necessarily true, while choice (E) must be false.

17. **The correct answer is (B).** In an experiment combining Y and Z, the rules stipulate that gaseous Z must not be combined with liquid Y. Thus, Z and Y are either both liquid, both gas, or Z is liquid while Y is gas. In each of the first two cases, liquid Y results. In the last case, gaseous Y results (because X is not used). Thus, Y may result from only one of two different experiments—combining liquid Y and liquid Z or combining gaseous Y and gaseous Z. Answer choices (A) and (C) are incorrect—liquid X and liquid Z may each result from any one of four different experiments. Answer choice (D) is incorrect because gaseous X is an impossible result (see question 3). Answer choice (E) is incorrect because only one experiment—combining gaseous Y and liquid Z—will produce gaseous Y.

18. **The correct answer is (C).** If either X or Z results from an experiment, it must be in liquid form (see general comments above). Thus, since the end result in this experiment is a gas, it must be gaseous Y. Gaseous Y can be produced only by combining gaseous Y and liquid Z. Liquid Z can be produced only by combining X and Y, although X and Y

may each be in either gas or liquid form. Thus, the only answer choice that cannot be used in any of the three experiments is gaseous Z.

```
GY  LZ      ?X  ?Y
 └──┘        └──┘
  GY          LZ
   └──────────┘
        GY
```

Questions 19–24: Multiple Row Game (Moderate):

The key to working through this game efficiently is to realize that H must occupy either seat 4 or seat 7. Why? D and H must sit next to each other. They cannot sit in row 1, since neither of them can drive the van. D cannot occupy a middle seat (that is, seat 4 or seat 7). Thus, H must occupy one of the two middle seats. Every question in this game includes this logical link as part of the analysis.

19. **The correct answer is (D).** In answer choice (A), D occupies seat 2; this is unacceptable, however, because D must sit immediately next to H (H cannot drive). In choice (B), H occupies seat 4. Since D must sit next to H, D must occupy seat 5 (seat 3 is occupied by E). This leaves no seat for G in either row 1 or row 2, violating the rule that "G will not sit in row 3." The arrangement indicated by answer choice (C) would place C in seat 4, which is one of the middle seats, violating the rule that C will not occupy a middle seat. In answer choice (E), C drives the van (the driver occupies seat 1), violating the rule that "either E, F, or G always drives the van."

20. **The correct answer is (C).** Since D will not sit in a middle seat, H must sit in one of the two middle seats (either seat 4 or seat 7), with D immediately next to H (in seat 3, 5, 6, or 8). Since C cannot sit in a middle seat, it is impossible for C and D to either sit next to each other or diagonally from each other.

21. **The correct answer is (A).** If seat 6 and seat 8 are empty, D and H (who must sit next to each other) must occupy row 2. Since D will not sit in a middle seat, H must occupy seat 4, while D occupies either seat 3 or seat 5.

22. **The correct answer is (D).** This question requires a bit of intuition or experimentation. To minimize the number of commuters who can converse, seat 4 must be empty—any commuter occupying seat 4 could converse with commuters in seats 2, 3, 5, 6, and 8. Assuming, then, that seat 4 is empty, H must sit in seat 7 with D in either seat 6 or 8. H can converse with D as well as with the commuter in either seat 3 or seat 5 (or both). Assuming that one of those two seats is empty, H can still converse with two other commuters (who in turn can converse with H). Therefore, at a minimum, three commuters (H, D, and one other under this "minimum conversation" scenario) can converse.

23. **The correct answer is (C).** Where is G sitting? G is not driving, since the rules prohibit the driver from conversing with another commuter. The rules also prohibit G from sitting in row 3. Thus, G must sit in seat 2, 3, 4, or 5. However, if G were to occupy seat 2 and converse with D, D would be in seat 4, which violates the rule that D cannot occupy a middle seat. Accordingly, G must sit in row 2. D, then, must sit in row 3, in either seat 6 or 8. In either case, H sits next to D in seat 7.

24. **The correct answer is (D).** H must occupy either seat 4 or seat 7 (see general comments above). If H were to occupy seat 4, then D would occupy either seat 3 or seat 5, and of course H could converse with D. However, H could not be limited to conversing with only one additional commuter. Thus, H must occupy seat 7 (and D must occupy either seat 6 or seat 8). Given that H occupies seat 7, the only way to limit H to conversing with only two others is to position the two empty seats among seats 3, 5, and 6. Accordingly, seats 1, 2, and 4 must be occupied (of course, seat I must be occupied in any event).

Practice Mini-test 4

In this mini-test, you will take a full-length Logical Reasoning section under actual test conditions. Allow yourself exactly 35 minutes to complete the 25 questions in this section.

SECTION IV: LOGICAL REASONING

NUMBER OF QUESTIONS: 25 • SUGGESTED TIME: 35 MINUTES

Directions: The questions in this section are based on the reasoning contained in brief statements or passages. For some questions, more than one of the choices could conceivably answer the question. However, you are to choose the best answer; that is, the response that most accurately and completely answers the question. You should not make assumptions that are by commonsense standards implausible, superfluous, or incompatible with the passage.

1. The nutrient value of animal products is indisputable. Complete protein—the kind with sufficient quantities of the eight amino acids—is found only in animal products. The human body cannot manufacture these eight amino acids, so they must be supplied through proper diet.

   Which of the following is the main point of the argument above?

   (A) Animal products are the main source of the eight amino acids that make up complete protein.
   (B) A proper diet must contain the eight amino acids.
   (C) Animal products must be included in a proper diet.
   (D) Amino acids cannot be manufactured by the human body.
   (E) Animal products are nutritious sources of food.

2. The earth-moon system, the satellites of Jupiter, and the moons of Saturn are all examples of planetary systems in which a satellite moves in the gravitational field of a much more massive body. In every one of these systems the satellite moves in an elliptical orbit.

If the statements above are true, they provide the most support for which one of the following?

(A) The more massive a body the more gravitational pull it exerts on another body.

(B) Only elliptical orbits can account for the various phases of the moon as seen from earth.

(C) Non-elliptical orbits violate the laws of celestial mechanics.

(D) The moons of the planet Uranus move in elliptical orbits.

(E) All celestial bodies move in elliptical orbits.

3. The mean price of new cars in Heavenly Hills is $38,563; in Cargo the mean price is only $23,769. Therefore, if you are in the market for a new car, you are likely to get a better deal on it in Cargo.

Which of the following best describes the flaw in the author's reasoning?

(A) The author's conclusion is based on a comparison that does not necessarily involve comparable things.

(B) The author assumes that the number of cars sold in Heavenly Hills is the same as the number sold in Cargo.

(C) The author has confused the mean average price with the median average price.

(D) The author assumes that new cars in Cargo are less expensive than new cars in Heavenly Hills.

(E) The author assumes that new car dealers in Cargo are more willing than Heavenly Hills dealers to make good deals on new cars.

4. Due to the fact that mean water temperatures in the oceans of the world have not changed significantly over the past century it is evident that the expected rise in global air temperatures as a result of ozone depletion has not yet begun.

Which of the following, if true, most substantially weakens the above argument?

(A) Ocean surface water temperatures fluctuate by as much as 20 degrees yearly.

(B) Air-to-water heat transfer is such that a rise of 10 degrees in air temperature will cause a rise of 1 degree of water temperature over a 24-hour period.

(C) Global ocean water temperatures are controlled mainly by polar ice.

(D) Global air temperatures have not varied significantly over the past decade.

(E) The rate of ozone depletion has been shown to be significantly less than as was first reported by scientists.

5. Flagrant violations of human rights were cited by the Astonian government as the official reason for ceasing to provide military support to the embattled country of Cretia. But, at the same time, military support continues to be provided to countries with far worse human-rights records than Cretia. Hence, despite the official explanation for this change in policy, this reversal cannot be accounted for solely by the Astonian government's commitment to human rights.

Which of the following, if true, would most strengthen the conclusion in the above argument?

(A) Cretia's neighboring countries recently entered into a nonaggression pact with one another.
(B) Astonia recently entered into long-range trade agreements with Cretia's neighboring countries.
(C) The newly elected head of the Cretian government is an avowed anti-Astonian.
(D) Cretia has a longer record of human-rights abuse than other countries to which military support is provided by Astonia.
(E) The Astonian government's decision to provide military support to a country is made mainly on the basis of the country's capability of defending itself from outside aggression.

6. It is commonly held in discussions of capital punishment that there is no evidence that the death penalty deters. This is simply untrue. We have an enormous amount of both informal and formal evidence—from everyday experience and from such "experiments" as increasing the fees for parking violations—that, as a general rule, the greater the punishment, the fewer people will behave in the punished way. Thus, it is perfectly reasonable to expect that the death penalty would have a more dissuasive effect than would life imprisonment.

Which of the following must be assumed for the above argument to be logically correct?

(A) Everyday experience shows that the death penalty deters.
(B) Life imprisonment does not act as a deterrent to murder.
(C) The death penalty is a greater punishment than life imprisonment.
(D) Potential murderers consciously weigh the alternatives beforehand and decide that the crime is worth life in prison, but not death.
(E) The more severe the punishment, the more it acts as a deterrent.

7. Since solid-state components of electronic devices are easily damaged by ionizing radiation, they would be useless in a nuclear war because they would not function properly. The crucial lesson to be drawn from this is that vital electronic equipment should not use solid-state components, but rather should use vacuum tubes or fiber optics.

Which of the following best expresses the main point of the passage?

(A) Electronic devices equipped with solid-state components will not function properly in a nuclear war.

(B) Vacuum tubes and fiber optics are better components for electronic devices than solid-state components.

(C) Electronic equipment should not be equipped with solid-state components.

(D) Vital electronic equipment should be equipped with vacuum tubes and fiber optics.

(E) Solid-state components of electronic devices are easily damaged by ionizing radiation.

8. Historians universally agree that all democracies in the past have eventually perished as a result of disputes between competing groups of special interests, coupled with gross inefficiency, waste and corruption in government, and a decline in the moral values of the society at large. Every day the news reports confirm that all of these maladies are currently present in the United States of America.

Given that the statements above are true, which of the following conclusions is most strongly supported?

(A) Communism is a better form of government than democracy.

(B) Nondemocratic societies do not suffer from the same problems as democratic societies.

(C) If the experience of past democracies is a reliable indicator, democracy in the United States is in decline.

(D) News reports generally focus only on negative news.

(E) In the future, the United States will be a dictatorship.

9. Card games requiring more than one player, such as poker and bridge, employ strategies aimed at outwitting the opponent; however, card games that are played alone, such as games of solitaire, do not. Hence, strategies that aim at outwitting an opponent are not an essential feature of all card games.

Which of the following most closely parallels the reasoning in the above passage?

   (A) Games of chance, such as roulette and craps, employ odds that are detrimental to the player, but favorable to the house. Since these are the only kinds of games that are found in gambling casinos, having odds that favor the house is an essential feature of all games played in gambling casinos.
   (B) Most aircraft have wings, but others, such as helicopters, do not. Hence, having wings is not an essential property of all aircraft.
   (C) Chez Bon's most celebrated features are its great food and extensive wine list. But, since these are features of many other fine restaurants as well, they are not the only features which define the essence of this outstanding restaurant.
   (D) It has been reliably reported that deer occasionally eat meat, but if deer were not primarily vegetarians they would have much different shaped teeth than they do. Hence, being a vegetarian is an essential feature of being a deer.
   (E) All cats are meat eaters and being a meat eater is the defining characteristic of being a carnivore. Hence, being carnivorous is essential to being a cat.

10. The average annual salary for executives at World-Wide Travel last year was $55,000, while the average salary for travel consultants was $47,000. The average annual salary for all employees was $38,000.

If the above information is correct, which one of the following conclusions can be properly inferred from it?

   (A) There were fewer executives than travel consultants at World-Wide Travel last year.
   (B) No travel consultants earned more than an executive last year.
   (C) There was at least one employee who earned less than the average for a travel consultant.
   (D) Some travel consultants earn more than the lowest paid executives.
   (E) All executives earn more than travel consultants.

QUESTIONS 11 AND 12 ARE BASED ON THE FOLLOWING PASSAGE.

An auto mechanic who is too thorough in checking a car is likely to subject the customer to unnecessary expense. On the other hand, one who is not thorough enough is likely to miss some problem that could cause a serious accident. Therefore, it's a good idea not to have your car checked until a recognizable problem develops.

11. Which one of the following, if true, casts the most doubt on the argument?

   (A) Mechanical problems that can cause serious accidents are easily detectable by a mechanic even before they become recognizable to the customer.

   (B) Due to the high cost of skilled labor, some auto garages limit the amount of time spent on auto checkups.

   (C) Drivers who are not trained mechanics generally have difficulty in recognizing that their car has a problem.

   (D) Many mechanics spend neither too little nor too much time when checking a car.

   (E) Most people cannot afford to have their cars checked for problems regularly.

12. Which one of the following, if true, provides the most support for the above argument?

   (A) The more complete the mechanical checkup, the more likely a problem, if present, will be discovered.

   (B) Some people have enough mechanical knowledge to recognize a problem with their car.

   (C) Not all tests performed by mechanics are time consuming and expensive.

   (D) Most mechanical problems that are potentially dangerous or expensive to repair cannot be detected by routine checkups no matter how thorough they are.

   (E) Many auto mechanics lie to customers about the mechanical condition of their cars.

13. A study of six patients who all suffer from a rare form of cancer revealed that though they all live in different locations in the county and have quite different medical histories, diet, and personal habits—two smoke cigarettes and three drink alcoholic beverages—they are all employed at a company that manufactures herbicides and pesticides. From this study it can be concluded that exposure to the chemicals produced by the company is the probable cause of the disease.

The argument proceeds by:

(A) reaching a general conclusion on the basis of insufficient evidence.

(B) isolating a common feature through a process of elimination and concluding that this feature is causally related to the event under investigation.

(C) reaching a general conclusion on the basis of the experiences of the six patients.

(D) providing information that allows the application of a general claim to a specific case.

(E) indirectly showing that exposure to the chemicals produced by the company is the likely cause by demonstrating that none of the other alternatives is the cause.

14. The College Board recently decided to recenter the scores on standardized college admission tests to reflect the composition of the test-takers. The College Board explained the recentering—lowering the definition of what is average—on grounds that students who take college admissions tests today—30 percent from minority groups and 53 percent women—cannot be expected to achieve the same test scores as the original reference group of 1941, which was predominantly white and 82 percent male.

Which of the following is an assumption on which the College Board's decision depends?

(A) Women and minorities have a lower level of general intelligence than white males.

(B) Admission tests are a lot more difficult today than they were in 1941.

(C) The original reference group of 1941 was not representative of the test-takers during that period.

(D) The definition of "average" has changed since 1941.

(E) Fewer people went to college in 1941 than do so today.

15. Seventeenth-century scientists argued that a void must exist in nature on the grounds that if there were no void, that is if all space were filled with matter, movement would be impossible. Movement would be impossible, they reasoned, because a body could not move unless it displaced another body. But to do this would require that the space occupied by the other body is empty, which it clearly is not because the other occupies it, thus movement is impossible.

Which of the following, if true, provides the most support for the scientists' conclusion?

(A) Instantaneous spatial displacement of one body by another is possible.

(B) Instantaneous spatial displacement of one body by another is impossible.

(C) Sequential spatial displacement entails that to move one body all other bodies would have to be moved.

(D) Sequential spatial displacement of one body by another is possible.

(E) Sequential spatial displacement of one body by another is impossible.

16. Given that the stated goal of environmentalists is to reduce the amount of carbon dioxide in the atmosphere while at the same time preserving existing plant life on earth, there are two very good reasons for harvesting living trees from old-growth forests. First, doing so would reduce the amount of carbon dioxide in the atmosphere for the simple reason that when old trees die they decompose, thereby releasing their stored carbon dioxide. Second, it would make room for more young trees which absorb carbon dioxide thereby further reducing the amount of carbon dioxide in the atmosphere.

Which one of the following, if true, most seriously weakens the above argument?

(A) Levels of carbon dioxide in the atmosphere have remained relatively constant over the past 100 years.

(B) Reduction in the amount of carbon dioxide in the atmosphere is necessary to reduce the "greenhouse effect."

(C) The amount of carbon dioxide released into the atmosphere through the decomposition of old trees is insignificantly small when compared to the amount released by agricultural waste.

(D) Old-growth forests are the habitat of many species which will not survive if these forests are destroyed.

(E) A reduction in the amount of carbon dioxide in the atmosphere is detrimental to plant life.

17. Analytic propositions provide no information about any matter of fact. This applies to all analytic propositions. In other words, they are entirely devoid of information about the world. It is for this reason that no empirical evidence can refute them.

Which of the following must be assumed for the above argument's conclusion to be properly drawn?

(A) The truth or falsity of analytic propositions cannot be determined by empirical evidence.

(B) Analytic propositions are neither true nor false.

(C) Analytic propositions are completely uninformative.

(D) Empirical evidence can only refute propositions that provide information about matters of fact.

(E) Propositions that are entirely devoid of information about the world are false.

18. Gasoline additives are designed to clean the electronic sensors in the ignition systems of modern automobiles. Because of the prevalent use of these additives in gasoline over the past decade, car manufacturers have been able to design engines that meet the stringent federally mandated emission standards. Unfortunately, current additives contain ingredients that threaten the ozone and will be illegal to use in the near future. Despite the fact that there is no likelihood that current emission standards will be changed, car manufacturers are confident that they will continue to be able to produce engines that meet them.

If the above statements are true, which of the following is the most strongly supported inference?

(A) New additives will be developed that do not contain ozone threatening ingredients.

(B) Gasoline-powered internal combustion engines will be replaced by hydrogen-powered engines.

(C) The electronic sensors in the ignition system will be eliminated.

(D) Smaller engines will be developed that are more fuel efficient.

(E) Gasoline powered engines will be outlawed in the near future.

19. Persons who do not control their cholesterol levels are more likely to have heart disease than those who do. However, even among those who do not control their cholesterol levels, the majority do not have heart disease. Therefore, to avoid heart disease, there is no need to adopt a diet that is low in cholesterol rather than one that is high in cholesterol.

The pattern of flawed reasoning displayed in the above argument most closely resembles the reasoning in which one of the following?

(A) People who swim every day are more likely to develop ear infections than those who jog. However, daily joggers are more likely to develop foot problems than swimmers. Hence, people who want to avoid foot problems and ear infections shouldn't jog or swim on a daily basis.

(B) There is no need to abstain from smoking to decrease the likelihood of contracting lung disease because even though smokers are more likely to die of lung disease than non-smokers, most smokers do not die of lung disease.

(C) Overweight people are more likely to die at a young age than persons who are physically fit. However, a surprisingly large number of young physically fit people die in sports-related accidents each year. Hence, to avoid an early death, it is probably best to be neither overweight nor physically fit.

(D) Crimes of passion are more likely to be committed by young people than old people. Yet many old people are capable of extremely strong emotional outbursts. Hence, middle-aged people are less likely to commit crimes of passion than either young people or old people.

(E) Persons who exercise daily are more likely to live longer than persons who do not exercise. But "daily exercise" means at least 20 minutes of strenuous aerobic exercise, not just walking around the block or bicycling to the store. For this reason, unless your willing to really work up a sweat every day, there is little reason to exercise daily.

20. Parents cannot be with their teenage children every minute of the day and, even if they could, they would not always be able to stop them from doing things that might cause harm to other people or other people's property. That's why they should not be blamed or punished for crimes that their teenage children commit.

Which of the following general principles, if established, would most help to justify the conclusion in the argument above?

(A) All activities that teenage children engage in should be supervised by adults.

(B) Teenage children should be treated as adults in the criminal justice system.

(C) People should be held accountable for only those actions over which they have control.

(D) Parents should supervise the activities of their teenage children as much as possible.

(E) Parents have the responsibility to teach their teenage children the difference between right and wrong.

21. Persons who advocate capital punishment typically do so on the grounds that it is a more effective deterrent than life imprisonment. So far this has not been conclusively established, but assuming for the moment that it is true, the question remains as to whether the goal of deterrence justifies the state-sanctioned murder of people who are under lock and key and are no longer a threat to anyone. Clearly, this is not something that any civilized society can condone, so it is simply erroneous to claim that this provides a valid reason for this barbaric form of punishment.

The method of the argument is to:

(A) discredit the argument in favor of capital punishment by showing that one of its premises is unacceptable because it leads to an unacceptable claim.

(B) discredit the argument in favor of capital punishment by questioning the motives of the persons who advance it.

(C) discredit the argument in favor of capital punishment by arguing that the fact that many people agree with the conclusion does not make it true.

(D) discredit the argument in favor of capital punishment by showing that the conclusion of the argument is assumed in the premises.

(E) discredit the argument in favor of capital punishment by showing that persons who advance the argument are uncivilized.

22. *Democratic Senator:* The fact that the Republicans have not articulated one good reason in support of their opposition to cuts in social security payments to the elderly shows that they are obviously in favor of them.

Which of the following best describes the flaw in the senator's reasoning?

(A) Arguing that there are only two possible alternatives to choose from, and since one can be eliminated the other must be true

(B) Arguing that a claim is true because of the lack of evidence that it is false

(C) Arguing that what is true of some members of a group must also be true of all members of the group

(D) Inferring a conclusion from unrepresentative or biased data

(E) Drawing a general conclusion from too small a sample of cases

23. Captive animals are more interesting research subjects than are wild animals. That's why researchers can learn more from studying captive animals than from studying wild animals.

Which of the following is an assumption upon which the above argument depends?

(A) Researchers study only subjects they are interested in.

(B) In general, the more that can be learned from a research subject, the more interesting it is to study.

(C) In general, the more interesting a research subject, the more that can be learned from studying it.

(D) Researchers learn less from studying subjects they are not interested in.

(E) In general, researchers prefer studying interesting subjects more than non-interesting subjects.

24. *George:* What benefit will taxpayers get from the installation of automated flight centers at privately owned airports? The answer is none, and that's why I am opposed to using taxpayer funds for this purpose.

Henry: I agree that there won't be any direct benefit to taxpayers from these projects, but the fact is that automatic flight centers will greatly increase the amount of traffic these airports can safely accommodate, and they are just too costly for private companies to install without government subsidies.

On the basis of their statements, George and Henry are committed to disagreeing about the truth of which of the following principles?

(A) Taxpayer funds should be used only to fund projects that benefit taxpayers.

(B) Airport safety should always take precedence over other factors when improving airports.

(C) Government subsidies should never be given to privately held companies.

(D) Automated flight centers should be installed at all airports.

(E) Taxpayer funds should only be used to fund those projects to which taxpayers have given their approval.

25. There is no such thing as one single scientific method. Instead, there is a jumble of methods ranging from careful observation and collection of data from which hypotheses are advanced to mere conjecture of the underlying causes. Moreover, no attempts to rationally justify the various methods of science as sources of truth have as yet proven fruitful. For these reasons it can be concluded that science is not preferable to religion or mythology when it comes to finding out the basic truths of the universe.

Which one of the following claims, if true, would most weaken the author's position in the passage?

(A) Science is based on reason, whereas religion and mythology are based on faith.

(B) Unlike religion and mythology, the various methods of science all yield accurate predictions, and yielding accurate predictions is an indicator of truth.

(C) Religion and mythology are based on superstition and ignorance.

(D) There is widespread agreement among scientists about the nature of the universe but little agreement among the practitioners of religion and mythology.

(E) More technological advances have been made in the past two centuries, during which science has reigned, than in the preceding twenty centuries, in which mythology and religion reigned.

ANSWER KEY AND EXPLANATIONS

1.	C	6.	C	11.	A	16.	E	21.	A
2.	D	7.	D	12.	D	17.	D	22.	B
3.	A	8.	C	13.	B	18.	A	23.	C
4.	C	9.	B	14.	A	19.	B	24.	A
5.	E	10.	C	15.	B	20.	C	25.	B

1. **The correct answer is (C).** This is a moderately difficult question requiring you to identify the main point or conclusion of an argument. In this passage, the main point or final conclusion of this argument is not overtly stated. The intermediate conclusion is stated in the last line—"so they must be supplied through proper diet." The pronoun "they" in this line refers to the eight amino acids, which, we were told earlier are found in sufficient quantities only in animal products. Since these eight amino acids can only be found in animal products and they are necessary for a proper diet, it can be concluded that animal products must be included in a proper diet. This is the main point of the argument and this is exactly what answer choice (C) asserts.

   Choice (A) is simply a restatement of the second sentence of the argument. This sentence functions as a premise—not a conclusion—in the argument. Choice (B) is an incorrect response. In this question you are asked to find the main point or final conclusion; this answer choice states an intermediate conclusion, not the final conclusion. Choice (D) is a generalization of one of the premises. In the passage we are told that the "human body cannot manufacture these eight amino acids." Choice (D) asserts this claim more broadly. Choice (E) is a restatement of the first sentence in the passage. It states neither a premise nor a conclusion of the argument; it functions merely to introduce the topic.

2. **The correct answer is (D).** This is a moderately difficult question that requires you to make an inference or draw a conclusion from a given premise. From the information given in the passage we can reasonably assume that Uranus and its moons constitute a planetary system. From this assumption and the claim that in all of the planetary systems mentioned the satellite moves in an elliptical orbit, we can infer that the moons of the planet Uranus move in elliptical orbits. This is exactly what choice (D) asserts.

   Choice (A) is unsupported by the passage. It states something that is true according to modern physics, but the premises in the passage do not provide any logical support for this claim. Choice (B) brings in information not mentioned in the passage. The phases of the moon as seen from earth are not discussed in the passage. Choice (C) makes too broad a claim. The information in the passage is restricted to laws governing planetary systems. Choice (E) is too broad. The passage concerns only planetary systems, not all celestial bodies.

3. **The correct answer is (A).** This is a moderately difficult question in which you must identify a reasoning error. The passage does not indicate whether the cars sold in Heavenly Hills were the in the same price range (i.e., similar makes and models) as the ones sold in Cargo. The mean price is simply the total dollar amount of the cars sold

divided by the number of cars sold. If the cost of each of the individual cars sold in Heavenly Hills was higher than those sold in Cargo, then the mean price would also be higher. For example, it could be that only one car was sold in each place—a high priced luxury car costing $38,563 in Heavenly Hills and a moderate priced compact car costing $23,769 in Cargo. In this case the mean price of cars in Heavenly Hills would be $38,563 and the mean price of cars in Cargo would be $23,769. From this example it can be clearly seen that choice (A) is the best answer because unless the cars are comparable, the author's conclusion that a person is likely to get a better deal in Cargo than in Heavenly Hills does not follow.

Even if the number of cars sold in both places were the same, it would not follow that a person would get a better deal in Cargo than in Heavenly Hills unless the cars were comparable, so choice (B) is incorrect. The median average price is simply the middle price in a series of prices with an odd number of items, or the price midway between the middle two prices in an even series. Given that the median price of new cars in Heavenly Hills was $38,563 whereas the median price in Cargo is $23,769, nothing could be inferred regarding the general prices of cars in either location. Since this is the case, a confusion of mean average price with median average price would not account for the flaw in the author's reasoning, so choice (C) is incorrect. Choice (D) is incorrect; the claim that new cars in Cargo are less expensive than new cars in Heavenly Hills is not an assumption in the argument, but a loose restatement of the conclusion. The argument in does not rely on the assumption in choice (E), so it is incorrect. At best, it is an inference that could be made from the conclusion of the argument.

4. **The correct answer is (C).** This is a moderately difficult question requiring you to assess the effect of additional information. The task in this problem is to find an answer that weakens the argument; that is, one that undermines the major assumption of the argument, attacks a stated premise, or that suggests an alternative conclusion that could be inferred from the premises. The major assumption in the argument is that water temperatures in the oceans of the world are controlled by global air temperatures. Choice (C) directly contradicts this assumption, and consequently, if true, substantially weakens the argument.

Choice (A) is consistent with the claim that "mean water temperatures in the oceans of the world have not changed significantly over the past century." While choice (B) is an interesting fact about air to water heat transfer, it is irrelevant to the argument. Consequently, its being true would have no effect on the argument one way or another. Choice (D) is consistent with the implied claim that global air temperatures have not risen over the past century. Choice (E) is incorrect because whether the ozone depletion rate is more or less than reported by scientists is irrelevant to the underlying assumption that water temperatures in the oceans of the world are controlled by global air temperatures.

5. **The correct answer is (E).** This is a challenging question requiring you to assess the effect of additional information. The task in this problem is to find an answer that strengthens the argument; that is, one that offers support for the major assumption of the argument or that provides additional evidence for the conclusion. Of the answer choices, response (E) is the best choice because it does the latter; that is, it provides a convincing rationale for the seemingly inconsistent action on the part of the Astonian government.

    Choice (A) is consistent with the claim that Cretia is an "embattled country." While this answer choice might provide a reason for Cretia's need for military support, it does not provide a rationale for the seemingly inconsistent action on the part of the Astonian government. Choice (B) is the second-best answer. It provides a plausible reason for the Astonian government's shift in policy, but to accept it as the best response we would have to make superfluous assumptions about how these trade agreements impact Astonia's foreign policy decisions. Choice (C) is the third-best answer. While it provides a rationale for Astonia's shift in policy, to accept it as the best response would require making a number of superfluous assumptions about the Astonian government's foreign policy making principles. Choice (D) conflicts with information provided in the passage regarding Cretia's human-rights record as compared to other countries. Moreover, the fact that Cretia has a worse record than other countries to which military support is provided by Astonia does not provide a convincing rationale for Astonia's change in policy towards Cretia.

6. **The correct answer is (C).** This is a relatively easy question in which you must identify assumptions employed in a specific argument. The argument stated in the passage is basically as follows:

    Premise: The greater the punishment, the fewer people will behave in the punished way.

    Conclusion: The death penalty will have a more dissuasive effect than would life imprisonment.

    The assumption required to fill the gap in the above argument is that the death penalty is a greater punishment than life imprisonment. This is exactly what choice (C) asserts.

    Choice (A) does not fill a logical gap in the argument. It is maintained in the passage that the death penalty deters. It simply provides additional evidence that this is the case. Choice (B) does not fill a logical gap in the argument. Whether or not life imprisonment acts as a deterrent to murder is irrelevant to the main point of the argument. Choice (D) does not fill a logical gap in the argument. It is consistent with the conclusion and may offer a rationale for the greater dissuasive effect of the death penalty. Choice (E) is a loose paraphrase of a stated premise of the argument—namely, "the greater the punishment, the fewer people will behave in the punished way."

7. **The correct answer is (D).** This is a moderately difficult question in which you must identify the main point or conclusion. The phrase "The crucial lesson to be drawn from this" signals the final conclusion of the argument. Choice (D) expresses a pared-down paraphrase of the sentence that immediately follows this phrase.

Choice (A) is a restatement of a premise in the argument. Choice (B) is too broad. The argument establishes only that vacuum tubes and fiber optics are better components for vital electronic devices than solid-state components. Choice (C) is also too broad. The argument establishes only that vital electronic equipment should not be equipped with solid-state components. Choice (D) is a premise in the argument.

8. **The correct answer is (C).** This is a relatively easy question requiring you to make inferences or draw conclusions from given premises. The task in this problem is to find the answer choice that is most likely to be true on the basis of the information stated in the passage. Basically what the stated information boils down to is that the United States suffers from all of the problems that led to the demise of other democracies in the past. Given this, the inference that the United States will likewise perish as a result of these problems is highly probable. Of all the answers, choice (C) comes closest to asserting this claim. It should be noted that while answer choice (C) requires that we assume that the United States of America is a democracy, this assumption is not, by commonsense standards, an implausible, superfluous, or incompatible assumption.

Choice (A) is incorrect. No mention of communism appears in the passage. To infer the claim asserted in this choice would require a number of superfluous assumptions. Choice (B) is also incorrect. No comparisons between non-democratic societies and democratic societies are warranted given the information stated in the passage. To infer the claim asserted in this choice would require numerous superfluous assumptions. The degree of likelihood that the claims asserted in choices (D) and (E) are true is indeterminable given the information stated in the passage.

9. **The correct answer is (B).** This is a moderately difficult question in which you must identify parallel reasoning. The reasoning in the passage runs basically as follows: X is not an essential feature of Y because it is not present in all Y's. Schematically, the argument looks like this:

Premise: Some Y's are X's.

Premise: Some Y's are not X's.

Conclusion: X is not an essential feature of all Y's.

The answer that most closely parallels this structure will be the best choice, so choice (B) is the best response. A close examination of the argument in choice (B) reveals exactly the same structure as the argument in the passage as is demonstrated below:

Premise: Some aircraft have wings.

Premise: Some aircraft do not have wings.

Conclusion: Having wings is not an essential feature of all aircraft.

Choice (A) is incorrect; its argument can be represented as follows:

Premise: All games played in gambling casinos have odds that are favorable to the house.

Conclusion: Having odds that are favorable to the house is an essential feature of all games played in gambling casinos.

The general structure of this argument is:

> *Premise:* All Y's are X's.
>
> *Conclusion:* X is an essential feature of all Y's.

This structure is not similar to the structure of the argument in the passage.

Choice (C) is incorrect; its argument can be represented as follows:

> *Premise:* Chez Bon has features A and B.
>
> *Premise:* Many other restaurants have features A and B.
>
> *Conclusion:* A and B are not the only features that define the essence of Chez Bon.

The structure of this argument is clearly not comparable to the structure of the argument in the passage.

Choice (D) is incorrect; its argument can be represented as follows:

> *Premise:* Deer must be vegetarians because of the shape of their teeth.
>
> *Conclusion:* Being a vegetarian is an essential feature of being a deer.

The structure of this argument is clearly not comparable to the structure of the argument in the passage.

Choice (E) is incorrect; its argument can be represented as follows:

> *Premise:* All cats are meat eaters.
>
> *Premise:* Being a meat eater is the defining characteristic of being a carnivore.
>
> *Conclusion:* Being carnivorous is essential to being a cat.

The structure of this argument is clearly not comparable to the structure of the argument in the passage.

10. **The correct answer is (C).** This is a moderately difficult question requiring that you make inferences or draw conclusions from given premises. The task in this problem is to find the answer choice that must be true or that is most likely to be true given the information stated in the passage. If executives and travel consultants were the only employees, the combined average for all employees would be $51,000. Since the passage states that combined average for all employees was $38,000, it can be inferred that there must have been other employees besides executives and travel consultants. Furthermore, it can be inferred that the average salary of these other employees was $12,000 $\left(\dfrac{\$55,000 + \$47,000 + X}{3} = \$38,000 \right)$. Moreover, while the number of other employees is indeterminable, since their average salary was $12,000 it can be inferred that at least one of them must have earned less than $47,000, so it follows that at least one employee must have earned less than the average for a travel consultant. This is exactly what answer choice (C) states.

Choice (A) is an incorrect response. Contrary to this claim, it is consistent with the information stated in the passage that there were more executives than travel consultants. This can be demonstrated with a simple example. Suppose there were three executives each earning $55,000. The average for executives in this case would be $55,000 as stated in the passage. Suppose further that there were only two travel consultants each earning $47,000. Again the average is as stated in the passage. In this hypothetical example the number of travel consultants is less than the number of executives.

Choice (B) is an incorrect response. Contrary to this claim, it is consistent with the information stated in the passage that some travel consultants earned more than some executives. For example, suppose there were only two executives at World-Wide Travel last year; one earned $85,000 and the other earned $25,000. In this case the average for executives is $55,000 as stated in the passage. Suppose further that there were only two travel consultants; one earned $60,000 and the other earned $34,000. Again the average salary for travel consultants is as stated in the passage. In this hypothetical example, a travel consultant earns more than an executive, clearly demonstrating that choice (B) cannot be inferred from the stated information. Choice (D) is an incorrect response. Contrary to this claim it is consistent with the information stated in the passage that no travel consultants earn more than the lowest paid executive. Choice (E) is an incorrect response. Contrary to this claim it is consistent with the information stated in the passage that some executives do not earn as much as some travel consultants.

11. **The correct answer is (A).** This is a moderately difficult question requiring you to assesses the effect of additional information. The task in this problem is to find an answer that weakens the argument; that is, one that undermines the major assumption of the argument, attacks a stated premise, or that suggests an alternative conclusion that could be inferred from the premises. Choice (A) attacks one of the stated premises of the argument (a mechanic "who is not thorough enough is likely to miss some problem that could cause a serious accident"). Since choice (A) contradicts one of the premises of the argument, accepting it as true effectively undermines or weakens the argument.

Choices (B), (C), (D), and (E) are incorrect; none of them asserts a claim that undermines an assumption of the argument, attacks a stated premise, or provides an alternative conclusion that could be inferred from the premises. Consequently, none of these answer choices weakens the argument.

12. **The correct answer is (D).** This is a moderately difficult question requiring you to assess the effect of additional information. The task in this problem is to find an answer that strengthens the argument; that is, one that offers support for the major assumption of the argument or that provides additional evidence for the conclusion. Choice (D) offers additional evidence for the conclusion. The claim that the thoroughness of routine checkups is inconsequential in detecting dangerous or costly mechanical problems provides an additional reason for waiting to have your car checked until a recognizable problem develops.

Choice (A) does not provide additional evidence for the conclusion nor does it offer support for the major assumption of the argument. Moreover, it is potentially inconsistent with the first premise which implies that unnecessary expense is to be avoided. Choice (B) is the second-best response. Choice (B) offers an additional reason why some people should wait to have their car checked until a recognizable problem develops. In the stated argument, however, the conclusion applies to all people, so choice (B) has minimal evidential value for the conclusion. Choice (C) does not provide additional evidence for the conclusion nor does it offer support for the major assumption of the argument. In fact, choice (C) provides a reason for not waiting until a recognizable problem develops to have your car checked. Choice (E) does not provide additional evidence for the conclusion nor does it offer support for the major assumption of the argument. Even if we accept the claim that many mechanics lie to their customers about the mechanical condition of their cars, it does not follow that they all do this. It is only this latter claim that could provide additional evidence for the conclusion.

13. **The correct answer is (B).** This is a moderately difficult question in which you must identify the method of reasoning used in the argument. The argument in the passage presents a textbook example of eliminative causal reasoning—reasoning in which a common causal factor is discovered through a process of elimination of possible factors. This is exactly the method described in answer choice (B).

    Choice (A) is an incorrect response. The conclusion of the argument in the passage applies only to the six patients in the study—it is not a sweeping generalization about all persons who suffer from the rare form of cancer mentioned. Given that this is the case, the evidence cited in the passage is sufficient to support it. Choice (C) is incorrect; no specific experiences shared by the six patients are cited in the passage as grounds for the conclusion. The conclusion is reached by finding a factor that all six patients share. No general claim is offered as a premise in the argument, so choice (D) is also incorrect. And no attempt is made in the passage to demonstrate or prove that other factors are not causally related to the disease, so choice (E) is incorrect. Alternative factors such as diet, personal habits, etc., are eliminated simply because they are not shared by all of the patients who suffer from the disease.

14. **The correct answer is (A).** This is a challenging question in which you must identify assumptions employed in a specific argument. There are, admittedly, a number of possible assumptions that could be operative in the College Board's decision, but, of the answer choices listed, choice (A) is the best. No premise is stated in the passage that explains why students who take college admissions tests today "cannot be expected to achieve the same scores as the original reference group of 1941." This is the gap in the argument that must be filled. Since the only difference between the two groups of test-takers that is cited in the passage is their composition, it is reasonable to assume that there is some difference between the two groups that somehow accounts for the expected difference in achievement. Choice (A) maintains that this difference is a difference in intelligence, thereby providing an explanation of why today's students cannot be expected to achieve the same scores as the 1941 reference group.

    Choice (B) does not fill the gap in the College Board's argument. The reasons offered in support of their decision focused only on facts about changes in the composition of the test takers. It would be superfluous to assume that the content of the tests had changed in ways which made them more difficult today than in 1941. Choice (C) also does not fill the gap in the College Board's argument. The reasons offered in support of their decision focused only on facts about changes in the composition of the test-takers. It would be superfluous to assume that the makeup of the reference group was not representative of the 1941 test takers. Choice (D) is not an assumption in the argument because it does not provide an explanation of why today's test takers cannot be expected to achieve the same scores as the 1941 reference group. Choice (E) may provide an explanation of the change in the composition of test-takers since 1941, but it would not explain why today's test takers cannot be expected to achieve the same test scores as the 1941 reference group.

15. **The correct answer is (B).** This is a challenging question requiring you to assess the effect of additional information. The task in this problem is to find an answer that strengthens the argument; that is, one that offers support for the major assumption of the argument or that provides additional evidence for the conclusion. The major assumption of the scientists' argument is that no two bodies can occupy the same space at the same time. Choice (B) provides support for the major assumption by ruling out the possibility of instantaneous spatial displacement of one body by another.

Choice (A) is inconsistent with the major assumption. If instantaneous spatial displacement of one body by another is possible, then one body would be able to occupy the space of another at the same time. Choices (C), (D), and (E) do not provide support for the major assumption, nor do they provide additional evidence for the conclusion.

16. **The correct answer is (E).** This is a moderately difficult question requiring you to assess the effect of additional information. The task in this problem is to find the answer that weakens the argument; that is, one that undermines the major assumption of the argument, attacks a stated premise, or that suggests an alternative conclusion that could be inferred from the premises. The major assumption of the argument is that the two elements of the stated goal of environmentalists are compatible with one another; that is, that preserving existing plant life and at the same time reducing the amount of carbon dioxide in the atmosphere are not conflicting aims. Choice (E) directly contradicts this assumption, and as a result weakens the argument.

Choice (A) is off-focus. The fact that the levels of carbon dioxide in the atmosphere have remained constant over the past 100 years is consistent with the stated premises of the argument. Furthermore, choice (A) does not undermine the major assumption of the argument, nor does it suggest an alternative conclusion that could be inferred from the premises. Choice (B) states a possible rationale for the environmentalists' concern to reduce the amount of carbon dioxide in the atmosphere, however, it does not provide information that would undermine the argument's major assumption, attack a stated premise, or provide an alternative conclusion that could be inferred from the premises. Choices (C) and (D) raise peripheral issues that are not addressed in the argument. Neither of these responses undermines the argument's major assumption, attacks a stated premise, or suggests an alternative conclusion that could be inferred from the premises.

17. **The correct answer is (D).** This is a relatively easy question in which you must identify assumptions used in a specific argument. The argument in the passage can be restated as follows:

> *Premise:* Analytic propositions do not provide information about any matter of fact.

> *Conclusion:* Empirical evidence cannot refute analytic propositions.

In this restatement, it is fairly obvious that the assumption that is required for the conclusion to be properly drawn is one that will link empirical evidence with propositions that provide information about matters of fact. Choice (D) provides this link, thus closing the gap in the stated argument. This closure is clearly demonstrated in the following reconstruction of the argument.

> *Premise:* Analytic propositions do not provide information about any matter of fact.

> *Assumption:* Empirical evidence can only refute propositions that provide information about matters of fact.

> *Conclusion:* Empirical evidence cannot refute analytic propositions.

Choice (A) is implied by the conclusion of the argument. It does not state an assumption of the argument. Choice (B) brings in information that is irrelevant to the stated argument. Choice (C) is a generalization of one of the stated premises. It does not state an assumption of the argument. Choice (E) is irrelevant to the stated argument.

18. **The correct answer is (A).** This is a moderately difficult question in which you must make inferences or draw conclusions from a given premise. The task in this problem is to find the answer choice that is most likely to be true given the information stated in the passage. The passage states that gasoline additives have enabled car manufacturers to design engines that meet the emission standards in the past. From this information it is reasonable to infer that this is the direction most likely to be taken in the future; that is, it is highly likely that new additives will be developed that do not contain ozone threatening ingredients.

Choices (B), (C), (D), and (E) are unsupported by the passage. There is no information in the passage that suggests that any of these responses is likely to be true.

19. **The correct answer is (B).** This is a moderately difficult question requiring you to identify parallel reasoning. The argument in the passage can be restated as follows:

> *Premise:* Persons who do not control their cholesterol levels are more likely to have heart disease than persons who do.

> *Premise:* Most persons who do not control their cholesterol levels do not have heart disease.

> *Conclusion:* There is no need to control one's cholesterol level in order to avoid heart disease.

Choice (B) is the best answer. The argument in this answer choice can be restated as follows:

Premise: Smokers are more likely to die of lung disease than non-smokers.

Premise: Most smokers do not die of lung disease.

Conclusion: There is no need to abstain from smoking in order to decrease the likelihood of contracting lung disease.

A comparison of this argument with the argument in the passage outlined above reveals a striking similarity in the structure of the premises and the conclusions of these arguments. Choice (A) is an incorrect response. Its argument can be represented as follows:

Premise: People who swim every day are more likely to develop ear infections than those who jog.

Premise: Daily joggers are more likely to develop foot problems than swimmers.

Conclusion: People who want to avoid foot problems and ear infections shouldn't jog or swim on a daily basis.

A comparison of this argument with the argument in the passage outlined above reveals significant differences in the premises and the conclusions of these arguments.

Choice (C) is incorrect; its argument can be represented as follows:

Premise: Overweight people are more likely to die at a young age than persons who are physically fit.

Premise: Many young physically fit people die in sports-related accidents each year.

Conclusion: It is probably best to be neither over-weight nor physically fit in order to avoid an early death.

A comparison of this argument with the argument in the passage outlined above reveals significant differences in the premises and the conclusions of these arguments.

Choice (D) is incorrect. Its argument can be represented as follows:

Premise: Crimes of passion are more likely to be committed by young people than old people.

Premise: Many old people are capable of extremely strong emotional outbursts.

Conclusion: Middle-aged people are less likely to commit crimes of passion than either young people or old people.

A comparison of this argument with the argument in the passage outlined above reveals a significant difference in the second premise and in the conclusion of these arguments.

Choice (E) is incorrect. Its argument can be represented as follows:

Premise: Persons who exercise daily are more likely to live longer than persons who do not exercise.

Premise: "Daily exercise" means at least 20 minutes of strenuous aerobic exercise.

Conclusion: Unless you are willing to do 20 minutes of strenuous exercise, there is little reason to exercise daily.

A comparison of this argument with the argument in the passage outlined above reveals a significant difference in the second premise and in the conclusion of these arguments.

20. **The correct answer is (C).** This is a relatively easy question in which you must identify the principle or principles that underlie or justify the reasoning used in the argument. The argument in the passage basically maintains that parents should not be held accountable for crimes their teenage children commit because they don't always have complete control over their actions. This argument can be represented as follows:

Premise: Parents don't always have complete control over the actions of their teenage children.

Conclusion: Parents should not be held accountable for crimes their teenage children commit.

The major assumption in this argument is that parents should be held accountable for only those actions performed by their teenage children over which the parents have control. This assumption is an instance of the general principle stated in (C).

Choice (A) would not help to justify the conclusion. The premise of the argument concedes that adult supervision is not sufficient to preclude the possibility of criminal action on the part of teenagers. Choice (B) would not help to justify the conclusion. The treatment of teenage children by the criminal justice system is irrelevant to the issue of whether or not parents should be held accountable for their children's actions. Choice (D) would not help to justify the conclusion. The premise of the argument concedes that even if parents supervise their teenage children, they might not be able to stop them from doing things that might cause harm to other people or their property. Choice (E) also would not help to justify the conclusion.

21. **The correct answer is (A).** This is a moderately difficult question in which you must identify the method of reasoning employed in the argument. In the passage the argument in favor of capital punishment is challenged on the grounds that its major premise leads to the unacceptable claim that murdering people "who are under lock and key and are no longer a threat to anyone" is justified. On this basis the major premise is rejected as unacceptable. Choice (A) best describes the method employed in this passage.

Choices (B), (C), (D) and (E) incorrectly describe the method of the argument in the passage. In each of these responses, issues that are irrelevant to the argument in the passage are addressed.

22. **The correct answer is (B).** This is a relatively easy question in which you must identify a reasoning error. In the argument in the passage, the Republicans' failure to articulate good reasons in support of their opposition to cuts in social security is taken as evidence that they are in favor of cuts in social security. Of all the answers, choice (B) best describes this reasoning error.

Choice (A) incorrectly describes the argument in the passage. No alternatives are mentioned in the passage. Choice (C) is an incorrect response. The argument in the passage does not conclude that all Republicans favor cuts in social security on the grounds that some do; it concludes this on the grounds that Republicans have failed to present evidence of their opposition to cuts in social security. Choices (D) and (E) incorrectly describe the argument in the passage. There are no cases or data presented in the passage.

23. **The correct answer is (C).** This is a moderately difficult question in which you must identify assumptions employed in a specific argument. The gap in the argument that needs to be filled is the relationship between interesting research subjects and subjects from which more can be learned. Choice (C) expresses this relationship and, as the following restatement of the argument clearly shows, fills the gap in the argument in the passage.

> *Premise:* Captive animals are more interesting research subjects than are wild animals.

> *Assumption:* The more interesting a research subject, the more that can be learned from studying it.

> *Conclusion:* Researchers can learn more from studying captive animals than from studying wild animals.

In choice (A), the denial of this claim is consistent with the information stated in the passage; consequently, it cannot be an assumption of the argument. Choice (B) states the required relationship in reverse. To satisfy yourself that this statement of the relation does not fill the gap in the argument, try it in the above restatement of the argument in the passage. In choice (D), the denial of this claim is consistent with the information stated in the passage; consequently, it cannot be an assumption of the argument. In choice (E), the denial of this claim is consistent with the information stated in the passage; consequently, it cannot be an assumption of the argument.

24. **The correct answer is (A).** This is a moderately difficult question in which you must identify principles that underlie or justify the reasoning used in the argument. George's opposition to the installation of automated flight centers at privately owned airports is based on the claim that, in this instance, taxpayers' funds will be used to do something from which they derive no benefit. The underlying principle George is appealing to is that taxpayers' funds should be used only to fund projects that benefit taxpayers. Henry responds that the fact that taxpayers won't benefit from the installation of the centers is not a compelling reason for not using taxpayers' funds to install them. This response to George's argument clearly indicates that Henry is not committed to the view that taxpayers' funds should be used only to fund projects that benefit taxpayers.

Choice (B) is an incorrect response. George and Henry could agree that as far as "other factors" are concerned, as a general rule airport safety should always take precedence when improving airports. George is committed to opposing only those improvements that are made with taxpayers' funds from which they derive no benefit. Choice (C) is incorrect; Henry clearly indicates his willingness to give government subsidies to privately held companies. George could conceivably be willing to do this as well so long as some benefit is realized by the taxpayer. George and Henry could conceivably agree that all airports should have automated flight centers, but disagree about how these centers should be funded, so choice (D) is incorrect. Choice (E) introduces issues that are not addressed in the passage.

25. **The correct answer is (B).** This is a moderately difficult question in which you must assess the effect of additional information. The task in this problem is to find an answer that weakens the argument—that is, one that undermines the major assumption of the argument, attacks a stated premise, or that suggests an alternative conclusion that could be inferred from the premises. The major assumption of the argument is that there are no additional reasons for preferring science over religion and mythology as a source of truth. Choice (B) undermines this assumption by pointing out that science differs from religion and mythology in that its methods yield accurate predictions and that this is a reliable indicator of truth.

Choices (A), (C), (D), and (E) do not assert any claim that undermines an assumption of the argument, attacks a stated premise, or provides an alternative conclusion that could be inferred from the premises. Consequently, none of these answer choices weakens the argument.

Practice Mini-test 5

In this mini-test, you will respond to a Writing Sample topic under timed conditions. Allow yourself exactly 35 minutes to complete your essay. Evaluate your essay using the scorecard in Lesson 12 and the two model responses provided.

WRITING SAMPLE

1 TOPIC • SUGGESTED TIME: 35 MINUTES

Adams Elementary, a private school for first grade through fifth grade, received a large donation, and different plans are being considered for the use of the funds. Write an argument in favor of one of the following two proposals, keeping in mind two guidelines:

- Adams Elementary School wants to improve its students' scores on standardized math, reading, and social-studies achievement tests.

- Adams Elementary School wants to preserve its reputation for innovation and for encouraging students' parents to become actively involved in their children's education.

One plan is to adopt a one-year program called "Back to Basics," developed and provided by Educare, a regional educational consulting firm. "Back to Basics" has been approved by the state's bureau of education and adopted by several regional elementary schools. The program emphasizes fundamental math and reading skills through the use of Educare's unique lesson plans, books, and other materials. The program is designed to implement the latest academic theories about how children learn. An integral feature of the program is its emphasis on hands-on learning and on group activities. As part of the program, Educare conducts monthly weekend workshops for the teachers to help them use the materials effectively in the classroom and to discuss and evaluate current motivational and instructional theories. Educare also arranges for periodic trips to local libraries and to the local Children's Science Museum.

The alternative plan is to establish a computer laboratory at the school. The laboratory would replace one of the existing classrooms, and the displaced class would be assimilated by one or more of the other classes. Currently, each classroom at Adams has one computer. The laboratory would increase the number of computers at the school by 200 percent. Funding is sufficient to provide state-of-the-art Internet access for two years and to acquire a basic educational-software library. Adams hopes to make the laboratory available to students, teachers, and their families during evenings and weekends. Funds are available to hire a computer consultant to monitor and troubleshoot the computer system part-time during school hours. While some of the teachers at Adams are interested in computers, insufficient funds are available to pay a teacher separately for providing computer instruction.

Use the space below to respond to the Writing Sample topic. Do not write in the margins.

_____

_____

_____

_____

_____

_____

_____

_____

_____

_____

_____

_____

_____

_____

_____

_____

_____

_____

_____

practice mini-test

EVALUATE YOUR WRITING SAMPLE

When you have completed your writing sample, evaluate it using the following techniques:

- Score your essay, referring to the scorecard in Lesson 12. Try to be as objective as possible. If you have trouble being objective, ask a friend or teacher to evaluate your essay for you.

- With a yellow highlighter, mark every sentence in which you accomplished nothing more than restating or paraphrasing the premise, criteria, or characteristics of the choices—that is, in which you merely rearranged and parroted back the facts to the reader. How great a portion of your essay did you highlight? Every sentence in yellow represents wasted space and wasted time that you want to use instead to formulate and present original ideas in the form of persuasive arguments.

- With a red pencil, circle or underline every grammatical error, awkward sentence, or other mechanical problem. If you're not sure what to circle, ask an English professor to do so. Does your essay look like a sea of red? If so, spend more time working on the mechanics of writing and on your writing style.

TWO MODEL ESSAY RESPONSES

Here are two model responses, one arguing for each of the two choices described in this mini-test's Writing Sample topic. As you read these responses, keep in mind the following:

- These essays are models in the sense that they would garner the highest accolades at law schools. Don't expect to write essays quite this polished in 35 minutes; these responses give you something to shoot for.

- That said, these essays aren't perfect. Regardless of how effective an LSAT essay is, there's always some room for improvement.

- These responses would fit in the two pages provided on the LSAT response sheet if handwritten.

- By virtue of the open-ended nature of the prompts, these responses cannot include every possible argument. In other words, effective arguments may have occurred to you that are absent in these model responses.

The topic is loaded with facts that allow for a great variety of effective arguments. These model responses include only some possible arguments, so don't be concerned if your essay includes arguments that differ somewhat from those presented in these models. Instead, focus on how you performed according to the scorecard in Lesson 12.

Model Response #1

(in favor of Back to Basics)

Adams should adopt the "Back to Basics" program. Its emphasis on basic math and reading skills would seem the most direct and effective way possible to improve achievement scores in those areas; and the program's approval by the state, along with its adoption by other schools, provides some assurance that the program will be effective. The alternative plan would be less effective in achieving this goal, since available time for each student in the lab would probably be quite limited, especially considering the problem of inadequate staffing. Finally, while computers may help to motivate some students, Educare's program also appears to provide fun, interactive learning experiences.

"Back to Basics" would also better preserve Adams' reputation—the use of new teaching theories and techniques would ensure its continued reputation for innovation, while the field-trip component of the program would allow for parent participation. While the computer-lab program might seem more innovative, without sufficient funding for upgrades and support, Adams could easily fall behind as technology advances.

In sum, "Back to Basics" is more likely to achieve the school's goals; test scores are more certain to improve, while the innovative and experiential nature of the program is sure to preserve the school's reputation.

Model Response #2

(in favor of the computer lab)

The computer lab is the better choice. Interactive software and Internet access not only is innovative but also will motivate students to develop the basic skills and knowledge needed for higher standardized test scores. Although regular classrooms would be more crowded, it might be possible to move computers from the classrooms to the lab to free up space. Doing so would also eliminate the distracting tendencies of computers from the classroom, allowing students to better focus on fundamentals. The problem of insufficient funds for computer instruction can be solved by soliciting parent volunteers, thus preserving Adams' reputation for parent involvement.

While "Back to Basics" appears consistent with Adams' reputation for innovation, it doesn't allow for much parent involvement, since parents are not likely to be familiar with the materials and methods. Although parents could become involved in field trips, such involvement may be too infrequent to be meaningful. Although "Back to Basics" may improve reading and math test scores, it fails to embrace social science. Furthermore, the weekend workshops may take their toll on the teachers who may quickly lose motivation and enthusiasm.

Thus, both the innovative and well-rounded education afforded by a computer lab, along with its attractiveness for parents and teachers, render this proposal the better choice for Adams.

STILL ROOM FOR IMPROVEMENT?

By now, you should have a fairly clear idea how effectively you respond to an LSAT Writing Sample topic. If you are not satisfied with your performance, take the following three remedial steps:

1. Review Writing Sample Lessons 12 and 13.

2. Rewrite the essay you wrote for this mini-test, limiting yourself to about 17 minutes. Unless your essay is either "limited" or "seriously flawed," don't start from scratch. Instead, try to refine and build upon your basic arguments and approach.

3. Based upon this mini-test's topic, write a new essay in which you argue for the choice that you argued against in your first essay. Evaluate that essay as you did the first one.

ANSWER SHEET PRACTICE TEST 6

SECTION I: READING COMPREHENSION

1. Ⓐ Ⓑ Ⓒ Ⓓ Ⓔ
2. Ⓐ Ⓑ Ⓒ Ⓓ Ⓔ
3. Ⓐ Ⓑ Ⓒ Ⓓ Ⓔ
4. Ⓐ Ⓑ Ⓒ Ⓓ Ⓔ
5. Ⓐ Ⓑ Ⓒ Ⓓ Ⓔ
6. Ⓐ Ⓑ Ⓒ Ⓓ Ⓔ
7. Ⓐ Ⓑ Ⓒ Ⓓ Ⓔ
8. Ⓐ Ⓑ Ⓒ Ⓓ Ⓔ
9. Ⓐ Ⓑ Ⓒ Ⓓ Ⓔ
10. Ⓐ Ⓑ Ⓒ Ⓓ Ⓔ

11. Ⓐ Ⓑ Ⓒ Ⓓ Ⓔ
12. Ⓐ Ⓑ Ⓒ Ⓓ Ⓔ
13. Ⓐ Ⓑ Ⓒ Ⓓ Ⓔ
14. Ⓐ Ⓑ Ⓒ Ⓓ Ⓔ
15. Ⓐ Ⓑ Ⓒ Ⓓ Ⓔ
16. Ⓐ Ⓑ Ⓒ Ⓓ Ⓔ
17. Ⓐ Ⓑ Ⓒ Ⓓ Ⓔ
18. Ⓐ Ⓑ Ⓒ Ⓓ Ⓔ
19. Ⓐ Ⓑ Ⓒ Ⓓ Ⓔ

20. Ⓐ Ⓑ Ⓒ Ⓓ Ⓔ
21. Ⓐ Ⓑ Ⓒ Ⓓ Ⓔ
22. Ⓐ Ⓑ Ⓒ Ⓓ Ⓔ
23. Ⓐ Ⓑ Ⓒ Ⓓ Ⓔ
24. Ⓐ Ⓑ Ⓒ Ⓓ Ⓔ
25. Ⓐ Ⓑ Ⓒ Ⓓ Ⓔ
26. Ⓐ Ⓑ Ⓒ Ⓓ Ⓔ
27. Ⓐ Ⓑ Ⓒ Ⓓ Ⓔ
28. Ⓐ Ⓑ Ⓒ Ⓓ Ⓔ

SECTION II: LOGICAL REASONING

1. Ⓐ Ⓑ Ⓒ Ⓓ Ⓔ
2. Ⓐ Ⓑ Ⓒ Ⓓ Ⓔ
3. Ⓐ Ⓑ Ⓒ Ⓓ Ⓔ
4. Ⓐ Ⓑ Ⓒ Ⓓ Ⓔ
5. Ⓐ Ⓑ Ⓒ Ⓓ Ⓔ
6. Ⓐ Ⓑ Ⓒ Ⓓ Ⓔ
7. Ⓐ Ⓑ Ⓒ Ⓓ Ⓔ
8. Ⓐ Ⓑ Ⓒ Ⓓ Ⓔ
9. Ⓐ Ⓑ Ⓒ Ⓓ Ⓔ

10. Ⓐ Ⓑ Ⓒ Ⓓ Ⓔ
11. Ⓐ Ⓑ Ⓒ Ⓓ Ⓔ
12. Ⓐ Ⓑ Ⓒ Ⓓ Ⓔ
13. Ⓐ Ⓑ Ⓒ Ⓓ Ⓔ
14. Ⓐ Ⓑ Ⓒ Ⓓ Ⓔ
15. Ⓐ Ⓑ Ⓒ Ⓓ Ⓔ
16. Ⓐ Ⓑ Ⓒ Ⓓ Ⓔ
17. Ⓐ Ⓑ Ⓒ Ⓓ Ⓔ

18. Ⓐ Ⓑ Ⓒ Ⓓ Ⓔ
19. Ⓐ Ⓑ Ⓒ Ⓓ Ⓔ
20. Ⓐ Ⓑ Ⓒ Ⓓ Ⓔ
21. Ⓐ Ⓑ Ⓒ Ⓓ Ⓔ
22. Ⓐ Ⓑ Ⓒ Ⓓ Ⓔ
23. Ⓐ Ⓑ Ⓒ Ⓓ Ⓔ
24. Ⓐ Ⓑ Ⓒ Ⓓ Ⓔ
25. Ⓐ Ⓑ Ⓒ Ⓓ Ⓔ

SECTION III: ANALYTICAL REASONING

1. Ⓐ Ⓑ Ⓒ Ⓓ Ⓔ
2. Ⓐ Ⓑ Ⓒ Ⓓ Ⓔ
3. Ⓐ Ⓑ Ⓒ Ⓓ Ⓔ
4. Ⓐ Ⓑ Ⓒ Ⓓ Ⓔ
5. Ⓐ Ⓑ Ⓒ Ⓓ Ⓔ
6. Ⓐ Ⓑ Ⓒ Ⓓ Ⓔ
7. Ⓐ Ⓑ Ⓒ Ⓓ Ⓔ
8. Ⓐ Ⓑ Ⓒ Ⓓ Ⓔ

9. Ⓐ Ⓑ Ⓒ Ⓓ Ⓔ
10. Ⓐ Ⓑ Ⓒ Ⓓ Ⓔ
11. Ⓐ Ⓑ Ⓒ Ⓓ Ⓔ
12. Ⓐ Ⓑ Ⓒ Ⓓ Ⓔ
13. Ⓐ Ⓑ Ⓒ Ⓓ Ⓔ
14. Ⓐ Ⓑ Ⓒ Ⓓ Ⓔ
15. Ⓐ Ⓑ Ⓒ Ⓓ Ⓔ
16. Ⓐ Ⓑ Ⓒ Ⓓ Ⓔ

17. Ⓐ Ⓑ Ⓒ Ⓓ Ⓔ
18. Ⓐ Ⓑ Ⓒ Ⓓ Ⓔ
19. Ⓐ Ⓑ Ⓒ Ⓓ Ⓔ
20. Ⓐ Ⓑ Ⓒ Ⓓ Ⓔ
21. Ⓐ Ⓑ Ⓒ Ⓓ Ⓔ
22. Ⓐ Ⓑ Ⓒ Ⓓ Ⓔ
23. Ⓐ Ⓑ Ⓒ Ⓓ Ⓔ
24. Ⓐ Ⓑ Ⓒ Ⓓ Ⓔ

answer sheet

SECTION IV: LOGICAL REASONING

1. Ⓐ Ⓑ Ⓒ Ⓓ Ⓔ
2. Ⓐ Ⓑ Ⓒ Ⓓ Ⓔ
3. Ⓐ Ⓑ Ⓒ Ⓓ Ⓔ
4. Ⓐ Ⓑ Ⓒ Ⓓ Ⓔ
5. Ⓐ Ⓑ Ⓒ Ⓓ Ⓔ
6. Ⓐ Ⓑ Ⓒ Ⓓ Ⓔ
7. Ⓐ Ⓑ Ⓒ Ⓓ Ⓔ
8. Ⓐ Ⓑ Ⓒ Ⓓ Ⓔ
9. Ⓐ Ⓑ Ⓒ Ⓓ Ⓔ

10. Ⓐ Ⓑ Ⓒ Ⓓ Ⓔ
11. Ⓐ Ⓑ Ⓒ Ⓓ Ⓔ
12. Ⓐ Ⓑ Ⓒ Ⓓ Ⓔ
13. Ⓐ Ⓑ Ⓒ Ⓓ Ⓔ
14. Ⓐ Ⓑ Ⓒ Ⓓ Ⓔ
15. Ⓐ Ⓑ Ⓒ Ⓓ Ⓔ
16. Ⓐ Ⓑ Ⓒ Ⓓ Ⓔ
17. Ⓐ Ⓑ Ⓒ Ⓓ Ⓔ

18. Ⓐ Ⓑ Ⓒ Ⓓ Ⓔ
19. Ⓐ Ⓑ Ⓒ Ⓓ Ⓔ
20. Ⓐ Ⓑ Ⓒ Ⓓ Ⓔ
21. Ⓐ Ⓑ Ⓒ Ⓓ Ⓔ
22. Ⓐ Ⓑ Ⓒ Ⓓ Ⓔ
23. Ⓐ Ⓑ Ⓒ Ⓓ Ⓔ
24. Ⓐ Ⓑ Ⓒ Ⓓ Ⓔ
25. Ⓐ Ⓑ Ⓒ Ⓓ Ⓔ

WRITING SAMPLE

_____

_____

_____

_____

_____

_____

_____

_____

_____

_____

_____

_____

_____

_____

_____

_____

_____

_____

_____

_____

_____

_____

_____

_____

_____

_____

_____

_____

_____

answer sheet

Practice Test 6

Section	Time	Number of Questions
Logical Reasoning	35 min.	25–26
Logical Reasoning	35 min.	25–26
Analytical Reasoning	35 min.	23–24
Reading Comprehension	35 min.	28
Writing Sample	35 min.	1 topic

Remember, except for the Writing Sample, which is always administered last, all other sections of the LSAT may appear in any order. To better simulate actual test conditions:

- Use scratch paper only during the writing section

- Use pencils or highlighters only (no pens), except when working on the Writing Sample section

- Do not work ahead or return to other test sections once you've completed work on them or time is up

practice test 6

SECTION I: READING COMPREHENSION

NUMBER OF QUESTIONS: 28 • *SUGGESTED TIME: 35 MINUTES*

Directions (as printed in test booklet): Each passage or passage pair in this section is followed by a group of questions to be answered on the basis of what is stated or implied in the passage(s). For some of the questions, more than one of the choices could conceivably answer the question. However, you are to choose the best answer; that is, the response that most accurately and completely answers the question.

QUESTIONS 1–7 ARE BASED ON THE FOLLOWING PASSAGE:

Line The region known as the Andean
cordillera, including the Northern and
Central Andes, is made up of many
mountain ranges, which include high
5 plateaus, basins, and valleys. The
Northern Andes contains several broad
ecosystems falling into four altitudinal
belts. Its northern subregion is distinguished by higher humidity and by
10 greater climatic symmetry between
eastern and western flanks. The
Central Andes are characterized by a
succession of agricultural zones with
varied climatic conditions along the
15 mountains' flanks and by large,
high-altitude plateaus, variously called
puna or *altiplano,* which do not occur
in the Northern Andes. The soil
fertility of the northern *altiplano* is
20 generally good. The western Central
Andean ranges are relatively arid with
desert-like soils, whereas the eastern
ranges are more humid and have more
diverse soils. The eastern slopes of the
25 Central Andes in many ways are
similar to the wet forests of the
Northern Andes. Unlike the Northern
Andes, however, these slopes have a
dry season.
30   In regions of consistent topography,
such as the flat Amazon basin, regional
climatic variation can be determined
from a few widely spaced measurements. Regional projections in the
35 Andean *cordillera* are quite difficult by
comparison. For example, while air
temperature generally decreases with
increasing altitude, variability of

mountain topography can produce
40 much lower than expected air temperatures. Nevertheless, some general
climatic patterns are discernible. For
example, with increasing distance
south of the equator the seasonality of
45 precipitation increases, whereas the
total annual amount generally decreases. Humidity commonly increases
with increasing altitude, but only to
some intermediate altitude, above
50 which it declines. The variability of
mountain terrain also affects precipitation, such that conditions of extreme
wetness and aridity may exist in close
proximity. Related to this temperature
55 gradient is a pattern of greater rainfall
at the valley heads, and less rain at
lower altitudes, resulting in part from
mountain "rainshadow effect."
    The weather patterns of the Andean
60 *cordillera* and Amazon basin in general
reflect movements of high- and low-
pressure cells associated with the
"Intertropical Convergence Zone," a
low-pressure trough that moves further
65 north and south on a seasonal basis.
Precipitation is high throughout the
year in the highlands and on the coast
in the Northern Andes. Coastal aridity
increases south of central Ecuador,
70 culminating in the Atacama desert of
northern Chile. In the Central Andes,
highland precipitation is seasonal, and
amounts are approximately half those
measured in the northern Andes. The
75 aridity of the Central Andean coastal
zone is the result of the drying effect of
the cold Pacific Humboldt current and
the southern Pacific high-pressure cell.
Much of the southern portion of the

80　Central Andes in Bolivia is also arid.
　　The dry season causes soil moisture
　　deficits and diminished stream flow
　　part of each year.
　　　　At the regional level, vegetation
85　patterns in the Northern and Central
　　Andes tend to reflect climatic zones
　　determined by latitude and altitude. At
　　the local level, however, this correspon-
　　dence becomes less precise, as local
90　variations in soil type, slope, drainage,
　　climate, and human intervention come
　　into play.

1.　In the passage, the author is con-
　　cerned primarily with

　　(A)　describing the climate and
　　　　topography of various regions of
　　　　the Andean *cordillera*.
　　(B)　discussing the factors affecting
　　　　the climate of the Andean
　　　　cordillera.
　　(C)　suggesting various alternative
　　　　explanations for the diversity of
　　　　climate among the various
　　　　regions of the Andean
　　　　cordillera.
　　(D)　examining the effects of topog-
　　　　raphy on the climate and
　　　　vegetation of the Andean
　　　　cordillera.
　　(E)　comparing the climate and
　　　　topography of the Northern
　　　　Andes to those of the Cen-
　　　　tral Andes.

2.　According to the passage, the
　　northern part of the high-altitude
　　plateaus is characterized by

　　(A)　fertile soil.
　　(B)　high relative humidity.
　　(C)　a succession of agricultural
　　　　zones.
　　(D)　extremes in air temperature.
　　(E)　an arid climate.

3.　Based on the passage, the air
　　temperatures in the Andean *cordil-
　　lera* are often "lower than expected"
　　(line 40) probably because

　　(A)　the Intertropical Convergence
　　　　Zone creates unexpected high
　　　　pressure cells.
　　(B)　the elevation varies dramati-
　　　　cally in the mountain regions.
　　(C)　prior measurements were based
　　　　upon inaccurate topographical
　　　　maps.
　　(D)　the humidity varies dramati-
　　　　cally in the mountain regions.
　　(E)　precipitation increases nearer to
　　　　the equator.

4.　Which of the following statements
　　finds the LEAST support in the
　　passage?

　　(A)　The northern subregion of the
　　　　Northern Andes is more humid
　　　　than the western subregion of
　　　　the Central Andes.
　　(B)　The soil in the northern
　　　　subregion of the Central Andes
　　　　is more fertile than the soil in
　　　　the western subregion of the
　　　　Central Andes.
　　(C)　The eastern subregion of the
　　　　Central Andes is more humid
　　　　than the western subregion of
　　　　the Central Andes.
　　(D)　The highlands of the Northern
　　　　Andes receive more precipita-
　　　　tion than the highlands of the
　　　　Central Andes.
　　(E)　The coastal subregion of the
　　　　Central Andes is less arid than
　　　　the southern subregion of the
　　　　Central Andes.

GO ON TO THE NEXT PAGE

5. Which of the following is NOT mentioned in the passage as a factor in the climate of the Central Andes *cordillera*?

   (A) The Intertropical Convergence Zone
   (B) The rainshadow effect
   (C) The southern Pacific high-pressure cell
   (D) Symmetry of the mountain ranges
   (E) The Pacific Humboldt current

6. Which of the following statements about vegetation patterns in the Andean *cordillera* is most strongly supported in the passage?

   (A) Local vegetation patterns are determined by the same factors as regional vegetation patterns.
   (B) Vegetation patterns vary more widely at the regional level than at the local level.
   (C) Vegetation patterns are affected by more factors at the regional level than at the local level.
   (D) Human intervention has a greater effect than either altitude or latitude upon vegetation patterns.
   (E) Some factors affecting vegetation patterns have only a local impact, whereas others have a broader impact.

7. Among the following, the passage would most logically continue by

   (A) describing the climate and topography of portions of the Andean *cordillera* other than the Northern and Central regions.
   (B) discussing how high- and low-pressure systems affect the climate of the Amazon.
   (C) exploring how proximity to the equator affects vegetation in the Andes *cordillera*.
   (D) identifying problems in determining the relation between soil type and vegetation in the Andean *cordillera*.
   (E) examining the effects of vegetation patterns on the topography of the Andean *cordillera*.

QUESTIONS 8–14 ARE BASED ON THE FOLLOWING PASSAGE:

Line Among the many other things it is, a portrait is a record of the personal and artistic encounter that produced it. It is possible for artists to produce
5   portraits of individuals who have not sat for them, but the portrait that emerges normally betrays the restrictions under which the artist has labored, even when the portrait is
10   simply a copy of someone else's work. In the many portraits of Queen Elizabeth I produced during her lifetime, the never-changing features of a monarch who refused to sit for her
15   court painters reflect not only the putative powers of an ever-youthful queen but also the physical remoteness of those attempting to depict her.
     Portraits are "occasional" not only in
20   the sense that they are closely tied to particular events in the lives of their subjects but also in the sense that there is usually an occasion—however brief, uncomfortable, artificial, or
25   unsatisfactory it may be—in which the artist and subject directly confront each other. Thus, the encounter a portrait records is most tangibly the sitting itself, which may be brief or
30   extended, collegial or confrontational. Cartier-Bresson has expressed his

passion for portrait photography by characterizing it as "a delicate rape," in sharp contrast to Richard Avedon's
35 conception of a sitting. While Cartier-Bresson reveals himself as an interloper and opportunist, Avedon confesses to a role as diagnostician and psychic healer—not as someone who
40 necessarily transforms his subjects, but as someone who reveals their essential nature. Both photographers appear to agree, however, that the fundamental dynamic in this process lies squarely in
45 the hands of the artist.

A quite different paradigm has its roots not in confrontation or consultation but in active collaboration between artist and sitter. This very different
50 kind of relationship was formulated most vividly by William Hazlitt in his 1823 essay titled "On Sitting for One's Picture." To Hazlitt, the "bond of connection" between painter and sitter
55 is most like the relationship between two lovers "in which their self-love finds an equal counterpart." Hazlitt fleshes out his thesis by recounting particular episodes from the career of
60 Sir Joshua Reynolds. According to Hazlitt, Reynolds' sitters, accompanied by their friends, were meant to enjoy an atmosphere that was both comfortable for them and conducive to the
65 enterprise of the portrait painter, who was simultaneously their host and their contractual employee. With artists like Reynolds, who I take to be a paradigmatic case, no fundamental
70 difference exists between the artist's studio and all those other rooms in which the sitters spin out the days of their lives. The act of entering Reynolds' studio—this social and aesthetic
75 encounter—did not necessarily transform those who sat for him. Collaboration in portraiture such as Reynolds' is based on the sitter's comfort and security as well as on his or her desire
80 to experiment with something new; and it is in this "creation of another self," as Hazlitt puts it, one that reflects the true self, that the painter's subjects may properly see themselves
85 for the first time.

8. Which of the following best expresses the central point of the first paragraph (lines 1–18)?

(A) True portrait artists know better than to copy other portraits.
(B) It is generally easy to discern between a copy of a portrait and the original work.
(C) The best portraits are those created while the portrait's subject is present.
(D) It is more difficult to paint a convincing copy of a portrait than is generally believed.
(E) Copies of a portrait are rarely as good as the original work.

9. In referring to Queen Elizabeth as "ever youthful" (line 16), the author implies in part that

(A) she instructed her court painters to paint her portrait in such a way that she appeared younger than she actually was.
(B) all portraits of the queen available for copying were painted when she was young.
(C) she died at an early age, and so all portraits of her depicted her as a young woman.
(D) her youthful appearance belied her actual age.
(E) artists who copied her portraits believed that she was younger than she actually was.

10. The author quotes Cartier-Bresson to

(A) refute Avedon's conception of a portrait sitting.
(B) support the claim that portrait sitting can be a confrontational encounter.
(C) provide one perspective of the portraiture encounter.
(D) show that a portraiture encounter may be either brief or extended.
(E) distinguish a sitting for a photographic portrait from a sitting for a painted portrait.

GO ON TO THE NEXT PAGE

11. Which of the following best characterizes the portraiture experience as
viewed by Avedon?

    (A) A collaboration
    (B) A mutual accommodation
    (C) A consultation
    (D) An uncomfortable encounter
    (E) A confrontation

12. A portrait artist operating under the
Reynolds paradigm would probably
disagree that

    (A) a portraiture sitting often
changes the way the sitter
views himself or herself.
    (B) the portraiture encounter
provides a means for both
artist and subject to display
their vanity.
    (C) a successful portrait depends
more upon the artist's initiative
than upon the subject.
    (D) the portrait sitting often
heightens the sitter's self-
knowledge.
    (E) the success of a portrait de-
pends largely upon whether the
artist and sitter are socially
compatible.

13. Of the following, it would be most
consistent with the information in
the passage to assert that Reynolds

    (A) may have provided a transform-
ing experience for some of
his sitters.
    (B) worked primarily with experi-
enced portrait subjects.
    (C) often painted portraits at his
subjects' homes.
    (D) was usually alone with his
sitters while he painted
their portraits.
    (E) painted portraits primarily of
friends and relatives.

14. Which of the following best expresses
the main idea of the passage?

    (A) The success of a portrait
depends largely upon the
relationship between artist
and subject.
    (B) Photographers and painters dif-
fer in their views regarding their
role in portrait photography.
    (C) The social aspect of portrait-
sitting plays an important part
in the outcome of the sitting.
    (D) Portraits, more than any other
art form, provide insight into
the artist's social relationships.
    (E) The paintings of Reynolds
provide a record of his success
in achieving a social bond with
his subjects.

QUESTIONS 15–20 ARE BASED ON THE FOLLOWING PASSAGE PAIR:

passage A

Line   Central to the restorationist critique of
environmental preservationism is the
claim that it rests on an unhealthy
dualism that conceives nature and
5   humankind as radically distinct and
opposed to each other. Dissatisfaction
with this dualism has for some time
figured prominently in environmentalists' unhappiness with mainstream
10   industrial society. However, the
writings of the restorationists themselves—particularly, Jordan and
Turner—offer little evidence to support
this indictment. In their view, preser-
15   vationists are imbued with the same
basic mind-set as the industrial
mainstream, the only difference being
that the latter exalts humans over
nature while the former elevates
20   nature over humans. While it is
puzzling that Jordan and Turner do
not see that there is no logic that
requires dualism as a philosophical
underpinning for preservation, more
25   puzzling is the sharpness and relentlessness of their attack on preservationists, accentuated by the fact that
they offer little, if any, criticism of

those who have plundered the natural
30 world.

    Nevertheless, the crucial question
about the restorationist outlook has to
do with whether the restorationist
agenda is itself faithful to the first
35 principle of restoration: that nature
and humanity are not separate but
rather fundamentally united. In their
categorical rejection of the old domination model, which sees humans as over
40 nature, in favor of a community-
participation model, Jordan and Turner
indeed prove themselves loyal.

passage B

Line The statements of the restorationists—
for example, Turner's description of
45 humans as "the lords of creation" and
Jordan's statement that "the fate and
well-being of the biosphere depend
ultimately on us and our relationship
with it"—do not cohere well with their
50 community-participation model for a
cogent environmental philosophy. The
restorationists might find another
holistic model—that of nature as an
organism—more serviceable. While
55 both models conceptualize nature as a
system of interconnected parts, an
organism's parts are wholly subservi-
ent to its life. If we could think of the
biosphere as a single living organism
60 and humans as its brain, we would
have a model that more closely fits the
restorationists' view.

    However, to consider humans as a
living earth's control center is to
65 ascribe to them a dominating role in
nature. Is this significantly different
from the domination model? After all,
neither view recognizes any limits to
the scope and range of legitimate
70 human manipulation in the world. This
does not mean that there are no
constraints; only beneficial manipulation should be undertaken. But it does
mean that nothing is off-limits. On the
75 other hand, restorationists no longer
view the world in the old dominationist
way as a passive and inert object, and
they conceive the controlling role of
humans in terms of healing rather

80 than conquest. And the restorationists
insist that the ideas that guide our
work in the world be drawn not solely
from a consideration of human needs
but also from an understanding of the
85 biosphere.

15. Passage A and passage B are similar
in that both provide a critique of

(A) a basic tenet of preservationism.
(B) certain claims of modern-day
environmentalists.
(C) the assumption of dualism
underlying the domination
model.
(D) certain writings of the restorationists.
(E) the dominationist view of the
human/nature relationship.

16. The author of passage A would
probably agree that preservationists

(A) have been unfairly criticized by
restorationists.
(B) have the same basic mind-set as
the industrial mainstream.
(C) base their ideas on an unhealthy dualism.
(D) are not critical enough of those
who have plundered the natural
world.
(E) have been unfaithful to the
principles upon which their
ideas are based.

17. The authors of the two passages would be LEAST likely to agree on the accuracy of which of the following statements about the restorationists?

    (A) They recognize clear limits to the scope of legitimate human manipulation of nature.
    (B) They assign to humans a controlling role in the world, which role they believe to be proper.
    (C) They require a more workable model for the relationship between humans and nature.
    (D) Their critique of preservationism is not well supported by logic.
    (E) Their program does not entirely coincide with their philosophical principles.

18. In asserting that the organic model might be "more serviceable" to the restorationists (line 54), the author of passage B implies that

    (A) the organic model is more consistent with the principle of restoration than the community-participation model is.
    (B) Turner's and Jordan's descriptions of the restorationists' program conform more closely to the organic model than to the community-participation model.
    (C) the organic model is more consistent with the restorationists' agenda than with the preservationists' program.
    (D) holistic models are more useful than the dualist model to the restorationists.
    (E) the organic model, unlike the community participation model, conceives nature as a system of interconnected parts.

19. The assertion that the activities of dominationists show a complete disregard for nature on their part

    (A) is supported in both passages, but more strongly in passage A than passage B.
    (B) is supported in both passages, but more strongly in passage B than passage A.
    (C) finds equally strong support in passage A and passage B.
    (D) is consistent with the information in passage A only.
    (E) is consistent with the information in passage B only.

20. Which of the following best expresses the relationship between passage A and passage B?

    (A) Passage A establishes the parameters of a debate, and passage B explores both sides of that debate.
    (B) Passage A identifies certain inconsistencies in a viewpoint, and passage B examines those inconsistencies in greater detail.
    (C) Passage A raises certain problems with a theory, and passage B discusses a partial solution to other problems with the same theory.
    (D) Passage A provides an historical perspective on a modern-day school of thought, and passage B compares its ideas with those of an older school.
    (E) Passage A introduces opposing viewpoints on an issue, and passage B evaluates each of those viewpoints.

QUESTIONS 21–28 ARE BASED ON THE FOLLOWING PASSAGE:

Line   To convince the warring and fiercely autonomous Iroquois nations to embrace his radical idea for an Iroquois Confederacy, Degandawida tied
5 the Confederacy to familiar Iroquois customs and institutions. He associated the notion of peace and partnership with the Iroquois custom by which the families of slain warriors adopted war
10 prisoners into the tribe. He used unquestioned social institutions as symbols, comparing the Confederacy to the traditional Iroquois clan in which several families share a "Longhouse"
15 and likening the Great Council, comprised of representatives from each nation, to the Longhouse's ever-burning Council Fire. And he assigned to each nation specific duties to
20 assuage its fear of losing national identity. For instance, the Iroquois tribe known as the Mohawks were given a veto while the Onondagas (another Iroquois tribe), who were
25 centrally positioned geographically, were made permanent hosts for meetings.

    Perhaps most persuasive to the Iroquois, however, was how Deganda-
30 wida's Confederacy replicated the power structure of the traditional Iroquois clan. Each of the five Iroquois nations was comprised of matriarchal clans in which the chiefs were men,
35 but the clan heads were women, and the chief's children were considered members of his wife's clan. Degandawida determined that the clan heads of each nation should select their Confed-
40 eracy representatives, thereby effectively precluding the possibility of Confederacy representatives passing their power on to their sons, as well as decreasing the likelihood that a
45 pro-war representative would be appointed.

    Iroquois unification under the Confederacy lasted about two centuries, until the 1776 American Revolu-
50 tion, when disagreement as to whether

to become involved in the war divided the Iroquois. Due to the success of the revolutionaries and the encroachment upon Iroquois lands that followed,
55 many Iroquois resettled in Canada, while those who remained behind lost the respect they had enjoyed among other Indian nations. The introduction of distilled spirits led to widespread
60 alcoholism and, in turn, to a rapid decline of the culture and population. The Quakers both impeded and contributed to this decline. By establishing American schools for the
65 Iroquois and by introducing them to modern agricultural and animal-husbandry techniques, the Quakers instilled some hope for the future while simultaneously undermining the
70 Iroquois' sense of national identity.

    Ironically (because the whites had introduced alcohol to the continent), it was the alcoholic half-brother of Seneca Cornplanter, the most outspo-
75 ken proponent among the Iroquois for assimilation of white customs and institutions, who revived the Iroquois culture. Around 1800, Handsome Lake, a former member of the Great Council,
80 established a new religion among the Iroquois that tied some aspects of Christianity to traditional Indian beliefs and customs. Lake's teachings quickly became firmly entrenched
85 among the Iroquois, sparking reunification and renewed confidence, while also helping to curb rampant alcoholism. Lake's influence is still evident today: many modern-day Iroquois belong both
90 to his religion and to one or another Christian sect. However, due partly to a long-standing mixture of Iroquois and Christian influences and partly to an absence of hierarchy, organization,
95 or even a name for Lake's religion, determining the extent of Lake's influence on modern-day Iroquois culture is problematic.

GO ON TO THE NEXT PAGE

21. In the passage, the author suggests that Degandawida "tied the Confederacy to familiar Iroquois customs and institutions" (lines 4–6) because

(A) the Iroquois nations that had already joined the Confederacy demanded that it reflect their longstanding traditions.

(B) the only aspects of Iroquois culture common among all the nations were the ones that preserved the traditional clan structure.

(C) many of the nations refused to join the Confederacy until Degandawida ceded his authority over the Confederacy to the Great Council.

(D) American revolutionaries threatened to force the Confederacy's member nations to disperse.

(E) the Confederacy's partnership principles were at odds with the Iroquois' penchant for autonomy and war.

22. Which of the following is NOT mentioned in the passage as a means by which Degandawida persuaded the Iroquois to join his Confederacy?

(A) Drawing an analogy between the Longhouse and the Confederacy

(B) Assigning each member nation its own specific duties

(C) Devising a system of representation that avoided family dynasties

(D) Likening the notion that enemies could become allies to the adoption of war prisoners

(E) Allowing each nation a veto in matters affecting all nations

23. In stating that the heads of the nations should select council representatives, thereby "decreasing the likelihood that a pro-war representative would be appointed" (lines 44–46)," the author implies that

(A) women were more likely than men to select peace-loving representatives.

(B) heads of the nations were less likely than heads of the individual clans to select pro-war representatives.

(C) war was more likely where power was passed down by a chief to his children.

(D) a chief's children were more likely than other members of the clan to favor war.

(E) children of clan heads were less likely than the chief's children to favor war.

24. Which of the following best characterizes the structure of the passage as a whole?

(A) A theory is presented and then applied to two related historical phenomena.

(B) Two historical figures are introduced; then the nature and extent of their influence are compared.

(C) The inception of an historical phenomenon is examined; then the subsequent development of the phenomenon is traced.

(D) Competing views respecting an historical phenomenon are presented and then evaluated based upon empirical evidence.

(E) An historical event is recounted; then possible explanations for the event are presented.

25. The passage mentions all of the following developments as contributing factors in the decline of the Iroquois culture EXCEPT:

(A) New educational opportunities for the Iroquois people in a non-Iroquois cultural milieu

(B) Divisive power struggles among the leaders of the Iroquois nations

(C) Introduction of new farming techniques

(D) Territorial threats against the Iroquois nations

(E) Discord among the nations regarding their role in the American Revolution

26. Among the following reasons, it is most likely that the author considers Handsome Lake's leading a revival of Iroquois culture to be "ironic" (line 71) because

(A) he was a former member of the Great Council.

(B) he was not a full-blooded relative of Seneca Cornplanter.

(C) he was related by blood to a chief proponent of assimilation.

(D) he was an alcoholic.

(E) his religious beliefs conflicted with traditional Iroquois beliefs.

27. Assuming that the reasons asserted in the passage for the decline of the Iroquois culture are historically representative of the decline of cultural minorities, which of the following developments would most likely contribute to the demise of a modern-day ethnic minority?

(A) A bilingual education program in which children who are members of the minority group learn to read and write in both their traditional language and the language prevalent in the present culture

(B) A tax credit for residential-property owners who lease their property to members of the minority group

(C) Increased efforts by local government to eradicate the availability of illegal drugs

(D) A government-sponsored program to assist minority-owned businesses in using computer technology to improve efficiency

(E) The declaration of a national holiday commemorating a past war in which the minority group played an active role

GO ON TO THE NEXT PAGE

28. Based upon the information in the passage, the author would probably agree that Degandawida and Handsome Lake most resembled each other in which of the following respects?

    (A) They combined traditional Iroquois religious beliefs and the most useful aspects of Christianity.

    (B) They drew upon their knowledge of Iroquois customs and traditions to formulate new cultural forms that attracted many Iroquois.

    (C) Their policies were aimed at uniting the Iroquois people against the white settlers.

    (D) Their efforts resulted in peace among the formerly feuding Iroquois factions.

    (E) Their teachings were largely responsible for a decline of alcoholism among the Iroquois population.

STOP   End of section. If you have any time left, go over your work in this section only. Do not work in any other section of the test.

SECTION II: LOGICAL REASONING

NUMBER OF QUESTIONS: 25 • SUGGESTED TIME: 35 MINUTES

Directions (as printed in test booklet): The questions in this section are based on the reasoning contained in brief statements or passages. For some questions, more than one answer choice could conceivably answer the question. However, you are to choose the *best* answer; that is, the response that most accurately and completely answers the question. You should not make assumptions that are by commonsense standards implausible, superfluous, or incompatible with the passage. After you have chosen the best answer, blacken the corresponding space on your answer sheet.

1. People who discontinue regular exercise typically claim that exercising amounted to wasted time for them. But this claim is born of laziness, in light of the overwhelming evidence that regular exercise improves one's health.

   Which one of the following statements, if true, most seriously undermines the conclusion of the argument?

   (A) Exercise has been shown to not only improve one's health but also increase longevity, or life span.
   (B) People who have discontinued regular exercise now make productive use of the time they formerly devoted to exercise.
   (C) People who are in good health are more likely to exercise regularly than people who are in poor health.
   (D) A person need not exercise every day to experience improved health from exercising.
   (E) People who are in poor health are less likely than other people to exercise.

2. Which one of the following provides the most logical completion of the passage below?

   More and more consumers are being attracted to sport-utility vehicles because they are safer to drive than regular cars, and because of the feeling of power a person experiences when driving a sport-utility vehicle. In its current advertising campaign, Jupiter Auto Company emphasizes the low price of its new sport-utility vehicle compared to the price of other such vehicles. However, this marketing strategy is unwise because

   _____.

   (A) consumers who purchase sport-utility vehicles associate affordability with lack of safety.
   (B) Jupiter would sell even more of these vehicles if Jupiter were to reduce the price of its sport-utility vehicle even further.
   (C) the retail price of Jupiter's most expensive luxury car is less than that of its new sport-utility vehicle.
   (D) most consumers who purchase sport-utility vehicles are also concerned about the reliability of their vehicle.
   (E) Jupiter's sport-utility vehicle is not as safe as those produced by competing automobile manufacturers.

GO ON TO THE NEXT PAGE

3. All college students read either literary classics or current best-selling books, but some readers of current best-selling books do not read literary classics because they do not appreciate these books. People who enjoy classical music do not find current best-selling books interesting, and therefore do not read them. Since Javier is a college student who enjoys classical music, he must appreciate literary classics.

Which one of the following, if added as a premise of the argument, would establish that the conclusion drawn in the last sentence is logically correct?

(A) Literary classics are more interesting than current best-selling books.

(B) All college students who appreciate literary classics read them as a habit.

(C) Literary classics are more interesting than classical music.

(D) All readers of literary classics have an appreciation for literary classics.

(E) All college students who find classical music enjoyable also read current best-selling books as a habit.

4. Only one pie can win first place at the annual pie-baking contest held at the county fair. Pies will be judged for flavor, freshness of ingredients, proper "doneness," and distinctness among the pies entered in the contest. The contest rules provide that only fruit-filled pies may be entered.

Which one of the following, if true, would best support the prediction that the winning pie at the pie-baking contest will be a cherry pie?

(A) More cherry pies than any other type of pie have been entered in the contest.

(B) Achieving proper doneness is more difficult with fresh cherries than with other pie ingredients.

(C) Fresh fruits are not available to any of the pie-baking contestants.

(D) Judges prefer the flavor of cherry pies over the flavors of other pies.

(E) Baking fresh cherries to their proper doneness results in over-baking the pie's crust.

5. Rivertown's historic Hill district used to be one of the city's main tourist attractions. Recently, however, the district's quaint older shops and restaurants have had difficulty attracting patrons. To reverse the decline in tourism to the district, Rivertown's City Council intends to approve construction a new shopping center called Hill Hub on one of the district's few remaining vacant parcels. However, the city's interests in attracting revenue from tourism would be better served were it to focus instead on restoring Hill district's older buildings and waging a publicity campaign touting the historically authentic character of the district.

The argument uses which one of the following argumentative techniques?

(A) Inferring certain merits of one course of action by disregarding the merits of another course of action

(B) Claiming that one of two distinct courses of action must be implemented to the exclusion of the other

(C) Pointing out that a certain condition must be satisfied to bring about a particular outcome

(D) Proposing a solution to a problem only be considering the potential drawbacks of an alternative proposal

(E) Questioning the basis for a proposed course of action by providing an alternative justification for that course

6. *Connie:* This season, new episodes of my favorite television program are even more entertaining than previous episodes; so the program should be even more popular this season than last season.

Karl: I disagree. After all, we both know that the chief aim of television networks is to maximize advertising revenue by increasing the popularity of their programs. But this season the television networks that compete with the one that shows your favorite program are showing reruns of old programs during the same time slot as your favorite program.

Which one of the following, if true, provides the most support for Karl's response to Connie's argument?

(A) What Connie considers entertaining does not necessarily coincide with what most television viewers consider entertaining.

(B) Entertaining television shows are not necessarily popular as well.

(C) Television networks generally schedule their most popular shows during the same time slots as their competitors' most popular shows.

(D) Certain educational programs which are not generally considered entertaining are nevertheless among the most popular programs.

(E) The most common reason for a network to rerun a television program is that a great number of television viewers request the rerun.

GO ON TO THE NEXT PAGE ➤

7. People are incurring more new types of ailments today partly because people are simply living longer. In response, pharmaceutical companies are developing new drugs for the prevention and treatment of these ailments. Our federal health insurance program for the elderly provides only partial coverage for only a small percentage of these new drugs. As a result, elderly people of modest financial means must essentially choose among their ailments. Proposed federal legislation would force pharmaceutical companies to lower their prices for these new drugs, so that more elderly people could afford them. If enacted, however, the law would undermine the health of our elderly citizens by stifling the development of new drugs for the prevention and treatment of other ailments afflicting these citizens.

The statement that elderly people of modest financial means must essentially choose among their ailments as a result of certain features of the federal health insurance program plays which one of the following roles in the argument?

(A) It is a claim that must be demonstrated to establish the argument's conclusion.
(B) It provides support for a position that the argument as a whole opposes.
(C) It provides additional but nonessential support for a premise of the argument.
(D) It is the conclusion of the argument.
(E) It is a principle from which the argument's conclusion is derived.

8. *Senator:*

Our current system of income taxation leaves middle-income households with no incentive to save and invest their earnings instead of spending discretionary income. Therefore, a median-income family is likely to spend income that it doesn't need to support itself rather than to invest that income in a home or in financial assets such as stocks and bonds.

Which one of the following best characterizes the flawed reasoning in the Senator's argument?

(A) It employs two different definitions of the same term to justify a conclusion.
(B) It assumes to be true that which has not been proven false.
(C) It assigns a single cause to a phenomenon that might have multiple causes.
(D) It appeals to considerations that are irrelevant to the argument at hand.
(E) It asserts a conclusion that is merely a reiteration of a premise.

9. A recent research study of state Y's prison system indicates that prisoners participating in the weekend furlough program are less likely to become repeat offenders after they are released than prisoners who do not participate in the program. The study confirms the researchers' hypothesis that weekend furlough programs at state prisons are an effective means of reducing crime.

Which one of the following, if true, would cast the most serious doubt on the hypothesis to which the last sentence above refers?

(A) The furlough program was available only to prisoners who had demonstrated good behavior while in prison.

(B) The crime rate in other states with similar furlough programs is lower overall than the crime rate in states without furlough programs.

(C) Whether the weekend furlough program is effective depends on how greatly one values the reform of any one prisoner.

(D) Less than half of the prisoners not involved in the furlough program become repeat offenders after they are released.

(E) Less than half of all the prisoners studied participated in the furlough program.

10. Very few software engineers have left MicroFirm Corporation to seek employment elsewhere. Thus, unless CompTech Corporation increases the salaries of its software engineers to the same level as those of Micro-Firm's, these CompTech employees are likely to leave CompTech for another employer.

The flawed reasoning in the argument above is most similar to the reasoning in which one of the following arguments?

(A) Robert does not gamble, and he has never been penniless. Therefore, if Gina refrains from gambling she will also avoid being penniless.

(B) If Dan throws a baseball directly at the window, the window pane will surely break. The window pane is not broken, so Dan has not thrown a baseball directly at it.

(C) If a piano sits in a humid room the piano will need tuning within a week. This piano needs tuning. Therefore, it must have sat in a humid room for at least a week.

(D) Diligent practice results in perfection. Thus, one must practice diligently to achieve perfection.

(E) More expensive cars are stolen than inexpensive cars. Accordingly, owners of expensive cars should carry auto theft insurance, whereas owners of inexpensive cars should not.

GO ON TO THE NEXT PAGE

11. In the city of Ocean View, escalating prices of single family homes are forcing more and more people who work in Ocean View and wish to purchase a home to move inland, where homes are more affordable. This trend is unhealthy for Ocean View, both economically and socially. But the city can reverse the trend by providing economic incentives for home-construction companies to build houses that are affordable to a greater percentage of Ocean view residents.

Which one of the following, if true, provides the most support for the argument in the passage?

(A) Workers who commute a short distance to work are more productive, on average, than workers who commute further.

(B) Most of Ocean View's workers would rather reside in Ocean View than in other areas.

(C) At present, there are a significant number of lots in Ocean View on which it is possible to build new single-family homes.

(D) The supply of rental housing in Ocean View currently exceeds the demand for such housing.

(E) Home builders generate a greater profit from building expensive homes than less expensive ones.

12. Everyone agrees that current and reasonable licensing requirements for child-care facilities are necessary to ensure public safety. Current licensing requirements for handgun ownership are far less stringent than those for operating child-care facilities. Yet the recent flurry of school shootings by young children using their parents' handguns shows that handgun ownership poses a significant potential threat to public safety.

The author is arguing that

(A) it would be reasonable to impose more stringent requirements for handgun ownership.

(B) parents of young children should not be allowed to own handguns.

(C) the legal requirements for obtaining a license for operating a child care facility are more stringent than those for handgun ownership.

(D) unlicensed child care and unlicensed handgun ownership both pose a potential threat to public safety.

(E) the recent school shootings would not have occurred were it not for lenient handgun ownership laws.

13. PharmaCorp, which manufactures the drug Aidistan, claims that Aidistan is more effective than the drug Betatol in treating Puma Syndrome. To support its claim, PharmaCorp cites the fact that one of every two victims of Puma Syndrome is treated successfully with Aidistan alone, as opposed to one out of every three treated with Betatol alone. However, PharmaCorp's claim cannot be taken seriously, in light of the fact that the presence of Gregg's Syndrome has been known to render Puma Syndrome more resistant to any treatment.

Which one of the following, if true, most strongly supports the allegation that PharmaCorp's claim cannot be taken seriously?

(A) Among people who suffer from both Puma Syndrome and Gregg's Syndrome, fewer are treated with Aidistan than with Betatol.

(B) Among people who suffer from both Puma Syndrome and Gregg's Syndrome, fewer are treated with Betatol than with Aidistan.

(C) Gregg's Syndrome reduces Aidistan's effectiveness in treating Puma Syndrome more than Betatol's effectiveness in treating the same syndrome.

(D) Betatol is less effective than Aidistan in treating Gregg's Syndrome.

(E) Neither Aidistan nor Betatol is effective in treating Gregg's Syndrome.

14. To save money, many manufacturers of chemical products decide to emit harmful chemicals into the environment instead of disposing of them safely. Often, these emissions are the obvious cause of health problems for people who live near the source of the emissions. Eventually, many manufacturers engaging in these activities are compelled by the courts to compensate their victims for these health problems.

Which one of the following is most readily inferable from the information above?

(A) Emitting harmful chemicals to reduce costs ultimately results in lower profitability levels than if the manufacturer refrains from emitting the chemicals.

(B) Manufacturers of chemical products place a higher value on saving money than on public health.

(C) These manufacturers will eventually discontinue emitting harmful chemicals into the environment.

(D) The courts consider the rights of those harmed by the emissions to be more important than the rights of chemical manufacturers.

(E) Those harmed by the emissions deserve to be compensated for the resulting health problems.

15. In a recent survey, nine out of ten people using Slim-Ease for two weeks as directed reported that they lost weight during this period. This fact surely proves that Slim-Ease is effective for anyone wanting to shed some unwanted pounds.

The claim made above depends on which one of the following assumptions?

(A) The survey participants were not using Slim-Ease immediately before the two-week period.

(B) The survey participants did not exercise during the two-week period.

(C) The survey participants were overweight before the two-week period.

(D) No other product is more effective than Slim-Ease to help lose weight.

(E) The survey participants' dietary and exercise habits were otherwise similar during the two-week period as before that period.

16. Human exposure to even low levels of nuclear radiation dramatically increases the likelihood of contracting some form of cancer. According to a research study involving a town near a former nuclear testing site, no person who resided in the town during the testing—which occurred more than sixty years ago—and who was under the age of ten during the testing lived beyond fifty years of age. However, some of the town's former residents who are now over fifty years of age are cancer survivors but resided in the town during the nuclear testing.

If the information provided is true, which one of the following must on the basis of it also be true about the town that is the subject of the research study?

(A) Some people who resided in the town during the nuclear testing do not remember the testing.

(B) The cancers contracted by the town's cancer survivors were not caused by exposure to nuclear radiation.

(C) Some of the town's former residents living today were over ten years of age during the nuclear testing.

(D) The nuclear testing resulted in the emission of lower levels of radiation than initially believed.

(E) Some of the town's residents died before turning fifty years of age due to causes other than cancer.

17. Veterinarians have developed a new cat food that contains medication that prevents hair balls from accumulating in a cat's stomach and digestive tract. Hair balls are generally not harmful to cats, but they do cause discomfort. When my cat eats this new medicated cat food, he develops an allergic reaction that, left untreated, can result in a harmful infection. I think it's best not to feed my cat the new medicated cat food.

The argument proceeds by

(A) calling into question certain evidence that supports the other side of an argument.

(B) pointing out that what is true of a group as a whole is not necessarily true of any single member of that group.

(C) recognizing that one event doesn't necessarily cause another one merely because the two events generally occur together.

(D) weighing two alternatives on the basis of known evidence and an unstated assumption.

(E) pointing out two alternate explanations for a particular phenomenon.

18. The emission of chlorofluorocarbons into the Earth's atmosphere has been shown to deplete the ozone layer in the atmosphere. Therefore, if we were to eliminate all sources of chlorofluorocarbon emission, we could successfully halt ozone layer depletion.

Which one of the following demonstrates a pattern of reasoning that is most similar to flawed reasoning in the argument above?

(A) When challenged to prove their psychic abilities, several of the world's most celebrated so-called psychics were unable to do so, clearly proving that the psychic phenomenon is fiction rather than fact.

(B) The theory that the Earth's temperature would be shown to be cyclical if measured over millions of years is convincing, in light of the fact that the extinction of the dinosaurs occurred due to changes in the Earth's temperature.

(C) Flag burning is ultimately in the state's interest as well as the individual's interest, because the First Amendment right to free expression was created for the purpose of preserving our democratic way of life.

(D) Any person suffering from phlebitis must take the drug Anatol to prevent the condition from worsening, as evidenced by the fact that doctors have used Anatol successfully for many years to treat and control phlebitis.

(E) Autopsies of the residents of Huiki Island killed by a recent volcanic eruption have shown excessive bone deterioration, which leads to my conclusion that the Huikan culture encourages a diet that promotes bone marrow disease.

GO ON TO THE NEXT PAGE

19. The high incidence of violence, either real or portrayed, shown on television today has often been cited as an explanation for the fact that violence is becoming increasingly common in our society. And, in fact, certain recent studies show that the incidence of televised violence has increased considerably over the past twenty years. However, other recent studies indicate that the level, while high, is only slightly greater than it was twenty years ago.

Which one of the following, if true, provides the best explanation for the discrepancy among the recent studies cited in the argument?

(A) Numerous studies of televised violence were conducted twenty years ago, and their results were not always in agreement.

(B) All of those involved in conducting the cited studies shared the same perception of what constitutes "violence" as shown on television.

(C) Television programs produced specifically for children account for a greater portion of all television programs today than twenty years ago.

(D) Many factors other than violence shown on television programs carry a significant impact on the incidence of violence in society.

(E) Over the last twenty years, the incidence of violence shown on television has increased more than in society as a whole.

20. In order for a new third-world democratic nation to achieve and maintain political stability, its government must afford its citizens the power to elect and remove the nation's leaders. After all, nation X is among the most stable countries in the world, and its government affords its citizens this power.

The argument is flawed in that it ignores the possibility that

(A) many third-world countries already grant their citizens the power to elect and remove their leaders.

(B) a large percentage of third-world countries have already achieved, and are maintaining, political stability.

(C) nation X's leaders are more popular among nation X's citizens than the leaders of most third-world countries are among their citizens.

(D) specific procedures for electing a nation's leaders vary significantly from one nation to another.

(E) nation X was already politically stable when its citizens were first afforded the power to elect and remove their leaders.

21. *Eva:* Our county's skating park interferes with horse shows that take place at the same showgrounds and which attract participants and spectators from outside the county. Skating activity has reportedly been responsible for a decline in the number of out-of-town visitors returning to our horse shows. Moreover, the skating park area could be put to good use to enlarge the equestrian arena, making for better horse shows that more people will want to see.

Frank: You are ignoring two important facts. As you know, the showgrounds are used for horse shows on only thirty days of the year, and the county's annual revenue from these shows is far less than from the skating park operation. Besides, our county's lands should serve county residents first and foremost.

Based on the statements provided, which one of the following best expresses the main point of disagreement between Eva and Frank?

(A) Whether the local economy is more important than the availability of the skating park

(B) Whether the horse shows generate more revenue for the county than the skating park

(C) Whether the showgrounds should be used simultaneously for horse shows and skating activity

(D) Whether the equestrian arena should be expanded to include the area now occupied by the skating park

(E) Whether the skating park is more popular among county residents than horse shows

22. No nation in the world has experienced as significant a decline in its Ziurba tree population as has our nation. Yet only our nation imposes a law prohibiting the use of Ziurba tree-bark oil in cosmetics. The purpose of this law in the first place was to help maintain the Ziurba tree population, at least in this nation. But the law is clearly unnecessary and therefore should be repealed.

Which one of the following, if true, most seriously weakens the conclusion drawn in the passage?

(A) This nation contains more Ziurba trees than any other nation.

(B) Ziurba tree-bark oil is not used for any consumer goods other than cosmetics.

(C) Corruption in this country has prevented full enforcement of this law.

(D) The demand for cosmetics containing Ziurba tree-bark oil is expected to decline in the future in other nations while continuing unabated in this nation.

(E) In this nation, some wild animals eat Ziurba tree bark, thereby contributing to their destruction.

GO ON TO THE NEXT PAGE

23. Recent activities among lobbyists suggest that illegal bribes to federal legislators for the purpose of influencing legislation that affects the financial interests of the private industries on whose behalf the lobbyists work is becoming increasingly pervasive. A proposed federal law would prohibit any individual who has been employed as a lobbyist on behalf of a particular industry from serving as the director of a government agency charged with regulating that same industry. However, some critics claim that, if passed, the law would prove counterproductive because it would prevent individuals who are the most knowledgeable about private industry from serving as government regulators.

Which one of the following, if established, would most logically serve as the principle appealed to in an argument countering the critics' claim?

(A) Those individuals most capable of objective, unbiased policy decisions should be the ones that hold power to regulate private industry.

(B) Government should vigorously regulate the activities of private industry whenever those activities pose a threat to public health or safety.

(C) Individuals who have served as lobbyists on behalf of private industry should generally be allowed to apply their knowledge to any legal undertaking, whether private or public.

(D) The financial interests of private enterprises should be weighed against the potentially harmful economic consequences of undue market control on the part of large businesses.

(E) In choosing elected representatives, voters should afford greater weight to their candidates' record of honest representation of their constituents' interests than to their specific knowledge and experience in a particular industry.

24. Babies who are breast fed instead of bottle fed until at least their first birthday are 70 percent less likely to become obese children than babies who are bottle fed but not breast fed. A child is obese if the ratio of the child's weight to height is among the highest 3 percent of all children. But breast feeding instead of bottle feeding during the first three months of a baby's life also reduces the likelihood that the baby will become an obese child.

Which one of the following can be most properly inferred from the information in the passage?

(A) Genetic propensity for obesity is not significant in determining whether a baby will become an obese child.

(B) Bottle feeding is more likely than breast feeding to result in obesity in children.

(C) Unless a baby is breast fed instead of bottle fed until at least its first birthday, the baby is likely to become an obese child.

(D) If a child is obese, there is a 70 percent likelihood that, as a baby, the child was bottle fed but not breast fed.

(E) Breast feeding is ineffective to prevent obesity unless it is continued until at least the baby's first birthday.

25. Vining University's teacher credential program should be credited for the high grade point averages of high school students who enroll in classes taught by Vining graduates. More new graduates of Vining's credential program accept entry-level positions at Franklin High School than at any other high school. And during the most recent academic year, just before which many of Franklin's teachers transferred to Valley View High School, the median grade point average of the students at Franklin has declined, while at Valley View it has increased.

The argument depends on which one of the following assumptions?

(A) The two high schools employ differing methods of computing student grade point averages.

(B) Neither high school has a peer tutoring program that would afford the school an advantage over the other in terms of student academic performance.

(C) Just before last year, more teachers transferred from Franklin to Valley View than from Valley View to Franklin.

(D) The teachers who transferred from Franklin to Valley View were replaced with teachers who are also graduates of Vining University's teacher credential program.

(E) The teachers who transferred from Franklin to Valley View last year were graduates of Vining's teacher credential program.

STOP End of section. If you have any time left, go over your work in this section only. Do not work in any other section of the test.

SECTION III: ANALYTICAL REASONING

NUMBER OF QUESTIONS: 24 • SUGGESTED TIME: 35 MINUTES

Directions (as printed in test booklet): Each group of questions in this section is based on a set of conditions. In answering some of the questions, it may be useful to draw a rough diagram. Choose the response that most accurately and completely answers each question.

QUESTIONS 1–5:

Each student in an art class has used at least one of six different colors of paint—green, white, red, yellow, blue, and orange—for a certain watercolor assignment. Each color was used by at least one student. The instructor has made the following observations about the students' use of colors:

> At least one student who used green also used white.
>
> None of the students used both green and orange.
>
> All students who used white also used either blue or yellow, but not both.
>
> All students who used red also used yellow.
>
> At least one student who used white also used red.
>
> All students who used yellow also used green.

1. It is NOT necessarily true that at least one student used both

   (A) blue and green.
   (B) white and yellow.
   (C) green and red.
   (D) white and green.
   (E) yellow and red.

2. If a particular student used only two colors, which of the following is a complete and accurate list of the possible pairs of colors used by that student?

   (A) Blue and green; green and yellow; white and blue
   (B) Orange and blue; green and yellow; blue and white
   (C) White and blue; green and blue; blue and orange; yellow and green
   (D) Green and blue; yellow and red; white and blue; orange and blue
   (E) Blue and white; yellow and green; orange and blue; white and green

3. What is the greatest number of colors that one student could have used?

   (A) Two
   (B) Three
   (C) Four
   (D) Five
   (E) Six

4. If a student used one color only, which of the following is a complete and accurate list of the possible colors that student could have used?

   (A) Blue
   (B) Orange
   (C) Orange or blue
   (D) Green or orange
   (E) Green, orange, or blue

5. Which of the following CANNOT be a complete list of the colors used by one student?

- **(A)** white, orange, blue
- **(B)** white, blue, green
- **(C)** yellow, green, blue
- **(D)** red, yellow, green, white
- **(E)** white, blue, green, yellow

QUESTIONS 6–11:

Five movie patrons—Anusha, Ben, Carrie, David and Estrella—are waiting in a single-file line to buy popcorn at the theater. Popcorn is available in four different box sizes: small, medium, large, and jumbo. Each movie patron may buy one and only one box of popcorn.

Anusha is further ahead in line than Estrella and will buy a smaller box of popcorn than David.

Ben will buy a smaller box of popcorn than Anusha.

Carrie is further ahead in line than Ben and will buy a larger box of popcorn than both David and Estrella.

Either Ben or Estrella, but not both, is further ahead in line than David.

6. Which of the following represents the order, from first to fifth, in which the five movie patrons could be waiting in line?

- **(A)** Anusha, Estrella, Carrie, David, Ben
- **(B)** Carrie, Anusha, Estrella, Ben, David
- **(C)** Anusha, Ben, Carrie, David, Estrella
- **(D)** Carrie, Anusha, David, Estrella, Ben
- **(E)** Anusha, David, Carrie, Estrella, Ben

7. If each of the last two movie patrons in line buys a medium box of popcorn, the second person in line is

- **(A)** Anusha
- **(B)** Ben
- **(C)** Carrie
- **(D)** David
- **(E)** Estrella

8. Which one of the following statements could be true?

- **(A)** The first person and the last person in line both buy a small box of popcorn.
- **(B)** The first person and the last person in line both buy a large box of popcorn.
- **(C)** The first two people in line both buy a medium box of popcorn.
- **(D)** The first two people in line both buy a large box of popcorn.
- **(E)** The last two people in line both buy a small box of popcorn.

9. Which one of the following may buy either a small, medium, large, or jumbo box of popcorn?

- **(A)** The first person in line
- **(B)** The second person in line
- **(C)** The third person in line
- **(D)** The fourth person in line
- **(E)** The fifth person in line

10. If the first movie patron in line buys the same sized box of popcorn as the fifth patron, with respect to how many of the five patrons can the patron's position in line and popcorn box size both be determined?

- **(A)** One
- **(B)** Two
- **(C)** Three
- **(D)** Four
- **(E)** Five

11. If sodas are free only to movie patrons who buy either a medium, large, or jumbo box of popcorn, which of the following must be entitled to a free soda?

    (A) The first person in line
    (B) The second person in line
    (C) The third person in line
    (D) The fourth person in line
    (E) The fifth person in line

QUESTIONS 12–17:

Eight dogs in an obedience class are learning to follow two commands: "heel" and "stay." Each dog is either a shepherd, retriever, or terrier, and each of these three breeds is represented among the group. All females among the group are retrievers. The results of the first lesson are as follows:

> At least two of the dogs have learned to follow the "heel" command.
>
> At least two of the dogs have learned to follow only the "stay" command.
>
> At least one of the dogs has learned both commands.
>
> Among the eight dogs, only terriers have learned to follow the "stay" command.

12. Which of the following two dogs CANNOT be in the group?

    (A) A male shepherd and a female retriever
    (B) A male terrier and a male shepherd
    (C) A male shepherd and a female retriever
    (D) A male retriever and a female terrier
    (E) A male terrier and a female retriever

13. If each dog has learned to follow at least one of the two commands, all of the following must be true EXCEPT:

    (A) All terriers have learned to stay.
    (B) All shepherds have learned to heel.
    (C) All retrievers have learned to heel.
    (D) All females have learned to heel.
    (E) All shepherds have not learned to stay.

14. If four of the dogs are male and four of the dogs are female, all of the following must be true EXCEPT:

    (A) One of the dogs is a shepherd.
    (B) Four of the dogs are retrievers.
    (C) Three of the dogs are retrievers.
    (D) Three of the dogs have learned to stay.
    (E) Four of the dogs have learned to heel.

15. If the group includes more shepherds than terriers, what is the minimum number of male dogs that have learned to heel?

    (A) Zero
    (B) One
    (C) Two
    (D) Three
    (E) Four

16. Which of the following statements CANNOT be true?

    (A) More of the dogs have learned to heel than to stay.
    (B) More of the dogs have learned to stay than to heel.
    (C) There are more shepherds than retrievers among the group.
    (D) There are fewer terriers than shepherds among the group.
    (E) There are more females than males among the group.

17. If each dog has learned to follow at least one of the two commands, and if exactly two dogs have learned to heel but not stay, which one of the following could be true?

    (A) Two of the dogs are female.
    (B) All of the dogs are male.
    (C) Only one male dog has learned to heel.
    (D) One female dog has learned to stay.
    (E) Two of the dogs are retrievers.

QUESTIONS 18–24:

A casting director for a movie about twins must select the cast from among nine actors—A, B, C, D, E, F, G, H, and J. Among the nine actors are three sets of twins: B and A are twins, C and D are twins, and E and F are twins. G, H, and J may each be selected for the cast only as "extras." A, B, E, G, and H are members of the actors union, but C, D, F, and J are not union members.

The director must include at least two sets of twins in the cast.

The director cannot assemble a cast that includes more actors that are union members than actors who are not union members.

A and B must both be included in the cast if either is included.

C and D must both be included in the cast if either is included.

At least one extra must be included in the cast.

18. Which of the following is an acceptable complete cast for the movie?

    (A) A, B, E, F, J
    (B) C, D, F, G, H, J
    (C) B, C, D, E, H, J
    (D) A, B, C, D, E, F, G
    (E) C, D, E, F, G, H, J

19. The cast must include which of the following?

    (A) D
    (B) J
    (C) F
    (D) H
    (E) E

20. If the director assembles the largest possible cast, all of the following must be included in the cast EXCEPT:

    (A) A
    (B) D
    (C) F
    (D) H
    (E) J

21. If G and only one other extra are selected for a cast of six actors, how many different combinations are possible for the movie's cast?

    (A) One
    (B) Two
    (C) Three
    (D) Four
    (E) Five

22. If the director selects both G and H for the cast, which of the following must be true?

    (A) A will not be a cast member.
    (B) F will be a cast member.
    (C) E will not be a cast member.
    (D) J will be a cast member.
    (E) B will not be a cast member.

23. If the director assembles a cast that contains the same number of union actors as non-union actors, under which of the following conditions can it be determined whether G and H are both cast members?

    (A) F is not a cast member.
    (B) A is a cast member.
    (C) B is not a cast member.
    (D) J is a cast member.
    (E) E is not a cast member.

24. Assume instead that E and F must both be selected for the cast. If all other conditions remain unchanged, which of the following statements is accurate?

    (A) If B is selected, J must be selected.
    (B) If G and H are both selected, J must be selected.
    (C) If A is selected, H cannot be selected.
    (D) If B and J are both selected, G cannot be selected.
    (E) If J is selected, B and D must both be selected.

STOP   End of section. If you have any time left, go over your work in this section only. Do not work in any other section of the test.

SECTION IV: LOGICAL REASONING

NUMBER OF QUESTIONS: 25 • SUGGESTED TIME: 35 MINUTES

Directions (as printed in test booklet): The questions in this section are based on the reasoning contained in brief statements or passages. For some questions, more than one answer choice could conceivably answer the question. However, you are to choose the *best* answer; that is, the response that most accurately and completely answers the question. You should not make assumptions that are by commonsense standards implausible, superfluous, or incompatible with the passage. After you have chosen the best answer, blacken the corresponding space on your answer sheet.

1. Bayside Aquarium plans to capture a great white shark and to display it at the aquarium, in the hope that doing so will help raise public awareness that this species of shark is in danger of extinction. But few such sharks have ever survived in captivity for more than one month. In all likelihood, then, this plan would amount to a waste of the aquarium's financial resources, which would be better directed toward other efforts to preserve the great white shark.

   Which one of the following, if true, would cast the most doubt on the conclusion above?

   (A) The expense involved in capturing a great white shark is difficult to predict.
   (B) Most visitors to the aquarium are already aware that the great white shark is an endangered species.
   (C) Certain other species of sharks are at greater risk of extinction than the great white shark.
   (D) Bayside Aquarium's shark habitat would resemble the species' natural environment far more closely than the shark habitats provided previously at other facilities.
   (E) Bayside Aquarium's popularity is due primarily to its large variety of sea life.

2. Equipment used by private biotechnology research firms becomes obsolete more quickly than any other business equipment, simply because biotechnology advances so rapidly. A proposed tax law would significantly enhance tax incentives for businesses in every industry to replace their old equipment with new equipment. In all likelihood, political lobbyists for the biotechnology industry were the instigators of this tax proposal. After all, other industries have not lobbied for the proposed law, and the biotechnology industry stands to benefit disproportionately from the bill's passage.

   The argument employs which one of the following argumentative techniques?

   (A) Drawing a general conclusion about what is possible in a certain situation based on information about what is not possible
   (B) Establishing that one particular piece of evidence is sufficient in itself to establish the truth of a particular assertion
   (C) Justifying a claim that one particular phenomenon is the cause of a certain event by ruling out certain other possible causes
   (D) Attempting to discredit an argument by calling into question the motivation of those who are asserting that argument
   (E) Relying on evidence of a certain kind of event occurring at the present time as a basis for claiming that it also occurred in the past.

GO ON TO THE NEXT PAGE

3. Which one of the following provides the best completion of the passage below?

Our nation's public policy dictates that our lands be put to their most economically productive uses. Although farm subsidies help farmers avoid bankruptcy during years in which they lose their crops due to natural disasters, in the long term, subsidies provide a disincentive for farmers to farm productively. Therefore, _____ .

(A) the farm subsidy system is ultimately to blame when a farm goes bankrupt.

(B) our nation's public policy should be modified to accommodate farm subsidies.

(C) farmers should strive to make more productive use of their farmland.

(D) in the long term, farmers would operate their farms more profitably without subsidies.

(E) the current farm subsidy system amounts to a violation of our nation's public policy.

4. Since the release of MicroTeam Corporation's newest version of its ActiveWeb software, more copies of this new version have been sold than any software product that competes with ActiveWeb. Therefore, MicroTeam Corporation's marketing campaign to promote the new version of ActiveWeb was highly effective.

Which one of the following, if true, provides the best indication that the conclusion in the argument is logically well supported?

(A) The number of potential purchasers of ActiveWeb and of products that compete with it has increased since the release of the new version of ActiveWeb.

(B) The number of products competing with ActiveWeb has diminished since the release of the new version of ActiveWeb.

(C) The new version of ActiveWeb corrected every known operational problem with previous versions.

(D) More copies of the new version of ActiveWeb have been sold than of any earlier version of ActiveWeb.

(E) Shortly after the release of the new version of ActiveWeb, a popular and influential magazine recommended a competing product over the new version of ActiveWeb.

5. The recent privatization of five public high schools in our state has clearly enhanced those high schools' educational effectiveness. The private firm that has assumed responsibility for administering these schools has done so at no additional cost to taxpayers. Moreover, last year, the number of graduating senior students, as a percentage of the entire senior class, was greater than ever before.

The argument's claim that privatization of the five high schools has enhanced their educational effectiveness relies on which one of the following assumptions?

(A) The percentage of senior-class students that graduated from these five schools was greater than the percentage that graduated the state's public high schools.

(B) High school teachers are more effective when they are paid higher salaries.

(C) Operating these five privatized schools costs taxpayers less per school, on average, than operating one of the state's public high schools.

(D) As a group, last year's graduating senior students deserved the academic grades that permitted them to graduate.

(E) The tardiness and absentee rates among students at these five schools have declined since the schools were privatized.

6. State X requires employers to pay hourly wage employees 50 percent more than their regular wage for every work hour in excess of eight, on any workday. State Y requires employers to pay these employees the same overtime rate, but only for work hours in excess of forty during any given week. Most hourly wage employees prefer to work in state Y over state X.

Based only on the statements above, which one of the following best explains why most hourly wage employees prefer to work in state Y over state X?

(A) Most hourly wage employees work at least five days per week.

(B) Most hourly wage employees prefer to work for employers that do not provide overtime work.

(C) Most hourly wage employees prefer to work for employers that provide overtime work.

(D) Overtime work hours for most hourly wage employees exceed regular work hours by at least 50 percent.

(E) Most hourly wage employees work less than forty hours per week.

7. Coffee consumption contributes to weight loss, no doubt about it. As proof, one need look no further than the typical coffee house, where you'd have difficulty finding a regular coffee customer with an obesity problem.

Which one of the following employs a method of reasoning most similar to the one employed in the argument above?

(A) Keeping regular company with a pet can help keep one's blood pressure at healthy levels. As a result, pet owners tend to live longer than other people.

(B) Excessive psychological stress is known to cause hair loss in men. However, most bald men have not led lives that are any more stressful than other men.

(C) More fatal vehicle accidents involve sport-utility vehicles than any other vehicle type. Therefore, sport-utility vehicles must be the most dangerous type of vehicle.

(D) Two particular diner patrons often eat dinner there at the same time. Therefore, these two patrons must leave work at about the same time.

(E) Students who study regularly are more likely to attain high grades than other students. Therefore, a student who does not study regularly is unlikely to attain high grades.

8. Currently, the supply of office buildings in this state far exceeds demand, while demand for single-family housing far exceeds supply. As a result, real estate developers have curtailed office building construction until demand meets supply, and have stepped up construction of single-family housing. The state legislature recently enacted a law eliminating a state income tax on corporations whose primary place of business is this state. In response, many large private employers from other states have already begun to relocate to this state, and according to a reliable study, this trend will continue during the next five years.

Which one of the following predictions is best supported by the information above?

(A) During the next five years, fewer new office buildings than single-family houses will be constructed in the state.

(B) Five years from now, the available supply of single-family housing in the state will exceed demand.

(C) Five years from now, the per capita income of the state's residents will exceed current levels.

(D) During the next five years, the cost of purchasing new single-family residential housing will decrease.

(E) During the next five years, the number of state residents working at home as opposed to working in office buildings will decrease.

9. *Gwen:* As we both know, the most popular restaurants among college students here in Collegetown are the ones that provide delivery service. So, local economic conditions, which rely on the student population, would improve if expensive Collegetown restaurants were replaced by less expensive ones that also provide delivery service.

   Jose: I disagree. After all, many expensive Collegetown restaurants also provide delivery service.

   Which one of the following best expresses the point of disagreement between Gwen and Jose?

   (A) Whether inexpensive restaurants are more popular among Collegetown students than expensive restaurants

   (B) Whether Collegetown should reduce the number of restaurants providing delivery service

   (C) Whether inexpensive restaurants in Collegetown should provide delivery service

   (D) Whether Collegetown students prefer delivery meal service over sit-down meal service

   (E) Whether inexpensive restaurants are popular among Collegetown students

10. Some of this year's Fairmount College graduates are eligible for the internship program with the district attorney's office. Any person meeting the eligibility requirements for this program is likely to gain admission to the local law school if he or she applies, whether or not that person actually participates in the internship program. However, only this year's Fairmount College graduates are eligible to participate in the internship program.

    If the information provided is true, which one of the following must, on the basis of it, also be true?

    (A) Any of this year's Fairmount College graduates who apply for admission to the local law school is likely to gain admission.

    (B) Some people likely to gain admission to the local law school would not have been eligible for the internship program.

    (C) Some of this year's Fairmount College graduates are likely to gain admission to the local law school if they apply.

    (D) Everyone who is eligible for the internship program graduated Fairmount College this year.

    (E) Unless a person is among this year's Fairmount College graduates, he or she cannot gain admission to the local law school.

11. More airplane accidents are caused by pilot error than any other single factor. The military recently stopped requiring its pilots to obtain immunization shots against chemical warfare agents. These shots are known to cause unpredictable dizzy spells which can result in pilot error. Since many military pilots also pilot commercial passenger airliners, the reason for the military's decision must have been to reduce the number of commercial airline accidents.

Which one of the following, if true, provides the most support for the conclusion drawn above?

(A) Recently, more pilots have been volunteering for the immunization shots.

(B) All commercial airline flights are piloted by two co-pilots, whereas military flights are usually piloted by only one.

(C) Military pilots are choosing to resign rather than obtain the immunization shots.

(D) Chemical warfare is likely to escalate in the future.

(E) Recently, the number of military pilots also piloting commercial airliners has declined.

12. Because of sharply escalating tuition at four-year colleges, debt on student loans has increased to the point that many new graduates are forced either to pursue graduate-level degrees, thereby postponing repayment of their student loans, or to pursue only the highest-paying jobs. As a result, fewer and fewer new graduates are entering important, but lower-paying, professions that require only a four-year degree. One influential educator has recommended that public universities expand undergraduate course offerings that prepare students for these lower-paying professions and establish higher admission standards for their graduate-level programs, thereby increasing the statistical likelihood that a new college graduate will enter one of these lower-paying professions.

On the basis of the premises advanced, which one of the following principles, if established, would provide the most justification for the educator's recommendations?

(A) A person's salary or other compensation for his or her vocation should be commensurate with the time spent preparing for that vocation.

(B) Financial aid should generally be more widely and readily available for four-year college education than for graduate-level education.

(C) College students should be encouraged to pursue whatever profession or other vocation that interests them, regardless of its potential financial rewards.

(D) Public universities should tailor their curricula primarily to meet the demands of present and prospective students.

(E) Lack of financial resources should not prevent college students with academic promise from pursing a graduate-level education.

13. According to life-insurance company statistics, nine out of ten alcoholics die before the age of 75, as opposed to seven out of ten non-alcoholics. A recent report issued by the State Medical Board recounts these statistics and concludes that alcohol addiction increases a person's susceptibility to life-threatening diseases, thereby reducing life expectancy.

The conclusion drawn by the State Medical Board depends on which one of the following assumptions?

(A) People who are predisposed to life-threatening diseases are more likely than other people to become alcoholic.

(B) The statistics cited exclude deaths due to other alcohol-related events such as automobile accidents.

(C) Alcoholism does not also increase a person's susceptibility to diseases that are not life-threatening.

(D) The life expectancy of that portion of the general population not characterized by alcoholism increases over time.

(E) The author of the report is not biased in his or her personal opinion about the morality of alcohol consumption.

14. Two years ago, a court found a certain cigarette manufacturer legally liable for the deaths of several thousand people who smoked the company's cigarettes, and ordered the company to pay a large sum to the families of those victims. The next year, the company's profits increased to record levels. The lesson for other large corporations is clear: Produce products that are unsafe or un-healthy for consumers, and your company will become more profitable.

The argument is most vulnerable to criticism on which one of the following grounds?

(A) It confuses the cause of an event with its effect.

(B) It generalizes about a group from what is true of one particular member of that group.

(C) It assigns a single cause to an event which is likely to have multiple causes.

(D) It relies on a questionable comparison between one group and another group.

(E) It assumes from the outcome of a particular event that the particular event is necessary to achieve that outcome.

practice test

15. A child's conception of whether certain behavior is right or wrong, referred to as "behavioral predisposition," is fully developed by the age of 10. During a person's teenage years, other teenagers with whom the person associates regularly have a significant influence on whether the person later acts in accordance with his or her predisposition. In other words, teenagers tend to mimic their peers' behavior. It is interesting to note that the vast majority of adult criminals also committed crimes as teenagers and associated primarily with other teenagers who later became adult criminals.

Which one of the following conclusions can most properly be drawn from the information above?

(A) A child's conception of whether certain behavior is right or wrong can change during the child's teenage years.

(B) Until a child becomes a teenager it is impossible to predict whether the child will eventually become an adult criminal.

(C) Law-abiding adults are unlikely to have developed a predisposition for adult criminal behavior.

(D) An adult criminal is likely to have been predisposed as a child to criminal behavior.

(E) Preteen children who are not predisposed to criminal behavior are unlikely to become adult criminals.

16. Last year, more job seekers applied for jobs with companies that regularly investigate their employees' personal medical histories than for jobs with companies that rarely do so. As a group, last year's job applicants were obviously unconcerned about the privacy of their medical records.

Which one of the following, if true, most seriously weakens the argument?

(A) A commonly known reason employers review employee medical files is to check for health problems that disqualify employees from receiving health insurance benefits.

(B) Job applicants have no way of knowing whether a prospective employer investigates its employees' medical histories.

(C) A certain proposed law, if enacted, would make it easier for employers to gain access to the medical histories of their employees.

(D) Information about which companies investigate their employees' medical histories, and which do not, is widely available to job seekers.

(E) The number of people applying for jobs last year was significantly greater than during most years.

17. *Company X spokesperson:*

Although several of our key managerial employees have left our company since we merged with our leading competitor two months ago, we have no reason to believe that a significant number of our other employees will follow suit. The employees who left our company since the merger did so because they received more attractive employment offers from other firms. However, virtually all of Company X's current employees are the same people who we employed prior to the merger, and our employee relations department just hired a highly respected consultant who specializes in employee relations, as well as taking other steps to ensure that these employees are content here.

An argumentative strategy that the spokesperson for Company X uses is to

(A) explain an apparent discrepancy between one piece of evidence and another by reconciling the two

(B) recharacterize certain facts in a way that is favorable to the argument

(C) appeal to the authority of an expert to confirm the reasonableness of a prediction

(D) call into question the relevancy of certain facts that might appear to undermine an argument

(E) show that a necessary condition for a predicted outcome has been satisfied

18. In the country of Xania, periods of political instability are always accompanied by a volatile Xania stock market and by volatility of Xania's currency compared to currencies of other countries. At the present time, Xania's currency is experiencing volatility. Hence, the Xania stock market must also be experiencing volatility.

Which one of the following allows the conclusion above to be properly drawn?

(A) Whenever Xania is politically stable, the Xania currency is stable as well.

(B) Whenever the Xania currency is stable, Xania is politically stable as well.

(C) Whenever the Xania stock market is unstable, Xania is politically unstable as well.

(D) Whenever the Xania stock market is unstable, the Xania currency is unstable as well.

(E) Whenever the Xania stock market is stable, the Xania currency is stable as well.

GO ON TO THE NEXT PAGE

19. Newspaper publishers earn their profits primarily from advertising revenue, and potential advertisers are more likely to advertise in newspapers with a wide circulation—a large number of subscribers and other readers—than with other newspapers. But the circulation of the newspaper that is currently the most profitable one in this city has steadily declined during the last two years, while the circulation of one of its competitors has steadily increased.

Any of the following, if true, would help explain the apparent discrepancy between the two statements above EXCEPT:

(A) Advertisers generally switch from the most widely circulated newspaper to another one only when the other one becomes the most widely circulated newspaper instead.

(B) Advertising rates charged by the most profitable newspaper in the city are significantly higher than those charged by its competitors.

(C) The most profitable newspaper in the city receives a significant portion of its profit from its subscribers as well from its advertisers.

(D) The circulation of the most profitable newspaper in the city is still greater than of any of its competitors.

(E) The number of newspapers competing viably with the most profitable newspaper in the city has increased during the last two years.

20. This county's current dumping ordinance, which requires that all refuse be hauled at least ten miles outside the city limits for dumping, should be repealed in the interest of public health. The purpose of the ordinance in the first place was to prevent the spread of Smith's Disease, which has been found to be most prevalent in regions near outdoor dumps. But the county funds used to maintain the roads to the dumping sites have been diverted from a proposed countywide education program for Smith's Disease awareness. This alternative use of the funds would have been more effective than the dumping ordinance in preventing the disease. The roads to the dumping sites are of no practical use other than for transport between the city limits and the dumping sites.

The statement that the roads to the dumping sites are of no practical use other than for transport between the city limits and the dumping sites plays which one of the following roles in the argument?

(A) It supports a claim that helps establish the argument's conclusion.

(B) It concedes a point of contention with the argument as a whole.

(C) It provides a reason to reject the conclusion of the argument.

(D) It illustrates a consequence of a claim used to support the conclusion.

(E) It confirms the limits of what the argument is attempting to establish.

21. Topical application of oil from the bark of aoli trees, which are quite rare and grow only in certain regions of South America, has been shown to be the only effective means of treating certain skin disorders. At the current rate of harvesting bark for aoli oil, however, aoli trees will become extinct within fifty years. Clearly, measures must be taken soon to reduce the demand for aoli oil; otherwise, fifty years from now it will no longer be possible to treat these skin disorders effectively.

Which one of the following, if true, most seriously weakens the argument?

(A) One of the skin disorders for which aoli oil is an effective treatment is caused by exposure to chemicals used in a manufacturing process that is quickly becoming obsolete.

(B) The bark of newly planted aoli trees can be harvested for oil within twenty years after the new trees are planted.

(C) The cause of skin disorders treatable with aoli oil is also the cause of certain other health problems which are treated effectively by ingesting aoli oil.

(D) In South America, aoli tree bark is widely used in making a variety of decorative craft items and utensils.

(E) Only people who live in the regions of South America where aoli trees are found suffer from skin disorders treatable with aoli oil.

22. A reliable survey indicates that college graduates change employers four times on average during the first ten years after college graduation. Therefore, to avoid employee turnover business administrators in charge of hiring new employees should favor job applicants who obtained college degrees at least ten years earlier over other job applicants.

The advice about how to avoid employee turnover rests on which one of the following assumptions?

(A) Employee turnover among businesses that hire employees without college degrees is greater than among businesses that hire only employees with college degrees.

(B) Job changes within the same company are less common than job changes from one employer to another.

(C) Employees who graduated from college at least ten years ago change employers less frequently on average than other employees.

(D) Most employees who leave their jobs do so upon either request or demand of their employers rather than by their own initiative.

(E) The survey excluded college graduates who interrupted their vocational careers to pursue advanced academic degrees.

23. *John:* If a person believes in the inevitability of success, then that person will surely succeed.

Jolanda: I disagree. According to a recent magazine article entitled "The 100 Most Successful Women in History," most of these 100 women did not believe they would ever become successful.

Which one of the following would be John's most logically convincing response to Jolanda's counterargument?

(A) Successful people are often viewed by others as unsuccessful.

(B) Success does not depend solely on whether a person believes in its inevitability.

(C) Success is inevitable for some people but not for others.

(D) Society's definition of success might have changed throughout history.

(E) None of the successful people listed in the magazine article were men.

24. No nation refusing to join the multinational free trade alliance can sustain the sort of economic environment needed for full employment among its citizenry. Country X has recently been experiencing less than full employment. I can only conclude that Country X refused to join the alliance.

Which one of the following demonstrates a pattern of reasoning most like the flawed reasoning in the argument above?

(A) All attentive students are rewarded with high grades in school. Alan is not attentive as a student. Therefore, he will not be rewarded with high grades in school.

(B) Every person seated in the front row can hear the coach's instructions to his players. Ursula can hear the coach's instructions. Therefore, Ursula must be seated in the front row.

(C) Anyone who claims to have been abducted by aliens is either not being truthful or is mistaken about whether he or she has been abducted by aliens. Sandy is always truthful. Therefore, she has not been abducted by aliens.

(D) Every legislator is in favor of the bill. Martha is not in favor of the bill. Therefore, she must not be a legislator.

(E) This sculpture is either priceless or a worthless fake. This sculpture is not a worthless fake. Therefore, it is priceless.

25. Among customers of breakfast restaurants, more order fruit for breakfast than any other menu item. However, an authoritative medical research laboratory has just reported that eggs do not pose as significant a health risk as previously thought. Since the report was issued, breakfast restaurant owners have been increasing the number of eggs they order from their suppliers. Surely, then, the amount of fruit these restaurant owners order from suppliers is declining.

Based only the information in the argument, which one of the following is the best reason for rejecting its conclusion?

(A) The argument confuses the cause of an event with its effect.
(B) The argument employs the same term in two different ways to justify its conclusion.
(C) The argument assumes a mutually exclusive relationship without any evidence of it.
(D) The argument relies on a potentially biased source of information.
(E) The argument appeals to considerations that are irrelevant to the argument.

S T O P End of section. If you have any time left, go over your work in this section only. Do not work in any other section of the test.

WRITING SAMPLE

1 TOPIC • SUGGESTED TIME: 35 MINUTES

> **Directions (as printed in test booklet):** The scenario presented below describes two choices, either one of which can be supported on the basis of the information given. Your essay should consider both choices and argue *for* one and *against* the other, based on the two specified criteria and the facts provided. There is no "right" or "wrong" choice: a reasonable argument can be made for either.

Nora, whose background is primarily in art and design, was last employed at a nationally recognized print and television advertising agency, responsible for graphic design work. She has been searching for a new job and has received two offers. Nora must now decide which offer to accept. Write an argument in favor of one of the following two choices, keeping in mind two guidelines:

- Nora hopes to find a job at which she can apply her artistic skills and talents.

- Nora wants to broaden her skill set by acquiring experience in public relations.

One job is for a long-time acquaintance who owns a building that she is currently converting into a small, upscale hotel. The hotel's ambiance and decor are to reflect the late Victorian style of the 1890s. The hotel will feature an art gallery that displays and sells original works depicting Victorian-era scenes. Nora would solicit and select works for the gallery, plan gallery events, and create watercolor images of the hotel's exterior and lobby for use on the home page of the hotel's Web site. Nora would also attend local community events in order to establish and maintain contacts with other local businesses and with the local arts community. Although a different employee will serve as concierge—responding to guests' questions, recommending local restaurants and attractions, and so forth—Nora may be asked to fill in for the concierge from time to time.

The other job is with Faulding Art Institute, an art school founded by a well-known sculptor and now owned and operated by a private foundation. Faulding's mission is to provide instruction in painting, drawing, sculpture, and mixed media to promising young artists. In response to the growing demand for training in computer-generated art and graphic design, Faulding has decided to expand its curricula to this area as well. Nora's initial job would involve marketing and promoting the new course offerings to prospective students—primarily through the use of display advertising in journals and magazines. Twice each year, Nora would attend a weeklong conference at which art educators discuss current and future trends in digital art. Once Faulding's new digital arts program is established, Nora would continue to perform various administrative functions for the digital arts program while also serving as a part-time art instructor at Faulding.

ANSWER KEY AND EXPLANATIONS

Section I: Reading Comprehension

1. B	7. C	13. A	19. B	24. C
2. A	8. C	14. C	20. C	25. B
3. B	9. B	15. D	21. E	26. C
4. E	10. C	16. A	22. E	27. D
5. D	11. C	17. E	23. A	28. B
6. E	12. C	18. B		

1. **The correct answer is (B).** This is a moderately difficult question in which you must identify the primary purpose or main idea of the passage. The bulk of the passage—the entire second and third paragraphs—is concerned with examining the factors affecting the climate of various portions of the Andean *cordillera*. The first paragraph provides a framework for this discussion by describing the climate and topography of the various regions.

   Choice (A) is too narrow. It indicates the author's purpose in the first paragraph only, omitting the discussion of the factors influencing climate. Choice (C) distorts the passage. Nowhere does the passage state or imply that competing explanations or theories exist to account for climatic differences among the different regions of the Andean *cordillera*. Also, the author is just as concerned with identifying the similarities among the regions as with discussing their differences. Choice (D) is off focus in two respects. First, although the author is concerned with the effects of topography on climate, topography is only one of several such factors discussed in the passage. Second, the effect of topography on vegetation is only briefly suggested in the final paragraph; since this topic is not explored in any detail, it is not fair to say that it is of primary concern to the author. Choice (E) is too narrow. Although the author does indeed discuss the similarities and differences in climate and topography between the two regions, the author is just as concerned (and probably more concerned) with the factors that affect the climate in both regions.

2. **The correct answer is (A).** This is a relatively easy question in which you must recall explicit information. The high-altitude plateaus are called *altiplano* (line 17). The passage states explicitly that the soil fertility in the northern *altiplano* is generally good (lines 18–20).

   Choice (B) confuses the information in the first paragraph. High relative humidity is mentioned as a feature of the Northern Andes and of the eastern portion of the Central Andes, but not of the northern plateaus. Choice (C) confuses the information in the first paragraph. Successive agricultural zones are mentioned as a characteristic of the Central Andes in general, not of any portion of the Central Andes in particular. Choice (D) confuses the information in the first and second paragraphs. Variations in air temperature are not discussed until the second paragraph and are not associated explicitly with any particular region of the Andes. Choice (E) confuses the information in the first and last paragraphs. An arid climate is mentioned as a characteristic of the western, coastal, and southern portions of the Central Andes but not specifically with the *altiplano* (i.e., plateaus).

3. **The correct answer is (B).** This is a relatively easy question requiring you to infer from or interpret specific information. The passage points out that while air temperature generally decreases as altitude increases, "variability of mountain topography"—i.e., dramatic changes in elevation—makes it difficult to determine temperature in any given spot from widely spaced measurements. It can be reasonably inferred from this information that an unexpected temperature would probably be the result of unexpected altitude.

    Choice (A) confuses the information in the passage. The topic of air pressure (discussed in the third paragraph) is unrelated to the question, which deals with information in the second paragraph. Choice (C) is a second-best response. In itself it is supported (at least in part) by the passage, insofar as the author implies that in measuring altitude in mountainous regions, "widely spaced measurements" do not provide an accurate report for areas between the measured points. However, nowhere in the passage is the reliability of older maps compared with that of newer maps. Choice (D) is also a second-best response. In itself, this answer choice is supported by the passage insofar as the author indicates a correlation between humidity and altitude (lines 47–50). However, the passage makes no correlation between humidity and air temperature. Thus, choice (D) calls for an unwarranted inference. Moreover, it does not respond to the question. Choice (E) also does not respond to the question. The relevant portion of the passage is not concerned with precipitation. Moreover, although choice (E) might be inferred from the information in the third paragraph, the passage makes no correlation between air temperature and precipitation.

4. **The correct answer is (E).** This is a moderately difficult question requiring you to infer from or interpret specific information. In lines 75–76, the author refers to the "aridity of the Central Andean coastal zone" as well as indicating (in lines 79–80) that "[m]uch of the southern portion of the Central Andes in Bolivia is also arid." However, nowhere does the author compare the two regions in this respect.

    Choice (A) is well-supported: the northern portion of the Northern Andes is characterized by "higher humidity" than other subregions (line 9), and the author mentions its "wet forests" in line 26. By contrast, the western portion of the Central Andes is described as "relatively arid with desert-like soils" (lines 21–22). Choice (B) is the second-best response. The author describes the soil fertility in the northern *altiplano* as "generally good" (line 20). Although the author does not specify in which subregion(s) the *altiplano* lie, the description in the passage suggests that they run in a north-south direction through the different regions. Thus, the "northern" *altiplano* are probably located in the northern subregion. By contrast, the passage describes the soil in the western subregion as "desert-like." Choice (C) is explicitly supported in the passage: the author describes the western portion of the Central Andes as "relatively arid" compared to the humidity of the eastern subregion (lines 22–23). Choice (D) is explicitly supported by the passage. In lines 73–74, the author states that the precipitation in the Central Andes measures approximately half of that in the Northern Andes.

5. **The correct answer is (D).** This is a relatively easy question in which you must recall explicit information. The only discussion of mountain symmetry is in the first paragraph, which mentions the symmetry in climate between the east and west flanks of the Northern Andes mountains. No mention is made anywhere in the passage of any symmetry with respect to the Central Andes mountains.

Choices (A), (B), (C) and (E) are all mentioned in the passage as factors affecting the climate of the Central Andes *cordillera*.

6. **The correct answer is (E).** This is a moderately difficult question in which you must infer from or interpret specific information. The question focuses on the information in the last paragraph. The author first notes that vegetation patterns correspond generally with climate (as determined primarily by latitude and altitude). Accordingly, altitude and latitude affect vegetation patterns throughout the region. Then, in the final sentence the author points out that, in spite of the general correspondence between climate and vegetation, local patterns may not correspond so precisely with climate, due to a number of local factors. Choice (E) accurately reflects the information in the final paragraph.

Choice (A) runs contrary to the information in the last paragraph. Regional patterns do not depend upon local variations; thus, fewer factors come into play in identifying these broader patterns. Choice (B) runs contrary to the information in the last paragraph. Regional patterns are broad patterns that do not take into account local variations (due to local factors). Thus, regional patterns will not vary to the extent that local patterns might. Choice (C) is unsupported. There is no evidence that vegetative patterns are affected by more factors in at the regional level or at the local level. The factors differ, but cannot be compared as categories ("regional" and "local"). Accordingly, choice (C) makes no sense. Choice (D) is an exaggeration. Although the author identifies human intervention as one factor that might distort the effect of climate (altitude and latitude) upon vegetation patterns, the author neither states nor implies that the impact of human intervention is greater than that of climate (altitude and latitude).

7. **The correct answer is (C).** This is a moderately difficult question in which you must extrapolate from or apply passage ideas. In the final paragraph, the author asserts that altitude and latitude (proximity to the equator) both determine climatic zones, as reflected in vegetation patterns. Accordingly, a more detailed discussion about why different forms of vegetation appear at different latitudes is a logical continuation.

Choice (A) ignores the direction of the final paragraph. Additionally, nowhere in the passage does the author suggest that regions other than the Northern and Central regions will or should be examined. Choice (B) ignores the direction of the final paragraph, returning instead to the Amazon, which was mentioned only in passing in the second and third paragraphs. Nowhere in the passage does the author suggest that a more detailed discussion of the Amazon climate will follow. Choice (D) is the second-best response. It is consistent with the content of the final paragraph, and thus is a better response than choices (A) or (B). Moreover, the author does suggest a relationship between soil type and vegetation. (Presumably, soil type determines what forms of vegetation will thrive.) However, the final paragraph neither indicates nor suggests any potential "problems" in determining such a relationship. Choice (E) appears at first glance to be a viable response, since it involves the same subject matter (i.e., vegetation) as the final paragraph. However, choice (E) is a bit nonsensical. It is unlikely that vegetation would have much of an effect upon topography; even if it did, nothing in the final paragraph indicates that this is the direction the discussion is likely to turn.

8. **The correct answer is (C).** This is a relatively easy question requiring that you infer from or interpret specific information. The main point of the first paragraph is that a portrait is (among other things) a record of the in-person encounter between artist and subject. Among the five answer choices, (C) comes closest to restating this point.

Choice (A) is not well supported. While the author may very well agree with this statement (especially in light of the author's interest in the viewpoints of certain eminent artists), the author makes no attempt in the paragraph (or anywhere in the passage) to draw a distinction between "true" artists and other artists. Choice (B) is supported by the author's assertion that a copy usually reveals the restrictions imposed on the artist. But this point merely elucidates the central point of the paragraph. Choice (D) is supported factually but is tangential to the paragraph's central point. Choice (E) is the second-best response. Based on the information in the paragraph, the author might very well agree that portrait copies aren't as "good" as an original portrait. However, it is why copies aren't as good that is the author's central point in the paragraph.

9. **The correct answer is (B).** This is a relatively easy question requiring you to infer from or interpret specific information. According to the passage, the queen refused to sit for her court painters. The author also makes clear that the "many portraits" of her were copies of other portraits. Thus, it can reasonably be inferred that the queen was relatively young when the "master" portrait(s)—i.e., the portrait(s) from which copies were painted—was (were) painted.

Choice (A) runs contrary to the information in the passage, which states that the queen refused to sit for her court painters. Choice (C) calls for an unwarranted inference. Just because all paintings of the queen depict her as a young person, it does not necessarily follow that she died when she was young. Choice (D) distorts the author's meaning. Considered in context of the discussion in the first paragraph, it is highly unlikely that the author's description of the queen as "ever youthful" should be taken to mean that the queen did not appear to age. Choice (E) is nonsensical. Artists copying pictures of the queen would probably depict the queen as she appeared in the "master" portrait, regardless of what age the copying artist believed the queen to be at the time.

10. **The correct answer is (C).** This is a relatively easy question requiring you to determine the function of a specific detail or piece of information. In the passage, the author compares and contrasts three different perspectives of the portraiture encounter: 1) Avedon's view, 2) Cartier-Bresson's view, and 3) Reynolds' view as interpreted and reflected by Hazlitt. Choice (C) properly expresses the function that the author's discussion of Cartier-Bresson (including the quote) serves in the author's overall discussion.

Choice (A) distorts the author's purpose as well as the meaning of the information in the passage. Although the author is explicit that Cartier-Bresson's conception is quite different from that of Avedon, the author is not concerned with "refuting" Avedon's conception—the author neither states nor implies that Avedon's conception is wrong or inaccurate in some way. The author is not arguing for one view over another, but is rather simply presenting different personal perspectives of the portraiture encounter. Choice (B) confuses the information in the passage. It is Avedon, not Cartier-Bresson, whose conception of the portraiture encounter is characterized as confrontational. Choice (D) confuses the information in the passage. The author states earlier in the paragraph that a sitting may either be "brief or extended, collegial or confrontational" (lines 29–30). The views of Cartier-Bresson and Avedon, discussed immediately thereafter, differ from each other in that Cartier-Bresson conceives his relationship with his sitters as confrontational, while Avedon views it as collegial. However, the author makes no further mention of the length of the sitting, either when describing the views of Avedon and Cartier-Bresson or in any other part of the passage. Choice (E) distorts the author's purpose and is unsupported by the passage. Nowhere in the passage does the author, either explicitly or implicitly, seek to distinguish between portrait photography and portrait painting.

11. **The correct answer is (C).** This is a moderately difficult question in which you must infer from or interpret specific information. In the first sentence of the third paragraph, the author distinguishes a "quite-different paradigm" (i.e., the case of Reynolds) from the conceptions of Cartier-Bresson and Avedon in that the Reynolds paradigm "has its roots not in confrontation or consultation but in active collaboration between artist and sitter" (lines 46–49). It is rather obvious from the quotation in the second paragraph that Cartier-Bresson conceives the encounter as "confrontational." Thus, the author seems to be characterizing an Avedon sitting as a "consultation."

Choice (A) confuses the information in the passage. It is the Reynolds paradigm discussed in the third paragraph, not Avedon's view, that the author characterizes as a "collaboration" (line 48). Choice (B) is a second-best response. Although the term "mutual accommodation" does not appear in the passage, this term suggests a relationship in which both artist and painter allow for the other's needs or desires. Such a description aligns much closer with Hazlitt's analogy of two lovers than with Avedon's view of the artist as diagnostician and psychic healer. Choice (D) is also a second-best response. According to the passage, Avedon confesses "uncomfortably" to his role as diagnostician and psychic healer (lines 38–39). It does not necessarily follow, however, that Avedon finds his encounters with his sitters to be uncomfortable; in this sense, choice (D) distorts the information in the passage. Choice (E) confuses the information in the passage. It is clear from the quotation in the second paragraph that it is Cartier-Bresson (not Avedon) who conceives the encounter as "confrontational."

12. **The correct answer is (C).** This is a challenging question in which you must infer from or interpret specific information. The author describes a sitting under the Reynolds paradigm as a "collaboration" (line 48) which is based in part on the sitter's "desire to experiment with something new" (lines 79–80), suggesting that the sitter and artist both play active roles in the process. Choice (C) runs contrary to this suggestion.

Choices (A) and (D) are both supported by the last sentence of the passage, which suggests that the portraiture experience provides the sitter with a new (and more accurate) view of himself or herself. Choice (B) is the second-best response. It is not as explicitly supported by the passage as the other incorrect responses. However, choice (B) is supported (albeit implicitly) by Hazlitt's analogy between the collaboration of artist and subject and the relationship between two lovers. Hazlitt describes both relationships as a sharing of each person's self-love (i.e., mutual displaying of each person's vanity). Choice (E) is implicitly supported. Hazlitt, as well as the author, seems to emphasize the importance of putting the sitter at ease socially—the artist is host as well as contractual employee, and collaboration (under the Reynolds paradigm) depends ("is based") upon the sitter's comfort. Choice (E) is thus a reasonable interpretation of the Reynolds paradigm.

13. **The correct answer is (A).** This is a moderately difficult question in which you must infer from or interpret specific information. According to the passage, "[t]he act of entering Reynolds' studio" . . . "did not necessarily transform those who sat for him" (lines 73–76). This statement allows for the possibility that some sitters were transformed in some manner (although the author does not state whether this was the case).

Choice (B) runs contrary to the information in the passage. According to the passage, the collaboration in portraiture such as Reynolds' is based in part upon the sitter's desire to experiment with something new (line 80). It is reasonably inferable, therefore, that many of Reynolds' sitters were not experienced in this area. Choice (C) runs contrary to the information in the passage. In mentioning "the act of entering Reynolds' studio" (lines 73–74) and that "no fundamental difference exists between the artist's studio and all those other rooms in which the sitters spin out the days of their lives" (lines 69–73), the author strongly suggests that Reynolds' portraits were created in his own studio rather than at the homes of his subjects. Choice (D) is explicitly contradicted by the passage, which states that Reynolds' sitters were "accompanied by their friends" (lines 61–62). Choice (E) is implicitly supported by various information in the third paragraph. Hazlitt and the author both emphasize the important role that establishing a social rapport played in the collaboration of Reynolds and his sitters. If Reynolds had limited his portrait subjects to friends and relatives, establishing a rapport would probably not have been necessary for his sitters' comfort. Also, the passage indicates that Reynolds' subjects were accompanied by their friends and suggests that this was necessary to help the subjects feel at ease. However, this probably would not have been necessary were Reynolds already a friend of his subjects.

14. **The correct answer is (C).** This is a moderately difficult question requiring you to recognize the main idea or primary purpose of the passage. Although it is difficult to articulate a single "main idea" or thesis of this Passage, the author seems to be most concerned with emphasizing that a portrait sitting is a social encounter, not just an artistic exercise, and that artists consider their relationship with their sitters to be somehow significant. Thus, choice (C) is a good statement of the author's primary point.

Choice (A) is the second-best response. It embraces the passage as a whole and properly focuses on the author's primary concern with exploring the relationship between artist and sitter. However, the passage does not discuss how or whether this relationship results in a "successful" portrait; thus choice (A) distorts the information in the passage. Choice (B) is off focus and calls for an unwarranted generalization. Admittedly, the author does claim that the Reynolds paradigm (described by Hazlitt as well as by the author in the third paragraph) is "quite different" (line 46) from the two paradigms discussed in the second paragraph, and the latter does indeed involve a painter (Reynolds) while the other two paradigms involve photographers (Cartier-Bresson and Avedon). However, nowhere in the passage does the author generalize from this fact that a portrait artist's approach or view depends upon whether the artist is a painter or a photographer. Choice (D) distorts the information in the passage and departs from the topic at hand. Although the passage does support the notion that a portrait might reveal something about the relationship between artist and sitter, the author neither states nor implies that a portrait reveals anything about the artist's other relationships. Moreover, nowhere in the passage does the author compare portraiture with other art forms. Choice (E) is too narrow and refers to information not mentioned in the passage. The passage is not just about Reynolds, but about the portraiture encounter in general. Also, the author does not comment on Reynolds' "success" or about how his relationship with his sitters may have contributed to his success.

15. **The correct answer is (D).** This is a relatively easy comparative reading question in which you must recall explicit information. Both passages clearly identify Jordan and Turner as restorationists, and both passages critique the writings of Jordan and Turner: passage A explains why their ideas are "puzzling," while passage B criticizes their statements as not cohering well with their announced principles.

Choices (A) and (B) are both incorrect because passage B provides no critique of environmental preservationism or of the claims of modern-day environmentalists. Choice (C) is incorrect for two reasons. First, it distorts the point in passage A that Turner and Jordan don't see that dualism is logically unnecessary for environmental preservationism. (Also, the author never mentions domination model in this context.) Secondly, passage B provides no direct critique of the dualism assumption. Choice (E) confuses the point in passage A that Turner and Jordan fail to criticize mainstream industry for plundering the natural world.

16. **The correct answer is (A).** This is a moderately difficult question in which you must determine the similarities (points of agreement) between the authors' viewpoints. In the first paragraph, the author of passage A criticizes Turner and Jordan for the "sharpness and relentlessness of their attack on preservationists." The author implies that other groups (for example, "those who have plundered the natural world") are more deserving of sharp criticism than the preservationists. In this sense, the author would probably agree that Turner and Jordan have unfairly criticized the preservationists.

Choice (B) confuses the passage information: it is Turner and Jordan, and not necessarily the passage's author as well, who claim that preservationists have the same basic dualist mindset as the industrial mainstream. Choice (C) expresses the viewpoint of environmentalists, and not necessarily of the passage's author. Choice (D) confuses the passage information. According to the author, it is Turner and Jordan—not the preservationists—who are insufficiently critical of those who have plundered the natural world. Choice (E) expresses the viewpoint of the author of passage B; the author of passage A expresses quite the opposite viewpoint (in the passage's final sentence).

17. **The correct answer is (E).** This is a moderately difficult question in which you must determine the similarities (points of agreement) between the authors' viewpoints. The author of passage A asserts (in the second paragraph) unequivocally that the restorationists prove themselves loyal to the first principle of restoration. However, the author of passage B claims quite the opposite—citing statements by Jordan and Turner that show an alignment with the domination model and that are at odds with the restorationists' community-participation model.

Choices (A), (B), (C), and (D) do not provide an assertion about the restorationists with which one author would clearly agree and the other would clearly disagree. Choice (A) completely confuses the information in passage B, which asserts that neither the domination nor the organic model recognizes any such limits. Choice (B) also confuses the information in passage B, which provides that the domination and organic models both assign such a role to humans. Choice (C) expresses the central idea of passage B, which runs contrary to the assertion in passage A that Turner and Jordan (the restorationists) are true to their model. Choice (D) expresses an explicit point that the author of passage A makes. However, the author of passage B does not directly address this issue, and so determining whether the author of passage B would agree with choice (D) calls for undue speculation. Passage B does suggest that there's a logical inconsistency in the restorationists' writings (because their statements do not accord with their principles), but this flaw in internal logic is not the problem to which answer choice (D) refers.

18. **The correct answer is (B).** This is a relatively easy question requiring you to infer from or interpret specific information. The author asserts that Turner's and Jordan's descriptions of restorationist activities "do not cohere well with [their] community-participation model." By following this assertion with the suggestion that another model might be more serviceable, the author implies that the restorationists' agenda is more consistent with this other model than with the community-participation model.

Choice (A) confuses the author's point that the organic model might reconcile what seems to be an inconsistency between the restorationists' statements and their announced principles. Choice (C) confuses the same point, which has nothing to do with the preservationists' program. Choice (D) confuses passage B with the discussion in passage A about dualism, which is any case is mentioned there as an assumption underlying certain models, not a model itself. Choice (E) contradicts the information in passage B, according to which both models conceive (conceptualize) nature in this way.

19. **The correct answer is (B).** This is a moderately difficult comparative reading question requiring you to infer from or interpret specific information. Passage B indicates the following (emphasis added): "the restorationists insist that the ideas that guide our work in the world be drawn *not solely from a consideration of human needs* but also from an understanding of the biosphere." The author provides this statement in the context of contrasting the dominationist and restorationist views. Hence, the strong implication here is that dominationists consider only human needs, and completely disregard nature, in their activities (their "work in the world"). Passage A refers to the industrial mainstream's "humans over nature" view and to the domination model as one "which sees humans over nature." This characterization implies that the

activities of dominationists show at least a comparative disregard for nature, but the implication that they show a complete disregard for nature is not nearly as strong.

Choices (A), (C), (D), and (E) are all incorrect for the same reason that choice (B) is the correct answer.

20. **The correct answer is (C).** This is a challenging comparative reading question in which you must identify the key issue, problem, or controversy that the two passages seek to address. Passage A first identifies one problem with the restorationists—their sharp critique of preservationism—which strikes the author as somewhat misplaced because they should also criticize the industrial mainstream, but they don't. Passage B focuses on a different problem with the restorationists: that they appear untrue to their principles in that some of their assertions seem to align with dominationist view. The passage then suggests that the restorationists embrace an organic model, which to some extent might help them distinguish their outlook from the industrial mainstream's humans-over-nature view.

Choice (A) departs completely from the gist of either passage (described above). Besides accomplishing other tasks, the two authors present contrary viewpoints on whether the restorationists' writings are true to their ostensible principles. To suggest, as choice (A) does, that one passage frames the issue while the other passage presents both sides of it amounts to a total distortion of this relationship. Choice (B) confuses an inconsistency suggested in passage A with a different inconsistency, examined in passage B. In passage A, its author suggests that the nub of the restorationist critique preservationism (that it rests on an unhealthy dualism) doesn't square with what the restorationists actually set about doing in their writings. In passage B, its author examines an inconsistency between the restorationists' statements (which suggest they are dominationists) and their principles (which run contrary to the dominationist model). Choice (D) distorts how the authors use various information in their respective passages. Passage A does examine what is probably a relatively "modern" movement: environmental preservationism. However, the passage makes no attempt to provide an historical perspective on this movement. By the same token, passage B does make a comparison involving the "old" domination model, but the comparison is with the organic model—not with preservationism or any other so-called "school of thought" discussed in passage A. Choice (E) grossly distorts the relationship between the two passages. Admittedly, both passages examine opposing viewpoints. However, the viewpoints that passage A compares are different than the ones that passage B compares, and both passages examine similarities between viewpoints just as much as differences. Besides, the key relationship between the two passages involves the difference of opinion between the authors of the two passages—not between others discussed in the passages.

21. **The correct answer is (E).** This is a relatively easy question requiring you to infer from or interpret specific information. The passage's first two sentences provide the answer to this question. To convince the Iroquois nations to join the Confederacy, Degandawida needed to tie the Confederacy's underlying "notion of peace and partnership," which was considered "radical" to "the warring and fiercely autonomous Iroquois nations," to established Iroquois traditions.

Choice (A) is not supported. The passage neither states nor implies that any Iroquois nation had already joined the Confederacy before Degandawida's attempts to tie it to certain Iroquois customs and institutions. Choice (B) contradicts the information in the passage. In the first two paragraphs, the author also mentions various other aspects of Iroquois culture that the nations shared—and to which Degandawida tied his Confederacy concept. Choice (C) is not supported. Nowhere in the passage does the author suggest that Degandawida ever had authority over the Confederacy or that he ever ceded any such authority. Choice (D) confuses the information in the passage. The author discusses the revolutionaries' encroachment on Indian lands and the resulting Iroquois dispersion in the third paragraph as one reason for the decline of the Iroquois nations—not in connection with the establishment of the Confederacy.

22. **The correct answer is (E).** This is a moderately difficult question in which you must recall explicit information. In the first two paragraphs, the author discusses various ways in which Degandawida tied the Confederacy concept to familiar Iroquois customs and institutions—to convince the Iroquois nations to embrace the concept. Choice (E) is the only response that is not supported explicitly by information in the first two paragraphs. Although the Mohawks were given a council veto in acknowledgment of their power, the passage does not indicate that any other nations were given veto power.

Choices (A), (B), (C), and (D) are all well supported. Choice (A): according to the first paragraph, Degandawida drew an analogy between traditional institutions—the Longhouse and Council Fire—and the concepts of the Confederacy and the Great Council to help the Iroquois appreciate the Confederacy's meaning and significance. Choice (B): in the first paragraph, the author tells us that each nation was assigned specific duties to ease its fear of losing national identity. Choice (C): according to the second paragraph, a system for selecting representatives by which the heads of the clans—i.e., the chiefs' wives—were to make the selections effectively precluded the possibility of representatives passing down their power to their sons. Choice (D): the second paragraph indicates that Degandawida compared the custom of adopting war prisoners into the captor's tribe to the peace-making process to persuade the Iroquois that long-standing enemies could lay down their arms and become brothers.

23. **The correct answer is (A).** This is a challenging question in which you must infer from or interpret specific information. The passage states that the clan heads were women, while the chiefs were men; the passage goes on to state that, according to Degandawida, the clan heads (women) rather than the chiefs (men) should select Confederacy representatives because the likelihood that a pro-war representative would be appointed would be decreased thereby. Among the five responses, the only response that is inferable from this information is that Degandawida believed the men to be more pro-war than the women—i.e., choice (A).

Choice (B) is unsupported and distorts the information in the passage. The author makes no comparison in terms of the propensity for war between clan heads and nation heads because a nation's heads and the heads of that nation's clans were one and the same. Statement (B) suggests, however, that a nation's heads and a clan's heads are two different groups.

Choice (C) confuses the information presented in the pertinent part of the passage. The author does not make a connection between family dynasties and the propensity for war.

Choice (D) is a second-best response. It is of the same nature substantively as choice (A). Qualitatively, however, choice (D) calls for an unwarranted inference. The passage does imply a connection between a chief's passing power down to his children and the children's propensity for war, but only insofar as men (e.g., chiefs) are more likely than women to choose pro-war representatives—see choice (A). However, the additional inference that a chief's children are more likely to favor war than all other clan members is unwarranted based upon the information in the passage. Although the passage supports the idea that women are less likely than men to select pro-war representatives, the passage does not suggest that, of the male population in a clan, a chief's children have the greatest propensity for war. Choice (E) is also a second-best response, but it is defective in much the same way as choice (D). The passage does imply a connection between a chief's passing power down to his children and the children's propensity for war, but only insofar as men (e.g., chiefs) are more likely to choose pro-war representatives than are women—see choice (A). Choice (D) suggests a comparison (in terms of propensity for war) between the chiefs' children and the children of the clan heads. However, the passage does not support the inference that children of a clan head will be less likely than any other member of the clan to want war.

24. **The correct answer is (C).** This is a moderately difficult question in which you must determine the main idea or primary purpose of the passage. The first and second paragraphs are concerned with the inception of the Iroquois Confederacy, while the third and fourth paragraphs outline the subsequent history of the Confederacy from its decline through its subsequent resurgence under Handsome Lake. Choice (C) recapitulates this overall structure.

Choice (A) is the second-best response. It could be argued that the author is presenting a "theory" as to how the Iroquois were swayed by Degandawida and later by Handsome Lake and that the "two related historical phenomena" mentioned in answer choice (A) refer to the inception of the Confederacy (under Degandawida) and its revival (under Handsome Lake). However, the author presents the information as historical facts rather than as theories—that is, the passage merely recounts historical events rather than seeking to explain them by way of a more fundamental theory. Moreover, choice (A) omits the discussion in the third paragraph concerning the decline of the Iroquois culture; in this sense, then, choice (A) is too narrow.

Choice (B) distorts the author's overall viewpoint. The author does "introduce" and examine the influence of two historical figures—Degandawida and Lake. However, the author makes no attempt to compare their influence. Also, although Lake is not mentioned until the last paragraph, choice (B) suggests that the two historical figures are introduced early in the passage. Choice (D) is unsupported. Nowhere in the passage are "competing views" presented or evaluated. Choice (E) is far too narrow and is unsupported. The passage does provide some explanation for the three phases (inception, decline, and revival) of the Iroquois history, but is the "historical event" to which answer choice (E) refers the inception of the Confederacy, its decline, or its resurgence? Since the passage discusses all three, this answer choice is far too narrow to reflect the overall structure of the passage.

25. **The correct answer is (B).** This is a relatively easy question requiring you to recall explicit detail. Nowhere in this passage does the author mention any power struggles among the leaders of the Iroquois nations. Although the third paragraph does refer to a dispute among the Iroquois leaders, the dispute involved the role that the Iroquois should play in the American Revolution—see choice (E).

Choices (A), (C), (D), and (E) are all explicitly mentioned in the third paragraph as factors contributing to the decline of the Iroquois culture.

26. **The correct answer is (C).** This is a relatively easy question requiring you to infer from or interpret specific information. In the final paragraph's first sentence, the author tells us that Cornplanter was an outspoken proponent of assimilation. The next sentence suggests in context that Handsome Lake was related to Cornplanter as a half-brother. The fact that Lake was responsible for the Iroquois reasserting their national identity is ironic, then, in light of Lake's blood relationship to Cornplanter.

Choices (A), (B), and (D) are all accurate statements, based upon the information in the passage. However, they do not respond to the question. Choice (E) runs contrary to the information in the passage and fails to respond to the question. Lake emphasized the similarities between Christianity and his brand of Iroquois religion; the passage does not deal with the differences between Christianity and the Iroquois' traditional beliefs. Moreover, even if choice (E) were supported by the passage, it is not the irony to which the author refers.

27. **The correct answer is (D).** This is a challenging question in which you must extrapolate from or apply passage ideas. According to the passage, the Quakers' introduction of new technology to the Iroquois was partly responsible for the decline of the Iroquois culture in that it contributed to their loss of national identity. Choice (D) presents a similar situation.

Choice (A) is the second-best response. Insofar as the children referred to in the scenario of this answer choice learn the language of the prevailing culture, assimilation and a resulting loss of ethnic identity might tend to occur. However, this sense of identity might be reinforced by their learning to read and write in their traditional language as well. Therefore, choice (A) is not as likely to lead to the demise of the minority group as choice (D), based upon the Iroquois' experience as discussed in the passage. Choice (B) is too vague and is not supported. Whether a government incentive to provide housing for members of the minority group actually undermines the group's sense of ethnic identity would probably depend upon whether the incentives result in integration or segregation. Moreover, since the passage does not address whether the Iroquois became geographically integrated (assimilated), choice (B) is not supportable. Choice (C) would probably carry the opposite result from the result that the question calls for. The scenario posed in answer choice (C) would actually contribute to the minority group's retaining its ethnic identity, at least based upon the information in the passage. According to the passage, the introduction of spirits to the Iroquois population led to rampant alcoholism, which in turn contributed to the culture's decline. Similarly, widespread drug abuse might have a similar effect today. Accordingly, any effort to curb such abuse—e.g., the scenario of choice (C)—would tend to impede rather than contribute to a decline. Choice (E), like choice (C), would carry a result opposite from the one that the question calls for. It is also unsupported. Any ceremony or holiday calling attention to the ethnic population as a distinct group and helping to bring the population together as a group under a shared experience would tend to reinforce a sense of identity. Moreover, the passage does not refer to any developments during the time of the Iroquois decline that might be similar in any way to the scenario of answer choice (E).

28. **The correct answer is (B).** This is a relatively easy question requiring you to infer from or interpret specific information. Both men had a thorough understanding of Iroquois traditions. Degandawida used Iroquois traditions as symbols to convey concepts and as models for the structure of his Confederacy, all with the goal of persuading the nations to join his Confederacy. Similarly, Lake's use of traditional religious beliefs helped convert the Iroquois people to his new religion.

Choice (A) is not supported. Although the author explicitly mentions that Handsome Lake combined Christianity and the traditional Iroquois religion, there is no indication in the passage of any similar efforts by Degandawida. Choice (C) is not supported. Although the policies of both men were indeed aimed at uniting the Iroquois, the author does not suggest that either man's efforts were directed toward establishing a force in opposition to the white settlers. Choice (D) is the second-best response. Statement (D) is only partly supported by the passage. Although Degandawida's efforts did result in a new and lasting peace among the Iroquois, the author does not make a similar claim with respect to Handsome Lake. Admittedly, the passage does mention a dispute among the Iroquois as to their proper role in the American Revolution. However, it is unwarranted to infer from this fact that the Iroquois factions were feuding amongst themselves just before Lake or that Lake's influence was responsible for some sort of new peace. Choice (E) is not supported. Although the passage does explicitly acknowledge Lake's influence in the decline of alcoholism among the Iroquois, no similar influence is mentioned with respect to Degandawida.

Section II: Logical Reasoning

1. B	6. E	11. C	16. C	21. D
2. A	7. B	12. A	17. D	22. C
3. D	8. E	13. A	18. D	23. E
4. D	9. A	14. B	19. A	24. B
5. B	10. D	15. E	20. E	25. E

1. **The correct answer is (B).** This is a moderately difficult question requiring you to assess the effect of additional information. The conclusion of the argument is that the claim made by those who have discontinued regular exercise is born of laziness; in other words, these people are making this claim because they are lazy. One effective way to refute the argument is to provide convincing evidence that directly contradicts the

conclusion. Choice (B) provides just such evidence, by showing that these people are not in fact lazy.

Choice (A) actually strengthens the argument, by providing evidence that exercise is not wasted time, especially considering that increasing longevity creates more time. In other words, the evidence that answer choice (A) provides weakens the claim made by those who have discontinued regular exercise that it is wasted time. Choice (C) provides no information that is not already inferable from the argument itself (specifically, from the stated premise that regular exercise improves one's health). Choice (D) is irrelevant to the argument, which provides no information suggesting that whether exercise is wasted time does not depend on how much time or how frequently one exercises. Choice (E) is irrelevant to the argument, which seeks to show why people discontinue regular exercise. Besides, choice (E) could just as likely be explained by the fact that people in poor health do not exercise because they cannot do so, not because they are lazy.

2. **The correct answer is (A).** This is a relatively easy question in which you must identify the conclusion of the argument. The passage boils down to the following:

   Premise: People buy sport-utility vehicles because they believe these vehicles are safe.

   Conclusion: To sell a vehicle, a manufacturer should not emphasize affordability.

Answer choice (A) provides the assumption needed to render the argument logically convincing:

   Premise: People buy sport-utility vehicles because they believe these vehicles are safe.

   Premise (A): People do not believe that affordable vehicles are safe.

   Conclusion: To sell a sport-utility vehicle, a manufacturer should not emphasize its affordability.

Choice (B) provides merely that Jupiter's sport-utility vehicle would be even more attractive were it priced lower; it contributes nothing to the explanation of why Jupiter should not emphasize affordability. Choice (C) provides a reason for Jupiter to de-emphasize the price of its sport-utility vehicle compared to the price of its luxury car, not compared to other sport-utility vehicles. Choice (D) provides a reason to emphasize reliability, but not a reason to de-emphasize affordability. It is possible, for example, that consumers are equally concerned about these two factors. Choice (E) provides a reason not to emphasize safety, but does not provide a reason not to emphasize affordability.

3. **The correct answer is (D).** This is a moderately difficult question in which you must identify assumptions employed in a specific argument. Based on the passage's premises, we can conclude that Javier reads literary classics. To also conclude that Javier appreciates literary classics—which is not the same thing as the mere fact of reading them—we must assume that all readers of literary classics appreciate this type of book. (College students may read literary classics based solely on reading requirements for courses they take for reasons other than appreciation of literary classics, for example.)

Choice (D) provides the additional premise needed to draw that conclusion, and this additional premise suffices.

Choices (A), (B), (C), and (E) do not provide a premise that substantiates the necessary assumption that all readers of literary classics appreciate these books.

4. **The correct answer is (D).** This is a relatively easy question in which you must assess the effect of additional information. One of the judging criteria is flavor. If the judges prefer the flavor of cherry pies over other flavors, this fact would increase the likelihood that a cherry pie will win the contest. Admittedly, flavor is only one judging criterion. Nevertheless, answer choice (D) is the best of the five choices.

Choice (A) does not firmly support any conclusion. On the one hand, the more cherry pies entered in the contest, the more statistically likely the winner will be a cherry pie. On the other hand, one of the judging criteria is "distinctness," and the more cherry pies entered, the less distinctive any cherry pie is likely to be. Choice (B) tends to support the opposite conclusion. If a fresh cherry pie is difficult to bake to proper doneness, then a fresh cherry pie is less likely to win the contest. Moreover, since freshness is also a judging criterion, a canned cherry pie is less likely to win, and therefore any cherry pie is less likely to win. Also, whether a pie is difficult to bake properly is not one of the judging criteria; in this respect, then, choice (C) is irrelevant. Choice (C) does not support any conclusion about the likelihood that a cherry pie will win. On the contrary, choice (D) provides evidence that none of the pies entered in the contest hold an advantage over any other with respect to one particular judging criterion. Choice (E) does not strongly support the conclusion. While a cherry pie that is fresh and is baked to the cherries' proper doneness is more likely to win as a result, a pie whose crust is overbaked (not baked to proper doneness) is less likely to win as a result.

5. **The correct answer is (B).** This is a moderately difficult question requiring you to determine the method of reasoning employed in the argument. The argument recommends one course of action (certain restoration and publicity efforts) over another (approving the Hill Hub project) to achieve the stated objective, without considering that might be possible to pursue both courses—in other words, that they are not mutually exclusive alternatives—thereby increasing the likelihood of achieving the objective.

Choice (A) is not an argumentative technique used in the argument. Although the argument does fail to acknowledge any merits of the proposal it rejects, it does not infer or even acknowledge any particular merits of the proposal it favors. Choice (C) is not an argumentative technique used in the argument. Although the argument does propose that one course of action would be more likely than another to bring about a desired outcome, the argument does not indicate that the course of action must be satisfied (is a necessary condition) for that outcome. Choice (D) is not an argumentative technique used in the argument. Although the argument does choose one proposed solution to a problem over another, it does not weigh any drawback of the proposal it rejects. Choice (E) is not an argumentative technique used in the argument. The argument does not consider the rationale (basis or justification) for either of the two proposals.

6. **The correct answer is (E).** This is a moderately difficult question requiring you to determine the effect of additional information on an argument. Karl's response relies on two alternative but interrelated assumptions: 1) the reruns are likely to be popular enough to compete with Connie's favorite program, and 2) Connie's favorite program will not in fact be popular. Answer choice (E) provides evidence that helps affirm both of these assumptions, by suggesting that the reruns might very well be popular enough to draw the viewing audience away from Connie's favorite program, thus rendering it less popular. Admittedly, choice (E) would provide even greater support if it explicitly indicated that one popular program can draw viewers away from another. Nevertheless, it is the best among the five answer choices.

Choice (A) does admittedly weaken Connie's argument. However, Connie's statement is vague about whether her favorite program is entertaining just to her or to many other people as well. If the latter is the case, choice (A) would provide no useful information to evaluate either Connie's argument or Karl's rebuttal. Moreover, we are not informed whether entertaining shows are necessarily popular. Without this additional information, this choice is not useful to evaluate either Connie's argument or Karl's rebuttal. Finally, while choice (A) tends to weaken Connie's argument, it fails to provide affirmative support Karl's rebuttal. Choice (B) provides some evidence that Connie's favorite might not be popular, thereby weakening Connie's argument that because the program is entertaining it will be popular. However, (B) allows for the possibility that Connie's favorite program will nevertheless be popular. Choice (C) would strengthen Karl's rebuttal only under the assumption that reruns are likely to be popular. In other words, choice (C) relies on the evidence provided by answer choice (A). Choice (D) would help support Karl's rebuttal only if the reruns to which Karl refers are educational programs that were very popular when originally aired and are likely to be popular as reruns. Yet we are not informed that this is the case. Thus, choice (D) is ineffective as it stands in supporting Karl's rebuttal.

7. **The correct answer is (B).** This is a challenging question in which you must determine the method of reasoning employed in the argument. The passage as a whole is an argument *against* the proposed legislation forcing pharmaceutical companies to lower their prices. The paragraph's final sentence is the conclusion of this argument. The statement to which the prompt refers (contained in the passage's third and fourth sentence) provides support for the proposed legislation (which the argument as a whole opposes): The fact that elderly people are forced to choose which medicines to buy and which to forego supports a law designed to remedy that problem.

Choices (A), (D), and (E) are incorrect essentially for the same reason: as a whole, the passage argues against the proposed law, which the statement at hand actually supports. Choice (C) mischaracterizes the statement at hand in a different way. The statement at hand does not merely support a premise. Rather, it is a claim that helps establish the need for proposed law. In other words, it is an intermediate conclusion for a position that the argument as a whole opposes.

8. **The correct answer is (E).** This is a relatively easy question in which you must detect a reasoning error. The first sentence of the argument is its premise, while the second sentence is its ostensible conclusion. However, despite the word "therefore" the second sentence is not a conclusion, since it provides no information that the premise (first sentence) does not already provide. In other words, the second sentence merely restates (reiterates) part of the premise, so the overall argument lacks a conclusion.

   Choice (A) is not supported. The argument does not rely on or otherwise employ multiple definitions of the same term. Choice (B) is not supported. The argument does not indicate that any of its assertions have not been proven false. Choice (C) is not supported. The argument does not rely on any cause-and-effect relationship. Choice (D) is not supported. No information in the argument could be characterized irrelevant.

9. **The correct answer is (A).** This is a moderately difficult question in which you are required to assess the effect of additional information. The argument relies on the assumption that the furlough program is responsible for, or at least contributes to, a prisoner's refraining from committing crimes after release. One effective way of weakening the argument is to refute this assumption, by providing evidence that the program does not contribute to the reform of prisoners. (A) provides strong evidence to this effect—specifically, that program participants are less likely than nonparticipants to commit crimes upon their release, regardless of their participation in the program.

   Choice (B) actually tends to support the argument by providing additional evidence, albeit weak, that furlough programs are effective in reducing crime. Choice (C) provides insufficient information to assess either the strength or weakness the argument. Choice (D) provides no useful information to determine whether or not the program is effective. Choice (E) raises the possibility the percentage of prisoners participating in the program *might* not be large enough to allow one to assess its effectiveness with a high degree of certainty. If the percentage is very low (for example, 5 percent) then answer choice (E) would significantly weaken the argument; but as this percentage approaches 50, it would actually tend to strengthen the argument. Thus, without additional information about the percent of prisoners participating in the program, choice (E) accomplishes little toward either weakening or supporting the argument.

10. **The correct answer is (D).** This is a moderately difficult question in which you must detect a flaw in parallel reasoning. The original argument's line of reasoning is essentially as follows:

    Premise: The well-paid engineers at CompTech do not quit their jobs.

    Conclusion: If MicroFirm engineers are not well paid, they will quit their jobs.

    You can express this argument symbolically as follows:

    Premise: All A's are B's.

    Conclusion: If not A, then not B.

    The reasoning is flawed because it fails to account for other possible reasons why MicroFirm engineers have not left their jobs. (Some B's might not be A's.) Answer choice (D) is the only one that demonstrates the same essential pattern of flawed reasoning. To recognize the similarity, rephrase the argument's sentence structure to match the essence of the original argument:

> *Premise:* All people who practice diligently (A) achieve perfection (B).

> *Conclusion:* If one does not practice diligently (not A) one cannot achieve perfection (not B).

Choice (A) reasons essentially as follows: One certain A is B. Therefore, if A then B. (This reasoning is flawed, but in a different respect than the reasoning in the original argument.) Choice (B) reasons essentially as follows: If A, then B. Not B. Therefore, not A. This reasoning is sound (not flawed). Choice (C) reasons essentially as follows: If A, then B. Therefore, if B, then A. (This reasoning is flawed, but in a different respect than the reasoning in the original argument.) Choice (E) is an argument from induction rather than deduction, and therefore cannot readily be expressed symbolically. Without additional evidence, it is impossible to determine the strength of the argument.

11. **The correct answer is (C).** This is a relatively easy question in which you must assess the effect of additional information. Answer choice (C) is the best response because it substantiates an assumption that is necessary for the argument. Unless it is possible to build more new homes in Ocean View to begin with, the argument's proposal—to build new homes that are affordable—would be impossible to implement.

   Choice (A) is irrelevant to the argument, whose final conclusion involves how to reverse the trend—not what the trend's consequences might be if it goes unchecked. Choice (B) has no effect on the argument, at least not without additional information. If, as a group, those workers who would rather reside in Ocean View than in other areas would also rather own their own homes than rent, then (B) would strengthen the argument. On the other hand, if this group would rather rent than own, then (B) would actually weaken the argument. Choice (D) tends to show that Ocean View workers, as a group, prefer home ownership over renting. To this extent, choice (D) strengthens the argument that if Ocean View homes were more affordable, then Ocean View workers would buy them. But the argument does not depend on an oversupply of rental housing; hence, choice (C) is a better response. Choice (E) actually tends to weaken the argument, by providing a clear disincentive for home builders to build inexpensive homes. The economic incentive that the argument proposes may or may not suffice to compensate for this disincentive.

12. **The correct answer is (A).** This is a relatively easy question requiring you to identify the main point or conclusion of the passage. The argument boils down to the following:

   > *Premise:* Child care license requirements are reasonable because they ensure public safety.

   > *Premise:* Handgun ownership laws are not as stringent as child care license laws.

   > *Intermediate Conclusion:* Current handgun ownership laws do not ensure public safety.

   > *Final conclusion:* More stringent handgun ownership laws would be reasonable.

   Answer choice (A) expresses the argument's final conclusion.

Choice (B) is not supported by the argument, which argues generally for more stringent handgun ownership requirements, not for prohibiting any specific class of people from owning handguns. Choice (C) merely reiterates one of the argument's stated premises. Choice (D) merely reiterates one of the argument's stated premises along with its intermediate conclusion; the argument's main point must embrace its final conclusion. Choice (E) is supported by the passage information only to a certain extent. The argument provides no information about whether the parents of the children responsible for the school shootings were able to obtain their handguns only because of the leniency of ownership requirements. Without this information, answer choice (E) is not inferable. In any event, it does not express the argument's final conclusion.

13. **The correct answer is (A).** This is a challenging question in which you are required to assess the effect of additional information. This argument relies on the assumption that Gregg's Syndrome is more prevalent among Puma Syndrome victims who take Betatol than among those who take Aidistan. Choice (A) essentially affirms this assumption, although it expresses it in a somewhat different way. Given that Gregg's Syndrome renders any Puma Syndrome treatment less effective, if victims who have both syndromes are treated with Betatol, while victims who have only Puma Syndrome are treated with Aidistan, then Aidistan will appear to be more effective, although the absence of Gregg's Syndrome might in fact be the key factor that explains the differing results.

Choice (B) would actually support PharmaCorp's claim that Aidistan is more effective than Betatol—by the same reasoning as above. Choice (C) provides no useful information, as it stands. Without additional information—about the number of people suffering from both syndromes who are treated with Aidistan compared to the number treated with Betatol—it is impossible to assess the effect of answer choice (C) on the argument. Choice (D) actually supports PharmaCorp's claim that Aidistan is more effective than Betatol. Given that Betatol is less effective in treating Gregg's Syndrome, the result is that Aidistan renders Puma Syndrome less resistant to treatment. (In other words, Aidistan is more effective in treating Puma Syndrome.) Choice (E) provides no useful information to compare the effectiveness of Aidistan with that of Betatol in treating Puma Syndrome.

14. **The correct answer is (B).** This is a moderately difficult question in which you must make an inference or draw a conclusion from given premises. The passage's first two sentences, considered together, suggest that the manufacturers probably knew about the risk to public health but, to save money, decided to emit the harmful chemicals anyway. In all likelihood, then, it's more important to them that they save money than help ensure that their chemicals do not harm the neighboring public.

Choice (A) depends on the assumption that the amounts saved by emitting the chemicals was less than the amounts paid to the victims. The passage information does not clearly support this assumption. Choice (C) depends on the assumption that the court awards will sufficiently deter the manufacturers from emitting the chemicals. The passage information does not clearly support this assumption. Choice (D) is certainly more inferable than its inverse. But it attributes certain value judgments to the courts that the passage does not clearly support. Choice (E) depends on additional assumptions that the court judgments and awards were fair—a highly subjective issue that the passage does not address.

15. The correct answer is (E). This is a relatively easy question requiring you to identify assumptions used in a specific argument. The claim in the second sentence relies on the assumption that all other factors in weight loss—such as exercise and dietary habits—remained unchanged from before the two-week period through the two-week period.

Choice (A) is not a necessary assumption; whether the survey participants were already using Slim-Ease is irrelevant in determining whether the product was effective during the two-week period. Choice (B) is not a necessary assumption. Even if the survey participants did exercise during the period, and even if exercise contributed to their weight loss, it is entirely possible that Slim-Ease also contributed to the weight loss. Also, it is entirely possible that exercise would not have contributed to weight loss in any event, depending on the amount and type of exercise. Choice (C) is not a necessary assumption. Without evidence to the contrary, whether a person is overweight to begin with is irrelevant to whether a particular product causes weight loss. Choice (D) is not a necessary assumption. The advertisement does not make any claims about the effectiveness of Slim-Ease compared to that of any other product. The advertisement merely claims that Slim-Ease causes weight loss.

16. The correct answer is (C). This is a challenging question in which you must make inferences or draw conclusions from given premises. The passage posits the following simple argument: If both of two conditions (exposure to the nuclear testing at an age under 10 years) are true, then a particular result (death before age 50) is certain. Given that this argument is true, any person alive today who resided in the town during the testing (and therefore was exposed to the resulting radiation) must have been at least 10 years old at the time. Here's the essence of the reasoning:

Premise: If both A and B, then C.

Premise: Not C.

Conclusion: Not both A and B.

Choice (A) is not a necessary conclusion. None of the premises in the passage draws any distinction based on whether a town resident remembers the testing. Choice (B) is not a necessary conclusion. It is entirely possible that some (and perhaps even all) of the cancers contracted by the town's surviving residents were caused either by the nuclear testing near the town (in which case the survivors were over 10 years of age during the testing) or were due to some other cause entirely. Choice (D) is not a necessary conclusion. None of the premises in the passage draws any distinction between low and higher levels of radiation exposure. Choice (E) is not a necessary conclusion. The premises do not preclude the possibility that the deaths of *all* of the town's residents who died before turning 50 years of age were caused by cancer.

17. The correct answer is (D). This is a relatively easy question in which you must determine the method of reasoning employed in an argument. The argument boils down to the following:

Premise: The new cat food alleviates discomfort.

Premise: The new cat food causes a potentially harmful allergic reaction.

Unstated Assumption: Discomfort caused by hair balls is preferable to a potentially harmful allergic reaction.

Conclusion: I won't feed my cat the new cat food.

The conclusion is merely a prescription based on the two premises and the unstated assumption indicated above.

Choice (A) inaccurately characterizes the argument, which neither presents nor alludes to any opposing argument. Choice (B) inaccurately characterizes the argument. Admittedly, the argument does identify a distinct group (cats) and one member of that group (the speaker's cat). However, the argument does not assert that what is true of cats generally is not true of this cat. (In particular, it is entirely possible that the new cat food causes an allergic reaction in all cats.) Choice (E) inaccurately characterizes the argument, which does not seek to provide more than one explanation (cause) for any particular phenomenon.

18. **The correct answer is (D).** This is a moderately difficult question in which you must detect an error in parallel reasoning. The original argument demonstrates essentially the following reasoning:

Premise: If chlorofluorocarbons are emitted, then ozone depletion will occur.

Conclusion: If chlorofluorocarbons are not emitted, then ozone depletion will not occur.

It is useful to express this reasoning symbolically as follows:

Premise: If A, then B.

Conclusion: If not A, then not B.

The reasoning is fallacious (flawed), because it fails to account for other possible causes of ozone depletion. (B might occur whether or not A occurs.)

Answer choice (D) is the only answer choice that demonstrates the same essential pattern of flawed reasoning:

Premise: If a person with phlebitis takes Anatol, the phlebitis will be controlled.

Conclusion: If a person does not take Anatol, the phlebitis will not be controlled.

Note that choice (D) begins with the conclusion, whereas the original argument begins with the premise. This fact makes no difference, however, in assessing the reasoning itself.

19. **The correct answer is (A).** This is a challenging question in which you are required to make inferences or draw conclusions from given premises. The discrepancy among the cited studies involves the extent of the increase in televised violence over the last twenty years. One possible explanation for the discrepancy is that the recent studies relied on different previous studies, which disagreed as to what the level was twenty years ago.

Choice (B) actually renders the discrepancy more inexplicable by eliminating one other possible explanation for it. Choices (C), (D), and (E) are irrelevant to the discrepancy among different studies as to the extent of the increase in the incidence of televised violence over the last twenty years.

20. **The correct answer is (E).** This is a moderately difficult question in which you must detect errors in reasoning. The argument suggests that the key to a third-world nation's political stability is to afford its citizens certain powers. However, the argument relies entirely on one observed case (nation X) in which both characteristics are present. To be convincing, the argument must at least show that these powers actually contributed to nation X's political stability. Choice (E) provides one plausible scenario in which these powers could have nothing to do with the nation's political stability.

Choices (A), (B), (C), and (D) are incorrect because each of these statements, even if true, would have no effect on the argument's line of reasoning.

21. **The correct answer is (D).** This is a relatively easy question in which you must identify the conclusion of the argument. Implicit in Eva's statements is her main point, or conclusion: the arena should be expanded to include the area now occupied by the skating park. Implicit in Frank's response is his main point, or conclusion: the skating park should not be removed.

Choice (A) is not clearly a point of disagreement. Frank argues that the skating park is more beneficial for the local economy; thus it is not an issue for Frank in any event. Choice (B) is not clearly a point of disagreement. Eva neither claims nor implies that the horse shows generate more revenue for the county than the skating park. Choice (C) is not clearly a point of disagreement. While Eva implies that skating should not occur at the same time as the horse shows, Frank does not address this issue. Choice (E) is not clearly a point of disagreement. Although Frank's statements strongly suggest his belief the skating park is more popular, Eva's statements do not provide sufficient information to indicate whether she would disagree.

22. **The correct answer is (C).** This is a challenging question requiring you to assess the effect of additional information on the argument. Choice (C) weakens the argument by providing some evidence that by clarifying an assumption. It is not the case that the mere passage of the law entailed full enforcement of the law; thus, the efficacy of the law cannot yet be judged. Moreover, repealing a partially enforced law may lead to even more destruction of Ziurba; hence the law may still be necessary. It cannot be concluded conclusively that it is *unnecessary*.

Choice (A) has no effect on the argument. The argument relies on a comparison involving the *rate of decline* in the tree population, not simply on the number of existing trees. Choice (B) actually *supports* the assertion that the law should be repealed. Specifically, if Ziurba tree-bark oil is *not* useful for other purposes, then a prohibition on its production is less critical than if the oil were useful for other purposes. Choice (D) doesn't address the argument. Whatever the level of demand, the law's efficacy in preventing Ziurba harvesting is what is at issue. Choice (E) is irrelevant to the argument, which seeks to show only why the law does not help preserve the Ziurba tree population. The mere fact that some other factor also contributes to the decline in the Ziurba tree population is beside the point.

23. **The correct answer is (E).** This is a moderately difficult question requiring you to identify principles that underlie or justify the reasoning in an argument. The point of disagreement between the proposed law's proponents and its critics is *not* whether corporate insiders will be susceptible to bribery if they become federal regulators. Instead, the issue here is which is a more desirable trait in a regulator: personal knowledge about how private industry works or personal integrity (insusceptibility to bribery). The critics' argument appeals to the principle that, on balance, the former is preferable, and so an argument countering their claim should appeal to the opposing principle: integrity is more important than knowledge.

    Choice (A) states a principle that would probably appeal to proponents of the proposed law, who are clearly concerned about regulators' vulnerability to bribery. However, since the principle does not help us to determine whether objectivity and integrity are more important than knowledge and experience, an argument countering the critics' claim would be better off relying on principle, as in answer choice (E). Choice (B) might very well be a principle that would appeal to proponents of the proposed law, who presumably believe that regulation of private industry is legitimate and important. However, like the principle in (A), it doesn't provide a firm basis for the assertion that objectivity and integrity are more crucial than knowledge and experience. Choice (C) states a principle that would appeal to the proposed law's critics, who favor allowing former industry insiders or lobbyists to serve as regulators. Choice (D) states a principle that might appeal to proponents of the proposed law, since it acknowledges a public interest that competes with the interests of private industry. (It is essentially an appeal to an anti-trust augment.) However, like (A) and (B), this principle does not serve as a strong basis for arguing against a person with insider knowledge of private industry serving as a regulator.

24. **The correct answer is (B).** This is a challenging question in which you must make an inference or draw a conclusion from given premises. The first and third sentences, considered together, strongly infer the conclusion expressed by choice (B). Admittedly, the passage does not rule out the possibility that babies who are breast fed during some portion of the first year other than the first three months are more likely than other babies to become obese. However, this possible scenario runs against the major thrust of the passage's argument. Thus, despite this remote possibility, choice (B) is the best answer.

    Choice (A) relies on information about genetic propensity not mentioned the passage, and therefore cannot reasonably be inferred based on the passage. Choice (C) is not inferable from the passage information. Choice (C) overlooks the possibility that babies who are breast fed during the first year but not up until the first birthday might nevertheless be *unlikely* to become obese children. (This answer choice exemplifies the following fallacy: If A, then B. Therefore, if not A, then not B.) Choice (D) confuses the statistic cited in the passage. It also over-generalizes by referring to all bottle-fed babies, rather than only to those who were bottle fed and not breast fed until at least their first birthday. Choice (E) directly contradicts the passage information, which provides that breast feeding instead of bottle feeding during the first three months can help prevent the baby from becoming an obese child.

25. **The correct answer is (E).** This is a moderately difficult question in which you must identify assumptions used in specific arguments. The argument relies on two important assumptions. One is that the teachers who transferred from Franklin to Valley View were Vining graduates; the other is that teachers who transferred from Valley View to Franklin were not Vining graduates. If neither or only one were the case, then it would be unreasonable to conclude that Vining graduates are responsible for high academic performance. Admittedly, these assumptions involve a matter of degree; for example, the greater the percentage of Vining alumni among the teachers transferring from Franklin to Valley View, the stronger the argument's conclusion. And, admittedly, (E) does not acknowledge this fact. Nevertheless, (E) provides the essence of one of these two crucial assumptions.

Choice (A) is irrelevant to the argument. The argument provides no evidence to suggest that the transferring teachers use any grading system other than the one used by all other teachers at their current school. Whether the schools differ in their grading methods is irrelevant, as long as each school has continued to use the same system consistently. Choice (B) is not a necessary assumption. Admittedly, if true, answer choice (B) would lend support to the argument, by ruling out one alternative explanation for the decrease in median GPA at one school and increase in median GPA at the other school. However, choice (B) rules out only this one single explanation, leaving available many other possible explanations. (For example, perhaps Valley View received significantly more funding than Franklin School last year, allowing Valley View to improved its computer lab, which in turn enhanced the median GPA of its students.) Choice (C) is not a necessary assumption. If true, it would appear to lend support to an argument that the teachers who transferred from Franklin are more effective teachers than those who transferred from Valley View to Franklin. However, we are not informed what percentage of the teachers who transferred in each direction were Vining graduates. Without this information it is impossible to determine the extent to which Vining's credential program can be credited with high academic performance of its alumni's students. Choice (D) can easily be ruled out as a necessary assumption because it actually *weakens* the argument, by providing evidence that Vining University contributes to *lower* grade point averages among its graduate's students.

Section III: Analytical Reasoning

1.	A	6.	A	11.	D	16.	E	20.	D
2.	C	7.	B	12.	D	17.	B	21.	C
3.	C	8.	C	13.	A	18.	E	22.	B
4.	E	9.	C	14.	E	19.	A	23.	C
5.	E	10.	E	15.	C			24.	A

QUESTIONS 1–5: SELECTION (EASIER)

Because the subjects of this game are linked together by a series of conditional statements, a flow-chart approach is appropriate. In the diagram below, statements about "at least one student" are signified by double-arrow dotted lines:

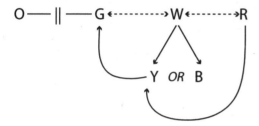

Since this game involves conditional rules, be aware of the contrapositive and related fallacies. For example, since all students using yellow also used green, it follows that if a student did not use green, he or she also did not use yellow (if not G, then not Y). However, it cannot be inferred that if a student used green, that student must have also used yellow (if G, then Y). In the diagram, the arrow flows only in one direction; it cannot be inferred that if a student did not use yellow, that student also did not use green (if not Y, then not G).

1. **The correct answer is (A).** Although at least one student using green must have also used white, it is possible that all such students used yellow rather than blue. Thus, choice (A) is not necessarily true. Choice (B) must be true because at least one student using white also used red, and all such students also used yellow. Choice (C) must be true. All students using red also used yellow, and all students using yellow also used green; thus all students using red also used green. Choice (D) must be true because at least one student who used green also used white—and vice versa. Choice (E) must be true because all students who used red also used yellow, and hence at least one student used both red and yellow.

2. **The correct answer is (C).** Answer choices (A) and (B) are incomplete lists. Answer choice (D) is incorrect because a student using yellow and red must have used green as well (a total of three colors). Answer choice (E) is incorrect because a student using green and white must have used a third color as well: either blue or yellow.

3. **The correct answer is (C).** A single student could have used four colors at most: green, red, yellow, and either blue or white.

4. **The correct answer is (E).** A student could have used orange only. In addition, a student could have used green only; although some students using green must also have used white, this student may have been one of those using green that did not use white as well. Finally, a student need not have used white to use blue, and so a student could have used blue only.

5. **The correct answer is (E).** A student using white could not have used both blue and yellow as well; thus, combination (E) is not possible.

QUESTIONS 6–11: SEQUENCE/ATTRIBUTE GAME (MODERATE)

This game involves a sequence (line position) that must be considered along with an attribute (popcorn box size) to answer most of the questions. Begin constructing the line position sequence with the last rule, since it calls for two alternatives:

```
B...D...E
E...D...B
```

Two unfixed core sequences may be constructed to display line position possibilities, and a single core diagram may be used to match the patrons to their box size:

```
(1) LINE POSITION (5)     BOX SIZE
                A          E
                ←
    C  B  D     E          C D A B
                C          j l m s
                ←
    A  E  D     B
```

The premise allows you to assign the following attributes to the patrons:

Carrie: jumbo

David: large

Anusha: medium

Ben: small

Since Estrella buys a smaller box than Carrie, Estrella must buy either a large, medium, or small box.

6. **The correct answer is (A).** Referring to the two line-position diagrams above, only answer choice (A) is consistent with either of the two diagrams. The sequence A-E-C-D-B, which choice (A) provides, complies with the bottom diagram.

7. **The correct answer is (B).** Estrella and Anusha are the only people that can buy a medium box. If Estrella and Anusha are the last two patrons in line, only one line-position sequence is possible: C-B-D-A-E. Thus, Ben is second in line.

8. **The correct answer is (C).** Only Anusha and Estrella may buy medium boxes, and they may appear first and second in line; thus choice (C) could be true. Choice (A) is false because only Ben and Estrella may buy a small box, but Ben and Estrella cannot appear first and last in line, in either order. Choice (B) is false because only David and Estrella may buy a large box, but David and Estrella cannot appear first and last in

line, in either order. Choice (D) is false because David and Estrella cannot be the first two people in line. Choice (E) is false because Ben and Estrella cannot be the last two people in line.

9. **The correct answer is (C).** Any of the five people could be third in line, and so the third person in line might buy any of the four sizes.

10. **The correct answer is (E).** Estrella must be either first or last in line, since Estrella and only Estrella buys the same size box as one of the others. Thus, the second line-position diagram above can be eliminated. Estrella must buy the same size box as the first person in line, who must be either Carrie or Anusha. However, Carrie must buy a jumbo box, while Estrella must buy a smaller than jumbo box. Thus, the five people must be in line in the following order, from first to fifth: A-C-B-D-E. Since Anusha and Estrella must buy the same size box, the box sizes for all five people can also be determined.

11. **The correct answer is (D).** We can infer from the information in the question stem that patrons who buy a small box of popcorn are not entitled to sodas. We know Ben buys a small box of popcorn, and the only other person who might buy a small box is Estrella. Neither Ben nor Estrella can be fourth in line. Hence, the fourth person in line must be entitled to a free soda.

QUESTIONS 12–17: COMPLEX ATTRIBUTE GAME (CHALLENGING)

This game is complicated by two conditional statements. The rule that all females among the group are retrievers infers its contrapositive: all shepherds and terriers are male. Similarly, the rule that only terriers have learned to stay infers its contrapositive: no shepherd or retriever has learned to stay. The following multiple-choice diagram provides for the various attributes of each of the eight dogs: which command(s) it has learned, its breed (uppercase letter), and its gender. Notice the conditional rules expressed to the right of the multiple-choice grid.

command	h	h	s	s	s/h						s
BREED	S/R	S/R	T	T	T				R	S/T	↓ T
gender			m	m	m				↑ f	↓ m	

12. **The correct answer is (D).** All females must be retrievers. Accordingly, all dogs that are not retrievers must be male; that is, terriers and shepherds must all be male.

13. **The correct answer is (A).** If one command must have been learned, then all dogs other than terriers must have learned to heel but not stay—because all dogs that have learned to stay are terriers. Thus, all retrievers and all shepherds have learned to heel but not stay. Thus, choices (B) and (C) must be true. Choice (D) means that all retrievers have learned to heel; that works. Choice (E) must be true as well, given that only terriers have learned to stay. However, it is possible for a terrier to have learned to heel but not stay; thus, answer choice (A) is not necessarily true.

14. **The correct answer is (E).** All dogs that other than retrievers must be male—that is, terriers and shepherds must all be male. There must be at least one dog of each breed among the group, and so one dog must be a shepherd, and three of the dogs must be terriers. (The remaining four dogs must, of course, be retrievers.) Thus, choices (A), (B), and (C) must be true. If a dog has learned to stay, the dog must be a terriers; thus, three dogs have learned to stay, and answer choice (D) must be true. Although at least three dogs have learned to heel, it is possible that as many as three dogs have learned neither to heel nor to stay. Thus, choice (E) is not necessarily true.

15. **The correct answer is (C).** At least three dogs must be terriers. Since each breed of dog must be represented at least once among the group, one of the dogs must be a retriever, while the remaining four dogs must be shepherds. One of the three terriers (all of which are male) has learned to heel. All four shepherds are male, and at least one of the four shepherds has learned to heel; otherwise, only three of the dogs at most could be shepherds. Thus, a minimum of two male dogs must have learned to heel.

16. **The correct answer is (E).** At least three dogs are terriers, all of which are male. At least one dog must be a shepherd, and all shepherds are male. Thus, at least four dogs must be male, and so it is not possible for there to be more females than males among the group. Choice (E) must be false.

17. **The correct answer is (B).** All dogs other than the two that have learned to heel but not stay must have learned to stay. All of those dogs (six in all) must be terriers and thus must be male. Since each breed must be represented among the group, of the two remaining dogs one must be a shepherd and the other must be a retriever. Both the shepherd and the retriever must have learned to heel but not stay. The shepherd must be male, although the retriever could be male or female.

QUESTIONS 18–24: SELECTION (CHALLENGING)

For this selection game, create a roster which incorporates the rules, at least to the extent possible. Indicate union members with upper-case letters and non-union actors with lower-case letters. List the three "extras" separately to avoid confusion. As in any logic game, ask yourself what else you can deduce from the original rules. In a selection game, determine whether any of the subjects must be selected and whether any of the subjects cannot be selected. Here, given that at least two sets of twins must be selected, C and D must both be selected. Why? If C and D were not selected, then A, B, E, and F (three of whom are union members), would all be selected; as a result, only two non-union actors (F and J) at most could be selected. However, the rules stipulate that at least as many non-union actors as union actors must be selected; thus, C and D must both be selected.

[AB] [ⓒ ⓓ] [E/f] ← at least 2 pair

G H i ⟵——— at least 1

(UNION ≤ non-union)

18. **The correct answer is (E).** Consider one rule at a time and eliminate answer choices that violate that rule. For example, considering the rule that at least two sets of twins must be selected, answer choices (B) and (C) can be eliminated. Answer choices (A) and (D) violate the rule that at least as many non-union actors as union members must be selected.

19. **The correct answer is (A).** C and D must both be selected (see general comments above).

20. **The correct answer is (D).** Since union members cannot outnumber non-union actors, the maximum number of actors that can be selected is eight. A bit of experimenting is required to determine who must be included in that group of eight. Assume first that all three sets of twins are selected. Since there are three union members and three non-union actors among the six twins, J (a non-union actor) and one other extra (either G or H) must be selected to complete the maximum cast. G and H cannot both be selected, since union members would thereby outnumber non-union actors. Assume next that all twins except E are selected; to maximize the total number of actors selected, all three extras may be selected. Considering both scenarios, E, G, and H are the only three actors that need not be selected for a cast of eight. Among these three, only H appears among the answer choices.

21. **The correct answer is (C).** First, remember that C and D must both be selected in any event. So your task here is to determine the number of possibilities for the remaining four members. Assuming first that G and H (but not J) are selected, E and F must both be selected for a cast of six, while neither A nor B can be selected. Why? If A and B are selected, or if E but not F is selected, the number of union members in a six-member cast would exceed the number of non-union actors. Thus, if G and H (but not J) are selected, the director can assemble only one possible six-member cast: {C D E F G H}. Next, assuming that G and J (but not H) are selected, two distinct six-member casts are possible: {C D G J A} or {C D G J E F}. The total number of distinct casts is three.

22. **The correct answer is (B).** C and D must both be selected (see general comments above). If G and H (both union members) are selected, then at least as many non-union actors as union actors must be selected among A, B, E, F, and J. Assuming A and B (both union members) are selected as a second set of twins, F and J (both non-union actors) must both be selected. Assuming A and B are not selected, then E and F will be selected as the second set of twins. In either event, F will be selected as a cast member.

23. **The correct answer is (C).** Assume that B is not selected. A cannot be selected, either. Accordingly, since at least two sets of twins must be selected, both E and F must be selected. In order for the cast to include the same number of union actors as non-union actors, G and H must both be selected.

24. **The correct answer is (A).** C and D must both be selected (see general comments above). If B is selected, then all six twins (three union actors and three non-union actors) must be selected. As a result, J must be selected; otherwise, union cast members would outnumber non-union cast members. Thus, answer choice (A) must be true. Choice (B) is not necessarily true. If both G and H are selected, J must be selected as

well only if A and B are selected. Choice (C) is not necessarily true. If A is selected, then all six twins (three union actors and three non-union actors) are selected. As a result, J (a non-union actor) must be selected, and so H may be selected without violating the rule that the cast must contain at least as many non-union actors as union actors. Choice (D) is not necessarily true, since it is possible to select all three sets of twins along with J and G, but not H, without selecting more union members than non-union actors. Choice (E) is not necessarily true, since a third set of twins (A and B) need not be selected.

Section IV: Logical Reasoning

1. D	6. A	11. D	16. B	21. B
2. C	7. C	12. C	17. D	22. C
3. E	8. A	13. B	18. A	23. B
4. E	9. A	14. B	19. E	24. B
5. D	10. C	15. D	20. A	25. C

1. **The correct answer is (D).** This is a relatively easy question in which you must assess the effect of additional information on the argument. The argument depends on the assumption that a great white shark would not survive at Bayside Aquarium long enough to have any significant impact on public awareness. Answer choice (D) provides evidence that helps refute this assumption. (Common sense tells us that a captive animal is more likely to survive in an environment similar to its natural habitat than in a different environment.)

   Choice (A) has no effect on the argument, at least without additional information. If the expense turns out small, then the plan might turn out to be a comparatively effective use of the aquarium's resources (thereby weakening the argument, in retrospect). But if the expense is great, than the plan might appear wasteful in retrospect (thereby strengthening the argument). Choice (B) actually strengthens the argument, by providing a reason why the plan would not in fact increase public awareness of the shark's plight and, therefore, would amount to a waste of financial resources. Choice (C) is irrelevant to the argument, which involves only great white sharks. Choice (E) tends to strengthen the argument. Adding another species to its collection would help sustain the Aquarium's popularity, thereby serving its objective of increasing public awareness of the shark's plight.

2. **The correct answer is (C).** This is a moderately difficult question in which you must identify the method of reasoning used in the argument. One premise of the argument is that other industries have not lobbied for the proposed law. Relying at least partly on this observation, the argument concludes that the biotechnology industry must have initiated it. In other words, the argument draws a conclusion as to what caused an event by eliminating certain other possible causes. (This reasoning is flawed, of course, because it fails to rule out the possibility that someone other than an industry lobbyist initiated the proposed law.)

Choice (A) is incorrect because the argument makes no claim as what is either possible or impossible, nor does it draw any *general* conclusion. Choice (B) is incorrect because the argument cites not just one but several pieces of evidence to support its conclusion and because it asserts its conclusion as "likely," not certain. Choice (D) is incorrect because the argument at hand does not present an opposing position, let alone attempt to discredit that position on any particular grounds. Choice (E) is unsupported. Although the argument does claim that a certain event (the instigation of a proposed law by biotechnology industry lobbyists) occurred in the past, that claim is based not on the occurrence of the same type of event at the present time but rather on the non-occurrence of certain other events (as well as on other evidence).

3. **The correct answer is (E).** This is a relatively easy question in which you must identify the conclusion of the passage. Although the passage's second premise (that farm subsidies discourage farm productivity) doesn't suffice to infer that they will in fact result in lower farm productivity, it does suggest that this result is probable to some degree. Given that a decrease in productivity would run contrary to public policy, it is reasonable to infer that farm subsidies are, or will be, responsible for a public-policy violation. Answer choice (E) expresses this conclusion.

Choice (A) goes beyond what is reasonably inferable from the passage; lower productivity levels do not necessarily result in bankruptcy, regardless of the reason for the lower levels. Choice (B) would require the additional, and dubious, assumption that a policy that promotes lower productivity levels is preferable to the current public policy. Choice (C) would require the additional assumption that the current public policy is a good one. (The passage provides no specific evidence to support that assumption.) Choice (D) conflates productivity with profitability. However, the passage provides no evidence that a productive farm (one that producing a significant crop yield) is likely to be profitable.

4. **The correct answer is (E).** This is a moderately difficult question in which you must assess the effect of additional information. The argument asserts essentially that it was the marketing campaign, and not some other factor, that was responsible for the high number of sales of the new version of ActiveWeb compared to competing products. One way to support the argument is to rule out one or more other factors that might have been responsible instead for this phenomenon. By implication, answer choice (E) provides just this sort of evidence. While *favorable* third-party reviews of ActiveWeb would serve to weaken the claim that the marketing campaign was the cause of the sales results, *unfavorable* reviews would accomplish just the opposite.

Choice (A) is irrelevant to the argument, which seeks to explain the success of the new version of ActiveWeb vis-à-vis competing products; the mere fact that the total market size has increased accomplishes nothing toward explaining this *comparative* success. Choice (B) has little effect on the argument, at least without additional information. On the one hand, *if* the decrease in the number of competitors was the direct result of MicroTeam's marketing efforts, then choice (B) would serve to *strengthen* the argument. On the other hand, by providing an alternative explanation for the sales comparison indicated in the argument's first sentence, choice (B) tends to *weaken* the argument. Choice (C) *weakens* the argument, by providing an alternative explanation for the sales comparison indicated in the argument's first sentence. Specifically, choice (C) provides evidence that it is the product itself, and not the marketing campaign, that is responsible for the product's comparative success in the marketplace. Choice (D) is not directly relevant to the argument. Admittedly, the fact that more copies of the new version of ActiveWeb have been sold than of any previous version *might* be explained by a successful marketing campaign. However, this fact could just as easily be explained by other factors.

5. **The correct answer is (D).** This is a moderately difficult question requiring you to identify assumptions used in a specific argument. The argument relies on an increase in graduation rates to conclude that the five privatized schools are "educationally effective." But if the schools' administration arbitrarily allows students to graduate, regardless of academic achievement, then any increase in graduation rates would not be meaningful. In other words, the argument depends on the assumption that the students deserved to graduate.

Choice (A) is irrelevant to the argument. The argument does not seek to compare *all* privatized schools with public schools. Choice (B) is not a necessary assumption. The fact that operating costs have not increased since privatization could that teacher salaries at these five schools have *not* increased. In any event, we have no information about teacher salaries pre- and post-privatization. Choice (C) is irrelevant to the argument for two reasons. First, taxpayer costs do not clearly relate to educational effectiveness. Second, the argument seeks to compare the effectiveness of the five schools after privatization with the effectiveness of *the same five schools* before privatization—not between these five schools and other schools, public or private. Choice (E) identifies factors that do not directly relate to educational effectiveness as measured by the percentage of the senior class that graduated. Thus, although if true, choice (E) might tend to support the argument, it is not a necessary assumption.

6. **The correct answer is (A).** This is a moderately difficult question in which you must make an inference or draw a conclusion from given premises. If an hourly wage employee works fewer than five days per week, the employee would need to work more than eight hours per day *on average* to qualify for overtime pay in state Y. On the other hand, the same employee would need to work more than eight hours per day *only on one day* to qualify for overtime pay in state X. Thus, employees working fewer than five days per week would prefer to work in state X. Given that most employees prefer to work in state Y, it is reasonable to conclude that most employees work at least five days per week.

Choices (B) and (C) are not inferable. Each of these two answer choices assumes that employers in one state provide overtime work while employers in the other state do not. However, the passage provides no information that might help affirm this assumption. Choice (D) confuses the use of the percentage cited in the argument. Choice (E) is not inferable. In fact, the *reverse* of choice (E) is readily inferable from the facts; that is, most employees probably work *more* than forty hours per week if they prefer to work in state Y over state X.

7. **The correct answer is (C).** This is a relatively easy question requiring you to identify parallel reasoning errors. The original argument bases a conclusion that one phenomenon causes another on an observed correlation between the two phenomena. The argument boils down to the following:

> *Premise:* X (coffee consumption) is correlated with Y (absence of obesity).

> *Conclusion:* X (coffee consumption) causes Y (absence of obesity).

Answer choice (D) demonstrates the same method of reasoning:

> *Premise:* X (sport-utility vehicles) are correlated with Y (fatal accidents).

> *Conclusion:* X (sport-utility vehicles) cause Y (fatal accidents).

Choices (A), (B), (D), and (E) fail to illustrate the same method of reasoning.

8. **The correct answer is (A).** This is a challenging question in which you must make an inference or draw a conclusion from given premises. The passage indicates that developers have curtailed construction of new office buildings until demand grows to meet supply, while stepping up construction of single-family houses. This evidence in itself strongly supports choice (A). Admittedly, it is possible that an influx of businesses from other states will deplete the current oversupply of office buildings and in fact create sufficient demand for new ones. Nevertheless, answer choice (A) is the best of the five.

Choice (B) is not readily inferable from the passage. First of all, it is entirely possible that businesses relocating to the state due to the favorable tax climate will bring their employees with them, in which case increasing demand for single-family housing might very well continue to outpace the rate at which developers construct new housing. Secondly, choice (B) assumes that the population of the state will not increase for some other reason. Choice (C) is not readily inferable. It is possible the large employers relocating to the state provide jobs whose compensation is low relative to the current average income. Also, other factors unrelated to the information in the passage might affect average income of state residents in the future. For example, an influx of retired persons might significantly increase the state's population while decreasing average income. Choice (D) is not strongly inferable. Admittedly, an increase in supply will exert downward pressure on price. However, this choice involves the cost of *new* housing, and other factors—including the costs of building materials and labor as well as the price and availability of older housing—can also affect the price of a new house. Without considering these factors, it is unfair to conclude that the price of new single-family houses will decline. Moreover, corporations relocating to the state will in all likelihood bring their employees with them, and demand for single-family housing might very well continue to outpace supply as a result. In this event the price of new homes might increase, not decrease. Choice (E) is not readily inferable from the passage. Although it is possible that the large corporations relocating to the state will employ many residents and thereby reduce the number of residents who work at home, the passage provides insufficient information to show that this will be the case. It is just as likely, for example, that most residents who work at home would continue to do so and that the number of self-employed residents who work at home will remain at current levels or perhaps even increase.

9. **The correct answer is (A).** This is a moderately difficult question requiring you to identify assumptions used in a specific argument. Gwen's argument relies on the assumption that expensive restaurants are not as popular among the college students as inexpensive restaurants. Jose provides one reason why expensive restaurants are not necessarily less popular among the college students, suggesting that the disagreement is about whether expensive restaurants are in fact less popular among the college students than inexpensive restaurants.

Choice (B) is irrelevant to the argument, in which Jose and Gwen disagree about whether the number of expensive restaurants should be reduced, not whether the number of restaurants providing delivery service should be reduced. Choice (C) is irrelevant to the argument, in which Jose and Gwen disagree about whether the number of expensive restaurants should be reduced, not whether inexpensive restaurants should provide delivery service. Choice (D) is not a point of disagreement between Jose and Gwen. On the contrary, the premise of Gwen's argument (first sentence) strongly suggests that Jose and Gwen agree on this point. Choice (E) misses the key point of disagreement: whether inexpensive restaurants are *relatively* popular *compared to* expensive restaurants among Collegetown students.

10. **The correct answer is (C).** This is a moderately difficult question in which you must make an inference or draw a conclusion from given premises. According to the argument, *any* person eligible for the internship program is likely to gain admission to the local law school if he or she applies, and some people eligible for the program are among this year's Fairmount College graduates. It follows logically that some of this year's Fairmount College graduates are likely to gain admission to law school if they apply. To follow these logical steps, it helps to express the premises and conclusion symbolically, as follows (E = eligible for the program), A = likely to gain admission to law school, F = Fairmount College graduate this year):

> *Premise:* All E are A.

> *Premise:* Some E are F.

> *Conclusion:* Some F are A.

None of the other choices provides a valid conclusion.

11. **The correct answer is (D).** This is a challenging question in which you must assess the effect of additional information on the argument. The argument concludes that the reason for the military's decision was to reduce pilot error during commercial flights. Answer choice (D) is the only one that supports this conclusion. Given that chemical warfare is likely to escalate in the future, it would seem that the military would continue to require immunization shots. But the military stopped requiring the shots. So the military's decision must have been based on some factor outweighing the potential danger of chemical warfare to pilots. One possible such factor is the increased danger of commercial airline accidents resulting from the immunization shots.

Choice (A) weakens the argument, by providing a plausible alternative reason why the military decided to no longer require the shots. Choice (B) weakens the argument. It provides evidence that pilot error is more critical during military flights than commercial flights. Accordingly, choice (B) shows that the reason for the military's decision to no longer require shots is that it endangers pilots during *military* flights, not commercial flights. Choice (C) weakens the argument, by providing a plausible alternative reason why the military decided to no longer require the shots. Specifically, the military wished to prevent more pilots from resigning. Choice (E) weakens the argument, by providing evidence that the danger that the immunization program poses for commercial airliners is less significant than it would be otherwise. This in turn makes it less likely that the military's decision was based on a concern for the safety of commercial flights.

12. **The correct answer is (C).** This is a moderately difficult question requiring you to identify principles that underlie or justify the reasoning used in the argument. The educator's recommendations are clearly intended to redirect college students away from graduate school and the highest-paying jobs and toward certain important but lower-paying professions. The premises strongly suggest that college students' career decisions are increasingly motivated by financial needs rather than by true vocational interests. The recommendations appeal strongly to the principle that those decisions should be motivated less by the former and more by the latter.

Choice (A) states a principle with which the educator may very well agree, but the premises simply do not support the conclusion that the recommended policies would serve to raise salaries in the lower-paying professions. Choice (B) also states a principle with which the educator might agree. However, the specific recommendations have nothing to do with financial-aid incentives or disincentives. Choices (D) and (E) state principles that would actually *undermine* one or both recommendations. What students currently appear to want is either graduate study or high-paying jobs. Following the principle stated in either choice (D) or choice (E) would only reinforce one or both preferences—quite the opposite of the intended impact of the recommended policies.

13. **The correct answer is (B).** This is a relatively easy question in which you must identify assumptions used in a specific argument. The argument relies on the assumption that alcoholics die relatively young only because alcoholism increases a person's susceptibility to life-threatening diseases, and not for other reasons as well. Answer choice (B) provides explicitly that those other possible reasons were ruled out in compiling the insurance statistics cited in the report.

Choice (A) need not be assumed for the argument's conclusion to be inferable. In fact, choice (A) actually weakens the argument, by reversing the causal connection (between alcoholism and susceptibility to life-threatening diseases) upon which the argument relies. Choice (C) need not be assumed for the argument's conclusion to be inferable. Even if alcoholism does increase a person's susceptibility to non-life-threatening diseases, this fact would have no effect on the causal connection between alcoholism and life-threatening diseases upon which the argument relies. Choice (D) need not be assumed for the argument's conclusion to be inferable. Even if the reverse of choice (D) were true—that is, life expectancy of the non-alcoholic population decreases over time—it is still entirely possible that alcoholism reduces life expectancy. Choice (E) need not be assumed for the argument's conclusion to be inferable. Even if the report's author is biased about the morality of alcoholism, that bias would serve to undermine the argument only if the bias affected the report itself. Yet the argument provides no evidence that this was the case.

14. **The correct answer is (B).** This is a relatively easy question requiring you to identify a reasoning error in the argument. The argument relies on events involving one particular corporation to reach a conclusion about an entire group (large corporations). The argument is unconvincing because a variety of factors affecting the law suit as well as the tobacco company's business the following year might very well not apply generally to other corporations.

Choice (A) is not a viable answer; no component of the argument mistakenly reverses cause and effect. Choice (C) distorts the cause-and-effect relationship which the argument seeks to describe. Specifically, it implies that the large court award in fact contributed to (was the partial cause of) the company's increase in profits the next year. However, the information provided in the argument does not support this notion, and common sense dictates just the opposite. Choice (D) distorts the argument, which does not seek to compare one group with another group, but attempts to generalize about all large corporations what is true about one large corporation. Although it does indeed draw an unfair analogy (questionable comparison), by assuming that what was true for one tobacco company would be true for other large corporations simply because of their similarity in size and business structure. But this is not the analogy described in answer choice (D). Choice (E) distorts the argument, which does not claim that corporations *must* produce unsafe or unhealthy products to increase profits.

15. **The correct answer is (D).** This is a challenging question requiring you to make inferences or draw conclusions from given premises. Based on the last sentence of the passage, we can conclude that juvenile criminals associate primarily with other juvenile criminals, and that adult criminals constitute the same group of people who were juvenile criminals. For (D) to *not* be readily inferable would require that most adult criminals associate primarily with law abiding peers as teenagers. But this contradicts what we know about adult criminals, based on the passage information. Thus, choice (D) is strongly inferable.

Choice (A) is not readily inferable. In fact, it is explicitly contradicted by one of the argument's stated premises (the first sentence). Choice (B) also is not readily inferable. Before we can determine whether the prediction to which it refers is "impossible" we would need to compare the significance of behavioral predisposition to the influence of a person's teenage peers. But the passage does not provide sufficient information for this comparison. (The passage indicates merely that the latter factor is "significant.") As with choices (A) and (B), choice (C) is not readily inferable. We do not know what percentage of law-abiding adults either lacked a childhood predisposition for adult criminal behavior and suppressed it through contact with non-criminal teenage cohorts or simply lacked the predisposition altogether. Unlike choice (D), choice (C) does not find *explicit* support in the passage; thus (D) is a better answer than choice (C). Choice (E) is not readily inferable. The passage information leaves open the possibility that most preteen children who are not predisposed to criminal behavior are later influenced by their teenage peers to act contrary to that predisposition and eventually become adult criminals.

16. **The correct answer is (B).** This is a relatively easy question in which you must assess the effect of additional information. The argument relies on the assumption that job applicants know which employers regularly investigate employee medical histories and which ones don't, but disregard this distinction in deciding to which companies they'll apply. Choice (B) directly refutes this assumption.

Choice (A) actually strengthens the argument. When applying for a job, if the applicant knows that her medical history might disqualify her for important job benefits, this fact would tend to show a lack of concern for keeping her medical history secret from the prospective employer. Choice (C) actually strengthens the argument's claim. Under the new law, employers (as a group) would be more likely to probe into the medical records of their employees. If job seekers realize this, whatever privacy concerns they might otherwise have had are less likely to be a factor, or concern, in choosing among prospective employers. Choice (D) helps to affirm the necessary assumption that choice (B), the correct choice, refutes. In other words, answer choice (D) accomplishes just the opposite of what the questions asks for. Choice (E) is irrelevant to the argument, which relies on a comparison between two different categories of job applicants, not between one year's applicant pool and another's.

17. **The correct answer is (D).** This is a challenging question requiring you to identify the method of reasoning used in an argument. The fact that certain employees were lured away from Company X by better offers suggests that Company X might expect other employees to do act similarly. The spokesperson responds to this unfavorable evidence by emphasizing certain differences (i.e., efforts now being made to prevent more attrition) that render the earlier departures of certain employees irrelevant now.

Choice (A) is not used as an argumentative strategy. There is no pair of facts in the argument that appear to contradict each other and that the spokesperson attempts to reconcile or explain. Choice (B) is not used as an argumentative strategy. The spokesperson makes no attempt to re-characterize, or put a favorable rhetorical spin, on any particular fact. Choice (C) is not used as an argumentative strategy. Although the spokesperson does cite the fact that an expert has been hired to help ensure that employees remain content, the argument does not go so far as to appeal to the expert in the sense of citing that expert's information or opinions for the purpose of bolstering the spokesperson's prediction. Choice (E) is not used as an argumentative strategy. Although the spokesperson does claim that the steps being taken (e.g., hiring the expert and other efforts) will prevent the further attrition on the scale of what occurred earlier, the argument does not claim that any of the steps are necessary to accomplish this goal.

18. **The correct answer is (A).** This is a challenging question in which you must identify assumptions used in a specific argument. The argument boils down to the following:

> *Premise 1:* If there is political instability, then the stock market is volatile (unstable).

Premise 2: If there is political instability, then the currency is volatile (unstable).

Premise 3: The currency is volatile (unstable).

Conclusion: The stock market is volatile (unstable).

The conclusion above requires the following additional premise:

Premise 4: If the currency is volatile (unstable), then there is political instability.

Only answer choice (A) provides this essential premise. Note that premise 4 above is essentially the same proposition as answer choice (A). In other words, the following two propositions are logically identical:

Premise 4: If A, then B.

Answer choice (A): If not B, then not A.

Choice (B) merely reiterates premise 2. In other words, the following two statements are essentially the same:

If A, then B.

If not B, then not A.

Choice (C) commits the following fallacy:

Premise: If A, then B.

Conclusion: If B, then A.

Choice (D) would lead to the conclusion that if the stock market is volatile (unstable), then the currency is volatile (unstable). In other words, choice (D) commits the same fallacy as choice (C):

Premise: If A, then B.

Conclusion: If B, then A.

Choice (E) merely reiterates the argument's conclusion. In other words, the following two statements are essentially the same:

If A, then B.

If not B, then not A.

19. **The correct answer is (E).** This is a moderately difficult question requiring you to make inferences or draw conclusions from given premises. Assuming the number of viable competitors has increased during the last two years, the likely result would be to draw circulation away from preexisting newspapers, including the most profitable one. Given that profitability depends primarily on advertising revenues and therefore on circulation, answer choice (E) actually exacerbates the discrepancy between the two statements.

Choices (A) and (D) help explain why the most profitable newspaper remains most profitable even though its circulation is declining: Advertisers have not yet begun to switch because the most profitable newspaper is still the most widely circulated. Choice

(B) helps explain the discrepancy. Although the argument provides that advertisers are more likely to advertise with widely circulated newspapers than with others, it is entirely possible that other factors, such as advertising rates that a newspaper charges, also affect which newspapers advertisers choose. Choice (C) helps explain the discrepancy, by identifying another source of profit. This in turn helps explain why the most profitable newspaper in the city remains the most profitable one, despite declining circulation. Admittedly, as circulation decreases so does subscriber revenue, and thus profit, and thus overall profitability. Yet the newspaper's profitability is still greater than it would be without the profit gained from its subscribers.

20. **The correct answer is (A).** This is a challenging question in which you must identify the method of reasoning used in the argument. The first sentence is the argument's conclusion: The dumping ordinance should be repealed. The next sentence presents the opposing viewpoint: the ordinance's rationale that Smith's Disease is most prevalent in areas near dumps. The fourth sentence presents a claim (the funds should be used differently) that supports the ordinance's repeal. The final sentence (to which the question refers) provides evidence that this claim is reasonable: To the extent that the roads to the dump sites are of no other practical use, the money used to maintain them should be redirected (e.g., to an education program).

    Choices (B) and (C) are incorrect because the statement at hand supports the line of reasoning leading to the argument's conclusion, not to an opposing position. Choice (D) is incorrect because it confuses the statement at hand with the claim it supports. The fact that roads to the dump are of no other use is not a consequence of any claim; rather, the claim the funds would be better used elsewhere is a logical consequence of the statement. Choice (E) is incorrect because the statement at hand provides clearly helps establish that the ordinance should be repealed in the interest of public health. In no respect does the statement "limit" this conclusion.

21. **The correct answer is (B).** This is a relatively easy question in which you must assess the effect of additional information. The argument assumes that the proposed course of action—reducing demand for aoli tree bark—is necessary to prevent total depletion of aoli tree bark within fifty years. However, the argument ignores the possibility of increasing the supply as an alternative means of achieving this goal. Answer choice (B) provides this alternative.

    Choice (A) actually strengthens the argument. The fact that a certain activity resulting in the use of aoli oil is becoming obsolete suggests a decline in demand for the oil in the future, and thus less urgency in taking steps to save aoli trees from extinction. Choices (C) and (D) tend to strengthen the argument as well, by providing evidence of an additional use for aoli bark. The more potential uses, the more likely that the rate of use will increase and hence that the bark will be depleted within fifty years. Choice (E) is irrelevant to the argument, which turns on the rate of use of aoli oil, not where the users of the oil reside.

22. **The correct answer is (C).** This is a relatively easy question in which you must identify assumptions used in a specific argument. The argument fails to explicitly provide that employees who are at least ten years out of college change employers less

frequently on average than other employees. This premise is essential to the argument's conclusion, and answer choice (C) supplies this additional premise.

Choice (A) is relevant to the argument, since the argument's conclusion appears to recommend college graduates of at least ten years over *all other job applicants (including college graduates as well as candidates without college degrees)*. However, choice (A) compares the job attrition rate among applicants without college degrees to the rate among all college graduates. The argument's conclusion recommends one group of college graduates over another. Since choice (A) does not distinguish between these two groups, it fails to provide a necessary assumption. Choice (B) is irrelevant to the argument, which seeks only to make a recommendation for reducing employee turnover, and not for minimizing the frequency of job changes within a company. Choice (D) is irrelevant as it stands. The argument provides no information about whether employees who graduated college at least ten years ago are more or less likely than other employees to leave their jobs at the request or demand of their employers, as opposed to leaving by their own initiative. Choice (E) is irrelevant to the argument, which seeks only to recommend one group of college graduates over other job applicants. Admittedly, whether recent college graduates are more or less likely than other college graduates to resign their jobs to pursue advanced degrees would be significant in determining how to minimize employee turnover. However, the survey involved only the former group, not the latter group. Thus, choice (E) would be relevant to the argument only under the additional assumption provided by answer choice (C).

23. **The correct answer is (B).** This is a moderately difficult question in which you must identify a reasoning error. John's statement does *not* logically infer, as Jolanda seems to think, that a person must believe in the inevitability of success to be successful. Choice (B) is an effective rebuttal for John because it points out Jolanda's apparent reasoning error.

Choice (A) would not be an effective rebuttal. Neither John's argument not Jolanda's response suggest that they disagree about the definition of success (specifically, whether one's success is defined by oneself or by others). Choice (C) would not be an effective rebuttal. Considered along with John's original statement, this answer choice would merely add that some people believe in the inevitability of success. This assertion does not directly address Jolanda's point that some successful people do not consider themselves successful. Choice (D) would not be an effective rebuttal. Neither John nor Jolanda appear to disagree about the definition of success. Choice (E) would not be an effective rebuttal. It would help make the point that some successful people (especially, some successful men) might consider themselves successful. However, this is not John's point.

24. **The correct answer is (B).** This is a moderately difficult question requiring you to identify parallel reasoning errors. The original argument boils down to the following:

Premise: If a country refuses to join the alliance, then that country will experience less than full employment.

Premise: Country X is experiencing less than full employment.

Conclusion: Country X refused to join the alliance.

To reveal the argument's structure (and its flawed reasoning), express the argument using symbols:

Premise: If A, then B.

Premise: X is B.

Conclusion: X is A.

This reasoning is fallacious (flawed), and answer choice (B) demonstrates the same basic pattern:

Premise: If a person is seated in the front row, then the person can hear the coach. (If A, then B.)

Premise: Ursula can hear the coach. (X is B.)

Conclusion: Ursula is seated in the front row. (X is A.)

Choices (A), (C), (D), and (E) fail to illustrate the same flawed method of reasoning.

25. **The correct answer is (C).** This is a moderately difficult question requiring you to identify reasoning errors. The argument relies on the implicit assumption that some customers who have been ordering fruit but not eggs are now ordering eggs but not fruit. But is entirely possible that customers will order both eggs and fruit; in other words, without evidence to the contrary, these two choices are not necessarily mutually exclusive. Admittedly, for *some* customers these choices might be mutually exclusive. Nevertheless, choice (C) is the best reason among the five listed for rejecting the argument's conclusion.

Choice (A) is nonsensical. The argument involves two cause-and-effect relationships: 1) the effect of the laboratory report on egg consumption, and 2) the effect of egg consumption on fruit consumption. Clearly, however, the argument does not confuse cause with effect in either of these two relationships. Choice (B) is not a good reason to reject the conclusion. Admittedly, the argument applies the word "order" to two different situations. But the argument does not *define* the word in two different ways and does not rely on two different definitions of the word. Choice (D) is not a good reason to reject the conclusion. Specifically, the argument provides no information suggesting that the laboratory (the source) is biased or even potentially biased. To the contrary, the argument provides that the report is "authoritative." Choice (E) is nonsensical. No information in the argument can reasonably be considered irrelevant.

Evaluate Your Writing Sample

When you have completed your writing sample, evaluate it using the following techniques:

- Score your essay using the scorecard in Lesson 12. Try to be as objective as possible. If you have trouble being objective, ask a friend or teacher to evaluate your essay for you.

- With a yellow highlighter, mark every sentence in which you accomplished nothing more than restating or paraphrasing the premise, criteria, or characteristics of the choices—that is, in which you merely rearranged and parroted back the facts to the reader. How great a portion of your essay did you highlight? Every sentence in yellow represents wasted space and wasted time that you want to use instead to formulate and present original ideas in the form of persuasive arguments.

- With a red pencil, circle or underline every grammatical error, awkward sentence, or other mechanical problem. If you're not sure what to circle, ask an English professor to do so. Does your essay look like a sea of red? If so, spend more time working on the mechanics of writing and on your writing style.

TWO MODEL ESSAY RESPONSES

Here are two model responses, each arguing for one of the two choices described in the Practice Test 6 Writing Sample topic. As you read these responses, keep in mind the following:

- These essays are models in the sense that they would garner the highest accolades at law schools. Don't expect to write essays quite this polished in 35 minutes; these responses give you something to shoot for.

- That said, they aren't perfect. Regardless of how effective an LSAT essay is, there's always some room for improvement.

- These responses would fit in the two pages provided on the LSAT response sheet if handwritten.

- By virtue of the open-ended nature of the prompts, these responses cannot include every possible argument. In other words, effective arguments may have occurred to you that are absent in these model responses.

Model Response #1

(in favor of the hotel job)

Nora should accept the hotel owner's job offer. Creating watercolor images for the hotel's Web site would afford Nora a direct and immediate outlet for her art talents. Selecting works for the art gallery, while perhaps not as artistically satisfying, would nevertheless call for the exercise of aesthetic judgment—a type of artistic skill. By comparison, the Faulding job fares poorly in serving Nora's first objective. Arranging for display advertising may be consistent with her previous job experience, but is this task creative in an artistic sense? Probably not. Admittedly, teaching art classes will no doubt involve demonstrating techniques for students. However, to teach art is mainly to direct others and evaluate results, which is no more artistically creative than critiquing art works submitted to a gallery.

The hotel job would better serve Nora's second objective as well. Public relations does, after all, mean engaging the public for the purpose of cultivating fruitful business relationships. Networking with the local business and arts communities amounts to just that. Although concierge duties are more in the nature of customer service, they nevertheless would expose Nora to the hotel's customers—i.e., the public. The Faulding job offers less in terms of public relations experience. The semi-yearly junkets are mainly for education, not to develop business relationships. And, implementing an advertising strategy for the new digital-arts program doesn't necessarily amount to public relations experience.

In sum, the hotel position is more likely to serve Nora's dual goals. Its artistic opportunities are more direct and immediate than the ones at Faulding, and the context in which Nora would deal with the public at the hotel amounts to public relations in a truer sense.

Model Response #2

(in favor of the Faulding job)

The Faulding job is the better choice. Applying her proven interest and talent in art is one of Nora's highest priorities. Once Faulding's new program is established, Nora will be able to turn a good part of her attention to her primary passion—art—in a way that allows her to expand her skill set as she wants. The creative outlet Faulding offers is even more compelling in view of the alternative. The hotel owner promises only a one-time watercolor project and a chance to scrutinize other artists' works; this may only frustrate Nora, who aims to directly apply her artistic skills and talents to her job.

As for Nora's interest in a public relations career, this path is experimental. It would be a shame to pass up a potential art teaching career for a chimera. Even assuming that Nora has an abiding interest in public relations, she could get a small taste of it at either job. In fact, the Faulding job arguably holds greater public relations promise, since Nora would network with a diverse and ever-changing group of people at the art conference.

In short, while Nora can indulge her curiosity about public relations at either job, only at Faulding would she be assured of exercising her art talents. On balance, then, the Faulding position is better for Nora.

Still Room for Improvement?

By now, you should have a fairly clear idea how effectively you respond to an LSAT Writing Sample topic. If you are not satisfied with your performance, take the following remedial steps:

- Review Writing Sample Lessons 12 and 13.

- Rewrite the essay you wrote, limiting yourself to 17 minutes. Unless your essay is either "limited" or "seriously flawed," don't start from scratch. Instead, try to refine and build upon your basic arguments and approach.

- Based on this topic, write a new essay in which you argue *for* the choice that you argued against in your original essay. Evaluate that essay as you did the first one.

APPENDIX

BEFORE, DURING, AND AFTER: AN LSAT CHECKLIST

Before, During,
and After:
An LSAT Checklist

In this Appendix, you will evaluate your practice test performance. We'll also provide you with a procedural checklist for the weeks leading up to your LSAT, for exam day, and for the weeks following the exam.

EVALUATING YOUR PRACTICE TEST PERFORMANCE

If you have not already done so, tally up your raw score for all four multiple-choice sections of Practice Test 6, referring to the answer keys on pages 389, 401, 413, and 418. Then evaluate that score using the score conversion table on page 6.

LSAT CHECKLISTS

The procedures, deadlines, and regulations discussed in this section are intended only to highlight some of the key steps in the process of getting ready for the LSAT. For the final word on everything related to the LSAT, be sure to consult the *LSAT/LSDAS Registration and Information Book.*

8 Weeks Before the Exam

Obtain the Registration Book. Use the form included in the book to register for the LSAT. Read the book from cover to cover. Most procedural questions about the LSAT and about the LSDAS are answered in the book.

Decide where you want to take the LSAT. A complete list of all available LSAT test sites is included in the Registration Book. On the LSAT registration form, you will be asked to specify your first two test-site choices. Most test takers prefer to take the exam at the nearest available location. However, if you are in college and away from your home, you may prefer to go home for an extended weekend and take the LSAT there, away from the distractions associated with the collegiate living environment. Another consideration is the testing accommodations themselves. Some testing rooms are equipped with long tables, others with standard classroom desks, while others are equipped with theater-style fold-away desktops. If possible, avoid a test site equipped with fold-away desktops.

appendix

Register early for the LSAT. Make sure that you register for the LSAT on or before the regular postmark registration deadline—4 to 5 weeks prior to the exam date. (Precise dates are specified in the Registration Book.) Late registration is permitted up to a certain date with payment of an additional late-registration fee. (Deadlines and fees are specified in the Registration Book.) Telephone registration with payment by credit card is permitted only for late registration. Walk-in (exam-day) registration is not permitted. Register as early as possible to ensure a seat at your first- or second-choice test site. Early registration is particularly crucial for the October exam, which is by far the most popular of the four exams offered during the year.

4 Weeks Before the Exam

Make a final determination about where you wish to take the LSAT. After registering for the LSAT and paying the registration fee, you can request a change of test site for an additional fee up until about 3 weeks prior to the exam.

2 Weeks Before the Exam

Look over your LSAT admission ticket. If you mailed your registration form by the postmark deadline but have not yet received your LSAT admission ticket in the mail, contact the testing service to be sure that your registration is being processed. When you receive your LSAT admission ticket, look it over to make sure that you are properly identified and have been assigned to an appropriate test site.

2 Days Before the Exam

Get a good night's sleep. Most people can get by without a lot of sleep for one day. Insufficient sleep is more likely to catch up with you on the second day.

The Day Before the Exam

Take the day off. Clear your mind and engage in relaxing activities. Don't think about or talk about the LSAT. Having already worked through this book, no amount of last-minute preparation for the LSAT will be of any real benefit.

Arrange for backup transportation to the test site. In case your first means of transportation is unexpectedly unavailable on exam day, make sure you have a "Plan B." Remember: automobiles do break down unexpectedly from time to time.

Go for a drive to the test site. Find the building and room where the test will be administered. If the building and room is open, go in and check out the facilities so that you know what to expect the next day. Check the size and style of the desks and chairs, check to see if there is a clock and whether there are vending machines, water fountains, and restrooms nearby. You will be under enough stress the next morning without worrying about finding your way around a strange place.

Set out everything you need for tomorrow. Have all of the following items ready to go before you retire for the night:

Required:

- One current form of photo identification that includes your signature

- Your LSAT admission ticket

- Two or three #2 pencils with good erasers

Recommended:

- Directions to the test site

- A silent timing device

- A highlighter pen

- Correction fluid

- A comfortable sweater, sweatshirt, or light jacket

- A non-electric pencil sharpener

- Snack foods (fruit, nuts, granola bars, etc.)

Set two alarms to wake you up on exam day. In case of an electrical-power outage, one alarm should be battery operated. Also, ask a friend to give you a wake-up call to ensure that you don't hit your alarm's snooze button and go back to sleep.

The Day of the Exam

Eat a good breakfast. No lunch break is provided during the exam. Be sure to eat enough to keep you going for at least five hours.

Leave early for the test site. The LSAT admission ticket will indicate when you should arrive at the test site. Make sure you depart early enough to arrive by that time.

Take along the morning newspaper. Plan on delays and idle time before (and possibly during) the LSAT. Keep your mind off the test by taking along some reading material to pass the time.

Don't forget your admission ticket, photo ID, etc. Review the list of items that you (should have) set out the day before to take with you to the test site. WARNING:

Don't inadvertently leave any of these items in your car at the test site. (Any LSAT supervisor will tell you that last-minute dashes back to the car for forgotten items are very common.)

What to do if you are ill on exam day. If illness or some other emergency prevents you from taking the exam, you do not need to contact the testing service or anyone at the test site to cancel. Your absence at the test site will not be reported per se, although cancellations are reported on your score report. Rest assured: the fact that you canceled the test or canceled your score will not adversely affect your chances of admission to law school.

Checking in. To be admitted to the test site you must present your admission ticket and one form of photo identification that includes your signature. An acceptable form of identification might include a driver's license, student identification card, or passport. The supervisor will check the examinee roster for your name.

Prepare to be thumbprinted. Sure, the testing service trusts you; but it does not trust the suspicious character seated next to you. Every test-taker is thumbprinted when checking in to help ensure that no registrant has sent someone else to take the test for them. After completion of all multiple-choice sections, testing staff members will check photo identification once again (to ensure that the individuals who checked in are the same individuals who actually took the complete exam).

Seating arrangements. The exam supervisor will separate test takers with empty desks or chairs to reduce the likelihood of cheating. You are not permitted to choose your own seat. Nevertheless, if your chair squeaks, or if you are seated near a drafty, poorly lit, or uncomfortable area, ask to move. Supervisors are instructed to honor all reasonable requests to relocate.

Bringing personal belongings into the testing room. Your personal belongings are permitted in the testing room but must be stowed under your desk or table at all times during the exam.

Beverages and food. Beverages are not permitted in the testing room. You are permitted to bring snacks into the testing room, but you must stow your snacks beneath your desk and cannot eat in the test room. If either during or between exam sections you wish to eat snacks that you brought, you must take your snacks outside the room and eat there.

Instructions and more instructions. Once you are settled in your seat, expect to spend at least 20 minutes filling in circles on your bubble-sheet to provide information about you and about the test you are taking. The supervisor will then review the testing procedures as well as the rules for examinee conduct. As with any standardized test, the exam supervisor will recite all instructions from a pre-written script.

All test booklets are not the same. On the cover of your test booklet will appear a large bold letter—either "A," "B," or "C"—that indicates which version of the LSAT you will be taking. Although the four scored sections will be identical for all test-takers, the test sections are ordered differently in different versions. Also, the trial section will vary among different versions. The primary purpose of administering different test versions is to prevent cheating.

Starting and stopping each section. The supervisor will keep time during each section and announce when you may start and stop each section. During each exam section, you are not permitted to work ahead or go back to other sections.

Recording your answers. You must record all your answers with a #2 pencil on a separate answer sheet provided by the supervisor. Answers recorded in the test booklet will not be scored. Be sure to blacken in an answer for every question, since there is no penalty for incorrect responses.

Timing devices. Silent timing devices are permitted. It is recommended that you take a watch with you to the exam, since there is no guarantee that there will be a functioning clock in the testing room.

Supervisor announcements concerning remaining time. The supervisor will issue one verbal 5-minutes-remaining warning during each exam section. The purpose of this warning is to allow you to adjust your pace so that you can finish the section and fill in all of the bubbles on your answer sheet.

Breaks between exam sections. A 10–15 minute break is provided after the third test section (1 hour, 45 minutes into the exam). At the completion of the multiple-choice portion of the LSAT, the testing staff will collect test booklets and distribute Writing Sample materials, so a break of sorts occurs at this point as well. Otherwise, there will be no break between test sections.

Leaving the room during the exam. You may leave the room at any time during the exam, although you must first obtain the supervisor's permission. If you do leave the room, you will not be permitted to make up that time. Be forewarned: A member of the testing staff might accompany you to and from the restroom!

Unexpected delays and problems. A variety of unexpected problems can interfere somewhat with the administration of the LSAT. Unexpected noise from the outside, windy or unusually cold or hot weather, and power failures are the most common uncontrollable problems. Some problems can be solved by relocating to another room in the building or to another building altogether. If any environmental problem occurs that might distract you, by all means bring the matter to the supervisor's attention.

Canceling your test at the test site. At any time during the test or immediately afterwards, you can cancel your test simply by completing a specified portion of the answer sheet. If you cancel your test in this manner, no score will be tabulated. Cancellations are irreversible; accordingly, think twice before hastily canceling your test while still at the test site. Instead, reflect for a day or two on your performance; the testing service allows you to cancel your score within 5 days after the test. As noted earlier, your score report will indicate cancellations, although canceled scores will not be included in the report. (Also remember that cancellations will not adversely affect your chances of admission.)

Take home some souvenirs of the LSAT. The supervisor will, of course, collect all test booklets after the exam. Remember, however, that a carbonless copy of your writing sample and the black pen provided for the Writing Sample section are yours to take home with you.

During the Week after the Exam

Request a refund if you do not take the exam. If you do not actually take the exam for which you register, a partial refund is allowed if requested in writing anytime before the exam or within one week following the exam.

Applying your registration fee to a later LSAT. If you decide to postpone taking the LSAT, for an additional fee the service will apply a portion of your registration fee to a subsequent exam, but only upon written request up until one week after the original exam date.

Canceling your test score. If you wish to cancel your score for the exam that you just took, the testing service must receive proper written notification of cancellation within 5 working days after the exam.

5 Weeks after the LSAT

Your LSAT score report. An LSAT score report is mailed to you 4 to 6 weeks after the exam. The report will include:

- A 5" × 8" copy of the entire exam (see the "NOTE" below, however), except for the Writing Sample Topic, a copy of which you took home with you on exam day

- Your raw score, your scaled score, and a conversion table to determine your percentile ranking

- Your response to each question and the correct response to each question

Thus, you will have all the information to assess your strengths and weaknesses on the exam. This should help you determine whether you should retake the test and, if so, what areas you should focus on in preparing for the test again.

NOTE: If you take the exam in December, you will not receive a copy of the exam. December exams are not disclosed.

About the Author

Mark Alan Stewart (B.A. Economics, J.D.; University of California, Los Angeles) is a preeminent authority and top-selling author of graduate-level entrance-exam preparation books. For more than a decade, Mr. Stewart was a consultant to schools in the University of California and California State University systems in graduate-level entrance-exam programs. His books on LSAT®, GRE®, and GMAT® preparation continue to be top sellers among aspiring law, business, and graduate students. His other book-length publications for graduate-level admissions include the following:

- *GRE–LSAT Logic Workbook*
- *GRE–LSAT–GMAT–MCAT Reading Comprehension Workbook*
- *GRE—Answers to the Real Essay Questions*
- *GMAT—Answers to the Real Essay Questions*
- *30 Days to the GMAT*
- *Words for Smart Test Takers*
- *Math for Smart Test Takers*
- *Perfect Personal Statements—Law, Business, Medical, Graduate School*

NOTES

NOTES

NOTES

NOTES

NOTES

Peterson's
Book Satisfaction Survey

Give Us Your Feedback

Thank you for choosing Peterson's as your source for personalized solutions for your education and career achievement. Please take a few minutes to answer the following questions. Your answers will go a long way in helping us to produce the most user-friendly and comprehensive resources to meet your individual needs.

When completed, please tear out this page and mail it to us at:

Publishing Department
Peterson's, a Nelnet company
2000 Lenox Drive
Lawrenceville, NJ 08648

You can also complete this survey online at **www.petersons.com/booksurvey.**

1. **What is the ISBN of the book you have purchased? (The ISBN can be found on the book's back cover in the lower right-hand corner.)** _____

2. **Where did you purchase this book?**
   ❑ Retailer, such as Barnes & Noble
   ❑ Online reseller, such as Amazon.com
   ❑ Petersons.com
   ❑ Other (please specify) _____

3. **If you purchased this book on Petersons.com, please rate the following aspects of your online purchasing experience on a scale of 4 to 1 (4 = Excellent and 1 = Poor).**

	4	**3**	**2**	**1**
Comprehensiveness of Peterson's Online Bookstore page	❑	❑	❑	❑
Overall online customer experience	❑	❑	❑	❑

4. **Which category best describes you?**
   ❑ High school student
   ❑ Parent of high school student
   ❑ College student
   ❑ Graduate/professional student
   ❑ Returning adult student
   ❑ Teacher
   ❑ Counselor
   ❑ Working professional/military
   ❑ Other (please specify) _____

5. **Rate your overall satisfaction with this book.**

Extremely Satisfied	Satisfied	Not Satisfied
❑	❑	❑

6. Rate each of the following aspects of this book on a scale of 4 to 1 (4 = Excellent and 1 = Poor).

	4	3	2	1
Comprehensiveness of the information	❑	❑	❑	❑
Accuracy of the information	❑	❑	❑	❑
Usability	❑	❑	❑	❑
Cover design	❑	❑	❑	❑
Book layout	❑	❑	❑	❑
Special features (e.g., CD, flashcards, charts, etc.)	❑	❑	❑	❑
Value for the money	❑	❑	❑	❑

7. This book was recommended by:
- ❑ Guidance counselor
- ❑ Parent/guardian
- ❑ Family member/relative
- ❑ Friend
- ❑ Teacher
- ❑ Not recommended by anyone—I found the book on my own
- ❑ Other (please specify) _____

8. Would you recommend this book to others?

Yes	Not Sure	No
❑	❑	❑

9. Please provide any additional comments.

_____

_____

_____

_____

_____

Remember, you can tear out this page and mail it to us at:

Publishing Department
Peterson's, a Nelnet company
2000 Lenox Drive
Lawrenceville, NJ 08648

or you can complete the survey online at **www.petersons.com/booksurvey.**

Your feedback is important to us at Peterson's, and we thank you for your time!

If you would like us to keep in touch with you about new products and services, please include your e-mail address here: _____